Completing Your Qualitative Dissertation

Third Edition

For
Israel Lippert (1902–1974)
Julia Esther Lippert (1906–1997)
Rosalind Ann Diamond (1941–1978)
All a constant source of energy, inspiration, and strength
Their spirit lives on.

And for my three children,
Carla, Brent, and Adam Bloomberg
In the hope that they will strive to realize their individual strengths
And always follow their dreams in the pursuit of fulfillment, peace, and happiness.

Praise for *Completing Your Qualitative Dissertation, Third Edition*

"I applaud the author for taking on the challenge of describing the conceptual/theoretical model. This piece of information alone will meaningfully improve doctoral students' ability to progress forward with writing their dissertations. The conceptual/theoretical model is one of the most misunderstood aspects of the dissertation, and yet the most important aspect of the dissertation because it anchors the study. But the single most impressive aspect of ***Completing Your Qualitative Dissertation*** is that the authors make sense of writing a qualitative dissertation in a way that will likely enhance the active and inactive students' ability to complete their dissertation."

—Antonio C. Cuyler, Florida State University

"I have used previous editions of this book and, while they have been excellent, I find the third edition to be the best resource for students that I've seen. The chapters are practical and applied, using a real life example throughout. There are even sections in each chapter that address frequent errors that students make. The third edition also provides a detailed description of various qualitative genres, making it easier for students to locate their own work within the book. This book will be required reading for each of my doctoral students, long before they start thinking about their dissertations."

—Kate de Medeiros, Miami University

"Students interested and/or committed in engaging in qualitative research would find ***Completing Your Qualitative Dissertation*** to be extremely informative and easy to read. Students need resources and tools to help with the thinking, collecting and analysis of rich qualitative data—of which can be found in almost every chapter of this text. This book does not lecture students but provides helpful tools to the assist in the collection of rich qualitative data. In addition, in many instances the students are actually able to see the tools and suggestions provided in the text in "action." When reading this text, the students are not left with figuring out next steps and how, this book provides a very clear road map."

—Kriss Y. Kemp-Graham, Texas A&M University

"In this third edition, I appreciated even more the intention the authors give to demystifying both the process of doctoral research and the rationale for the dissertation as a culminating product. It is heartening to have experienced researchers and teachers provide such clarifying and encouraging support to novices, particularly those whose progress through the complicated journey of becoming a qualitative researcher has become stymied and who are thereby feeling demoralized or despairing of ever completing their research work. The challenges of providing good research advisement stood out for me in reading this revision, so even though the book is primarily designed for a graduate student audience, I have already recommended the third edition to my faculty colleagues within counselor education who are looking for a way to better transition excellent clinicians into excellent qualitative researchers for the counseling profession."

—Karen Mackie, University of Rochester

"This third edition is a valuable guide for doctoral students. Theoretical and often abstract elements of the dissertation process are translated into clear and practical steps that students can take and instructors can share on the road toward successful completion of the dissertation."

—Amira Proweller, DePaul University

"Completing Your Qualitative Dissertation is well written and clear. There is an enjoyable mix of scholarly and informal tone that should engage students well. Figures and tables are useful and are appropriate and well placed or referenced within the manuscript. I especially like the use of related examples and included resources. I also like that the authors enumerate common student errors or mistakes in each chapter."

—Nathan R. Templeton, Texas A&M University

Completing Your Qualitative Dissertation

A Road Map From Beginning to End

Third Edition

Linda Dale Bloomberg

Marie Volpe
Columbia University

Los Angeles | London | New Delhi
Singapore | Washington DC

Los Angeles | London | New Delhi
Singapore | Washington DC

FOR INFORMATION:

SAGE Publications, Inc.
2455 Teller Road
Thousand Oaks, California 91320
E-mail: order@sagepub.com

SAGE Publications Ltd.
1 Oliver's Yard
55 City Road
London EC1Y 1SP
United Kingdom

SAGE Publications India Pvt. Ltd.
B 1/I 1 Mohan Cooperative Industrial Area
Mathura Road, New Delhi 110 044
India

SAGE Publications Asia-Pacific Pte. Ltd.
3 Church Street
#10-04 Samsung Hub
Singapore 049483

Printed in the United States of America

ISBN 978-1-5063-0769-5

Acquisitions Editor: Helen Salmon
Editorial Assistant: Anna Villarruel
eLearning Editor: Katie Bierach
Production Editor: Laura Barrett
Copy Editor: Renee Willers
Typesetter: C&M Digitals (P) Ltd.
Proofreader: Theresa Kay
Indexer: Wendy Allex
Cover Designer: Anupama Krishnan
Marketing Manager: Nicole Elliott

This book is printed on acid-free paper.

15 16 17 18 19 10 9 8 7 6 5 4 3 2 1

• Contents at a Glance •

• Contents •

PART II • CONTENT AND PROCESS: A CHAPTER-BY-CHAPTER ROAD MAP   81

Chapter 5 • Introduction to Your Study   85

Chapter 6 • Developing and Presenting Your Literature Review   103

PART III • NEARING COMPLETION   281

Chapter 11 • Some Final Technical Considerations   283

Chapter 12 • Defense Preparation and Beyond   299

• List of Tables •

• List of Figures •

• List of Appendices •

Note: Those appendices that are completed samples of the various templates provided throughout this book, are included in the companion website at study.sagepub.com/bloomberg3e. This includes appendices E, G, H, K, L, M, N, O, P, S, T, U, V, W, X, Y, AA, BB, CC, DD, EE, FF, GG, indicated here with an asterisk.

• Preface •

Who Should Read This Book?

This book is essentially a *dissertation in action*—an explanation and illustration of content and process. It is geared primarily for doctoral students in the social sciences (education, psychology, sociology, social work, nursing, community development, management, etc.) who are about to embark on or who are already conducting a qualitative research study. This book is for you if

- You are contemplating entering a doctoral program and want to know more about what lies ahead in terms of conducting research and writing a dissertation.
- You are enrolled in a doctoral program; having difficulty identifying a sound, researchable topic; and hence unable to develop your dissertation proposal.
- You have completed all the course requirements and are about to begin the research but are unsure of how and where to get started.
- You are stuck in some part of the research process and are unable to make progress toward completion of your dissertation.
- You have just about abandoned the idea of ever completing your dissertation for whatever reason.

During most doctoral programs, there is a heavy emphasis on the theoretical concepts that form the basis of research. Having completed all the required research courses, as well as having passed a certification examination, there is an expectation that doctoral students have mastered the various aspects of research design and methodology. However, once students are "out on their own" to complete their dissertations, they are often unclear about appropriate style, content, and/or procedures and are uncertain as to how to proceed. As a result, every university and college has a significant number of what are commonly referred to as all-but-dissertation (ABD) students, those who never manage to complete the dissertation—the culminating product needed to fulfill the requirements to graduate with a doctorate. If you suspect that you might fall into this category, then read on.

We have witnessed and experienced many of the frustrations voiced by students confronted with the academic challenge of writing a dissertation. How do I select a suitable topic? How do I narrow and focus an idea? What exactly is a research problem? How do I go about formulating a research purpose? How and in what ways do the research questions relate to the study's overall purpose? How do I conduct a literature review? How do I manage and analyze my data? In response to these and other challenges, we have developed what we call "road maps" for understanding the content of the dissertation and navigating through the iterative, recursive, and often messy dissertation process, from its inception to its ultimate successful completion.

Completing a dissertation is fraught with many challenges, both personal and professional. These challenges often lead to a sense of confusion and feelings of inadequacy, incompetence, and frustration. Overwhelming feelings such as these can often spiral to despondency and apathy. It is at this level that many of the students with whom we spoke find themselves. Faced with life's demands and compounded with the stresses of academic rigor, students often bow out, putting aside their dissertations, sometimes forever.

This book represents our combined efforts to facilitate an understanding of the dissertation process so that the student feels confident and competent in successfully pursuing its completion. Our experience has been shaped by our work with our own students through the dissertation advisement process. We have been fortunate to draw on and benefit from the feedback and insight of colleagues and students who saw the value of a book such as this.

One challenge in compiling a book of this nature is to acknowledge that institutional requirements vary. There is no universally agreed-on format, and each school has its unique structural regulations regarding the dissertation. Moreover, each academic program differs, and in fact even each advisor or sponsor usually has her or his own requirements as well. Although dissertations can vary in form and length, depending on the institution, they do share basic components. All dissertations must have an introduction, a review of the relevant literature, a review of methodology, a presentation of findings, a presentation of analysis and interpretation, and a presentation of conclusions and recommendations. In this book, although we address each of these components comprehensively as separate chapters, we are aware that in some institutions or programs some of these components might be combined in the same chapter. As such, readers should always adhere to the guidelines set by their own institutions and be mindful of the preferences of their own advisors.

The Purpose of This Book

Completing Your Qualitative Dissertation: A Road Map From Beginning to End fills an important gap in the qualitative research literature by specifically addressing the fast-growing practice of qualitative postgraduate dissertations in colleges and universities throughout the world. Many students struggle to complete qualitative research projects because the research itself is inherently messy. To address this challenge, the authors have distilled decades of experience into a first-of-its-kind, highly practical reference for graduate students. Students often think that the dissertation writing process is simple. We wish we had a simple answer to the question: How to portray the process as doable without neglecting the complexity? This is what this book hopes to achieve!

Logical and systematic thinking is necessary to successfully complete a qualitative dissertation. Completing the dissertation will depend on your ability to successfully master both the content and the process. Aside from offering clear guidelines as to the necessary content, the intent of this book is to shed light on structure and style, thereby making the dissertation process organized and manageable. The purpose of the book is to assist you at whatever stage you find yourself. You might be right at the beginning of the process, unable to select a topic that is interesting and/or researchable. You might already have a topic, but are unsure of how to focus it narrowly and articulate a researchable problem. You might have covered a lot of ground already, even having collected and analyzed some of your data, but are feeling stuck, lost, or adrift. Writing a dissertation is a process, but not one that is neat and linear. Our intent is to help you better understand the various elements involved in the qualitative dissertation process and be able to address these elements appropriately and effectively.

Our hope, and the motivation behind this book, is that we make the process of conducting research and writing a dissertation more understandable and, hence, manageable. Moreover, our hope is that the process is a meaningful one for you. A dissertation is intended to be an academically rigorous process, the completion of which demonstrates that you are qualified to join a research community whose members carry the title "Dr." As we see it, a dissertation should not be viewed as a punishment. Rather, it is a unique opportunity to choose a topic of your own interest, to learn more about it, and to make a contribution to existing bodies of knowledge in your field. We understand the frustrations and difficulties involved in taking on a project of this magnitude. We understand the level of commitment required and the sacrifices that you have made to get to this point. We also understand how important it is for you to complete your dissertation so that you do not remain ABD forever. Therefore, the goal of this book is that you are able to produce a dissertation, and so we offer this step-by-step guide from inception to completion. Our sincere hope is that this book helps you understand the process, embrace it, and succeed!

The cover illustration abstractly depicts the typical doctoral graduation gown sleeve with three velvet stripes, and doctoral cap—the black velvet tam with the golden tassel. The blue hue represents the color of the graduation gown of Columbia University where both authors obtained their doctorates. (And the touch of orange represents the sun at the end of the long dissertation journey; something to dream of and strive for!) Academic regalia, colloquially known as the "cap and gown" or "graduation robes," are the formal attire worn by degree candidates and holders during various ceremonial occasions. The history of the cap and gown dates back over 800 years to scholars in medieval Europe. Around this time, students and professors began organizing themselves into guilds, and three distinct groups emerged: the apprentices (bachelor of arts), the teachers (master of arts), and the teachers who had completed postgraduate work (doctorate). The style of robes and dress became standardized as a gown with a hood. Today's cap and gown are based on 14th- and 15th-century styles that were particularly popular with students and teachers at Oxford and Cambridge universities in England. American commencement rituals and graduation dress have been in place since colonial times and were standardized by the intercollegiate code in 1895. Doctoral graduates traditionally wear robes with a velvet stripe that extends down the front panel, as well as three velvet stripes across the sleeves in colors indicating the area of study. In addition, instead of the mortarboard that is characteristic of bachelor's and master's degree status, those receiving the doctoral degree traditionally wear a black velvet tam with a small golden tassel. With these images in mind, you have something concrete to aspire to in striving to reach the pinnacle of academic achievement: your doctorate!

How This Book Works

In this book, we offer a series of road maps that are designed to help you steer your way through the various activities that constitute the process of writing a qualitative dissertation. At each juncture of the process, the road maps allow you to clarify your objectives, understand and tackle the task at hand, and check on what you have accomplished before you proceed to the next step.

At the heart of the book is a series of chapters that models the typical progression of a dissertation. Each chapter is illustrated by examples that give the reader an understanding of what the actual write-up would look like. Emphasis throughout the book is on conceptual understanding as it relates to the practical aspects involved in navigating the dissertation process. To begin, we use an actual research problem, which is the problem that confronts you, the reader. You are reading this book because you have not yet managed to complete your dissertation. This same problem is the example that will be addressed as the basis of discussion throughout this book. This problem is referred to insofar as it relates to each step of the dissertation process, and as such you will see a common thread running throughout each of the chapters. We proceed from articulating the problem statement, through developing a research purpose and associated research questions. Based on the research problem, we formulate appropriate data collection methods, analyze and synthesize data, and present conclusions and recommendations. In effect, the problem that is used in this book provides a model for you in conducting and writing up your own dissertation.

As you prepare to navigate the dissertation process, please be aware of three caveats:

First, the approach throughout is to emphasize conceptual understanding as it relates to the practical aspects involved in navigating the dissertation process. As such, this approach bears some caution as it may be seen as an attempt to reduce the complexity and "messiness" of qualitative research by way of a series of simplified "how-to" offerings. The many tables and checklists that are provided in this book might imply that the process is linear. However, this is certainly not the case! It is difficult for many students to understand that even a roadmap is a guideline only, and sometimes routes must be retraced or detours developed in order to avoid or navigate unexpected roadblocks. Although our intent is to demystify the dissertation process, we do not sacrifice intellectual rigor for the sake of simplification. This book is not intended to be a quick fix, nor do we offer an easy recipe for success. In our experience, completing a dissertation is a rigorous and demanding process. It is iterative, unpredictable, and in many respects, recursive. However, with the development of a clearer understanding, sharpened competencies, and a set of resources to guide you, the dissertation is, in fact, doable.

As a second caveat, the reader is reminded throughout that there are various institutional differences and requirements regarding the structure of a dissertation. Be aware that while most institutions will approach the dissertation in common ways, at the same time there are differences in terms of the organization and presentation, and also distinct differences in terms of what and how qualitative language and terminology are used. This book presents information as guidelines that are meant to be flexible per institutional expectations and requirements, and subject to modification depending on your institution, department, and program. As such, this book is meant to be a guide rather than a prescriptive one-fits-all approach.

A third caveat is that although we do offer a general structure regarding the writing of a dissertation, we do not believe this structure should stifle students' creativity. Creativity comes into play through your own initiative in how you design your instruments, develop your conceptual frameworks and related coding schemes, present your findings, and analyze, interpret, and synthesize your data. That said, however, qualitative research must not be viewed as an exercise in creative writing when it is, in fact, an exercise in conducting a research project that is integrative and intellectually rigorous. Rigor and structure are necessary and essential in order to account for subjectivity and keep creative speculation in check.

We realize that readers of this book are at different stages of the dissertation process. Our advice is that you start off by finding your own entry point and depending on where you are in the dissertation process, begin at the chapter that is most relevant to you. If you are just starting out on your research study, with no clearly defined topic, you should start reading this book from the beginning. If you are further along in the research process, choose to focus on those chapters that are most relevant to your unfolding experience. We readily acknowledge that researchers never move in a linear fashion. Conducting research and writing a dissertation are not like strolling along a clearly marked path. Rather, this process is iterative and recursive, looping back and forth, with many unanticipated events along the way. This book is intended, through its road maps, to walk you through that process and through the confusion.

Organization of This Book

This book is organized in three parts. Part I, "Taking Charge of Yourself and Your Work," is the point of entry and constitutes a broad introduction to the complex task of writing a dissertation. Part I offers an overview of the steps involved in thinking about and preparing for the dissertation process. The objective of Part I is fourfold: (a) demystify and clarify the dissertation process while maintaining intellectual rigor and the highest ethical standards; (b) expand students' understanding and appreciation of both the content and the process pertaining to conducting qualitative research and producing a sound defensible dissertation; (c) demonstrate the *skills* needed to conduct and write up the study; and (d) recognize, appreciate, and adopt the *attitudes* that will contribute to the success of the research project. Part I consists of four chapters:

Chapter 1, "A Complete Dissertation: The Big Picture," provides *a cursory glance* at the constitution of an entire dissertation by way of a comprehensive outline of all key elements for each section of the dissertation. This chapter is a precursor of what is to come, with each element being more fully developed and explained further along in the book.

Chapter 2, "Gearing Up: There Is Method in the Madness," introduces the *mindset* that is required to create the physical and mental "space" necessary to begin the dissertation process in as methodical a manner as possible. The chapter includes a discussion about the strengths and limitations regarding identification and choice of topic, as well as clarification regarding appropriate advisor-student collegial relationships and mutual responsibility. The chapter also begins the process of developing the skills involved in establishing and managing a realistic and doable timeline.

Chapter 3, "Choosing a Qualitative Research Approach," discusses the implications of choosing an appropriate qualitative research approach based on the study's problem, purpose, and research questions. We strive for conceptual understanding of the logic behind choice of research approach including knowledge claims and tradition of inquiry by clarifying and explaining the most commonly used current and cutting-edge qualitative genres or inquiry traditions with an emphasis on researcher reflexivity and insights into the critiques of each tradition. The chapter provides an overview of the historical development and current status of qualitative inquiry and illustrates the primary characteristics of qualitative research and how these characteristics compare and contrast with the characteristics of quantitative and mixed methods approaches.

Chapter 4, "A First Step: Developing Your Proposal," explains the logic and reasoning behind developing a sound and comprehensive research proposal, by providing an in-depth understanding of the content of a three-part proposal so that students can make direct application to their own research. Included in this chapter is a comprehensive set of guidelines regarding academic writing skills, as well as sections that clarify expectations and issues regarding academic integrity and that provide guidelines regarding institutional review board (IRB) certification and approval.

The chapters of Part II, "Content and Process: A Chapter-by-Chapter Road Map," narrow and focus the scope of the discussion and direct the reader's attention to the discrete aspects involved in conceptualizing and addressing the research and writing process. Each of the chapters of Part II provides comprehensive instructions with respect to the content of a specific dissertation chapter, and how to develop that content. Instructions also pertain to understanding the process involved in setting up each dissertation chapter. The "Application" section of each chapter in Part II demonstrates what a completed chapter of a dissertation should look like by way of a consistent research example that is carried throughout all of the chapters. Although the application section of each chapter represents a model of application, in a real dissertation, the reader is reminded that the discussion would need to be elaborated as required.

At the outset of Part II, and throughout the chapters that constitute Part II, we are careful to point out that while most institutions will approach the proposal and dissertation in common ways, at the same time there are differences in terms of the organization and presentation, and distinct differences in terms of what and how qualitative language and terminology are used. This book presents information as guidelines that are meant to be flexible per institutional expectations and requirements and are subject to modification depending on your institution, department, and program.

The chapters that make up Part II are organized in such a way as to reflect and describe the actual chapters of a dissertation. Part II consists of six chapters:

Chapter 5, "Introduction to Your Study," explores the foundational elements that are necessary in the first chapter of a dissertation, which is the introduction to the study. This includes how to formulate a researchable problem statement and align this with the purpose and research questions. Also covered are the additional components of the first chapter of a dissertation, such as researcher assumptions, anticipated outcomes, overview of approach, rationale and significance, and clarification of terminology used.

Chapter 6, "Developing and Presenting Your Literature Review," provides an understanding of the function and purpose of a literature review, describes the role of a research-based critical literature review in a dissertation, and outlines the skills related to the various steps involved in conducting and presenting a thorough and systematic review of the literature, including identifying and retrieving relevant material and sources and analyzing, evaluating, and synthesizing ideas found in the literature. This chapter also addresses the conceptual framework as an integral element of the research process and provides detailed explanation regarding how to think about developing this and how it functions with regard to analysis.

Chapter 7, "Presenting Methodology and Research Approach," offers a guide for tackling the dissertation's methodology chapter. Key components of the methodology chapter are identified and explanation is provided regarding how each component of the research methodology must be developed and presented. This chapter illustrates how all of the components combined form a logical, interconnected sequence and contribute to the overall methodological integrity of the research study.

Chapter 8, "Analyzing Data and Reporting Findings," demonstrates how to write and present the findings of a research study. The challenge of qualitative analysis lies in making sense of large amounts of data—reducing raw data, identifying what is significant, and constructing a framework for communicating the essence of what the data reveal. This chapter begins with a conceptualization of qualitative data analysis and goes on to identify the specific strategies involved in analyzing qualitative data. Detailed explanations are provided regarding how to organize, reduce, and prepare raw data through coding and categorization; how to formulate clear and precise findings statements based on analysis of the data; and how to report and present findings in a clear, comprehensive, and systematic manner.

Chapter 9, "Analyzing and Interpreting Findings," explains how to analyze and interpret findings of the research. This chapter demonstrates how to integrate and synthesize the findings with the literature and to present the meaning behind those findings, which is the essence of the research. The chapter offers explanations regarding the concept of qualitative analysis and how to analyze and interpret the findings of the research. Included is also an explanation and description regarding the concept of synthesis as an ongoing process and how to go about presenting a final integrated synthesis.

Chapter 10, the final chapter of Part II, "Drawing Trustworthy Conclusions and Presenting Actionable Recommendations," presents the ways in which to address the last chapter of a dissertation: conclusions and recommendations. Included is an explanation of what conclusions are as distinct from findings and interpretations, as well as suggestions for thinking about and developing sound conclusions and practical, actionable, and research-based recommendations. The chapter also offers the researcher ideas for a final reflection statement.

Part III, "Nearing Completion," addresses the final stage of the dissertation process by explaining all the activities that need to take place when nearing completion of the dissertation and by providing guidelines regarding how to most effectively engage in these final activities including preparing for a successful defense. Part III is designed to bring a sense of closure to the dissertation process and to offer some suggestions for moving beyond the dissertation. It consists of two chapters:

Chapter 11, "Some Final Technical Considerations," focuses on the technical considerations involved in the final stages of the dissertation process. Here we offer advice and suggestions around the concept of alignment with regard to an entire dissertation. We also provide instruction and guidelines with regard to crafting an appropriate dissertation title, devising a dissertation abstract, proofreading, editing, and comprehensive assembly of the manuscript. This chapter also includes a comprehensive final checklist of activities.

Chapter 12, "Defense Preparation and Beyond," offers guidelines and suggestions regarding pre-dissertation preparation including choosing a committee and preparing for a successful defense. The chapter also offers guidelines and suggestions regarding post-defense preparation, including possible avenues for the presentation and publication of the research.

Defining Features of This Book

Some books on writing a dissertation explain the process in overcomplicated language—the classic textbook scholarly writing style that tends to mystify and overwhelm the reader. Other books on the subject make assumptions that by following a set of instructions the reader will somehow know how to conduct the process and do not take into account the inherent messiness of qualitative research. Still others offer way too many unrelated examples and fail to provide sufficient detail and strong examples of the various elements involved. All these versions are difficult to learn from. Included in *Completing Your Qualitative Dissertation: A Road Map From Beginning to End* are a number of useful and reader-friendly features that set this book apart:

- A real researchable problem is illustrated up front and is carried through each chapter to demonstrate each step of the dissertation process. By using a real problem, we model what a real dissertation should look like. Carrying one research problem throughout the chapters allows the reader to follow the same idea as it threads through all the different sections required in a dissertation.

- The focus throughout is on conceptual understanding as it relates to the practical aspects involved in navigating the dissertation process.
- Chapter objectives are outlined at the start of each chapter.
- The purpose of each chapter is twofold: to provide instruction and to demonstrate application. In this way, the chapters are, in effect, a dissertation in action. Each chapter of Part II mirrors the respective chapters of an actual dissertation. Chapters 5 through 10 set up the study and constitute the study's framework. Each of these chapters is presented in two sections: Section I provides instructions regarding the specific content of each chapter and how that content is developed. Section II is the application that demonstrates what a written-up chapter would look like based on the content developed.
- In the instruction section of each chapter, road maps in the form of tables, figures, and checklists are provided throughout the book. These afford the reader, at a glance, overviews at each stage of the research-writing process. These road maps are our own creation and have not been previously published.
- Based on the idea of road maps, we emphasize the use of working tools to clarify thinking and organize and present the data. Within each instruction section, we include templates for how to go about creating these working tools. In the appendices, we include various completed examples that offer the reader some idea of what the finished products might look like.
- There is an emphasis throughout the instruction sections on how to store and manage information.
- Although the objective of each application section is to illustrate the content of an actual dissertation, what is presented is not a full-blown dissertation chapter, but a representation or model of what the chapter should look like. The reader is constantly reminded that in a real dissertation the discussion would need to be more extensively expanded.
- We acknowledge and reinforce throughout the book that there are often institutional and/or program-related differences vis-à-vis the dissertation process. The processes described do not apply universally. This is particularly pertinent with respect to the nature of advisement, committee structure, proposal requirements, and methodological requirements.
- Where appropriate, we flag possible instances of differences in the content and structure of the dissertation so that students are aware of these.
- Where appropriate, we point out qualitative language and terminology that allows for differences among doctoral programs and higher education institutions.
- Where appropriate, we point out instances where qualitative traditions or genres might differ in application among themselves. This is particularly pertinent with respect to literature review and analysis of data.
- Each chapter concludes with an integrative summary discussion. These discussions highlight key concepts and issues raised in the chapter, as well as providing segues or transitions from one chapter to the next.

- A quality assessment checklist is provided for each chapter. This checklist is a supplement to the narrative and serves to review what needs to be accomplished before proceeding to the subsequent chapter. A final comprehensive checklist for the complete document is also provided.

- Each chapter includes an annotated bibliography for easy referral to additional up-to-date, cutting-edge, and relevant sources. In preparing this book, we have done extensive research and literature reviews, and we share sources that have been found to be most useful. In many cases, this includes seminal works in the field, but we also include works that are less well known and that we consider worthwhile and relevant.

- A comprehensive checklist of all the activities that constitute the entire dissertation process is provided on the inside of the back cover. This is a practical tool intended to help students get started on the process and keep themselves in check at every stage along the way.

The companion website **study.sagepub.com/bloomberg3e** provides free access to SAGE journal articles and other resources relevant to materials in the book. The website also includes a list of 101 questions that provide a comprehensive overview of the dissertation process in all its many varied components. The intent is that these questions will stimulate critical thinking, reflection, and dialogue, thereby motivating doctoral students or prospective doctoral students to seek and consult additional relevant texts and resources in order to delve deeper into the many issues raised. These questions might also be used to prompt discussion between doctoral students and their advisors. In addition, the website includes access to all tools and templates referenced and illustrated in the book, which are downloadable for ease of use.

New to the Third Edition: Chapter-by-Chapter Changes

This third edition of *Completing Your Qualitative Dissertation: A Road Map From Beginning to End* follows a similar structure to both the successful first edition published in 2008 and second edition published in 2012, and continues to offer doctoral students comprehensive guidance and accessible and practical tools for navigating each step in the recursive and iterative qualitative dissertation process. While key features that distinguish the book's unique approach are retained, this third edition responds to developments in the field as well as reviewer feedback. Two key elements are new to the third edition:

- Throughout, there is a greater focus on application to a broader range of qualitative traditions or genres. In the previous editions, case study was the dominant focal point. This broader coverage is reflected throughout the chapters (particularly Methodology and Analysis; Chapters 7, 8, and 9) as well as in the selected annotated bibliographies at the end of each chapter.

- There is a greater attempt throughout all the chapters to reiterate the iterative and nonlinear nature of qualitative research and the dissertation and model recursive behavior by continually referring the reader back to previous instruction regarding key concepts and processes. This was one of the reviewer suggestions that was greatly appreciated. Key concepts and processes include the following: Reflexivity especially with regard collaborative/critical approaches; portraying the process as doable without neglecting the complexity of the research and writing process; institutional differences in terms of style, content, process, and other specific requirements; and constant reminders regarding academic writing requirements.

Substantially rewritten for the second edition, Part I—"Taking Charge of Yourself and Your Work"—presents the initial steps involved in thinking about and preparing for the complex dissertation process. Included are four new separate chapters that address the knowledge, skills, and attitudes required to successfully complete the required work, as well as a new figure for visualizing and conceptualizing the entire dissertation process.

- An *all new* Chapter 1, "A Complete Dissertation: The Big Picture" (based on Bloomberg, 2009), outlines each content element involved in the dissertation process and includes "reasons," "quality markers," and "frequent errors" for each element. This broad guideline overview is a precursor of what is to come, with each element being more fully explored and developed further along in the book. Chapter 1 also now includes a new section for evaluating the quality of a qualitative dissertation, and toward this end, two new rubrics have been added.
- Chapter 2, "Gearing Up: There Is Method in the Madness," provides additional information and practical tips regarding organizing and managing the research project, additional details regarding choice of research topic, as well as expanded discussion pertaining to students and faculty as partner stakeholders in the dissertation process. In addition to choosing an advisor, the chapter elaborates on standards of good advisement practice, including student and faculty responsibilities, expectations, and obligations. Organizing and managing the project is also outlined in chart form for easy reference.
- Chapter 3, "Choosing a Qualitative Research Approach," deals with choosing an appropriate qualitative research approach and includes new sections on the history and landscape of qualitative research. This chapter now incorporates additional detailed and more critical discussion around the seven qualitative traditions or genres that are presented (case study, ethnography, phenomenology, grounded theory, narrative inquiry, action research, and postmodernism), with a greater focus on comparative analytic and representational strategies. There is also an increased emphasis on reflexivity, representation, positioning, and voice as integral features of critical and participatory qualitative research.

Additional details pertaining to the key defining features of qualitative research as a field of inquiry have also been added to enhance greater understanding of the nuances of this field of inquiry.

- Chapter 4, "A First Step: Developing Your Proposal," includes additional updated references to a variety of style manuals used in the social sciences, guidelines for strong academic writing, and expanded discussion around plagiarism in academic and professional contexts, including accidental plagiarism and ways to avoid this offense, as well as expanded discussion around IRB application and approval. New academic writing resources and Internet resources have been added. The discussion around developing the proposal has been extended, with additional reference to the integral function of the conceptual framework throughout the dissertation. The lengthy chapter summary has been reorganized and broken into smaller segments for ease of usability.

The chapters of Part II, "Content and Process: A Chapter-by-Chapter Roadmap," continue to mirror the chapters of an actual dissertation. Chapters 5 through 7 set up the study and constitute the study's framework. As pointed out in Part I, these three chapters form the research proposal. Chapters 8 through 10 discuss how to analyze and present the data that are collected.

- Chapter 5, "Introduction to Your Study," remains largely unchanged except for greater discussion around the significance of the research problem and the addition of new figures and updated references. The application section, particularly the research problem, has been updated to include current references. As mentioned at the outset, and again in subsequent chapters, the reader is continually reminded that while most institutions will approach the proposal and dissertation in common ways, there are differences in terms of the organization and presentation of the proposal and dissertation, and distinct differences in terms of what and how qualitative language and terminology are used.
- In appreciating how doctoral students often struggle to comprehend the nature of the conceptual framework, a notion that is largely abstract due to lack of uniform and consistent definitions, additional discussion in Chapter 6, "Developing and Presenting Your Literature Review," serves to enhance and clarify this integral and significant aspect that has significant implications for the design and analysis of qualitative research. There is expanded discussion regarding theoretical definitions, how to develop a conceptual framework and how it functions in analysis, different ways of going about creating the framework, and its value and potential limitations in terms of its permeation throughout the research and dissertation. In addition, there is an expanded section regarding literature synthesis (and how this differs from summary), information regarding annotated bibliographies and digesting scholarly sources, as well as extended discussion around exploring and evaluating web resources.

- Chapter 7, "Presenting Methodology and Research Approach," remains largely unchanged except for additional discussion regarding sampling, issues of validity and trustworthiness, limitations, and delimitations. There is reiteration of the importance that while most institutions will approach the dissertation in common ways, at the same time there are differences in terms of the organization and presentation, and also distinct differences in terms of what and how qualitative language and terminology are used. As such, this is an important consideration in terms of planning, conducting, and writing up the research study.

- Chapter 8, "Analyzing Data and Reporting Findings," continues to acknowledge analytic distinctions among traditions and genres, emphasizing how each tradition is sensitive to particular analytic methods and strategies. There is additional discussion regarding issues involved in qualitative analysis, including selecting codes and presenting categories of findings on a macro thematic level. New references to various qualitative data analysis software resources are included, as well as an overview of the most commonly used analytic software packages currently available, including description of key features and practical relevance vis-à-vis the various qualitative genres.

- Chapter 9, "Analyzing and Interpreting Findings," provides additional material and references regarding data analysis and representation within the different qualitative approaches, development of analytic categories, and trustworthiness and credibility of researcher interpretation. Additional emphasis is placed on interpretation and reflexivity.

- In Chapter 10, "Drawing Trustworthy Conclusions and Presenting Actionable Recommendations," additional strategies have been researched for drawing original conclusions from qualitative data, and related trustworthiness issues are elaborated upon.

Reorganized and restructured, Part III, "Nearing Completion," focuses on the final stages of the dissertation process, and now includes two new stand-alone chapters:

- Chapter 11, "Some Final Technical Considerations," deals with various technical considerations and expands on what an abstract is and the art and science, or "how-to," of crafting an effective and comprehensive abstract. Additional details pertaining to the dissertation's appendices are also included. In addition, new to the second edition, and retained in this third edition, is an all-inclusive and comprehensive quality assessment checklist for the complete dissertation.

- Chapter 12, "Defense Preparation and Beyond," deals with the challenges encountered in pre- and post-defense preparation. The chapter remains largely unchanged, except for the addition of new resources pertaining to journal publication. The second edition saw additional defense questions pertaining to the study's conceptual framework, and regarding post-defense preparation, a greatly expanded section devoted to the presentation and publication of dissertation research with the inclusion of new resources and references.

New organization and structure throughout this third edition includes

- Where possible, sections where the narrative was too dense have been reorganized and additional headings and/or subheadings have been included so that the reader can more easily follow the text.
- Revised format and easier access for "Application" sections of Chapters 5 through 10.
- To the degree possible, "Application" sections have been updated to include most current references.
- Updated tabulated "quality assessment checklists" for each chapter as well as a final detailed and extensive summary checklist. Previously long checklists are now clustered in chart form and as such, are more user-friendly and accessible.
- Updated references, citations, and websites throughout that include new and cutting-edge research and practice, as well as attention to new editions of previously cited works.
- Inclusion of new and updated annotated bibliographies throughout, which provide broad coverage of all seven qualitative traditions included in the book. In order to remain relevant and accessible, all outdated annotations were discarded. A total of 21 new and current annotations were added.
- Additional revisions to existing charts for organizing and managing data.
- Updated and reformulated appendices where necessary.
- Additional appendices, including two extensive rubrics for evaluating the quality of a completed dissertation and literature review. These rubrics are referenced in Chapter 1 where reasons for inclusion, evaluative quality markers, and frequent errors regarding all aspects of the dissertation are included. These rubrics will hopefully be highly useful to both professors and doctoral students.

The companion website **study.sagepub.com/bloomberg3e** an ancillary package designed by lead author Linda Dale Bloomberg to accompany this text, provides free access to SAGE journal articles and other resources relevant to materials in the book. The website also includes a list of 101 questions that provide a comprehensive overview of the dissertation process in all its many varied components. The intent is that these questions will stimulate critical thinking, reflection, and dialogue, thereby motivating doctoral students or prospective doctoral students to seek and consult additional relevant texts and resources in order to delve deeper into the many issues raised. These questions might also be used to prompt discussion between doctoral students and their advisors. In addition, the website includes access to all tools and templates referenced and illustrated in the book, which are downloadable for ease of use.

• Acknowledgments •

*C*ompleting Your Qualitative Dissertation: A Road Map From Beginning to End is meant as a tribute to the resolve of the countless doctoral students with whom we have worked and continue to work, and from whom we have learned so much. This book could not have been conceptualized without being a part of their experiences. Of special importance to the completion of this work are the doctoral students who we interviewed, and who candidly shared their experiences and insights, thereby providing the rich qualitative data for the book's application sections.

Many thanks to those who have contributed in various ways to the enhancement and reorganization of this third edition: Helen Salmon, acquisitions editor, for her constructive feedback and suggestions, and for her ongoing support, collaboration, and expertise at all stages of this project; Anna Villarruel, editorial assistant, for her support and assistance; Laura Barrett, production editor, for her efficiency and professional support in overseeing the editing process; Renee Willers, copy editor, for her time, thoroughness, and attention to detail in refining and editing the entire manuscript; and Katie Bierach, eLearning editor, for her support with producing and overseeing the book's companion website. It has been a pleasure to work with this team of professionals.

Great appreciation goes to SAGE Publications for recognizing the value of this book, and as with the first and second editions, for working tirelessly and collaboratively to prepare this third edition for publication in record time. The success of the previous editions of this book is indeed gratifying, as is the ongoing positive feedback that I continue to hear from students and faculty alike in various parts of the world. My hope is that this third edition will continue to offer the support, structural framework, and guidelines that doctoral students seek in their journey along the long road of developing and defending a rigorous qualitative dissertation.

Special mention of gratitude to Corinne Broomberg, Maxine Benjamin, Vivienne Goldcwajg, Mandy Goldin, Fay Lewis, Brenda Hoffman, Clive Goldin, Mark Weinberg, Liora Krug, Gina Shomalistos, Debbie Levinson, Melissa Sacks, Mieko Kobayashi, Sheryl Westerman, and Janet Schatten; in everlasting appreciation of their friendship, love, and support. And special thanks to Roberta Louis Goodman, teacher, colleague, and mentor, for her ongoing guidance and encouragement over the years.

SAGE Publications and the author gratefully acknowledge the contributions of the following reviewers: Antonio C. Cuyler, Florida State University; Kriss Y. Kemp-Graham, Texas A&M University–Commerce; Nathan R. Templeton, Texas A&M University–Commerce; Marilyn J. Bruin, University of Minnesota; Kate de Medeiros, Miami University; Karen L. Mackie, University of Rochester; and Amira Proweller, DePaul University. In addition, we acknowledge the many faculty members and doctoral students at various institutions who have taken the time to critically evaluate this text and provide their generous endorsement of its value.

• About the Authors •

Linda Dale Bloomberg, lead author, is former adjunct faculty and dissertation advisor in adult learning and leadership at Teachers College, Columbia University. As senior researcher for the South African Human Sciences Research Council and National Institute for Personnel Research, Dr. Bloomberg's work focused on change management, diversity initiatives, and enhanced workplace learning. She currently teaches qualitative research in graduate programs, serves as dissertation advisor, and also serves as consultant to various research, higher education, and nonprofit advisory boards. She is founder of Bloomberg Associates and ILIAD (Institute for Learning Innovations and Adult Development), and a cofounder of Columbia University's Global Learning and Leadership Institute. She has authored and edited numerous publications in the fields of organizational evaluation, qualitative research, leadership development, adult learning, and distance education. She is currently working on *Executive Coaching: Supporting Adult Development and Implications for Learning and Leadership.* Dr. Bloomberg holds master's degrees in counseling psychology, organizational psychology, and Jewish education. In 2006, she received her doctorate in adult education and organizational learning from Columbia University.

Marie Volpe is adjunct faculty in adult learning and leadership at Teachers College, Columbia University, where she teaches dissertation seminars and serves as advisor to doctoral candidates. She conducts workshops for teachers in Mongolia and lectures on qualitative research methods at Suzhou University, China. After a career spanning 35 years with Exxon Corporation, where she held the position of manager of education and development, Dr. Volpe embarked on a second career in higher education, in which she has practiced for the past 20 years. She has contributed to publications in the areas of staff development and informal learning in the workplace. She received her master's in organizational psychology and doctorate in adult education from Columbia University.

SAGE | 50 YEARS

SAGE was founded in 1965 by Sara Miller McCune to support the dissemination of usable knowledge by publishing innovative and high-quality research and teaching content. Today, we publish over 900 journals, including those of more than 400 learned societies, more than 800 new books per year, and a growing range of library products including archives, data, case studies, reports, and video. SAGE remains majority-owned by our founder, and after Sara's lifetime will become owned by a charitable trust that secures our continued independence.

Los Angeles | London | New Delhi | Singapore | Washington DC

TAKING CHARGE OF YOURSELF AND YOUR WORK

PART I

T he intent of this book is to demystify and clarify the dissertation process while maintaining intellectual rigor and the highest ethical standards of research. Part I presents the initial steps involved in thinking about and preparing for the complex dissertation process by expanding appreciation and understanding of both the content and the process pertaining to conducting qualitative research and producing a sound defensible dissertation. This work is intellectually rigorous, requiring intensive thinking, preparation, and planning, and is very much a matter of having tenacity, perseverance, and patience. Completing a dissertation is, in fact, a process of continuous learning because for most people, conducting research and writing a document such as this is a first-time endeavor, an undertaking for which there is little experience. By the end of the process, you will indeed have learned as much about yourself and how to conduct research as you will have learned about the subject of your inquiry. Chapter 1 provides an overview of all key elements for each section of the dissertation—that is, a precursor of what is to come further along in this book. Chapter 2 addresses the knowledge, skills, and attitudes required to successfully complete the required work. Chapter 3 discusses the implications of choosing an appropriate qualitative research approach in an attempt to develop conceptual understanding of the logic behind choice of research approach. Chapter 4 explains the process and content involved in developing a sound and comprehensive research proposal.

The following figure depicts the cyclical and complex qualitative dissertation process in its entirety. This figure demonstrates the iterative nature of qualitative research, by illustrating the relationships between and among multiple components. The figure also sheds light on the continuum of movement between technical (micro), practical (macro), and conceptual (meta) levels of thinking and explains the inherent hierarchy of activities that constitute the complex dissertation process.

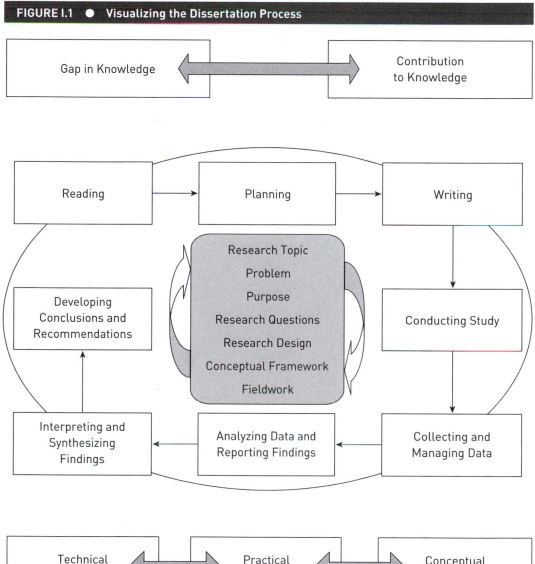

FIGURE I.1 ● Visualizing the Dissertation Process

Source: This figure first appeared in Bloomberg, L. D. (2010). *Understanding qualitative inquiry: Content and process* (Part II). Unpublished manuscript.

A Complete Dissertation

The Big Picture

Chapter 1 Objectives

- Provide *a cursory glance* at the constitution of an entire dissertation.

- Offer a comprehensive outline of all key elements for each section of the dissertation—that is, a precursor of what is to come, with each element being more fully developed and explained further along in the book.

- For each key element, explain reason for inclusion, quality markers, and frequent or common errors.

Overview

Following is a road map that briefly outlines the contents of an entire dissertation. This is a comprehensive overview, and as such is helpful in making sure that at a glance you understand up front the necessary elements that will constitute each section of your dissertation. Reasons for inclusion, quality markers, and frequent errors are included for each element of the dissertation. This broad overview is a prelude to the steps involved in each of the chapters that are described and demonstrated in Part II. While certain elements are common to most dissertations, please note that dissertation requirements vary by institution. Toward that end, students should always consult with their advisor and committee members to ascertain any details of any of the elements that might be specific or particular to institutional or departmental requirements. Finally, a rubric for evaluating a complete qualitative dissertation and a rubric for specifically evaluating the quality of a literature review are included.

Front Matter

Order and format of front matter may vary by institution and department.

- Title page
- Copyright page (optional)
- Abstract
- Dedication (optional)
- Acknowledgments (optional)
- Table of contents
- List of tables and figures (only those in chapters, not those in appendices)

Title Page

The title gives a clear and concise description of the topic and/or problem and the scope of the study. The title page will show the title; the author's full name; the degree to be conferred; the university, department, and college in which the degree is earned; and the month and year of approval. Margins for the title page and the entire document are left—1.5 inches; right, top, and bottom—1 inch. Also, the title should be in all capitals.

Reason The title both guides and reflects the purpose and content of the study, making its relevance apparent to prospective readers. The title is also important for retrieval purposes enabling other researchers to locate it through a literature search.

Quality Markers A well-crafted title conveys the essence and purpose of the study. The title should include the type of study ("An Analysis") and the participants. Use of keywords will promote proper categorization into databases such as ERIC (the Education Resources Information Center) and Dissertation Abstracts International.

Frequent Errors Frequent title errors include the use of trendy, elaborate, nonspecific, or literary language, and grandiose or unrealistic expectations (e.g., "Finally, a Solution to . . .").

Copyright Page (optional)

Copyright is the legal right of an owner of created material to control copying and ownership of that material. Authors of research documents who wish to protect their writing through copyright may do so. A student may file a claim to copyright by corresponding directly with the U.S. Copyright Office (Library of Congress, 101 Independence Avenue S.E., Washington, DC 20559-6000).

The copyright symbol (©) should appear with author's name and year centered between the margins on the lower half of the backside of the title page. Below the copyright line, include the statement "All Rights Reserved."

Abstract

The abstract, limited to 350 words, is a concise summary description of the study, including statement of the problem, purpose, scope, research tradition, data sources, methodology, key findings, and implications. The abstract is written after the dissertation is completed and is written from the perspective of an outside reader (i.e., not "My dissertation examines" but "An examination of…").

The page numbers before the text are in Roman numerals. The abstract page is the first page to be numbered, but as iii. All Roman numerals should be centered between the left and right margins, and 1 inch from the bottom of the page. The title of the page, "ABSTRACT," should be in all capitals and centered between the left and right margins and 2 inches from the top.

Reason The abstract's inclusion in Dissertation Abstracts International (which mandates a 350-word limit) makes it possible for other researchers to determine the relevance of this work to their own studies. Over 95% of American dissertations are included in Dissertation Abstracts International.

Quality Markers Marks of quality include conciseness and accuracy. The abstract should also be written in the third person (active voice without the personal pronouns *I* and *we*). Generally, the first sentence of an abstract describes the entire study; subsequent sentences expand on that description.

Frequent Errors Inclusion of irrelevant material (i.e., examples, information extraneous to the dissertation itself), exclusion of necessary material (i.e., problem, purpose, scope, research tradition, data sources, methodology, key findings, and implications), and incorrect format are frequent abstract errors.

Dedication and Acknowledgments (optional)

These pages are optional, although most dissertations include a brief acknowledgment of the contributions of committee members, colleagues, friends, and family members who have supported the students' research. "ACKNOWLEDGMENTS" should be capitalized and should appear centered between the left and right margins, 2 inches from the top. Text should begin two line spaces after "ACKNOWLEDGMENTS."

The dedication page is separate from the acknowledgments page. If included, the dedication text should be centered between the left and right margins and between the top and bottom margins; it should also reflect a professional nature. Do not include the title "DEDICATION" on the dedication page.

Table of Contents

An outline of the entire dissertation, listing headings and subheadings with their respective page numbers, the table of contents lists all chapters and major sections within chapters and all back matter with page numbers.

The heading "TABLE OF CONTENTS" is centered between the left and right margins, 2 inches from the top of the page. The listing begins one double space below and even with the left margin. Leader dots are placed from the end of each listing to the corresponding page number. All major titles are typed exactly as they appear in the text. When a title or subtitle exceeds one line, the second and succeeding lines are single-spaced and indented two spaces. Double spacing is used between major titles and between each major title and its subtitle.

The table of contents may be followed by any of the following, if needed, and any of these subsequent lists are formatted in the same manner as the table of contents:

- List of tables
- List of figures
- List of illustrations
- List of symbols

Reason The table of contents assists the researcher in organizing the material while promoting accessibility for the reader.

Quality Markers The headings and subheadings clearly and concisely reflect the material being presented. Headings and subheadings are parallel grammatically (i.e., "Introduction," "Review of Literature" not "Introduction," "Reviewing the Literature"). The headings and subheadings in the table of contents are worded exactly the same as those headings and subheadings in the text.

Frequent Errors Frequent errors include lack of parallelism in headings and subheadings, as well as wording in the table of contents that does not match wording in text.

Dissertation Chapters

Order and format of dissertation chapters may vary by institution and department.

1. Introduction
2. Literature review
3. Methodology
4. Findings
5. Analysis and synthesis
6. Conclusions and recommendations

Chapter 1: Introduction

This chapter makes a case for the significance of the problem, contextualizes the study, and provides an introduction to its basic components. It should be informative and able to stand alone as a document.

- **Introduction:** The introduction includes an overview of the purpose and focus of the study, why it is significant, how it was conducted, and how it will contribute to professional knowledge and practice.
- **Problem statement:** The problem indicates the need for the study, describes the issue or problem to be studied, and situates it in a broader educational or social context. The problem statement includes a brief, well-articulated summary of the literature that substantiates the study, with references to more detailed discussions in Chapter 2.
- **Statement of purpose:** Describing the research purpose in a logical, explicit manner, the statement of purpose is the major objective or intent of the study; it enables the reader to understand the central thrust of the research.
- **Research question(s):** Research questions are directly tied to the purpose. They should be specific, unambiguously stated, and open-ended. These questions cue readers to the direction the study will take and help to delineate the scope of the study.
- **Overview of methodology:** This section outlines the methodological type or approach, the research setting, the sample, instrumentation (if relevant), and methods of data collection and analysis used.
- **Rationale and significance:** Rationale is the justification for the study presented as a logical argument. Significance addresses the benefits that may be derived from doing the study, thereby reaffirming the research purpose.
- **Role of the researcher:** This section explains the role of the researcher in planning and conducting the study.
- **Researcher assumptions:** This section makes explicit relevant researcher assumptions, beliefs, and biases (if applicable).
- **Definition of key terminology:** Some terms may be unfamiliar to readers. In addition, the meanings of certain terms can vary depending on the context, conceptual framework, or field of study. Making terms explicit adds precision and ensures clarity of understanding. These terms should be operationally defined or explained; that is, be sure to make clear how these terms are used in *your* study.
- **Organization of the dissertation:** This brief concluding explanation delineates the contents of the remaining chapters in the dissertation.

Reason The introduction sets the stage for the study and directs readers to the purpose and context of the dissertation.

Quality Markers A quality introduction situates the context and scope of the study and informs the reader, providing a clear and valid representation of what will be found in the remainder of the dissertation. Discussion is concise and precise.

Frequent Errors Errors occur when the introduction does not clearly reflect the study and/or its relationship to the proposed problem and purpose, or it does not stand alone as a document.

Chapter 2: Literature Review

This chapter situates the study in the context of previous research and scholarly material pertaining to the topic, presents a critical synthesis of empirical literature according to relevant themes or variables, justifies how the study addresses a gap or problem in the literature, and outlines the theoretical or conceptual framework of the study. A dissertation does not merely restate the available knowledge base of a particular topic, but adds to or augments it.

- *Introduction:* The introduction describes the content, scope, and organization of the review as well as the strategy used in the literature search.
- *Review of literature:* This section accomplishes the following:
  - is clearly related to the problem statement, purpose, and research questions;
  - states up front the bodies of literature that will be covered, and why;
  - reviews primary sources that are mostly recent empirical studies from scholarly journals and publications, as well as secondary sources;
  - is logically organized by theme or subtopic, from broad to narrow;
  - synthesizes findings across studies and compares and contrasts different research outcomes, perspectives, or methods;
  - notes gaps, debates, or shortcomings in the literature and provides a rationale for the study; and
  - provides section summaries.

- *Conceptual framework:* The conceptual framework draws on theory, research, and experience, and examines the relationship among constructs and ideas. As such, it is the structure or heuristic that guides your research. In essence, the conceptual framework provides the theoretical and method-ological bases for development of the study and analysis of findings. When appropriate, a graphic depiction of the model is included, showing the relationships between concepts, ideas, or variables to be studied.
- *Summary:* A comprehensive synthesis of the literature review should complete this section.

Reason This chapter provides a strong theoretical basis for the dissertation by ana-lyzing and synthesizing a comprehensive selection of appropriate related bodies of literature. The review of literature should build a logical framework for the research, justify the study by conceptualizing gaps in the literature, and demonstrate how the study will contribute to existing knowledge. The review serves to situate the dissertation within the context of current ongoing conversations in the field. The conceptual framework guides the research and plays a major role in analysis of findings.

Quality Markers A comprehensive and thoughtful selection of resources that cover the material directly related to the study's purpose and background, not the full scope of the field, is considered a mark of a quality literature review. All relevant primary sources and empirical research studies are cited (these are preferable to secondary sources, which are interpretation of the work of others). The writer adopts a critical perspective in discussing the work of others and provides a clear analysis of all available related research. Relevant literature is critiqued, not duplicated, and there is a clear connection between the purpose of this study and the resources included. The conceptual framework's role and function are clear: The conceptual framework clearly draws on theory, research, and experience, providing conceptual coherence to the research. Another quality marker is the correct use of American Psychological Association (APA) format, citations, and references throughout.

Frequent Errors Frequent errors include insubstantial breadth of review (i.e., insufficient number or range of resources; failure to include relevant primary sources) and insubstantial depth of review (i.e., use of nonscholarly material; inability to demonstrate clear understanding of resources). Another error is that the review reads more like a catalog of sources than a synthesis and integration of relevant literature. There is also a tendency to eliminate literature that contradicts or questions the findings of the dissertation's study. Other errors include incorrect or insufficient citation of sources, resulting in accidental plagiarism, and presentation of a diagrammatic conceptual framework with no accompanying narrative explanation.

Chapter 3: Methodology

This chapter situates the study within a particular methodological tradition, provides a rationale for that approach, describes the research setting and sample, and describes data collection and analysis methods. The chapter provides a detailed description of all aspects of the design and procedures of the study.

- *Introduction:* The introduction restates the research purpose and describes the organization of the chapter.
- *Rationale for research approach:* This section describes the research tradition or paradigm (qualitative research) and the research methodology (phenomenology, case study, action research, etc.) with a rationale for their suitability regarding addressing the research questions, and citing appropriate methodological literature.
- *Research setting and/or context:* This section describes and justifies selection of the research setting, thereby providing the history, background, and issues germane to the problem.

- ***Research sample and data sources:*** This section
  - explains and justifies the sample used and how participants were selected (including population and sampling procedures);
  - describes the characteristics and size of the sample and provides other pertinent demographic information; and
  - outlines ethical considerations pertaining to participants, shedding light on how rights of participants were protected, with reference to conventions of research ethics and the IRB (institutional review board) process.

- ***Data collection methods:*** This section describes and justifies all data collection methods, tools, instruments, and procedures, including how, when, where, and by whom data were collected.

- ***Data analysis methods:*** This section describes and justifies all methods and tools used for analysis of data (manual and/or computational).

- ***Issues of trustworthiness:*** This section discusses measures taken to enhance the study, as well as credibility (validity) and dependability (reliability).

- ***Limitations and delimitations:*** This section identifies potential weaknesses of the study and the scope of the study. Limitations are external conditions that restrict or constrain the study's scope or may affect its outcome. Delimitations are conditions or parameters that the researcher intentionally imposes in order to limit the scope of a study (e.g., using participants of certain ages, genders, or groups; conducting the research in a single setting). Generalizability is not the goal of qualitative research; rather, the focus is on transferability—that is, the ability to apply findings in similar contexts or settings.

- ***Summary:*** A comprehensive summary overview covers all the sections of this chapter, recapping and highlighting all the important points. Discussion is concise and precise.

Reason The study is the basis for the conclusions and recommendations. In many ways, it is what makes the difference between a dissertation and other forms of extended writing. A clear description of the research sample, setting, methodology, limitations, and delimitations and acknowledgment of trustworthiness issues provide readers with a basis for accepting (or not accepting) the conclusions and recommendations that follow.

Quality Markers A quality study achieves the purposes outlined in the introduction's research problem and research questions. The relationship of the research paradigm and type of data collection and analysis used in this study is clear. All relevant information is clearly articulated and presented. Narrative is accompanied by clear and descriptive visuals (charts, figures, tables).

Frequent Errors Errors occur when data are not clearly presented; the study is not applicable to purposes outlined in the introduction; and methods of gathering and analyzing data and trustworthiness issues are insufficient or not clearly explained.

Chapter 4: Findings

This chapter organizes and reports the study's main findings, including the presentation of relevant quantitative (statistical) and qualitative (narrative) data. Findings are often written up in different ways depending on the research tradition or genre adopted.

- ***Introduction:*** The introduction provides a brief summary of and rationale for how data were analyzed. It describes the organization of the chapter according to research questions, conceptual framework, or thematic categories.
- Findings build logically from the problem, research questions, and design.
- Findings are presented in clear narrative form using plentiful verbatim quotes, and "thick description." Narrative data are connected and synthesized through substantive explanatory text and visual displays, if applicable, not simply compiled. Some tables and figures may be deferred to the appendices.
- Headings are used to guide the reader through the findings according to research questions, themes, or other appropriate organizational schemes.
- Inconsistent, discrepant, or unexpected data are noted with discussion of possible alternative explanations.
- ***Summary:*** This section explains in summary form what the chapter has identified and prepares the reader for the chapters to follow by offering some foreshadowing as to the intent and content of the final two chapters.

Reason The challenge of qualitative analysis lies in making sense of large amounts of data, reducing raw data, identifying what is significant, and constructing a framework for communicating the essence of what the data reveal. The researcher, as storyteller, is able to tell a story that is vivid and interesting and at the same time accurate and credible. This chapter is the foundation for the analysis, conclusions, and recommendations that will appear in the next and forthcoming chapters.

Quality Markers Markers of a quality findings chapter include clear, complete, and valid representation of the data that have emerged as a result of the study and effective use of graphs, charts, and other visual representations to illustrate the data. Findings are presented objectively, without speculation—that is, free from researcher bias. Presentation and structure in this chapter are neat, precise, and related to the study's qualitative tradition or genre.

Frequent Errors Errors occur when study findings are manipulated to fit expectations from research questions, or when researcher bias and/or subjectivity is apparent. Other frequent errors include poor or invalid use of visual representation and findings not overly generalized.

Chapter 5: Analysis and Synthesis

This chapter synthesizes and discusses the results in light of the study's research questions, literature review, and conceptual framework. Finding patterns and themes is one result of analysis. Finding ambiguities and inconsistencies is another. Overall, this chapter offers the researcher an opportunity to reflect thoroughly on the study's findings and the practical and theoretical implications thereof.

- ***Introduction:*** The introduction provides an overview of the chapter's organization and content.
- ***Discussion:*** This section provides an in-depth interpretation, analysis, and synthesis of the results and/or findings.
  - Analysis is a multilayered approach. Seeking emergent patterns among findings can be considered a first round of analysis. Examining whether the literature corresponds with, contradicts, and/or deepens interpretations constitutes a second layer of interpretation.
  - Issues of trustworthiness are incorporated as these relate to and are applied throughout the analysis process.
  - Discussion may include interpretation of any findings that were not anticipated when the study was first described. Establishing credibility means that you have engaged in the systematic search for rival or competing explanations and interpretations.
  - This section restates the study's limitations and discusses transferability of the findings to broader populations or other settings and conditions.

Reason Analysis is essentially about searching for patterns and themes that emerge from the findings. The goal is to discover what meaning you can make of them by comparing your findings both within and across groups, and with those of other studies. Interpretation that is thoughtful and compelling will provide the opportunity to make a worthwhile contribution to your academic discipline.

Quality Markers There is no clear and accepted single set of conventions for the analysis and interpretation of qualitative data. This chapter reflects a deep understanding of what lies beneath the findings—that is, what those findings really *mean*. Interpretation is presented systematically and is related to the literature, conceptual framework, and interpretive themes or patterns that have emerged. A key characteristic of qualitative research is willingness to tolerate ambiguity. As such, examining issues from all angles in order to demonstrate *the most plausible* explanations is an indication of high-level analysis. Integrity as a researcher is given credence by inclusion of all information, even that which challenges inferences and assumptions.

Frequent Errors Frequent errors include analysis that is simple or shallow. Synthesis is lacking; there is no clear connection to other research literature or theory. Credibility and/or plausibility of explanations is in question. The chapter is poorly structured, presented, and articulated.

Chapter 6: Conclusions and Recommendations

This chapter presents a set of concluding statements and recommendations. Conclusions are assertions based on findings and must therefore be warranted by the findings. With respect to each finding, you are asking yourself, "Knowing what I now know, what conclusion can I draw?" Recommendations are the application of those conclusions. In other words, you are now saying to yourself, "Knowing what I now know to be true, I recommend that . . ."

- Conclusions are based on an integration of the study findings, analysis, interpretation, and synthesis.
- Concluding statements end the dissertation with strong, clear, concise "takeaway messages" for the reader.
- Conclusions are not the same as findings; neither are conclusions the same as interpretations. Rather, conclusions are essentially conclusive statements of what you now know, having done this research, that you did not know before.
- Conclusions must be logically tied to one another. There should be consistency among your conclusions; none of them should be at odds with any of the others.
- Recommendations are actionable; that is, they suggest implications for policy and practice based on the findings, providing specific action planning and next steps.
- Recommendations support the belief that scholarly work initiates as many questions as it answers, thus opening the way for further practice and research.
- Recommendations for research describe topics that require closer examination and that may generate new questions for further study.

Reason This chapter reflects the contribution the researcher has made to the knowledge and practice in his or her field of study. In many ways, it provides validation for the researcher's entrance into the ranks of the body of scholars in the field.

Quality Markers Clearly stated and focused concluding statements reflect an integration of the study findings, analysis, interpretation, and synthesis. Recommendations must have implications for policy and practice, as well as for further research, and *must* be doable. The reasonableness of a recommendation depends on its being logically and clearly derived from the findings, both content and context specific, and most important, practical and capable of implementation.

Frequent Errors Overgeneralization of importance or relevance sometimes leads to grandiose statements. Other frequent errors include the lack of a clear link to the review of literature, or recommendations that have no clear usefulness for practice and future research; that is, they are not "doable."

Epilogue, Afterword, or Final Thoughts

This final section offers the researcher an opportunity to reflect on the overall process, review the findings that have emerged, and share any new learning and insights that she or he has developed over the course of the research and writing process. How do you personally value the research experience? What are the lessons you have learned from conducting the study? What insights, knowledge, and inspiration have you derived from conducting this study?

Back Matter

Appendices

Appendices contain all research instruments used, as well as any relevant additional materials such as sample interview transcripts, sample coding schemes, summary charts, and so forth. Each item that is included as an appendix is given a letter or number and listed in the table of contents.

References

The list of references includes all works cited in the dissertation in alphabetical order by author and in proper APA format. All sources that are quoted, summarized, or paraphrased, as well as all other sources of information (text, visual, electronic, personal, etc.), must be correctly cited using APA parenthetical citation format within the dissertation. All sources must also be correctly listed on the references page. Proper citation serves several purposes: It attributes work fairly to the author, places the dissertation within the context of the literature in the field, and provides readers with a quick resource for locating and accessing sources that were used.

Evaluating the Quality of a Qualitative Dissertation

Now that you have some idea of the core elements that are required for the various sections of your dissertation, two rubrics are included for your convenience. These will hopefully provide you with useful information pertaining to the different levels of quality of a qualitative dissertation. In undertaking a research study the intent is to produce findings that will make a contribution to knowledge and ultimately make a difference in a discipline, practice, or policy. Quality must be evident in both the processes of the research, as well as in the final product; that is, your dissertation.

These two rubrics are by no means exhaustive since, as stressed previously, different institutions have different requirements and criteria, and there is no "one size fits all." The intention is that these are tools that will provide you with some idea of what the evaluation of a completed dissertation may involve. Appendix A is a rubric for evaluating a completed qualitative dissertation. Appendix B is a rubric for evaluating a completed literature review. Please use these rubrics as guides only in assessing or evaluating the quality of your own work and in determining where limitations may lie and where improvements can be made.

Gearing Up

There Is Method in the Madness

Overview

Undoubtedly, if you are reading this book, you are a continuous learner; it is the reason you decided to pursue a doctoral degree in the first place. It takes a certain amount of courage to take on this work because in many ways it is fraught with uncertainty. For those of you who are just starting out and for those who need to restart and continue, it can seem an overwhelming process. Truth be told, everyone who has ever embarked on this journey most likely has experienced a certain amount of anxiety, if not downright fear. Will I know how to do this work? Will I be up to the task? What if I fail? Ah, what if I succeed? Will it meet my expectations? These are some of the cobwebs that cloud our vision and stand in our way. It is OK to feel anxiety and fear. As a matter of fact, these feelings are natural as long as they do not debilitate us.

One way not to become overwhelmed is to look at the entire process of completing a dissertation as an incremental one. It is like the novice skier, who recognizes that a good way not to be overwhelmed by the sheer size of the mountain is to traverse it—going from side to side, conquering it bit by bit. It is a matter of taking one step at a time and finding out what is needed at each step along the way. That is what this book is all about—giving you the information you need and helping you to develop the skills required along the way to complete this work.

So let us take up our journey and begin by getting ourselves energized and organized mentally and physically. Begin by adopting a reflective stance—think about those things, personal and professional, that have caused you to procrastinate, get stuck, or even abandon the work. Attempt to come to terms with those obstacles. Persistence and determination are what it takes to finish. Develop a sense of urgency about completing your dissertation. No matter how talented you are, if you don't have a sense of urgency, develop it now! Make plans to deal with the real challenges that you face, and determine to move beyond your own self-imposed obstacles by taking action. Commit to acting despite your apprehensions and commit to developing an "I can do this" attitude; become your best friend and not your own worst enemy. This is of paramount importance. Once you have the right mind-set and attitude, you can begin to get organized.

Organizing and Managing Your Project

Your dissertation is an iterative (and often messy) project that will extend over a period of time. Therefore, successful completion requires careful organization and planning. To begin the process of getting organized, you need to create a "workspace" for your dissertation—a physical as well as a mental and intellectual space. You will also begin to create a system for organizing and managing your work on this project by developing a writing routine and by starting to keep records of information as well as of your thinking.

Creating a Workspace

Find a place where the dissertation is the only thing that you do. Find a space that works for you. A space where you can minimize distractions is key. This might be a coffee shop, the library, or an empty office at your workplace. The important thing is to find a space that for the time you dedicate to writing, only your dissertation exists. Having done this, you can then begin to plan time dedicated to writing and make this a concrete commitment by structuring time for writing. Remember, making specific plans to block off time for writing is a mental and emotional commitment.

And alerting people to your plans and taking concrete steps to structure your time builds in a social and physical commitment. You are then certainly more likely to write! And that's the goal!

Creating your new workspace means that you also should begin identifying writing resources. In addition to purchasing the relevant textbooks, become familiar with online library databases as they will become invaluable as well. Your computer, in connection with your university library system, is a literature searching and bibliographic management tool. An ongoing literature review begins right from the beginning stages of topic identification; continues with reviews of research methodologies, specific methods of data collection, and issues of trustworthiness; and carries through to the final stages of analysis and synthesis. In addition, you have to produce a bibliography or reference list that is formatted correctly and in perfect synchronization with the materials referenced in the body of your dissertation. This ongoing literature review can indeed be one of the most time consuming of all the dissertation challenges. It is certainly worth taking the time to become familiar with using your library's computerized search capability, as well as with the variety of software programs that allow you to efficiently perform the tasks of referencing your materials. We just briefly mention this now so that you can start adding these thoughts to your new mental workspace. Further details pertaining to some of the more commonly used electronic library databases for the social sciences are presented as Appendix C.

Managing the Data

As you begin your research and as you live with your study, you will begin to gather and accumulate a diverse array of material that has potential relevance. As you become immersed in your work, you will continue to be inundated with large amounts of information, including formal documents, correspondence, photocopies of articles, pieces of reflective writing, class notes, reading notes, discussion notes, handouts, and memos, as well as other miscellaneous scraps of paper. All of this information is the precursor to the final data. It is the raw material of the inquiry that will be of use later. You certainly do not want to lose any of your material, nor do you want to drown in it. Organizing and managing dissertation-related "stuff" right from the beginning is essential to getting on track and staying focused. In this regard, you will need to make sure that it is sorted systematically, stored safely and securely, and will be easily retrievable when you need to access it.

There are various systems for handling information at a practical level, and based on your learning style preference, different methods will seem more appealing. Those of us who are more visual and tactile like to print hard copies of everything and have the physical "evidence" in our hands. Some people "file" material in stacks or neatly labeled files or folders. Still others are less inclined to file manually, preferring to set up electronic folders in which to store information by way of emerging topics or chapters. Regardless of which method you choose, organizing your material well is a crucial step in the overall research process. By organizing your material, you will be able to easily retrieve your sources now and in the future, group similar sources together, and possibly identify potential patterns or links within your research topic.

In addition to storing various forms of information, you also should make sure that you keep the various drafts of your dissertation. During the process of writing your dissertation, drafts will need to be edited and refined. As you make revisions and update earlier versions, you will find yourself continually writing and rewriting. These drafts are important and should not be discarded. It is possible that you may want to revisit some text of an earlier version to check on something you have written. In addition, as your research and writing progress, by comparing drafts you can keep a check on your progress, as well as note any developments in your understanding of certain issues and phenomena. Therefore, before making revisions, original drafts should be kept intact, and each revised version should be labeled, dated, and stored in a designated file or folder for easy retrieval.

Whatever methods work best for you and whatever strategy of information management you choose, your computer will become your best friend throughout the dissertation process. Using your computer, you can catalogue, record, and manage multiple forms of information. Becoming familiar with your computer and technological resources before you start your research will save you much time and frustration. Developing computer literacy and mastering the software does add another layer of learning to an already intensive experience, but one that is well worth the effort. If you feel overwhelmed in this regard, you might want to seek technical assistance.

In addition, no matter what kind of computer system or software package you are working with, a necessary and, in fact, absolutely essential consideration is that you are—right from the beginning—vigilant in saving information. This goal can be accomplished by regularly and frequently backing up your files by way of copying them to your hard drive, as well as to a disk or flash drive, or by saving them to an online storage system such as Dropbox or Google Drive. You can never back up too much! Many people recommend printing out hard copies of completed sections in addition to saving electronic copies. As useful as they are, computers are not infallible. They can and do crash. Losing material can be a devastating setback in the dissertation process.

Planning Your Time

You might finally be ready to write your dissertation, but every time you sit down to work, you're seized with "writer's block." Most people have a romantic image of a writer as someone who writes during spontaneous bursts of creativity. Unfortunately, few writers write only when they feel inspired, and waiting for inspiration is impractical when you are working on a long-term project such as a dissertation. If you work on your dissertation only when you feel like it, the project will never be completed. It certainly requires self-discipline to always be ready to write on certain days whether you feel inspired or not and to stick to self-imposed deadlines. Yet the right plans and routines can make self-discipline an extremely easy thing to establish. Effective planning is key to gaining better control over one's writing. Organizing our time makes writing far less stressful, and helps us actually accomplish goals we might otherwise consider out of our reach. When thinking about planning time and establishing realistic time-lines, you should be thinking of continuing the same approach to time management as when completing your coursework, which was an essential step in the doctoral process, and which enabled you to reach the point of embarking on your dissertation. Similarly, after completing the coursework, you will now need to develop a system of planning your writing times and adhering to the schedule. Figure 2.1 is an example of a schedule-planning tool.

By providing this essentially amorphous and iterative process with some structure, a structured timetable makes writing more predictable and therefore less intimidating and allows you to pace yourself. Scheduling your time allows you to develop a plan for writing a "done" dissertation. (Remember, the best dissertation is a "done" disser-tation!) Schedules also help reduce the pressure associated with deadlines as well as the tendency to procrastinate. Moreover, setting a schedule also helps integrate your writing into the rest of your life, which is important. There are some basic principles for developing an effective writing schedule:

- Make a list of your regular activities, and within that context, decide how much time you hope to devote to your writing. If you've never tried a weekly schedule before, be open to adjustment. Try to create a balance between writing and other activities.

- Identify the times and days when you are most productive and least likely to be interrupted. For example, if you know you are tired in the afternoon, don't schedule your writing times then. Find your ideal time slots that can become sacred for writing.

- Working on a dissertation entails ample opportunities to doubt whether you can actually complete the task. Intimidated by the great distance from their goal, many scholars break down and never complete their dissertations. Yet even the most "impossible" tasks can be managed if broken into several smaller (and less intimidating) tasks. Setting smaller benchmarks or "chunks" along the road to your ultimate goal helps you proceed one step at a time, while alleviating the tremendous pressure of having to constantly grapple with your entire project. Having divided your dissertation into smaller segments also allows you to plan how long you need to spend on each segment and project when you might complete your entire manuscript.

- It is important to set a comfortable, relaxed pace that allows you to avoid pres-sure. The best way to maximize your sense of accomplishment and minimize your experience of disappointment is to set goals that are within your reach. You also need to build into your timetable some slack time for when you are sick or overburdened with unanticipated commitments. Moving along slowly should not prevent you from being prolific. Even days when you write only one page ultimately add up. The secrets are perseverance and persistence, which are much more important than speed.

FIGURE 2.1 ● Sample Schedule-Planning Tool

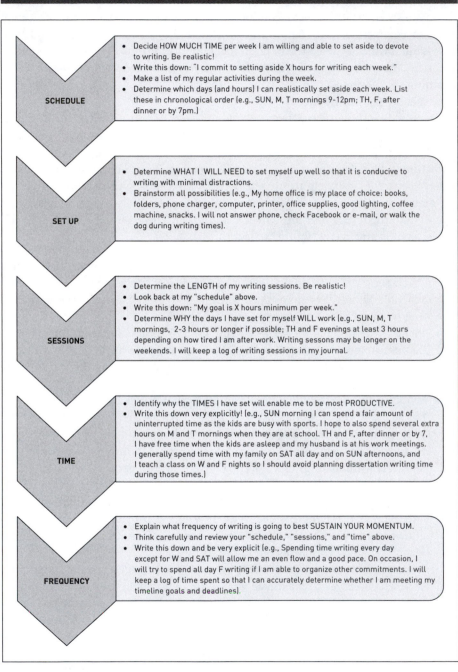

SCHEDULE
- Decide HOW MUCH TIME per week I am willing and able to set aside to devote to writing. Be realistic!
- Write this down: "I commit to setting aside X hours for writing each week."
- Make a list of my regular activities during the week.
- Determine which days (and hours) I can realistically set aside each week. List these in chronological order (e.g., SUN, M, T mornings 9-12pm; TH, F, after dinner or by 7pm.)

SET UP
- Determine WHAT I WILL NEED to set myself up well so that it is conducive to writing with minimal distractions.
- Brainstorm all possibilities (e.g., My home office is my place of choice: books, folders, phone charger, computer, printer, office supplies, good lighting, coffee machine, snacks. I will not answer phone, check Facebook or e-mail, or walk the dog during writing times).

SESSIONS
- Determine the LENGTH of my writing sessions. Be realistic!
- Look back at my "schedule" above.
- Write this down: "My goal is X hours minimum per week."
- Determine WHY the days I have set for myself WILL work (e.g., SUN, M, T mornings, 2-3 hours or longer if possible; TH and F evenings at least 3 hours depending on how tired I am after work. Writing sessons may be longer on the weekends. I will keep a log of writing sessions in my journal.

TIME
- Identify why the TIMES I have set will enable me to be most PRODUCTIVE.
- Write this down very explicitly! (e.g., SUN morning I can spend a fair amount of uninterrupted time as the kids are busy with sports. I hope to also spend several extra hours on M and T mornings when they are at school. TH and F, after dinner or by 7, I have free time when the kids are asleep and my husband is at his work meetings. I generally spend time with my family on SAT all day and on SUN afternoons, and I teach a class on W and F nights so I should avoid planning dissertation writing time during those times.)

FREQUENCY
- Explain what frequency of writing is going to best SUSTAIN YOUR MOMENTUM.
- Think carefully and review your "schedule," "sessions," and "time" above.
- Write this down and be very explicit (e.g., Spending time writing every day except for W and SAT will allow me an even flow and a good pace. On occasion, I will try to spend all day F writing if I am able to organize other commitments. I will keep a log of time spent so that I can accurately determine whether I am meeting my timeline goals and deadlines).

- Figure out how to maintain your momentum. Be sensitive to the "flow" of your writing. With a large project such as a dissertation, try to minimize the number of times when you have to interrupt your writing for more than a day at a time.
- Finally, be sure to have in your mind a deadline for your project. Setting deadlines is the most effective way of closing open-ended tasks. Indeed, in helping overcome indefinitely receding horizons, a deadline is a writer's best friend.

Tracking Your Thinking

Up to this point, much of the discussion has focused on the practical details of the organization and management of dissertation-related material. Aside from keeping track of information, you need to keep track of your thinking. Just as it is important to have the relevant material on file, so it is important to keep a record of your changing thoughts about the literature and its relevance to your emerging research topic, as well as about the research process in general. One way to ensure that you preserve your reasoning and thinking and are able to spell out the development of your ideas is to keep a research journal. Recording your thinking means that you will accumulate material that can be revisited and drawn on and that can form a substantial part of the methodology and analysis chapters of your dissertation. Keeping careful records also implies an open-minded and critical approach and provides ideas for future directions of your work. In addition, by making your reasoning transparent, you contribute to what Lincoln and Guba (1985) refer to as an "audit trail," which provides useful material for making validity claims for your study.

Journaling allows you to be meticulous about keeping an orderly record of your research activities and your productivity. Journaling also engenders a reflective stance (Miles & Huberman, 1994), which offers the opportunity to create a record of your experiences—your insights, speculations, hunches, questions, methodological and analytical concerns, tentative interpretations, and so on. In the qualitative inquiry process, you as the researcher and writer are the main instrument of data collection and data analysis. It is your task to provide personal insight into the experience under study. Integral to the notion of *self as instrument* is a capacity for reflection. The act of reflection, as Dewey (1916) suggests, affords the potential for reconstructing the meaning of experience that actually yields learning. In effect, a journal provides a solid link to and keeps track of the many levels of experience that are involved in the dissertation process. In the qualitative dissertation, what you bring to the inquiry is as important as what you discover as you live with your project. The quality and credibility of the dissertation indeed rests on your capacity for insightful conceptual reflection.

Developing a Support System

Although much of the work involved in the dissertation process—in both the researching and writing phases—is done independently, you need not feel you must "go this alone"; you should not isolate yourself. As a resourceful doctoral candidate, you need to create a dissertation support system that contributes to your success by providing emotional and academic support. Support systems include various options such as dissertation groups, a dissertation "buddy" (someone with whom you are compatible and who has a similar work ethic to your own and who you feel might be more efficient than a larger group), and virtual support groups (operated through online chat rooms, online editorial critiques, and online coaching and/or mentoring). There are many people who have the potential to promote your progress. In our experience, we have found the graduate student network to be a particularly valuable resource. It is to your advantage to reach out to graduates and other professionals and colleagues who you believe might be helpful to you in this regard. This becomes especially important in the burgeoning online environment where students are working outside the parameters of a traditional classroom, a context where isolation and lack of connection might be particularly prevalent.

Table 2.1 outlines the steps necessary to embark on the dissertation process in a methodical and organized manner. Once you have your mental and physical house in order, and with strong personal commitment and the will to succeed in completing your dissertation, you are ready to take the first step or resume wherever you may have left off in the process.

Identifying and Developing a Researchable Topic

Finding Your Topic

The starting point for any research project, and indeed the first major challenge in conducting research, is coming to some decision about a sound, doable topic. The topic is the subject of inquiry around a particular research problem that your study will address. For some, choosing a topic can be an exciting process; finally, you have the opportunity to pursue an area in which you have long been interested. For others, generating and selecting a topic can be a frustrating and somewhat overwhelming experience. Commonly, students consider a few potential topics before finally settling on one.

Finding a research topic that is interesting, relevant, feasible, and worthy of your time may take substantial effort, so you should be prepared to invest your time accordingly. Considering your options, doing some background work on each option, and ultimately settling on a topic that is manageable will spare you many of the frustrations that come from attempting research on a topic that, for whatever reason, may not be appropriate. The criterion of feasibility is especially important when choosing a dissertation topic. You don't want to settle on a topic and then find out that the study you were imagining can't be done, or the survey or assessment instrument you need can't be used. You also want to make sure that you select a topic that will allow you to be an objective researcher. If you select a topic that you have worked closely on for many years, make sure you are still open to new information, even if that information runs counter to what you believe to be true about the topic. It is very important to think about these considerations beforehand so that you don't get stuck during the dissertation process.

Task	Why?	Action Steps
Create your own "dissertation space."	Successful completion requires careful organization and planning. Structure is important. To begin you should create a physical and mental "space."	1. Set aside a physical workspace that is dedicated to your dissertation. Find a place where the dissertation is the only thing that you do. 2. Set aside times to work on your dissertation. 3. Create your mental workspace; develop an "I can do this!" attitude.
Create a *system* for organizing and managing your work.	As you become immersed in your work, you will continue to be inundated with large amounts of information. You do not want to lose any material, nor do you want to drown in it. Organizing and managing dissertation-related "stuff" right from the beginning is essential to getting on track and staying focused.	1. Start collecting and storing any and all material that is potentially related to your topic. 2. Keep records of all relevant information. 3. Make sure that all material is sorted systematically and stored securely so it will be easily retrievable. 4. Choose the storage method that works best for you. File all information manually or electronically. Be consistent in your filing!
Save all drafts.	As you make revisions and update earlier versions, you will be continually rewriting. Drafts should not be discarded. You may want to revisit earlier versions in order to check on previous thinking and strategies.	1. Keep clear records of all drafts. 2. Be vigilant in saving all drafts systematically and methodically.
Keep track of your thinking.	The quality and credibility of the dissertation rests upon your capacity for insightful conceptual reflection. Just as it is important to have relevant material on file, so is it important to keep a record of your changing thoughts about the research process. Journaling engenders a critically reflective stance, a key characteristic of qualitative research. Recorded reflection provides ideas for future directions of your work, and also contributes to an "audit trail," providing useful material for making validity claims. Keeping careful records makes your reasoning transparent—both to yourself and to your readers. What happens throughout the research process is a vital source of data: A research diary contributes significantly toward a substantial part of the methodology chapter of your dissertation.	1. Keep track of your thinking by way of journaling, writing memos, or keeping a research diary. 2. Keep a running log of all conversations you have with colleagues and advisors. This log should include important details and suggestions, as well as your reflections, reactions, and ideas.

(Continued)

TABLE 2.1 ● (Continued)

Task	Why?	Action Steps
Track your productivity as a way to motivate you to write.	Goal setting can be hard: Our goals can be too big. Or they can be too small. We set goals that are just right when we set them, and then life happens and we might miss our targets. This can be very frustrating and demotivating.	1. Record what you do each day or part of the day. In a week, you will have a list of things you've done, rather than a list of near and entire misses. So much more motivating! 2. Paying attention to what you're tracking might reveal useful patterns about where and when you were most productive and what kinds of settings that happened in. And you can try and do more of that.
Forgive yourself! Understand and accept the necessity of slow movement and messiness as groundwork for productivity.	The research and writing process is iterative, recursive, and messy, with challenges (detours and roadblocks) along the way that can impede—or even stall—our progress. We tend to become discouraged if we move slowly and are not so productive in some parts of our writing. Being discouraged leads to frustration, and frustration takes away energy, and lack of energy depletes motivation. And so productivity suffers.	1. Change the way you think and you will change the effect on your writing. The slow and messy parts are all part of building a foundation of thinking and writing so that further along, you work faster and better. 2. Pay attention to the patterns of your writing process. This will help prevent you from feeling demotivated when writing slows down. 3. Trust that you will gather momentum and accelerate if you can shift your thinking to understand and accept this iterative and often messy process.
Save, save, save!	The importance of saving material cannot be underestimated. Loss of information and data can be extremely stressful and time consuming, not to mention detrimental to your final product. Develop the habit of saving!	1. Be vigilant and methodical with regard to file naming. 2. Regularly and frequently back up all your files by way of copying them to an external hard drive, disk, flash drive, or backup web location. 3. Make sure that your computer is set up for consistent autosave and backup.
Identify and store all writing resources.	Ongoing literature review begins from the beginning stages of topic identification and carries through to the final stages of analysis and synthesis. In addition, you will have to produce a bibliography or reference list that is formatted correctly and that is in perfect synchronization with the materials referenced in the body of your dissertation. Making notes on your reading should be an active and critical process.	1. Maintain clear records of relevant resources including books and journals. 2. Keep track of all your reading, making critical notes as well as being very careful to accurately list all references and citations. 3. Become familiar with online library databases. The university library system is an essential literature search and bibliographic management tool. 4. Explore different software program options that allow efficient referencing of your materials.
Develop a collegial support network.	While much of the work in the dissertation process will be done independently, you do not need to "go this alone," nor do you have to work in isolation. This becomes especially significant in the online environment. Research is essentially a collaborative endeavor rather than a solo process. The graduate student network is a valuable resource for collaboration, sharing of resources, and dialogue.	1. Students should always be encouraged to build support systems and seek guidance from advisors and peers. 2. In addition, be sure to reach out to graduates and other professionals and colleagues who you believe might be helpful to you as you navigate the lengthy dissertation process.

As Tracy (2010) describes it, "Good qualitative research is relevant, timely, significant, interesting, or evocative. Worthy topics often emerge from disciplinary priorities and, therefore, are theoretically or conceptually compelling. However, worthy topics just as easily grow from timely societal or personal events" (p. 840). When judging the significance of a study's contribution, researchers gauge the current climate of knowledge, practice, and politics, and ask questions such as "Does the study expand knowledge and insight?" "Deepen understanding?" "Improve practice?" "Generate ongoing research?" "Liberate or empower?" Tracy (2010) explains that the significance of qualitative research can be conceptualized in various ways: Theoretically significant research builds theory, or extends or problematizes current theoretical assumptions. Such contributions offer new and unique understandings that emerge from the data analysis—conceptualizations—that help explain social life in unique ways and may be transferred to other contexts. In doing so, the study builds on past research but provides new conceptual understandings that can be used by future researchers. Heuristic significance moves people to further explore, research, or act on the research in the future. Research is heuristically significant when it develops curiosity in the reader, inspiring the need for new discoveries. Heuristic significance also implies an influence on audiences, including policy makers, research participants, or the lay public, to engage in action or change—in this way creating an overlap with practical significance. Practically significant research asks whether the knowledge derived by the research is useful in shedding light on or framing a contemporary issue. Does the knowledge produced by the research empower participants to become more critically reflective, thereby challenging assumptions and perspectives and viewing society in new ways? Does the research provide a story that might liberate individuals from injustice or in some way transform their lives? Another means toward achieving significance is through engaging research methodology in novel, creative, or insightful ways—methodological significance. A research project that incorporates methodologically significant approaches may not only lead to theoretical insights and practical usefulness but also contribute to future researchers' practice of methodological craft skills.

In selecting a topic, most students focus on trying to be original and exhibiting the desire to contribute to the existing knowledge base. Most universities and doctoral faculties agree that a dissertation should be an original piece of research and should make a significant contribution to the field. At the outset, it is important to remember, however, that making an original contribution does not imply that there need be an enormous "breakthrough." In social science research, the discovery of new facts is rarely an important or even challenging criterion. Rather, research is a process of searching or re-searching for new insights; it is about advancing knowledge or understanding of a practice or phenomenon. In fact, it is perfectly acceptable to model your research on a previous study and develop some aspect of it or even replicate it. Replicating a previous study or aspects of a previous study is appropriate because knowledge accumulates through studies that build on each other over time.

When thinking of finding a researchable topic, it may be helpful to begin by completing a cursory review of available scholarly sources. This is a necessary step that will provide you with an understanding of the availability of literature on the proposed topic or topics you may have in mind. Looking at previously published dissertations is another good way to gauge the level of research and involvement that is generally expected at the dissertation level. Previously published dissertations can also be good sources of inspiration for your own dissertation study. The literature review of a dissertation contains a wealth of information. Not only can the literature review provide topic ideas by showing some of the major research that has been done on a topic, but it can also help you evaluate any topics that you are tentatively considering. From your examination of literature reviews can you determine if your research idea has already been completed? Has the theory that validates your study been disproved by new dissertation research? Is your research idea still relevant to the current state of the discipline? Literature reviews can help you answer these questions by providing a compact and summative description of a particular research area. Similar to scholarly articles, many dissertations will suggest areas of future research. Paying attention to those suggestions can provide valuable ideas and clues for your own dissertation topic. It is important to note that dissertations are not considered to be peer-reviewed documents, so be sure to carefully review and evaluate the information presented.

In seeking a topic, you should remember that the objective of doing a dissertation is to obtain the credentials by demonstrating that you understand and can therefore conduct good research. The dissertation should not be centered on any grandiose ideas that you want to pursue—that can come later at another point in your life. For the purpose of successfully completing your dissertation, the focus should be on a sound topic—one that is crystal clear and concise.

For the most part, identification of what to study evolves slowly as you become immersed in a variety of concepts, philosophies, and theories. The way to begin developing a researchable topic is to look around you at the activities in which you are involved and to draw on your own personal and professional experiences. Most students find that they can best access areas in which they already have substantial expertise or familiarity with practice in the field or existing research. Once you have identified an area of interest, begin to examine and become familiar with the available literature related to your topic. Especially useful are reviews of literature found in journals specifically committed to publishing extensive review articles, as well as policy-oriented publications that discuss current and emerging issues. In addition, all discipline areas have their own encyclopedias, yearbooks, and handbooks, most of which can be accessed on the Internet. You also might take time to look over earlier dissertations and seek previous studies that in some respects mirror your own interests and topic.

In addition to seeking out relevant literature, engage in conversation with colleagues and peers to hear different perspectives about pertinent issues and to begin to sharpen your topical focus. Generating and selecting a viable topic is a complex process that involves various competing factors. As you may notice throughout this book, our predisposition toward research and writing is that both are highly inter-active processes. Seeking the feedback and critique of academic advisors, faculty committee members, and colleagues is, in our experience, an integral part of the dissertation process.

Refining and Honing Your Topic

Once you have identified a general area of interest, you will need to begin narrow-ing your topic. The process of developing a researchable topic is a process of idea generation—the movement from a general interest "out there" toward a more clearly refined idea around a researchable problem. It is important that the problem becomes specific and narrow enough to let you master a reasonable amount of information. If your problem is too broad—that is, if you try to take on too many aspects of one problem—you will encounter a data glut, which makes the reporting of findings and analysis of your data extremely difficult and tedious.

Refining the problem to be addressed calls for reflecting on whether that pro-blem *can* and *should* be researched in the first place. First, whether the problem can or cannot be researched involves giving some thought to the practical feasibility or *do-ability* involved (Marshall & Rossman, 2015). Important judgments will have to be made regarding the possibility of access to potential sites and potential research populations, availability of sources of information, the researcher's knowledge and skills, and the availability of time and resources at your disposal to collect and analyze data over a sustained period of time. Second is the question of *should*. This question is complex and brings various factors into play. Considering the *should-do-ability* of a study calls into consideration the practical as well as the theoretical implications of pursuing a research problem (Marshall & Rossman, 2015). You therefore need to take the following aspects into account:

1. Potential audience. Who would appreciate the worth of my study? Who would care enough to read it? Who would be interested?

2. Intellectual value and worth of the study. What, if any, is the wider significance of this research? Who would benefit by this study? Would a study in this area contribute to the ongoing conversation in a particular social science discipline or applied field? Would the study generate theoretical and/or conceptual under-standing? What, if anything, would be the significance for policy? Will the study contribute to the development of professional practice?

3. Personal and professional goals. Will this study further my personal and pro-fessional interests? Will it enhance my career and/or career change? Will the research problem sustain my interest over the ensuing months and years?

4. Ethical considerations. Does the research involve practices or strategies that might embarrass or harm participants? Are there any political risks to others or me in reporting fairly and accurately the findings and outcomes of the potential study?

Undertaking a dissertation is a rigorous and long-term engagement, in terms of both conducting the fieldwork and working with the data. Although the dissertation need not necessarily be one's "life's work," caring about the topic at hand and having a compelling interest to learn what is not yet known are critical to sustaining motivation and commitment and hence, momentum. The sooner you can begin to narrow your research interests and identify and develop a topical focus, the better. Having a fairly good idea of the area in which you will be situated, you will most productively be able to utilize your time to refine your research problem and so further the dissertation objectives.

Students often labor over coming up with a dissertation title at the early stages of dissertation work. It is a good idea to create what is, in effect, a "working title," as you think about your topic and hone your problem, and to refine this title as your study proceeds. A title generally captures the major thrust of your research. A working title becomes a guiding focus as you move through your study. Keeping notes or journaling about how and why your title changes over time is a useful exercise because it tracks developments in your thinking as your study progresses. A more extensive discussion regarding selecting a final dissertation title is included in Part III of this book.

Seeking Suitable Advisors

One of the most important tasks of a doctoral candidate is finding a suitable advisement team. Each university has a different system in this regard, and you need to make sure of your institution and/or program's policies and procedures. At some universities, the doctoral committee structure is based on an apprenticeship model and is used as a vehicle to guide the student from coursework through the dissertation defense. The dissertation committee in effect becomes the group of faculty responsible for your progress right from the beginning of the process, with all members contributing to the development of an acceptable dissertation. The committee is usually a hierarchical organization, with each member of the committee having a different responsibility vis-à-vis your research. At some universities, you work with an advisor (sponsor) and a second reader from the proposal stage onward; when you have almost completed your dissertation, a dissertation committee needs to be formed.

Ideally, the doctoral committee is composed of faculty with different areas of expertise and whose resources you will be able to tap in the process of working on your dissertation. Again, this is a matter of institutional difference. In some instances (but not always), you can select your committee from among those in your department and related departments, those whose courses you have taken, and/or those whose work bears some relation to the focus of your dissertation. Some faculty may be members of other programs or other schools within your university. In other instances, choice of committee may be more tightly constrained. In some cases (but not always), experts beyond your university are chosen. It is strongly advised that you be clear about your own institutional requirements so you can follow the necessary protocol and take into account acceptable policy and procedures. Additional details regarding selecting and forming your dissertation committee are included in Part III of this book.

Remember that your advisor or dissertation chair will hopefully be your mentor, principle guide, and primary resource throughout the dissertation process. Therefore, you need to spend time looking for the kind of authentic educator you feel confident can help you. Take the time to do some research, ask others about their experiences, and find out as much as you can about the faculty at your institution and their areas of interest. Considerations in looking for the right advisor, sponsor, or dissertation chair include

- **Expertise**—Your advisor need not be a content expert with regard to your particular topic, but should be a process expert. In this case, you may select a second reader who is a content expert, and in this way, you would have a strong combination of resources.
- **Chemistry**—You need to feel comfortable with a prospective advisor and confident that you will be able to develop a good working rapport with him or her. There also need to be good lines of communication between your sponsor and your second reader so that you are hopefully never caught in the middle trying to resolve different perspectives.
- **Access and availability**—You may find the kind of expertise you are looking for in a prospective advisor and feel comfortable with that faculty person, but he or she may be so busy that it makes getting advisement time and feedback difficult and even frustrating.
- **Understanding**—All too often, and inadvertently, one's work is interrupted by life issues. As such, you should strive to find someone who is willing to provide you with understanding and encouragement from the sidelines, and who knows when to push you to start moving again. Above all, this person must have a genuine interest in helping you succeed.

Once you select an advisor, sponsor, or dissertation chair, be proactive in establishing and maintaining a good working relationship. Keep her or him apprised of your status along the way by regularly sending progress reports. This communication serves to maintain contact throughout and is a strategy for gaining the necessary support and feedback as you proceed to tackle your dissertation.

Finding just the right advisor is a tall order, and you might be wondering what happens if you do not make the right selection or if you are appointed an advisor who is not the right fit for you. Many students are afraid to change advisors because they view it from a political perspective. It is often acceptable to make changes by going through the correct channels, seeking out the most appropriate person within your department, and asking for his or her help and advice. Remember, if you do make changes, be sure to give your existing advisor the respect and courtesy of informing him or her of your desire to change. Be aware, too, that some departments discourage changing advisors or dissertation committee chairs, and may not even allow it. The view in these instances is that doctoral students need to know when an issue warrants a change and when they may simply be overreacting to "tough-love" advising.

Stakeholder Responsibility and Standards of Good Practice

As a graduate research student, and key stakeholder in the process, you have a right to expect the following:

- Orientation seminars dealing with the dissertation process and requirements and policies that are entailed.
- Identification of a doctoral committee with a designated doctoral advisor and second reader.
- A graduate handbook that outlines and explains all departmental policies, expectations, and deadlines pertaining to supervision of doctoral students. This handbook might include rights and responsibilities of doctoral students, as well as procedures for changing advisors and/or filing grievances.
- Verbally communicated or written documentation (memo, e-mail, letter) from your advisor regarding expectations, recommendations for best practices, and deadlines for deliverables.

Supervision has become increasingly recognized as a professional skill that requires training and monitoring. In addition to committee chairs, most university departments have faculty members who serve as dissertation advisors and who are responsible for ongoing guidance and support throughout the research process. This includes informing students about institutional and departmental regulations, requirements, and policies (and changes and updates when these occur); keeping students updated about responsibilities, deliverables, and deadlines; and assisting students with completing and timeously submitting all official documentation. Obtaining a doctorate cannot be achieved without the necessary institutional support, structure, and guidance. Qualitative research itself poses additional potential dangers posed by inherent lack of structure, and so regular and structured supervision becomes increasingly critical. As a student, you would not want to spend months or even years in the field only to realize that you have not collected appropriate and relevant amounts of material and/or conducted appropriate and relevant analytic procedures to qualify for a grounded and defensible dissertation. As such, *you* need to take the initiative to (a) become familiar with the structure and policies of your department and (b) consult with your chosen advisor on a regular and consistent basis about your progress as well as the challenges you may encounter. As you advance through the process you will certainly come to realize that there is no substitute for self-discipline and orderly thinking, and that your professional working relationship with your advisor is a key factor in this process.

Students and faculty are partner stakeholders in the dissertation process. Producing a quality dissertation is expected to require creation, review, feedback, and revision of numerous successive drafts. Each draft submitted for review to the dissertation advisor and/or committee members should reflect the student's best efforts in light of accumulating knowledge, experience, and feedback. In turn, the final product and the quality thereof are a reflection, too, of the guidance and support of faculty. As such, both student and faculty have a stake in the process and its final outcome: a successful defense and a quality product that has contributed new knowledge and insights to the field and that is hopefully worthy of enhancing practice and/or prompting further research.

Advisors expect doctoral students to

- Work independently.
- Think critically and conceptually.
- Submit drafts as needed.
- Be available for regular meetings at mutually convenient times.
- Be honest about their progress.
- Choose to follow advice and guidelines, or offer valid reasons for not choosing to do so.

Therefore, student responsibilities include

While students receive guidance from their dissertation chairs and committee members, they are ultimately responsible for the timely completion and successful defense of a high-quality (i.e., defensible and publishable) dissertation. The following guidelines will assist students in accomplishing this goal:

1. Establish and sustain a collegial working relationship with your advisor.
2. Create, revise as needed, and adhere to a dissertation project plan (including timeline). The project plan should be developed and revised in close consultation with the advisor.
3. If a conflict with the advisor arises, first address the conflict directly with the advisor. If the conflict remains unresolved, arrange a meeting with the chair (or committee member) and the program director or another appropriate third party.
4. When writing the dissertation, enable the advisor to provide timely and helpful review and feedback by submitting quality work at each revision.
5. Carefully consider feedback from the advisor. Initiate and engage in conversation to better understand and evaluate feedback. Explain to the advisor any decision made to adapt or reject feedback, and remain open to further feedback.
6. Assure and appropriately evidence compliance with all relevant research regulations (e.g., federal and institutional) regarding human subjects.

7. Understand that hired assistance is acceptable under certain circumstances. An editor may be hired to provide aid during the writing process; however, the help received should be limited to editing assistance for narrative already created and revised.

8. Consider hiring a statistician for guidance and input regarding statistical analysis and interpretation as needed. Students are expected to conduct their own data auditing to assure quality data input. The dissertation should include clear and accurate documentation of the type and extent of assistance received.

9. Prepare for and defend the dissertation proposal and demonstrate capacity to successfully complete and defend the dissertation according to the proposed timeline.

10. Defend the dissertation to the satisfaction of the dissertation committee and in accordance with established program procedures.

11. Assuming successful defense, present the final written dissertation with proper paper, binding, style, and format, according to program and institutional guidelines.

Doctoral students expect their advisors to

- Supervise and advise.
- Read their work in advance of meetings.
- Be available when needed at mutually suitable times.
- Be both supportive and constructively critical.
- Have thorough knowledge of the field of qualitative research and the chosen research genre or tradition.
- Have good knowledge of the research area.
- Be genuinely interested in the topic and/or the contribution that the research study may potentially make to the field.

Therefore, faculty responsibilities include

While students are ultimately responsible for the timely completion and successful defense of a high-quality (i.e., defensible and publishable) dissertation, dissertation faculty members are responsible for providing support and critical feedback throughout this dissertation process. The following guidelines will assist students' understanding and expectations regarding faculty's responsibility in providing support and guidance:

1. Engage dissertation students in extensive conversations to explore and eventually focus on a meaningful and significant dissertation topic. Through focused conversations students should broaden and deepen their thinking and understanding around potential contribution to their topic of choice.

2. Assure that the dissertation progresses with the following characteristics: (a) The dissertation topic holds personal and professional meaning for the

student as well as significance and value to the field; (b) dissertation work progresses within a conceptual framework developed through significant consideration of prior work (i.e., literature review); (c) research and/or guiding questions are developed in relation to both the dissertation topic and the conceptual framework; (d) research methodologies are appropriate to the research topic and questions and support qualitative research principles; (e) dissertation findings, analyses, and conclusions are consistent with collected data; (f) limitations of methodologies are explicitly recognized and explained; (g) research and writing style are appropriately scholarly; and (h) the final dissertation product is worthy of reviewed publication.

3. Assure appropriate compliance with all relevant human subjects research regulations (e.g., federal and institutional).

4. Provide students with timely written and/or oral review and feedback on submitted dissertation drafts with a view toward guiding successful and timely completions of a high-quality (i.e., defensible and publishable) dissertation and defense.

5. Assure adequate preparation for proposal-related hearing or qualifying exam and dissertation defense by guiding and challenging student thinking and writing throughout their dissertation work and by asking fundamental and challenging questions throughout the dissertation process.

6. Provide guidance to students' development of the dissertation project plan—slowing or accelerating the timeline as required to assure timely completion of a high-quality (i.e., defensible and publishable) dissertation.

7. Conduct the dissertation defense and notify the student and program chair of results (pass or not pass) according to established program procedures.

Establishing a Realistic Timeline

One of the major challenges of completing the dissertation is developing and honing the habit of thinking critically. Another challenge is the practical application of ideas, including the need to systematically plan the study, collect and analyze the data, and write up the dissertation. The ability to focus, problem solve, and make informed decisions at every step of the way will bring your study to completion. Time is part of the equation.

Clearly, the more time you devote to carefully thinking about, planning, and completing your study, the more effective your discipline will be. Because the time commitment required of an individual doing qualitative research is substantial, you need to pace yourself from the beginning. Be sure to keep your goals realistic, or you will set yourself up for failure. As such, be honest about the time that particular tasks might take to complete and what other life demands are competing with the dissertation demands. Aside from time constraints, you also need to plan carefully for what can be achieved given your available resources (e.g., personal and financial support). Finally, you must consider developing realistic deadlines with regard to institutional constraints. For example, many university departments are typically understaffed during the summer months and over winter vacation. Expecting feedback from advisors, gaining approval from review boards, or even attempting to set meeting times with research participants at these particular times of the year would be somewhat unrealistic.

A timetable for work may or may not be formally required by your committee, but it is an effective way to manage your time and keep you on track. In line with the ski metaphor mentioned earlier, it is important that you set yourself a time frame within which to complete each section of the dissertation. Just as the experienced skier traverses the terrain, benchmarking is fundamental to success in the dissertation process, too. In developing realistic deadlines, we recommend that students "chunk" the tasks in conjunction with a multiyear calendar. Create a system whereby you work on parts that contribute to the whole—chapter-by-chapter or even one part of a chapter at a time. The dissertation journey is essentially about achieving milestones one step at a time.

A useful guiding principle is to always have a sense of your next step. Identifying the various stages in the process, pacing yourself, and documenting your achievement of goals and subgoals along the way are important and will contribute to keeping you task oriented and focused. Having some sense of how your progress is moving you closer and closer to completion will help to keep you motivated. In this regard, we recommend marking your progress on a checklist that you create for yourself. A sample checklist appears on the inside back cover.

It is especially critical that you not lose momentum once formal coursework has ended. At this moment of being out there on their own, many students experience overwhelming feelings and are unsure of how to proceed. The longer they remain fixed and unmoving, the more their inclination to start on the dissertation wanes; the longer this continues, the more difficult it becomes to get going again.

You also should bear in mind that, in most institutions, once a student is certified and becomes a doctoral "candidate," he or she usually has a designated number of years in which to complete the dissertation, or else he or she will have to be recertified (which involves retaking the "certification" or "candidacy" exam—a most unappealing thought). In any event, although extensions may be granted for extenuating circumstances, to get an extension, a student usually has to demonstrate that she or he has been making significant progress. This is all the more reason to take the time to develop a timeline, stay on task, and set realistic, appropriate, and reasonable goals. After all, this doctoral program is a once-in-a-lifetime venture, and you surely want to succeed.

In following up with our students as to their progress, we often hear, "I'm still reading." Reading widely indeed allows you to become knowledgeable and proficient in a specific domain. Although reading is essential, it can sometimes be an avoidance mechanism when it is time to write. It is now time to start *writing* your dissertation. The sooner you begin writing, the easier it is to continue writing and the more rapidly your dissertation is likely to progress. Adopt a do-it-now attitude and get started!

3

Choosing a Qualitative Research Approach

Chapter 3 Objectives

- Discuss the implications of choosing an appropriate qualitative research approach based on the study's problem, purpose, and research questions.

- Offer conceptual understanding of the logic behind choice of research approach including knowledge claims and tradition of inquiry.

- Clarify and explain the most commonly used current and cutting-edge qualitative genres or inquiry traditions.

- Illustrate the primary characteristics of qualitative research and indicate how these compare and contrast with the characteristics of quantitative and mixed methods approaches.

Overview

Choice of research approach is directly tied to research problem and purpose. As the researcher, you actively create the link among problem, purpose, and approach through a process of reflecting on problem and purpose, focusing on researchable questions, and considering how to best address these questions. Thinking along these lines affords a research study methodological congruence (Richards & Morse, 2013). A research problem should not be modified to fit a particular research approach. You cannot assume a particular qualitative approach regardless of your research problem. In other words, research approach follows research problem; the appropriate research approach is the one that best fits with your research problem.

Qualitative research addresses the question of "what." Knowing what something is entails a conceptualization of the matter under investigation as a whole and in its various parts. Knowing what something is also involves the conceptualization of its "how"; that is, its process and unfolding. Importantly, qualitative research includes an understanding of context, circumstance, environment, and milieu. As Wertz et al. (2011) explain, knowledge of the "what" may be implicit or explicit, carefully established or uncritically assumed, and informally or formally acquired. Deep understanding about what a subject matter is, in all its real world complexity, and an ability to describe, explain, and communicate that understanding lies at the core of qualitative research.

Qualitative research is suited to promoting a deep understanding of a social setting or activity as viewed from the perspective of the research participants. This approach implies an emphasis on exploration, discovery, and description. Quantitative research, in contrast, is applied to describe current conditions, investigate relationships, and study cause–effect phenomena. Both research approaches involve complex processes in which particular data collection and data analysis methods assume meaning and significance in relation to the assumptions underlying the larger intellectual traditions within which these methods are applied.

Table 3.1 provides a summary overview of qualitative research, illustrating its primary characteristics and indicating how these compare and contrast with the characteristics of quantitative and mixed methods approaches. For a detailed comparison between the key characteristics of qualitative, quantitative, and mixed methods approaches refer to Creswell (2014).

The History of Qualitative Research

The fierce methodological struggles, often referred to as "the paradigm wars" of the 1970s and 1980s (Denzin & Lincoln, 2013a, 2013c; Ercikan & Roth, 2006; Reichardt & Rallis, 1994), have fallen away. The global community of qualitative researchers has now found itself midway between two extremes; mixed methodologies and calls for scientifically based research, on the one side, renewed calls for social justice inquiry from the critical social science tradition, on the other (Denzin & Lincoln, 2013c). With all of the debate surrounding it, qualitative research has emerged as a field of inquiry that crosscuts disciplines and subject matter, encompassing a complex interconnected family of concepts, terms, and assumptions. Qualitative research is situated within a complex historical field that crosscuts at least eight historical "moments" characterized by successive waves of epistemological theorizing. Denzin and Lincoln (2013c) define these "moments" as traditional (1900–1950), the modernist or golden age (1950–1970), blurred genres (1970–1986), the crisis of representation (1986–1990), postmodern (1990–1995), postexperimental inquiry (1995–2000), the methodologically contested present (2000–2010), and the future, (2010–). This eighth moment, in which we find ourselves currently, is concerned with moral discourse and asks that the social sciences and the humanities become sites for critical conversations about race, gender, class, democracy, globalization, freedom, complexity, and community. And so the field of qualitative research continues to transform itself.

TABLE 3.1 ● Choosing a Qualitative Research Approach

	Quantitative Research	Qualitative Research	Mixed Methods
Research paradigm	Postpositivist	Constructivist, critical theory/advocacy	Pragmatic
Strategy/ tradition/genre of inquiry	Descriptive, correlational, causal/ comparative, and experimental research	Case study, grounded theory, ethnography, narrative inquiry, discourse analysis, phenomenology, action research, postmodernism, and poststructuralism	• Sequential design can be exploratory or explanatory • Concurrent design triangulates methods
Research purpose	• Seek consensus (the norm) • Examine topic in order to quantify results • Investigate relationships and cause–effect phenomena	• Seek range and variation in findings • Delve into the "essence" of the topic	• A combination of quantitative and qualitative methods is needed to fully understand a problem
Researcher role	• Adopts an *etic* (outsider) point of view • Seeks to test or verify theory • Identifies variables, makes predictions, and seeks specific evidence that will support or disconfirm hypothesis • Believes that research can be value-free • Attempts to remain unbiased, objective, and impartial	• Adopts an *emic* (insider) point of view • Seeks to discover and understand meaning of experience • Adopts a flexible stance and is open to change • Is reflective about own voice and perspective • Acknowledges personal values, and brings own experience to bear on the study • Is active and involved	• Appreciates how quantitative and qualitative data might complement each other • Develops a rationale for integrating aspects of qualitative and quantitative research • Decides whether to prioritize one or the other type of approach or to consider them equally important
Research design	• Hypothetic-deductive: Research is about "idea testing" • Design is determined up front and follows systematic procedures • Large samples are selected randomly • Study is conducted under controlled conditions • Usually involves some form of pre- and posttest • Little opportunity for creativity outside prestructured research design	• Inductive: Research is about "idea generation" • Design is proposed up front, but is open and emergent, rather than rigid and fixed to permit exploration • Small samples are selected purposefully • Research takes place within natural contexts • Real-world situations are studied as they naturally unfold • Researcher-designed framework allows for flexibility and creativity	• Design combines quantitative structure and qualitative flexibility • Borrows distinct elements from both quantitative and qualitative approaches • Purposeful or random sample selection • Researcher-designed framework allows for innovation or creativity
Methods of data collection	• Uses existing instrumentation • Experimentation follows rigid guidelines	• Researcher as instrument • Methods are emergent and flexible	• Research questions determine the methods • Instruments yield multiple forms of information that can be triangulated

(Continued)

TABLE 3.1 ● (Continued)

	Quantitative Research	Qualitative Research	Mixed Methods
	• Survey includes closed-ended questions, scales, and ranking order checklists • Instruments yield performance data, observational data, attitude data, and census data	• Instruments include observation, surveys, interviews, documents, focus groups, and critical incidents • Questions are generally open ended • Multiple methods are combined to achieve triangulation	• Research employs both quantitative and qualitative practices • Statistical as well as textual analysis is used
Methods of data analysis	• Deductive design reduces data to precise numerical indices • Statistical analysis occurs after all data have been collected • Researcher offers causal explanations • Analytic process is linear and unidirectional	• Inductive design leads to holistic, richly descriptive findings • Analysis is based on identifying themes and patterns • Phenomena are understood as holistic and complex systems and are viewed within particular social and/or historical contexts • Researcher tries to authentically depict the voices of participants while remaining reflexive and politically aware • Context sensitivity and understanding allows for interpretation • Analysis is iterative, cyclical, and ongoing	
Issues of trustworthiness	• Seeks to uphold scientific standards of validity and reliability • Seeks to generalize results from research sample to the larger population	• Seeks to establish credibility and dependability by way of triangulation and other strategies • Seeks to explain transferability of findings to other similar contexts	• Decisions are made according to methods used
Presentation of findings	• Charts, graphs, and diagrams are used to display results • Discussion explains and augments visual displays	• Thick, rich description is the primary mode of data presentation • Visual displays are used to augment the narrative discussion	• Both quantitative and qualitative modes of presentation are used to illustrate the research design and to portray and describe findings

Source: This table first appeared in Bloomberg, L. D. (2007). *Revisiting research approaches.* Unpublished manuscript.

Note: Although qualitative research is presented here as one broad approach, it must be remembered that each tradition or genre has its own peculiarities and nuances. Moreover, although qualitative research as an overall approach is based on certain central assumptions, it also is characterized by an ongoing discourse regarding the appropriate and acceptable use of terminology. Current thinking over the years has caused some qualitative researchers to develop their own terminology to better reflect the nature and distinction of qualitative research, whereas others still borrow terminology from quantitative research.

Defining Features of Qualitative Research

Any definition or conceptualization of qualitative research must work within the complex historical field. Qualitative research means different things in each of the eight moments. Nonetheless, some key generic defining characteristics are applicable to the field as a whole:

- Qualitative research involves an interpretive naturalistic approach to the world. Qualitative researchers study things and people in their natural settings, attempting to make sense of or interpret phenomena in terms of the meaning people bring to them.
- Qualitative research is grounded in a philosophical position that is essentially constructivist in the sense that it is concerned with how the complexities of the social and cultural world are experienced, interpreted, and understood, in a particular context, and at a particular point in time. The intent of qualitative research is to examine a social situation or interaction by allowing the researcher to enter the world of others and to attempt to achieve a *holistic* understanding.
- The researcher strives to describe the meaning of the findings from the perspective of the research participants. To achieve this goal, data are gathered directly from the participants. Since description, understanding, interpretation, and communication are the primary goals, the researcher is the primary instrument for data collection and data analysis.
- An underlying assumption of qualitative research is that rich data that is nested in a real context can be captured only by way of the interactive process between the researcher and the research participants. Since understanding is the primary goal, the researcher is the primary instrument for data collection and data analysis. However, the subjective lenses that *both* the researcher and research participants *together* bring to a qualitative study form the context for the findings.
- Qualitative research involves the collection and study of a variety of empirical materials that describe routine and problematic moments and meanings in individuals' lives. Accordingly, qualitative researchers employ a wide range of interconnected interpretive practices in an endeavor to achieve a better understanding of the subject matter at hand.
- Design flexibility is a significant hallmark of qualitative methodology. Adjustment and iterativity are two related hallmarks. In the qualitative research process, instrumentation can be modified when necessary to explore new insights and to address revised research questions.

Qualitative research, as a set of interpretive activities, privileges no single methodological practice over another. As such, consensus has gradually emerged among qualitative researchers that, rather than universally advocate any single methodological approach for all research, the challenge is to appropriately match the research approach to purposes, questions, and issues. Thus, as a researcher, you are obliged to understand those theoretical principles that shape the logic of your inquiry. Understanding the logic behind a research approach allows your study to be appropriately positioned within an inquiry tradition and also lays the foundation for supporting your study's findings. Preliminary steps in formulating a research approach include (a) assessing the knowledge claims that the researcher brings to the study based on her or his theoretical perspectives and (b) identifying the strategy or tradition of inquiry that informs the procedures of the research.

Knowledge Claims

A knowledge claim implies certain assumptions about what the researcher will learn during the inquiry and how she or he will learn. These claims might be called *research paradigms* or *worldviews*—that is, a basic set of beliefs and assumptions that guide action. Philosophically, researchers make claims about what knowledge is (ontology), how we know what we know (epistemology), what values go into knowing what we know (axiology), and the processes for studying knowledge (methodology). There are essentially four core paradigms that inform qualitative research and that identify how worldviews shape the conceptualization, practice, and nature of research.

Postpositivism

Postpositivism is referred to frequently as "the scientific method," "quantitative research," or "empirical science." It refers to the thinking that developed from logical positivism, a school of thought that maintains that all knowledge can be derived from direct observation and logical inferences based on that observation (Phillips & Burbules, 2000). Postpositivism reflects a deterministic philosophy, and the problems studied by postpositivists typically examine causes that influence or affect outcomes. Thinking within this paradigm is reductionistic. The belief is that there are laws or theories that govern the world and that these can be tested and verified. Thus, research typically begins with a theory and a set of hypotheses, and the intent is to test ideas. Research is concerned with causal relationships, and the aim is to advance the relationship between variables. The knowledge that develops through a postpositivist lens is based on careful observation and measurement. Results of a study either support or refute the theory. Being objective is an integral component of inquiry, and standards of reliability and validity are important.

Social Constructivism/Interpretivism

Social constructivism challenges the scientific-realist assumption of postpositivism that reality can be reduced to its component parts. The basic tenet of constructivism is that reality is socially, culturally, and historically constructed (Lincoln & Guba, 1985, 2000; Neuman, 2000; Schwandt, 2000). Therefore, research attempts to understand social phenomena from a context-specific perspective. Social constructivists view inquiry as value-bound rather than value-free, meaning that the process of inquiry is influenced by the researcher and the context under study (Lincoln & Guba, 1985).

The central assumption of this paradigm is that reality is socially constructed, that individuals develop subjective meanings of their own personal experience, and that this gives way to multiple meanings. Therefore, it is the researcher's role to understand the multiple realities from the perspectives of participants. The only way to achieve this understanding is for the researcher to become involved in the reality of the participants and to interact with them in meaningful ways. Thus, constructivist researchers often address the "process" of interaction among individuals. They also focus on the specific contexts in which people live and work to understand particular cultural and historical settings. The constructivist researcher's role is essentially that of "passionate participant," as the facilitator of multivoice reconstruction (Lincoln & Guba, 2000). Constructivist researchers recognize and acknowledge that their own background shapes their interpretation, and they thus "position" themselves in the research to acknowledge their own cultural, social, and historical experiences. Rather than starting with a theory (as in postpositivism), researchers pose research questions and generate or inductively develop meaning from the data collected in the field.

Critical Theory

The critical theory paradigm, which also is referred to as an advocacy, liberatory, or participatory framework, includes feminist perspectives, racialized discourses, queer theory, and disability inquiry. It has a clear focus on social justice (Creswell, 2014). This framework arose during the late 1980s from the critique that postpositivist assumptions imposed unfair structural laws and theories that did not fit marginalized or disenfranchised individuals or groups. In addition, the critique of constructivism is that it did not go far enough in advocating for an action agenda to address the injustice and inequality inflicted on those who have become the passive object of inquiry.

Critical theorists view research as intertwined with politics, and therefore advocate that research contain an integral action agenda that will bring about reform that will change the lives of the research participants and the institutions and communities in which they live and work, as well as the researcher's life (Brookfield, 2005). Critical perspectives involve research strategies (e.g., action research, participatory action research, and narrative analysis) that are openly ideological and have empowering and democratizing goals. It is assumed that the researcher will engage participants as active collaborators in the inquiry so as not to further marginalize them as a result of the inquiry. To achieve this, participants are typically involved in designing questions, collecting data, and analyzing and interpreting information. Advocacy means providing a platform for research participants so that their voice can be heard and their consciousness can be raised. The goal of research is to create political debate and discussion to empower people to take action, to bring about change in existing social structures and processes, and to reconceptualize the entire research process.

Pragmatism

Pragmatism arises from the work of Peirce, James, Mead, and Dewey. Pragmatism is not committed to any one research philosophy or paradigm. For the many forms of pragmatism, knowledge claims arise out of situations, actions, and consequences, rather than from antecedent conditions (as in postpositivism). There is a concern with practical application and workable solutions to research problems (Patton, 2015). Instead of methods being important, the problem is primary. Researchers posit that research is contextually based and typically employs both quantitative and qualitative approaches to understand the problem. Pragmatic researchers propose that, within the same study, methods can be combined in creative ways to more fully or completely understand a research problem. It is contended that researchers should be free to choose the methods and procedures that best meet their needs and purposes and that the research questions should determine the methods used (Krathwohl, 1998). Pragmatists thus adopt multiple data collection and data analysis methods.

Qualitative Research Traditions or Genres

In addition to assumptions about knowledge and operating at a more applied level are genres or traditions of inquiry that provide specific direction for procedures in a research design. These genres or traditions, in turn, contribute to decisions regarding research design and research methods.

Strategies of inquiry associated with quantitative research invoke postpositivist perspectives. Such strategies include descriptive research (involves collecting data to test hypotheses or answer questions about the current status of the subject of inquiry), correlational studies (involves collecting data to determine whether and to what degree a relationship exists between two or more quantifiable variables), causal-comparative research (attempts to determine the cause or reason for existing differences in the behavior or status of groups of individuals), and experimental research (includes true experiments as well as less rigorous experiments or quasi-experiments). In both strategies, at least one independent variable is manipulated, other relevant variables are controlled, and the effect on one or more dependent variables is observed. Although there are variations among these strategies regarding their goals and their data collection procedures, what is common among them is that all quantitative strategies collect and analyze numerical data to explain, predict, and/or control phenomena of interest.

Qualitative research is a broad approach to the study of social phenomena and is based essentially on a constructivist and/or critical perspective (Denzin & Lincoln, 2013a, 2013c), with some researchers (Maxwell, 2012) adopting a more *critical realist* stance. Qualitative research is pragmatic, interpretive, and grounded in people's lived experiences. Qualitative research is typically enacted in naturalistic settings, focuses on context, and is emergent and evolving. Qualitative researchers view social worlds as holistic and complex, and as such, they rely on complex reasoning that moves dialectically and iteratively between deduction and induction (Marshall & Rossman, 2015). Within the qualitative approach, there are a variety of traditions or genres (the word *strategy* is more suited to quantitative research), each distinguished by specific form, terms, and focus regarding what constitutes inquiry within the qualitative paradigm. While each of these genres or disciplinary traditions is naturalistic, interpretive, and increasingly critical, and draws upon multiple methods, each rests on somewhat different assumptions about what constitutes inquiry within the qualitative interpretive paradigm. Each qualitative tradition and each individual researcher has ways of defining a research topic, critically engaging the literature on that topic, identifying significant research problems, designing the study, and collecting, analyzing, and presenting the data so that it will be most relevant and meaningful.

Qualitative research is in itself a field of inquiry that crosscuts disciplines and subject matters (Denzin & Lincoln, 2011, 2013c). Creswell (2013) identifies five main traditions: case study, ethnography, phenomenology, grounded theory, and narrative research. To that list, we add action research and postmodernism/poststructuralism. There are others, but they are more content-specific such as various types of textual analysis, including conversation analysis and discourse analysis, as well as different critical approaches, including feminist theories, critical race theory, queer theory, and disability theories (Creswell, 2013). It is important to acknowledge that traditions are not always wholly separate and may overlap. Moreover, to complicate matters, each tradition is not necessarily an agreed-upon "whole," and distinctions and divisions have come to characterize some traditions.

Although all of qualitative research holds a number of characteristics and assumptions in common, there are variations in how a qualitative study might be designed and what the intent of the study might be. Just as the choice of research approach is directly tied to and fits with the research problem, purpose, and research questions, so is the choice of qualitative research tradition. In other words, choice of research tradition follows research problem and purpose.

Following is a descriptive and critical overview of some of the most current qualitative traditions or genres. As you read further, you will notice that the primary differences among these traditions lies essentially in the particularities of the philosophical and methodological underpinnings, the social context that is examined, the data collection methods, the unit of analysis, and the data analysis strategies. In all of the traditions, it is imperative to consider one's beliefs about the world (ontology) and the nature of knowledge (epistemology), and to reflect on how these impact one's approach to the study of the world and knowledge. Knowing this, you will be in a better position to align your philosophy and methodology with the purpose of your research. There are some excellent texts that cover these traditions in great detail, and it is recommended that once you are familiar with the basic tenets of these traditions and have a clearer idea of your study's research design, you seek and explore more in-depth literature on your tradition of choice.

Case Study

As a form of qualitative research methodology, case study is an intensive description and analysis of a bounded social phenomenon (or multiple bounded phenomena), be this a social unit or a system such as a program, institution, process, event, or concept (Creswell, 2013; Lichtman, 2014; Merriam, 1998, 2009; Stake, 1995; Yin, 2014). Case study is both a methodology (a type of design in qualitative inquiry) and an object of study (Creswell, 2013). Case study is an exploratory form of inquiry that affords significant interaction with research participants, providing an in-depth picture of the unit of study. The researcher explores the bounded system (or bounded systems) over time through in-depth data collection methods, involving multiple data sources. Since case study methodology is a broad definition of a choice of research focus, it can be used with numerous methods and accompanying philosophical positions (Mills & Birks, 2014). As such, a highly interpretivist approach may choose to emphasize participant observation by conducting field ethnography, while a more realist approach could elect to conduct surveys or interviews. A key consideration in case study methodology is to ensure that the researcher's selected methods are aligned with their particular ontological and epistemological beliefs. Since there are many research philosophies, the range of methods that can be applied are equally numerous.

What is common to case study is the production of a detailed description of a setting and its participants, accompanied by an analysis of the data for themes, patterns, and issues (Merriam, 1998, 2009; Stake, 1995). Three variations exist in terms of case analysis (Creswell, 2013): the single instrumental case study (research focuses on an issue or concern in one bounded case), the collective or multiple case study (multiple case studies illustrate an issue or concern), and the intrinsic case study (the focus is on the case itself because the case presents a unique situation).

Data collection in case study research is typically extensive and draws on multiple methods of data collection including document review, observation, interviews, focus groups, surveys, and critical incidents.

In a case study, triangulation is critical in attempting to obtain an in-depth understanding of the phenomenon under study and adds rigor, breadth, and depth to the study and provides corroborative evidence of the data obtained. In triangulation the researcher makes use of multiple and different sources and methods, and these are reported as part of the study's methodology, including peer review or peer debriefing (which provides an external check of the research process) and member checks (where participants' views are solicited regarding the credibility of findings, analyses, and interpretations).

Analysis of data can be holistic or embedded—that is, dealing with the whole or parts of the case (Yin, 2014). Thematic analysis is not for purposes of generalizing beyond the case but rather for rich description of the case in order to understand the complexity thereof. As Merriam (1998) points out, analysis is rich in the context of the case or setting in which the case presents itself. When multiple cases are examined, the typical analytic strategy is to provide detailed description of themes within each case (within-case analysis), followed by thematic analysis across cases (cross-case analysis). Selecting a case (or cases) to study requires that the researcher establish a rationale for a purposeful sampling strategy, and clear indications regarding the boundaries of the case. In many instances, case studies may not have clear beginning and end points, and deciding on boundaries that adequately surround the case can be challenging. In addition, a caveat of case study research is that generalizability is not the goal, but rather *transferability*—that is, how (if at all) and in what ways understanding and knowledge can be applied in similar contexts and settings. With regard to transferability, Patton (1990) talks of "context-bound extrapolations," which he defines as "speculations on the likely applicability of findings to other situations under similar, but not identical, conditions" (p. 489). Toward this end, the qualitative researcher attempts to address the issue of transferability by way of thick, rich description that will provide the basis for a qualitative account's claim to relevance in some broader context (Schram, 2003). As with any other methodology, the case study is not itself an inherently flawed approach. Rather, it is when the methodology used is an inappropriate fit for the research questions and design.

Ethnography

Ethnography, as both a method and a product, has multiple intellectual traditions, located in diverse disciplines. The researcher studies an entire cultural or social group in its natural setting, closely examining customs and ways of life, with the aim of describing and interpreting cultural patterns of behavior, values, and practices (Van Maanen, 1988, 1995, 2006). As Creswell (2013) points out, there are various forms of ethnography including confessional ethnography, life history, autoethnography, feminist ethnography, critical ethnography, ethnographic novels, and visual ethnography including photography, video, and electronic media. Rooted in cultural anthropology, ethnography involves extended observations of the group, most often through the researcher as participant observer becoming immersed in the day-to-day lives of the participants.

Fieldwork is a cornerstone of ethnography, typically involving the researcher's participation in a community or setting over an extended period of time. To produce a holistic "cultural portrait," the researcher gains access to the group through "gatekeepers" and "key informants." Both the process and the outcome of research ethnography are ways of examining a culture-sharing group as well as the final written product of that research. Ethnographers study the meaning of the behavior, interaction, and communication among members of the culture-sharing group. The goal of analysis is to seek patterns and irregularities, examining data for explanations of the studied phenomenon. Approaches to analysis can include cultural analysis, thematic analysis, narrative analysis, content analysis, and discourse analysis (Mills & Birks, 2014). The final product of analysis is a holistic cultural portrait of the group that incorporates participants' views (*emic*), as well as the researcher's views (*etic*). As a result, the reader learns about the culture-sharing group from the participants themselves as well as from the perspective of the researcher. The final product usually advocates for the needs of the group or suggests changes in society so as to address the needs of the group. Products may also include performances, poems, artworks, and so on.

Geertz (1973) coined the term "thick description" with an emphasis on the need to understand and elaborate the symbolic import of what is observed and systematically documented during fieldwork. This approach added an interpretive element to ethnography in an effort to enhance the quality of ethnographic texts. A reflexive stance therefore becomes imperative so that researchers remain accountable for their positions of authority, and their ethical responsibilities relative to representation and interpretation. As Creswell (2013) points out, ethnography poses challenges to use for the following reasons: The researcher needs grounding in cultural anthropology and the meaning of the social-cultural system. Data collection is extensive and requires much time involving prolonged immersion in the field. There is also the possibility that the researcher will "go native"; that is, the researcher will become immersed in the group and as such be unable to complete the study, or alternatively become compromised by the study.

Phenomenology

Phenomenology may be conceived as a philosophy and a method. The purpose of phenomenological research is to investigate the meaning of the *lived experience* of people to identify the core essence of human experience or phenomena as described by research participants. Phenomenologists are committed to understanding what our experiences in the world are like; experience (*verstehen*) is to be examined as it actually occurs, and on its own terms (Smith, Flowers, & Larkin, 2009). Phenomenology does not endeavor to develop a theory to explain the world; rather, the aim is to facilitate deeper insight to help us maintain greater contact within the world (Smith et al., 2009; van Manen, 1990). Rooted in the philosophical perspectives of Husserl (1859–1938) and subsequent philosophical discussions by Heidegger (1889–1976) and Merleau-Ponty (1908–1961), phenomenological research involves studying a small number of subjects through extensive and prolonged engagement to develop patterns and relationships of meaning (Moustakas, 1994). In this process, the researcher "brackets" her or his own experiences to understand the participants' experiences (van Manen, 1990). The notion of bracketing is considered one of the key elements that distinguish Husserlian phenomenology. Heidegger, Husserl's pupil, moved phenomenology from a descriptive to an interpretive endeavor, focusing on the hermeneutic perspective, which recognizes that human existence is always embedded in a world of meanings. Therefore phenomenology becomes hermeneutical when its method becomes interpretive rather than purely descriptive (Mills & Birks, 2014). Gadamer (1960) explains the *hermeneutic circle,* whereby a text is understood by reference to the context in which it was generated; the text, in turn, produces an understanding of the originator and context. Parts of the text are understood by reference to the whole, and the whole is understood in terms of its parts.

Phenomenologists focus on describing what all participants have in common, the basic purpose of research being to reduce individual experiences with a phenomenon to a description of the universal essence (van Manen, 1990). In phenomenological research, the researcher is a writer, as the craft of writing is central to this design. Writing is intricately linked to analysis, as the researcher attempts to capture the essential characteristics of the phenomenon. Van Manen (1990) discusses phenomenological research as a dynamic interplay among various core research activities: First, the researcher focuses on a phenomenon or lived experience that is an "abiding concern" (p. 31). The researcher, in taking on a reflexive stance, reflects on essential themes that constitute the nature of this lived experience. The researcher then writes a description of the phenomenon, maintaining a strong relationship to the topic of inquiry. Phenomenology is not only description, however; it is also an interpretive process in which the researcher interprets the meaning of the lived experience. As Moustakas (1994) points out, the concept of *epoche* involves bracketing one's own experiences as much as possible to take a fresh perspective vis-à-vis the phenomenon under consideration; however, this state is seldom perfectly achieved. The researcher then analyzes the data by reducing information to significant statements or quotes and combines these into thematic categories. Following analysis, the researcher develops a *textural description* of the experiences of participants, as well as a *structural description* of their experiences, to produce a combination of descriptions in order to convey an overall essence of the phenomenon.

While phenomenology provides a structured approach toward deep understanding of a phenomenon as experienced by several individuals, there are some critiques of this form of inquiry: Phenomenology requires some understanding of broader philosophical assumptions, and these should be identified and explained by the researcher. Moreover, bracketing personal experiences is difficult, if not impossible. As Creswell (2013) points out, perhaps rather than strive to bracket experiences the researcher should decide how and in what ways her or his own personal understanding can be introduced into the study and usefully incorporated in the analysis. Quality and rigor have also become key areas of critique of phenomenology. Ongoing scholarly attention ensures that phenomenology as a method continues to develop, and that strategies for researchers to ensure rigor and research quality will continue to be refined and enriched.

Grounded Theory

Grounded theory is most appropriately employed in studies where little is known about a phenomenon of interest. The purpose of grounded theory is to inductively generate theory that is grounded in, or emerges from, the data. Theory can be defined as "an explanatory scheme comprising a set of concepts related to each other through logical patterns of connectivity" (Schwandt, 2015). The goal is to move beyond description and to have the researcher generate or discover a theory of a process, an action, or an interaction grounded in the views of the research participants

(Corbin & Strauss, 2015). Study participants would all have experienced the process, and the development of theory might explain practice, or provide a framework for further research. A core component is that theory development is generated by or "grounded" in data from the field—especially in actions, interactions, and social processes (Corbin & Strauss, 2015).

To examine changing experiences over time and to describe the dimensions of experience, research involves multiple recurrent stages of data collection and the refinement of abstract categories of information (Charmaz, 2014, 2015; Corbin & Strauss, 2015). Two primary characteristics of grounded theory are the *constant comparative method* of data analysis (i.e., the ongoing comparison of data with emerging categories) and *theoretical sampling* of different groups to maximize the similarities and differences of information. The objective is to generate theory from the data or modify or extend existing theory. The researcher integrates categories into a theoretical framework that specifies causes, conditions, and consequences of the studied process. Through theoretical sampling coupled with theoretical sensitivity, the researcher strives to ensure that the raw data is reflected or grounded in the final theory produced. Grounded theory data analysis involves a number of strategic methods that facilitate the development of a theory that is grounded in the data. Researchers typically begin with *open coding*—that is, coding data for major categories of information. From this type of coding, *axial coding* emerges—that is, identification of one open coding category as the "core phenomenon." This process gives way to *causal conditions* (factors that cause the "core phenomenon"), *strategies* (actions taken in response to the "core phenomenon"), *contextual and intervening conditions* (situational factors that influence the strategies), and *consequences* (outcomes as a result of the strategies). The final step in the process is *selective coding*; that is, the researcher develops propositions or hypotheses that interrelate the categories or assembles a story line that describes the interrelationships among categories.

Thus the theory developed by the researcher is articulated toward the end of the study, and this theory hopefully has explanatory power to make a significant contribution in terms of knowledge building and potential practical application. Critiques of grounded theory include researcher ability to set aside or suspend theoretical ideas so that the analytic substantive theory can emerge. In addition, the researcher faces the difficulty inherent in determining when categories are saturated or when the theory is sufficiently detailed.

Narrative Inquiry

Narrative research has many forms, incorporates a variety of practices and applications, and is rooted in different social disciplines (Creswell, 2013; Mills & Birks, 2014). To begin, it is important to understand that narrative inquiry as a research genre can be employed successfully in multiple disciplines, and no two narrative studies will look alike. Paramount in any narrative research is the necessity to "think narratively," as narrative inquirers structure a self-narrative through living, telling, re-telling, and reliving (Connelly & Clandinin, 2006). A biographical study is a form of narrative inquiry in which the researcher records the experiences of another's life. Autobiography is written and recorded by those who are the subjects of the study.

The narrative researcher is immersed in the complexity of the multiple layers of stories we as human beings live day to day. As a method, narrative research begins with the experiences as expressed in lived and told stories of individuals or cultures. In this form of research, the researcher studies the lives of one or more individuals through the telling of stories, including poetry, play, or performance. Life history is an integral research technique, as developed by the Chicago School of Sociology. The information gleaned from the story or stories is then retold or "restoried" by the researcher into a "narrative chronology" in order to provide the meaning of experiences (Creswell, 2014). As Chase (2005) points out, one approach is to make use of paradigmatic reasons including how individuals are enabled or constrained by social resources. A second approach is to emphasize the variety of forms found in narrative research practices (Creswell, 2013). Ultimately, the narrative combines views from the participants' lives with those of the researcher's life, culminating in a collaborative narrative (Andrews, Squire, & Tamboukou, 2013; Clandinin, 2006; Connelly & Clandinin, 2006; Daiute, 2014). Paramount to all narrative work is the centrality of relationship in the research process and recognition of the sacredness of the stories that participants share and trust within the research environment (Mills & Birks, 2014). It is important to remember that narrative research does not lead to conclusions and certainty. Uncertainty and tension guide the work, and rather than produce conclusive findings, the process offers understanding and meaning.

There is an inherent reflexivity in narrative research that demands the attention of the researcher and the participant collaborators as the story emerges and evolves through multiple iterations. Each researcher will bring his or her own epistemological and ontological views to the study. And so multiple issues arise in collecting, analyzing, and telling individual stories, not least of all being how the researcher is positioned in the narrative. As Pinnagar and Daynes (2006) ask, Who owns the story? Who has the right to tell it? Who can change it? Whose version is convincing? What happens when narratives compete? As a community, what do stories do among us?

Action Research

Action research is a systematic, collaborative, and democratic orientation toward inquiry that seeks effective solutions to complex problems that people confront in their communities and organizations (Denzin & Lincoln, 2013c; McNiff, 2014; Mertler, 2012; Reason & Bradbury, 2008; Stringer, 2014). Especially valuable to those involved in professional, organizational, and community research, action research focuses on specific situations that people encounter by engaging them in collaborative relationships and working on developing localized solutions. Action research, being about collaborative and democratic practices, makes it essentially political (McNiff, 2014). As McNiff (2014) explains, "Action research is political because it aims to influence processes of change. This means engaging with different forms of politics including the politics of research in general, of the social context, of the researcher, and of the potential reader" (p. 14).

McNiff (2014) describes action research as "research in action on action for action" (p. 9). The goal of action research is, through systematic questioning and feedback, to open new "communicative spaces" (Reason & Bradbury, 2008) so that people may increase the effectiveness and meaningfulness of their work. Action research encompasses a set of consciously collaborative and democratic strategies for generating knowledge and designing action in which trained experts in social research and other stakeholders work together. Many different data collection methods are used, including observation, interview, and focus group. The action research routine provides a simple yet powerful cyclical framework—research, reflection, action—that enables people to commence on a shared and productive process of inquiry in a stepwise fashion and to build greater detail into procedures as the complexity of issues increases. This approach is based on the assumption that all stakeholders—those whose lives are affected by the problem under study—should be involved in the research process in order to inform understanding and subsequent action. As such, knowledge production unfolds and proceeds as a collective process, actively engaging people who have previously been the "subjects" of research to collectively investigate and reconcile their own situation.

The protocol is therefore iterative, cyclical, and participative in nature and is intended to foster deeper understanding of a given situation, starting with conceptualizing and particularizing the problem and moving through several interventions and evaluations. The purpose of data analysis in action research is two-fold: to produce understanding or theory and to inform future action. When practitioners use action research, it has the potential to increase the amount they learn consciously from their experience; the action research cycle can be regarded as a learning cycle. Action research studies also often have direct and obvious relevance to improving practice and advocating for change.

Action research has been subject to various criticisms over the years within the social scientific community. Some of these criticisms include that action research does not meet criteria of valid scientific methodology, that it is little more than refined common sense and not rigorous empirical research, and that it blurs an important distinction that should be maintained between theory and practice (Schwandt, 2015). Moreover criticisms of action research have also postmodern perspectives, these being focused on issues of legitimacy, including voice, representation, power, control, and subordination (Stringer, 2014).

Postmodernism/Poststructuralism and Critical Theory Research

In the past two decades, a critical turn has taken place in the social sciences, humanities, and applied fields, with scholars challenging the historical assumptions of neutrality in inquiry, asserting that all research is interpretive and fundamentally political. It is increasingly argued that research involves issues of power and that traditionally conducted social science research has silenced, marginalized, and oppressed groups in society by making them the passive objects of inquiry. Postmodernism views the world as complex and chaotic, and reality as transitional and multiply constructed. Postmodernism is skeptical of narratives, viewing these as containing power-laden discourses developed for the maintenance of dominant ideas or the power of individuals, institutions, or theories. In this approach, truth is multifaceted, and subjectivity is paramount. In recognition of the socially constructed nature of the world, meaning rather than knowledge is sought because knowledge is seen as constrained by the discourses that were developed to protect powerful interests. As social construction is seen to dominate knowledge, meanings are recognized as individual creations that require deconstruction and negotiated interpretation. Deconstruction of grand narratives is viewed as an important way of removing their power (Grbich, 2013).

Critical approaches that have emerged include critical ethnography, queer analysis, critical race analysis, feminist research methods, cultural studies, and multimodal studies. Inquiry is seen as contributing to radical change or emancipation from oppressive social structures, either through sustained critique or through direct advocacy and action taken by the researcher, often in collaboration with participants. Reflexive subjectivity of the researcher—that is, constant reflective and self-critical processes—is an essential component of data collection and data analysis. The researcher and the researched are not considered separate entities; through interpretation, their constructed meanings become interwoven (Grbich, 2013).

Poststructuralism, with its emphasis on language, forms a subset of postmodernism (Creswell, 2013; Denzin & Lincoln, 2013a, 2013c; Grbich, 2013; Marshall & Rossman, 2015). Poststructuralism developed in reaction to structuralism, which sought to describe the world in terms of systems of centralized logic and formal structures. In the creation and communication of meaning, language is viewed as an integral and key process. Words are seen as providing patterns of meaning and deep structures that exist and operate within a cultural system. With structuralism and poststructuralism, as reported in Fontana and Frey (2008) and Grbich (2013), two data analytic approaches have emerged for use by qualitative researchers: discourse analysis (developed by Foucault, 1972), in which the dominant ways of writing and speaking about a particular topic become set in place over time and require historic tracking to identify who has benefited from a particular discourse and who has become marginalized as a result of it; and deconstruction (developed by Derrida, 1976, 1981), which involves textual unraveling through acceptance of the multiple meaning of words in order to break down boundaries and re-create text. Poststructuralism has been critiqued in terms of the complexities it engenders, in particular its tendency toward nihilism—deconstruction of the deconstructed text (Grbich, 2013).

The Current Landscape of Qualitative Research

Qualitative research, as outlined in Denzin and Lincoln (2013c), is an emergent and fluctuating field of inquiry. Now in its "Eighth Moment," the field is characterized by renewed calls for social justice inquiry from the critical social science tradition. As mentioned previously, despite its complexity, there are some common core elements that characterize qualitative research. In summary, qualitative research involves the collection, analysis, and interpretation of narrative and visual (non-numerical) data to gain insight into a particular phenomenon of interest. Taking place within natural or non-manipulated settings, qualitative research allows for complex social phenomena to be viewed holistically.

An underlying assumption of qualitative research is that rich data that is nested in real context can be captured only by way of the interactive process between the researcher and the research participants (Creswell, 2014; Denzin & Lincoln, 2013c; Marshall & Rossman, 2015; Patton, 2015; Rossman & Rallis, 2012). The researcher strives to describe the meaning of the findings from the perspective of the research participants; to achieve this goal, data are gathered directly from the participants. Since description, understanding, interpretation, and communication are the primary goals, the researcher is the primary instrument for data collection and data analysis (Creswell, 2014; Merriam, 2009; Rossman & Rallis, 2012).

While the concepts of objectivity and subjectivity are no longer meaningful in qualitative research, strategies that may be collectively labeled as "reflexive practices" abound in the qualitative methodological literature (Roulston & Shelton, 2015). These strategies focus on examining one's subjectivity and biases and reflecting on how these shape the research process. "Researcher as instrument" raises important ethical, accountability, and social justice issues, including intersubjectivity, power, positioning, authorship, and voice. Importantly, the reflexive researcher understands that a reflective stance is an imperative; that is, reflexivity implies the explicit self-consciousness on the part of the researcher, including social, political, and value positions. O'Dwyer and Bernauer (2014) define reflexivity as "a researcher's conscious awareness of . . . cognitive and emotional filters comprising their experiences, world-views, and biases that may influence their interpretation of participants' perceptions" (p. 11). May and Perry (2014) explain reflexivity this way:

> Reflexivity is not a method, but a way of thinking or critical ethos, the role of which is to aid interpretation, translation, and representation. It does not legislate or seek closure and cannot be confined to one element of the research process, bracketed, or appended; it is an iterative and continuous characteristic of good research practice. (p. 111)

May and Perry (2014, pp. 111–120) go on to describe two different yet interrelated dimensions of reflexive practice: endogenous and referential reflexivity. The former refers to the ways in which the actions and understandings of the researcher contributes to the modes in which research practices are constituted, whereas the latter refers to how we think and act in our own social and cultural milieus, particularly within academic disciplines and communities.

Maintaining a reflexive approach ensures a critical review of the involvement of the researcher in the research and how this impacts the processes and outcomes of the research. After all, it is only through the analysis of your subjectivity by way of a judicious process of reflectivity that you can guide your own actions in a more insightful way. Important, too, are representational issues; that is, how the "other" will be represented. As such, research becomes a *dialogic* process, with the subjective lenses that *both* the researcher and research participants bring to a qualitative study as part of the context for the findings. Collaborative, participatory, and critical research designs such as action research and cooperative inquiry problematize positioning and representation within research accounts by engaging participants' responses to the researcher's findings and analyses. This establishes both the researcher and the "researched" as the instrument. This conversation between researcher and participants enables better understanding of the complexities of power, privilege, positionality, ownership, and interpretive authority in human scientific research.

Choosing a Qualitative Approach

It should be clear that each qualitative methodology is founded on a particular philosophy of thought that influences the type of research design and methods used. As Mills and Birks (2014) put it,

> The position of the researcher is the bridge between philosophy, methodology, and the application of methods. Thus the alignment between the research question, chosen methodology and personal philosophy, and the ability of the researcher to be reflexive in relation to the research is critical to ensure congruence in the study that will be manifested in the products of the research. (p. 27)

Having decided on a qualitative research approach, you will proceed to design your study within the framework of one of the traditions or genres of qualitative inquiry. Thus, the components of the design process (e.g., the theoretical framework, research purpose, and methods of data collection and data analysis) reflect the principles and features that characterize that tradition. However, one need not be so rigid as to not mix traditions, employing, for example, a grounded theory analysis procedure within a case study design or conducting a hermeneutic phenomenological inquiry (van Manen, 1990). We recommend that you have some knowledge of the available traditions before making a choice and that you understand each one as rigorous in its own right before combining them.

An important assumption that underlies qualitative research is that the world is neither stable nor uniform, and therefore, there are many truths. Qualitative data are analyzed inductively, requiring flexibility in the research design—one of the hallmarks of qualitative research. Data analysis often occurs concurrently with data collection. As the data are analyzed, the researcher seeks patterns and common themes. Qualitative research is iterative. That is, there is a continuous movement between data and ideas.

Qualitative research reports include detailed descriptions of the study and clearly express the participants' voices. Qualitative research seeks to establish credibility and dependability and is concerned with the issue of transferability; that is, how and in what ways the findings of a particular study might apply or be useful in other similar contexts.

With a researchable problem in mind and with a clear idea of what qualitative research involves, you are in a position to think about carrying your ideas further and consolidating these ideas in terms of developing a dissertation proposal.

Annotated Bibliography

Creswell, J. W. (2013). *Qualitative inquiry and research design: Choosing among five traditions* (3rd ed.). Thousand Oaks, CA: Sage.

This book explores the distinctive features and guiding assumptions of each of the five major qualitative research traditions or genres—narrative research, phenomenology, grounded theory, ethnography, and case study—and the types of qualitative research that fall within each genre. Each tradition or genre is fully explored along philosophical, theoretical, and practical lines. Various phases of research design inherent in each of the five traditions are compared, from conceptualization to analysis and interpretation. Included are comparisons among theoretical frameworks, methodologies for employing standards of quality, strategies for writing introductions to studies, collection and data analysis methodology, narrative writing, interpretive approaches, and verification of findings. The emphasis throughout is on the variation among the five traditions, offering the reader insights into and understanding of the inherent philosophical underpinnings, interpretive frameworks, theories, assumptions, and practices. New to this edition is expanded discussion around research questions for the genres, key ethical issues, as well as technological developments in data collection. Especially useful are Creswell's rich examples from the fields of human services, education, sociology, and psychology; the comprehensive list of additional readings for each of the five traditions; sample exercises to practice specific skills introduced in each chapter; and the comprehensive glossary of definitions of terminology presented by research tradition.

Denzin, N. K., & Lincoln, Y. S. (2011). (Eds.). *Handbook of qualitative research* (4th ed.). Thousand Oaks, CA: Sage.

Representing some of the best thinking from leading scholars in the field, the fourth edition of this handbook continues to define the present and shape the future of qualitative research. Built on the foundation of the landmark first edition, published in 1994, this handbook represents a comprehensive and transdisciplinary overview of the state of the art for the theory and practice of qualitative inquiry. This publication provides a wealth of resources, philosophies, methods, and perspectives, and as such, is a useful companion for those on their own qualitative research journeys. Written largely within a critical framework, contributors address social justice issues, demonstrating how qualitative research can make a powerful impact in bringing about positive social change. Part I locates the field of qualitative inquiry in 21st-century context. Part II highlights paradigms and perspectives in contention. Part III includes research strategies, with Part IV focusing specifically on methods of collection and analysis of empirical materials, and Part V on the art and practices of interpretation and presentation. The final part deals with potential future directions of qualitative research with its multiple vicissitudes. Included throughout the text are thought-provoking examples of studies and their application, with the contributors examining relevant histories, philosophies, controversies, and current practices associated with cutting-edge qualitative genres.

Denzin, N. K., & Lincoln, Y. S. (Eds.). (2013c). *The landscape of qualitative research* (4th ed.). Thousand Oaks, CA: Sage.

This edition aims to situate the ever-changing and emergent field of qualitative research in context. It offers background on the field, beginning with a detailed historical overview, and then moving to the politics and ethics of qualitative research, paradigmatic controversies and contradictions in the field, and finally, ideas regarding the future and potential of qualitative research as a tool for combatting repression and oppression. This edition isolates the major historical and contemporary paradigms now structuring and influencing qualitative research in the human disciplines. Action research is highlighted as a collaborative and democratic research and teaching strategy that can reform social science knowledge production, and as such, is strongly promoted as a major alternative strategy for social research. The chapters move from competing paradigms (positivist, postpositivist, constructivist, critical theory) toward specific interpretive perspectives, including feminisms, radicalized discourses, cultural studies, critical humanism, and queer theory. The final section on the future of qualitative research is particularly enlightening and informative, and includes a chapter on teaching the new emergent dynamic and ever-evolving field of qualitative research. Overall, this edited text provides clear and interesting context to the field of qualitative research in all its facets, and does an excellent job of portraying the transformations that currently define the field, and that continue to gain momentum.

Gibson, G., & Hartman, J. (2014). *Rediscovering grounded theory*. Thousand Oaks, CA: Sage.

This is a re-evaluation of the origins of grounded theory, and provides a philosophical clarification of its key ideas and techniques. By returning to the original ideas of Glaser and Strauss, the authors answer questions such as "What should grounded theory look like?" "How do I recognize grounded theory?" and "How do I produce good grounded theory?" The book includes detailed analysis of current literature, an analysis of the core aspects in grounded theory, real world examples and applications, and a detailed glossary. This text offers a good grasp of what a grounded theory study should look like. It takes the reader through the process of building grounded theory, writing up a grounded theory study, and generating theory. The book also explains best practices for critically evaluating the quality of grounded theory research. This text offers useful and valuable background information as well as practical strategies and skills.

Lichtman, M. (2014). *Qualitative research for the social sciences*. Thousand Oaks, CA: Sage.

This text provides a well-rounded and practical view of qualitative research focusing on the diverse ways that qualitative researchers can design and implement studies. The author employs a conversational writing style that covers a full range of methodologies and viewpoints about the field, with myriad examples within the various traditions of qualitative research—ethnography, grounded theory, phenomenology, case study, action research, narrative theory, and mixed methods. Each section concludes with key discussion issues, with questions to stimulate discussion related to important topics, as well as modules that include activities for practicing and extending new ideas. Part one presents theoretical concepts, historical overview, hallmarks of qualitative research, ethical issues, and qualitative research approaches. Part two of the book focuses on planning and conceptualizing a qualitative study and provides step-by-step coverage of the entire research process beginning with thinking and reflecting on the task at hand, reviewing relevant literature, and selecting appropriate methods of data collection. Included is coverage of social media as a tool to facilitate research or as a venue for study (Chapter 8). Part three deals with the final product, with a focus on data analysis, communication and presentation of findings, and evaluation of the research process and final product. This book is highly recommended as a comprehensive and user-friendly go-to guide for those embarking on the qualitative research process, as well as for those familiar with the field who are in search of new conversation and dialogue in the field. The text includes an open-access study site that provides links to resources.

Marshall, C., & Rossman, G. B. (2015). *Designing qualitative research* (6th ed.). Thousand Oaks, CA: Sage.

This text addresses the complexity, flexibility, and controversies of qualitative research's many genres by way of a thorough overview of the process of designing and reporting a qualitative study. While maintaining a focus on the proposal stage, the book takes readers from selecting a research genre through building a conceptual framework, data collection and interpretation, and arguing the merits of the proposal. Extended discussions cover strategies that researchers can use to address the challenges posed by postmodernists, feminists, and critical race theorists, as well as others who interrogate historical qualitative inquiry. Included is thoughtful discussion on trustworthiness and ethics, in addition to dealing with time, resource, and political stressors inherent to the research process. There is an excellent section on specialized data collection methods that includes distance-based research (such as e-mail interviews), implications of postmodernism, integrating archival material, combining research methods, and creative avenues for presenting research findings. Included in the book are vignettes that illustrate common methodological challenges faced by contemporary qualitative researchers and ways of thinking about and addressing these. The authors expand on the methodological challenges involved and offer extended coverage of ethics, data analysis, and research design techniques. Throughout, the authors emphasize the importance of being systematic, but also inspire readers with potential "Aha!" moments and opportunities to do research in close connection with people and communities. This work is an excellent introduction to qualitative research, providing issues to consider, as well as comprehensive guidance for preparing and planning a well-grounded research proposal.

Maxwell, J. (2012). *A realist approach for qualitative research*. London: Sage.

This is a book that should be read by qualitative researchers at any stage of their career and by those critical of the qualitative and realist approach to social science, such as that which Maxwell supports. The book is divided into three sections, which deal with the critical realist stance for qualitative research, realism, and qualitative methods and applications of realism. The first section provides a convincing account of the foundations and tenets of the realist approach. Key issues inherent in qualitative research are discussed, including understandings of culture in relation to interactional and societal orders; causal relationships in qualitative analysis; and complexities with regard to concepts such as positionality and "voice." The second section of this book goes on to discuss a realist approach to the more familiar components of qualitative research including research design, access and field relationships, analysis of qualitative data, and building and substantiating social scientific claims. The third section of the book continues in this vein, providing exemplars of the realist stance and demonstrating conclusions that might otherwise be drawn if alternative approaches were adopted. Readers will of course respond differently to the critical realist position presented in this book. However, the systematic manner in which this position is developed and explicated consistently and clearly throughout the book—by Maxwell, one of the key figures in qualitative research literature—serves as an important and relevant text for researchers all orientations within the ongoing qualitative research discourse.

Mills, J., & Birks, M. (Eds.). (2014). *Qualitative methodology: A practical guide*. Thousand Oaks, CA: Sage.

This edited volume focuses on the theoretical underpinnings of major qualitative methodologies: action research, discourse analysis, critical ethnography, grounded theory, historical research, case study, narrative research, and phenomenology. The aim of this book is to provide a practical guide to the very early stages of designing a qualitative study, with the reader being introduced to key concepts as building blocks of this process. Qualitative methodologies as opposed to qualitative methods are the main focus of the book, and the reader is reminded upfront that the two terms have very different meanings: A methodology is a set of principles and ideas that inform the design of a research study, whereas methods are practical procedures and techniques used to generate and analyze data. Part one of the book addresses the foundations of qualitative research, including its historical development, and the concepts of a generic qualitative research process. Part two scaffolds the reader's learning by examining eight qualitative methodologies. The authors acknowledge that qualitative research studies are not always clear-cut, and that qualitative researchers will often draw upon a range of research traditions. The focus is on philosophical underpinnings, positioning of the researcher, and alignment of philosophy and methodology with purpose and methods. Part three examines the details involved in planning a qualitative study, including strategies for writing a proposal, ethics, and appraising the quality of a qualitative study. Useful case studies and activities are included in each section.

Reason, P., & Bradbury, H. (Eds.). (2008). *Handbook of action research*. Thousand Oaks, CA: Sage.

Action research is a participatory approach to inquiry that provides people with the means to take collaborative and systemic action to confront and work toward resolving specific problems. The editors make it clear up front that action research is conceptualized not so much as a *methodology* but rather as an *orientation toward inquiry* that seeks to create and engender engagement, curiosity, and question posing through gathering evidence and testing practices. Drawing on rich examples written by leading researchers from a range of social science disciplines, this handbook enables the reader to appreciate the diversity of ideas and practices that make up the family of action research. Through the comprehensive collection of examples provided, what is clearly demonstrated is that action research is an *inquiry-in-action approach* that engages people in collaborative relationships, opening the way for dialogue, critical reflection, and action. In reading through this book, action research becomes increasingly understood as a living and emergent process that cannot be predetermined, but that changes and develops as those engaged deepen their understanding of the issues to be addressed and develop their capacity as co-inquirers both individually and collectively. As such, it becomes clear that the outcomes of action research can be transformational and create positive communal, organizational, societal, or organizational change. For those seeking an action research approach, this text is highly recommended as groundwork reading in that it provides a thorough understanding of the key concepts, nuances, paradigms, epistemologies, and grounding perspectives that are inherent in and that inform this research approach. The text illustrates how different researchers have applied this practice in their work, and also addresses some of the competencies that may be required for the initiation and conduct of this type of research.

Rossman, G. B., & Rallis, S. F. (2012). *Learning in the field: An introduction to qualitative research* (3rd ed.). Thousand Oaks, CA: Sage.

This book is a clearly written and straightforward introduction to qualitative research. The authors creatively integrate the scientific and artistic dimensions of qualitative research, explaining how the research process unfolds from planning and design, through fieldwork and data gathering, to the presentation of findings, analysis, and interpretation. To help the reader better visualize and grasp the complexities inherent in the research process, the authors introduce each chapter with discussions among three "characters"—students whose research projects demonstrate the challenges and excitement of qualitative inquiry. The underlying theme cutting across all the chapters is that research is a process of learning and that the utility of research requires clarity of purpose. This book is excellent for novice researchers, and introduces the puzzles and tensions that one faces in embarking on a qualitative study, offering some assistance in grasping the core concepts, issues, and complexities involved.

Silverman, D. (Ed.). (2011). *Qualitative research* (3rd ed.). Thousand Oaks, CA: Sage.

This edited volume draws on a list of leading international scholars in the field, each of whom writes on her or his own specialized area in qualitative research. The book is, in essence, a conceptual and technical tool kit: It provides a guide to the latest developments in qualitative research, covering a broad range of methods in depth, from approach (i.e., how to think about doing research) to practice (i.e., how to conduct research). The book as a whole is based on a number of underlying assumptions, and these are addressed explicitly or implicitly by each of the contributing authors. Among these assumptions are the congruence of analytical perspectives and methodological issues and the consequent requirement to go beyond a purely cookbook version of research methods; the need to broaden the conception of qualitative research beyond issues of subjective meaning, and toward issues of language, representation, and social organization; the search for ways of building linkages between social science traditions rather than dwelling in opposed camps; and the commitment to dialogue between social science and the broader community about bringing about real social change rather than a facile acceptance of topics defined by what are taken to be "social problems." All chapters include Internet links, reflective questions, and additional recommended reading.

A First Step

Developing Your Proposal

Overview

A completed proposal is the point at which you present and justify your research ideas to gain approval from a faculty committee to proceed with your study. Once your proposal has been approved, you are ready to embark on the research. Holding the proposal meeting represents a vital step in the dissertation process. At this meeting, you and your committee will discuss your proposed study relative to its scope, significance, design, and instrumentation. You also agree on expectations and procedures for the study's duration.

As Marshall and Rossman (2015) point out, when writing a proposal for a qualitative research study, three interrelated concerns need to be addressed: "do-ability" (that is, considerations of feasibility), "should-do-ability" (that is, consideration of potential significance and ethics), and "want-to do-ability" (that is, considerations of sustained and sustaining interest). In essence, a well-planned and logical proposal should indicate (a) whether the research design is clearly explained, credible, and achievable; (b) why others should be interested in the research; and (c) whether you as the researcher are capable and willing to conduct the proposed research.

The proposal is a well-thought-out written action plan that identifies (a) a narrowly defined and clearly written problem statement; (b) a purpose statement that describes how the problem will be addressed; (c) research questions that are tied to the purpose and when answered, will shed light on the problem; (d) a review of the literature and relevant research to determine what is already known about the topic; and (e) data collection and data analysis methods. Rather than merely descriptive specifications of what you will do, a qualitative proposal should present a clear argument that explains and justifies the logic of your study. In effect, a dissertation proposal is a "working document on the way to the production of a dissertation" (Kilbourn, 2006, p. 530). Although a proposal is mandatory, it also is the means to obtain feedback from advisors before implementing your study, and this feedback is usually useful in improving the proposed study. Typically, you will write multiple drafts of your proposal. Based on the feedback you receive, you will continue to work toward an increasingly more integrated presentation of the different components guiding the proposed study.

The dissertation proposal is defended orally after copies of the proposal are submitted to the committee members. This process is subject to the policies of the department and/or university, however, and the defense can take place weeks or even months after the submission of the proposal. The oral defense of the dissertation proposal centers on the candidate's ability to indicate that her or his research project is feasible, relevant, and doable. Faculty advisors are not so much "testing" the candidate as helping develop and refine the proposal. Ideally, the proposal defense is a dialogue between you and your committee, the product of which is richer understanding of your proposed research in its many facets. A completed proposal approved for execution and signed by all members of the sponsoring committee constitutes a bond of agreement between you and your advisors. The approved proposal describes a study that, if conducted competently and completely, should provide the basis for an extensive research report (the dissertation) that will meet all the standards of acceptability. However, remember that design flexibility is one of the hallmarks of qualitative research. Although you are expected to make a convincing and persuasive case for the research, and while the proposal is a contractual document, it is also a working document—a preliminary and evolving outline of the research plan. Therefore, as the research progresses, you should remain open to the possibility that some changes or modifications will, in all likelihood, have to be made along the way.

Proposal Components

At the outset, please note that while most institutions will approach the proposal and dissertation in common ways, at the same time there are differences in terms of the organization and presentation and distinct differences in terms of what and how qualitative language and terminology are used. This book presents information as guidelines that are meant to be flexible per institutional expectations and requirements and subject to modification depending on your institution, department, and program.

Some universities make specific demands regarding the format of proposals, whereas others provide more general guidelines for form and content. You will no doubt have to attend carefully to the variations that reflect the expectations and requirements of your particular institution (Creswell, 2014; Marshall & Rossman, 2015; Maxwell, 2013; Schram, 2003). The chapters in Part II of this book provide more elaboration on each of these sections. Note, too, that proposals are written in the future tense because they are proposing research that has not yet taken place. Once you have carried out your study and proceeded to write up your dissertation, be sure to change your writing to the past tense.

Introduction to the Study

The introduction includes the context or background for your study, the problem statement, the purpose of the study, your research questions, the research approach, researcher assumptions and expertise, significance of and rationale for the study, and explanation of key terminology. All of these components are discussed in detail in Chapter 5. The introductory section serves three major purposes. First, it orients your readers by providing them with the context leading to the problem that you are addressing and the overall purpose of your inquiry. Second, it identifies your research questions and the research approach you are adopting. Third, it begins to frame the study by explaining what has led you to focus on your topic, conveying a personal orientation as well as a more general sense of the rationale and significance of the study. In summary, the introduction sets the stage for explaining and justifying the research. It should draw readers into your inquiry while orienting them to its nature and purpose.

Literature Review

The literature review includes contemporary debates and identifies what is already known about your topic and/or problem and what consensus or lack there is around your topic and/or problem under study. Literature is reviewed to identify other relevant research so that you can situate your work within the literature, as well as draw from existing literature to inform your study. The literature review helps develop the argument for your study by showing how your study is part of a larger conversation and/or part of a broader theoretical scheme. Following the review, it is recommended that you present a conceptual framework, which is designed to guide your study. The categories of the conceptual framework are tied directly to the research questions. These are the same categories under which your data are sorted. The conceptual framework is not an abstract model. It is, in fact, a working tool. These categories continue to evolve and become further refined as data emerge.

To establish a solid framework for doctoral study, you are required to discuss the theory, or theories, that support each of the presented constructs in your aligned problem and purpose statements and research questions. As a doctoral-level candidate, you are expected to include a cohesive, meaningful, and comprehensive conceptual framework in your dissertation proposal. The proposal should include an overview of the broad conceptual and/or theoretical area under which the research falls and discuss how the proposed research fits within the larger body of research in the field. Discussion specifically includes important issues, perspectives, and if appropriate, controversies and theoretical tension in the field. Your discussion should reflect knowledge and familiarity with both historical and current literature. Once a draft of your conceptual framework section is written, the next step is to ask yourself several important questions:

1. Is the theoretical support relevant to my topic?
2. Are the seminal and contemporary theoretical sources appropriately described, supported, and cited?
3. Does the section clearly reflect consideration of my proposed study's theoretical assumptions and principles? In other words, have I described the current study's theory so that the theory is clear to the outside reader? Have I considered the theoretical assumptions from several angles?
4. Is there any theoretical controversy or problematic issue missing or not adequately discussed?
5. Is the theoretical framework presented in a cohesive and integrated way?

If you answer in the affirmative to each of these questions, the section is complete. If the answer is no to any of the questions, you will need to rework this section of your proposal. When the answer to each of these questions is yes, it is likely that the conceptual framework for the current study is appropriate and comprehensive.

The conceptual framework is, in our experience, one of the most misunderstood pieces in the dissertation puzzle. Hence, more about understanding, developing, and presenting the conceptual framework is explained in great detail in Chapter 6.

Methodology

The methodology section includes an overview of the research design, information needed and sources of data, a proposed research sample, plans and methods for data collection and data analysis, and a rationale for the methods to be used. The strategies you intend to employ for both collecting and analyzing data are determined by the particular qualitative tradition that you have adopted for the study; thus, in your discussion, you need to demonstrate these connections. In addition, there should be some mention of how you intend to deal with issues of trustworthiness (validity/credibility and reliability/dependability), anticipated ethical issues and your plans for dealing with them, dissemination and policy relevance as applicable, and an explanation regarding how you intend to communicate your findings, as well as limitations and delimitations and some plans for addressing these issues.

The methodology section of the proposal, therefore, helps further develop the argument for your study by showing how and in what ways you will go about conducting your study. Although research proposals do not always necessitate the collection of data, it is often recommended that you include in your proposal intentions to conduct pilot studies, which will constitute preliminary findings in advance of your actual research. By doing the "spadework" and by saying, "I tried it, and here is how it worked," you demonstrate the availability of participants, the practicality of procedures, and your skills and capabilities as a researcher. Moreover, pilot studies have additional benefits. As Locke, Spirduso, and Silverman (2000) point out, "The modest pilot study is the best possible basis for making wise decisions in designing research" (p. 74). It is important to remember that pilot studies if included in the proposal will only be conducted *after* the proposal has been approved and IRB permission secured. Details regarding IRB protocol and requirements are discussed further on in this chapter.

Additional Elements

In addition to the three parts of the proposal outlined previously, we recommend the inclusion of a clear title, a tentative chapter outline for the dissertation, and a detailed projected timetable for your research. Both of the latter elements illustrate that you are able to plan and think ahead. The proposed chapter outline indicates logic, structure, and clarity. The timeline will convince the reader that you have given serious thought to the tasks involved and the time needed to complete each task. The timeline will help the reader (and you) judge the feasibility of the proposed study and may suggest implications for logistics and practicality that might not be immediately apparent in the body of the proposal. In addition, you need to attach as appendices all necessary and relevant information, such as a copy of IRB (or similar body) approval for your proposed study, tailored consent forms with a clear outline of the steps you will take to protect research participants, projected instruments and forms to be used in pilot studies, projected coding schemes and projected matrices, and any other appropriate documents.

Of course, proper use of references and citations is necessary, too. It is important to note that citations from the literature constitute the beginning of a more comprehensive list of references that is continuously being developed as you proceed through each chapter and will culminate in a final set of references at the end of the dissertation. Attention to updating your list of references throughout your study is indeed a critical discipline in carrying out research. This task can be accomplished manually, but should you prefer there are also software programs that can assist in creating a list of bibliographic references including EndNote (www.endnote.com), ProCite (www .procite.com), and RefWorks (www.refworks.com). These programs can be thought of as an online filing cabinet and can be used to store citation information and format bibliographies in American Psychological Association (APA) style.

A proposal requires a logical structure. The conceptual and methodological parts of the proposal need to make sense in relation to one another, and the writing must be clear and concise. You need to think carefully about the relationship between the various parts of your proposal and how they are aligned. This keen sense of inter-relatedness not only provides your readers with a cohesive picture of the proposed project, but also helps you, as the researcher and writer, to conceptualize the entire process involved.

It is important to point out that this understanding of structural interrelationship, while implying clear definition and cohesiveness, does not necessitate a rigid frame-work. It is vital that your proposal preserves the design flexibility that is characteristic of qualitative research. Qualitative researchers need to remain flexible and attuned to emergent data. In this regard, you should expect that, before it evolves toward its final form, your proposal will most likely undergo many drafts as you refine your thinking. The thinking, writing, and rewriting involved in developing a sound proposal will help you to develop a logic and a plan that will continue to guide and direct your research. As such, the time and energy spent in writing a clear and persuasive proposal that is carefully explained, theoretically sound, methodologically thoughtful, and practically grounded will reap rewards throughout the dissertation endeavor.

You may have heard the term *elevator speech*. This refers to your ability to clearly and concisely answer the question, "What is your study about?" If somebody asks you this, for example in an elevator, you would not have very long to explain the essence or gist of your study. This is where you have to be crystal clear about your research problem and purpose statement as these convey the study's context, rationale, goals, and objectives. Preparing this speech at the proposal stage also provides you with clarity about what it is you are seeking to achieve with your study and reinforces the study's rationale and significance.

Guidelines for Academic Writing

A dissertation is the combination of performing research and writing about your research to describe and explain it. As a researcher and writer, knowing how to best express your ideas in written form to convey them to the reader becomes an essential skill. The impact of any research is likely to be enhanced if you are able to write well about your work. The dissertation requires a high level of scholarly writing. Although not everyone enjoys scholarly writing, nor is everyone good at it, you have to get into the mode of writing for a particular audience—the academic community. Academic or scholarly writing is, in essence, writing that is clear, concise, precise, and bold. Above all, good writing is a function of good thinking.

Clarity, Coherence, and Cohesiveness

Whatever chapter of your dissertation you are busy with, it is important that you spend time planning not only *what* you will write, but also *how* you will write. Creating an outline or "mind map" that traces the path of your argument is one way to begin thinking about this. Creating outlines is an effective way to organize your thinking and sequentially guide your writing. In writing your dissertation, your intention is not only to demonstrate your knowledge of the topic, but also to capture the interest of and guide the reader throughout so that she or he understands and can follow your train of thought. To ensure that your paper is user-friendly, aim for clarity and logic:

- In your introductory section, write a paragraph that describes your outline. This paragraph lets readers know where you will take them. A strong introduction as well as a strong conclusion (described further on) will help readers to see the significance of your work.
- Make use of headings and subheadings to provide structure to your writing. These are useful in communicating the key ideas to the reader. Crowding makes reading difficult and unpleasant.
- Resist jargon. Jargon excludes and mystifies the reader. Do not assume that all readers understand specialized language. If you must use a specialized term, be sure to explain it.
- Build coherence through connecting sentences. Every sentence should be a logical sequel to the one that preceded it.
- Use transitions or segues to trace the path of your argument and to guide the reader. Transitions are "bridge sentences" between paragraphs and help make your discussion easy to follow.
- Organize your thoughts in a coherent, well-constructed paragraph. Create paragraphs that contain one main idea only. Begin each paragraph with a topic sentence, followed by supporting sentences that illustrate, elaborate, explain, and clarify your main idea.
- Each paragraph should logically and sequentially lead to the next. Remember to pay particular attention to the last sentence of each paragraph because this is the springboard to the subsequent paragraph.
- Paragraphs should not be overly long because this overwhelms the reader. If a paragraph is one page or more, break it into two or more paragraphs.
- Make sure that each section and/or chapter ends by summarizing and integrating the main points and themes. The summary allows the reader to come away with a clear understanding of what you have written and what will follow.

After writing each paragraph, it is helpful to read it aloud. In this way, you can check for syntax, as well as for coherence and flow. In academic writing, it is essential that you are clear and precise. In reviewing your work, ask yourself, "Is what I am reading really what I intended to write? Does it say what I mean it to say?" If a written passage sounds awkward, you might need to add new words, phrases, or sentences to establish clearer connections. You also should watch out for sharp breaks where the reader is left "hanging"; in these cases, you should consider restructuring the sentence or phrase.

In reading aloud, watch for any assumptions and unsupported statements. In these cases, the reader might ask, "Who says so?" You must provide evidence to support what you say. In dissertation writing, you have to get in the habit of writing defensively. In other words, you need to stop after each paragraph and ask yourself: "Have I provoked any questions in the reader's mind?" This step is important because the process in the defense of a qualitative dissertation is one of questioning and challenging any assumptions you may have made. As soon as you provoke questions in the reader's mind, she or he begins to lose confidence in your argument and may even go looking for more questions. That is the last thing you want to happen.

Reading aloud also allows you to check for grammatical errors:

- Make sure that you use complete sentences, not fragmented ones.
- Do not use unwieldy, run-on sentences. Long, complicated sentences force the reader to decide which of the points you are making should be emphasized. Each sentence should contain one thought only. Aim for short, clear, and crisp sentences.
- Check for incorrect use of punctuation, which can affect meaning.
- Be consistent in your tenses.
- Place descriptive words and phrases as close as possible to the words they describe, or they may inadvertently describe the wrong word.
- Be careful not to end a sentence with a preposition (*to, from, with,* etc.).
- Whenever possible, use the active rather than the passive voice. The active voice reduces wordiness and is more direct, giving vitality and force to your writing.
- Look for unnecessary adjectives and delete vague qualifications such as *very.*
- Remember that academic writing is formal writing. As such, slang expressions, colloquialisms, and idioms are not appropriate.

Format and Style Requirements

A research report must consistently follow a selected system for format and style. Format refers to the general pattern of organization and arrangement of the report. Style refers to appropriate writing conventions and includes rules of grammar, spelling, capitalization, and punctuation to be followed in preparing the report. Most colleges and universities require the use of a specific style—either their own or that in a published style manual. You need to make inquiries regarding your particular department's recommended style preference. The most frequently used style manuals in the social sciences are included as Appendix D.

Regardless of which manual you use, you are expected to adhere to its rules meticulously. Early on in the dissertation process, you should become familiar with your required manual and use it consistently throughout. Mastering the manual's technical nuances early on (such as the use of headings, footnotes, tables, and figures) will save you considerable time and effort in the long run.

Be especially careful to follow the manual's guidelines regarding citation of references. It is imperative that all citations be completely accurate. For example, APA style (2010) recommends, when citing a study with three to five authors, including all authors' names for the first citation and using only the first author's name followed by *et al.* for all subsequent citations. When citing a study with six or more authors, use *et al.* after the first author's name—even if it is the first citation, with no comma before *et al.* Especially important is that, from the beginning, you remain vigilant in updating your reference list each time you add a citation. Do not imagine that you will remember to do so later. Searching for "lost" references is time-consuming and very frustrating.

For specific APA reference examples refer to Chapter 7 (pages 193–224) of the *Publication Manual of the American Psychological Association* (6th ed.). For information about citing references in-text refer to pages 174–179. The following Internet resource provides valuable information regarding APA style and reference examples: http://www.apastyle.org/manual/supplement/index.aspx. In addition to general format and style requirements, there are books that deal specifically with the rules and principles of writing. These offer useful suggestions regarding sentence construction and word choice. Although writers tend to have their own favorites, we have found Strunk and White's (2000) *Elements of Style* and Hacker's (2014) *Writer's Reference* to be extremely helpful guides.

A note regarding use of first-person *I* in your writing: Generally, writing in the active voice is recommended. In qualitative research, in particular, the researcher is the main research tool or instrument. The unique style and narration of the researcher is an integral part of the study, and as such, the first-person *I* is sometimes used. According to some (but not all) views, this usage can be justified in a qualitative research report, as opposed to *the researcher* or *the author*, which tends to sound distant and uninvolved. Because there may be different preferences regarding the use of the first person, we strongly advise that you check with your advisor before proceeding to write.

Although different style manuals emphasize different rules of writing, several rules are common to most. The most common rules include the following:

- Do not use contractions.
- Avoid being too colloquial or too informal.
- Avoid overuse of sophisticated vocabulary. Communicate complex ideas in the simplest way possible.
- Italicize all statistical symbols and abbreviations.
- Spell out all numbers from one to nine and use numerals for those 10 and above.
- Spell all Latin abbreviations correctly.
- Use lists selectively and sparsely. Too many lists appear as an attempt to avoid writing.
- Double-space your work throughout.

Tables and figures are often included in a dissertation to augment the narrative, thereby enabling the reader to more clearly understand the issues being discussed. These graphic organizers are somewhat distinguished from one another:

- Tables are typeset, rather than photographed, from artwork supplied by the author. Tables consist of text only and are frequently used to present quantitative data. Tables offer precise details, including percentages and whole numbers and should always include group size (i.e., $N = ...$).
- Figures are typically used to convey structural or pictorial concepts. Figures can be line graphs, bar graphs, pie graphs, maps, drawings, and photographs. Choose a figure if you want to reinforce the point you are making by way of a strong image.

Tables and figures are used to present material in summary form and should add clarity to the overall presentation of the report. Indeed, readers of dissertations are often drawn to graphic displays of information. Tables and figures follow their related textual discussion and are referred to by number. If you choose to use displays of any sort, make sure that they are appropriately included and do not unnecessarily disrupt the flow of the text. The potential usefulness and importance of visual displays suggest a need to dedicate time and care in creating them. Tables and figures should be uncluttered and self-explanatory; it is better to use two tables (or figures) than a single overcrowded one. If you choose to include tables and figures, be sure to contact your style manual for correct format and usage.

Proofreading and Editing

Always proofread your work. The goal of proofreading is to enable you to find and correct your own errors in thought and organization. After writing each section, examine your sentences for clarity and grammar. In an effort to present an organized, logical, and coherent argument, be prepared to spend time editing and reediting as you "polish" your narrative, correct sentence structure, and trim excess wordiness and redundancy. You will find yourself writing and rewriting throughout the process of doing your dissertation. Writing multiple drafts of a manuscript is part of the writing process and is standard practice for most writers.

If you feel that you need assistance with writing, be sure to contact your instructor for additional resources and guidance. It should be obvious that the expectations for correctness and accuracy in academic writing are high. If you feel that you are unable to meet these demands at your current level of writing proficiency, you may need to seek outside assistance. It is quite acceptable to hire an editor or a proofreader to help meet academic writing expectations. In addition, most universities offer writing classes and/or workshops.

A dissertation is indeed a "creation" or "construction" that takes effort and time. Constructing a dissertation is both an art and a science and takes thoughtful and careful planning. A good dissertation is built on solid outlines and is constructed logically and sequentially, paragraph by paragraph. This process includes paying close attention to style, format, and precise language. Most important, your writing should flow logically and smoothly. You do not want to lose the reader.

Integrity Matters

The strength of your writing rests on your ability to refer to and incorporate the work of others. It is imperative, however, that you attribute recognition to all and any sources of information that you use. There are few intellectual offenses more serious than plagiarism in academic and professional contexts. A charge of plagiarism can have severe consequences, including expulsion from a university or loss of a job, not to mention a writer's loss of credibility and professional standing.

Plagiarism is commonly defined as submitting material that in part or whole is not entirely one's own work without attributing those same portions to their correct source; that is, plagiarism is the uncredited use (both intentional and unintentional) of somebody else's words or ideas. Plagiarism is presenting someone else's words or ideas as your own. The following are *all* examples of plagiarism:

- Quoting or paraphrasing material without citing the source of that material. Sources can include websites, magazines, newspapers, textbooks, journals, TV and radio programs, movies and videos, photographs and drawings, and charts and graphs—that is, any information or ideas that are not your own.
- Quoting a source without using quotation marks—even if you do cite it.

Deliberate plagiarism—that is, copying the work of others and turning it in as your own, or falsifying data—is considered cheating. But there is also another kind of plagiarism—accidental plagiarism. This occurs by carelessly and/or inadequately citing ideas and words borrowed from another source.

In all academic work, and especially in our writing, we are building upon the insights and words of others. A conscientious writer always distinguishes clearly between what has been learned from others and what he or she is personally contributing to the reader's understanding. To avoid plagiarism, it is important to understand how to attribute words and ideas you use to their proper source. In this regard you must be certain to give credit whenever you make use of any of the following:

- Another person's idea, opinion, or theory.
- Any facts, statistics, graphs, or drawings—any pieces of information—that are not common knowledge.
- Quotations of another person's actual spoken or written words.
- Paraphrase of another person's spoken or written words.

Strategies for Avoiding Plagiarism

Note Taking

- Read the entire text and summarize it in your own words. Then paraphrase important points and copy usable quotes. Enclose quotes in quotation marks.
- Make sure to always carefully distinguish between material that is quoted, material that is paraphrased, material that is summarized, and your own words and ideas.
- As you paraphrase, make sure you are not just rearranging or replacing a few words.
- Check your paraphrasing against the original text to be certain that you have not accidentally used the same phrases or words, and that the information is accurate.
- Include in your notes all the information you will need to cite your sources.
- Copy all source information into your working bibliography.
- Print any webpages you use. Write the URL and the date on the webpage if it is not included on the printout.

Citing Sources *You must cite the source of every quote, every paraphrased passage, and every summarized idea you use in a research paper.* Commonly known facts, such as dates or definitions, do not need to be cited unless you take those facts directly from a specific reference source. If you're not sure whether a source should be cited, include it just in case. Sources must be cited throughout the body of the paper:

- Copy quoted material exactly, enclose it in quotations marks, and name the author immediately before or after the quote. Use the same procedure for summarized or paraphrased material, but omit the quotation marks.
- Cite the source information (title, publisher, date, etc.) for the quote or paraphrased or summarized information either in parentheses within the text or in a footnote.
- List on a reference page at the end of your paper the information for all the sources you have cited. (This is not the same as the bibliography. The bibliography is a list of all the sources you used—both those you cited and those you used for research but did not cite directly.)

A Note About Attributions or Citations The two most commonly used attribution systems—Modern Language Association (MLA) and American Psychological Association (APA)—consist of two parts: (a) a reference or works cited list at the end of the document, giving precise information about how to find a source, and (b) parenthetical citations immediately following the material you are citing. Professors and disciplines may vary as to the preferred style for documenting ideas, opinions, and facts, but all methods insist upon absolute clarity as to the source and require that all direct quotations be followed by a citation. It is sometimes difficult to judge what needs to be documented. Generally, knowledge that is common to all of us, or ideas that have been in the public domain and are found in a number of sources, does not need to be cited. Likewise, facts that are accepted by most authorities do not require a citation. It is often wrongly assumed that if one finds material on the web, that material is in the public domain and does not need to be cited. However, the same guidelines apply to all sources you use in your work: electronic or print, signed or unsigned.

Gray areas always exist, and sometimes it is difficult to be sure how to proceed. If you are in doubt, err on the side of over-documentation. For proper use of quotations, refer to your style manual. There is no fixed rule regarding when and how much to quote and paraphrase. If you quote and cite too often, you may seem to offer too little of your own thinking. If you quote too little, readers may think that your claims lack support, or they may not be able to see how your work relates to that of others. However, there are some general rules of thumb, as outlined by Booth, Colomb, and Williams (2008): Use direct quotations when you are using the work of others as primary data or when the specific words of your source are of particular significance. Paraphrase sources when you can say the same thing more clearly or when you are more interested in conveying the general idea than in how it is expressed by a particular source. Do not quote because you think it is easier or you think you lack the authority to speak for your sources. Make your own argument with your own claims, reasons, and evidence.

Institutional Review Board Approval

The IRB is concerned with studies desiring to implement research development, evaluation, and testing characterized as a systematic investigation to develop or contribute to generalized knowledge of research or the public (U.S. Department of Health and Human Services [HHS], 2005). Any research designed to research human subjects, interact with human subjects, provide interventions for human subjects, obtain identifiable information about living subjects, or observe and record private behavior of human subjects must come under the jurisdiction of the governing board of institutional research.

The logic and necessity of protecting the dignity and personal and/or professional safety of research participants is widely accepted among social scientists today (although this was not always the case historically). Abuse of research subjects in the name of science has led to the establishment of commonly agreed-upon codes of research ethics. While there are some variations across disciplines and national boundaries, key principles are fundamental. These include (a) voluntary participation, (b) identity protection of research participants and locations, (c) disclosure to participants of potential risks and benefits associated with the research, and (d) obtaining informed consent. All studies conducted under the auspices of federally funded educational and research institutions are required to receive IRB approval. As such, IRBs have emerged in accredited academic institutions of higher education as bureaucratic entities responsible for the regulation, governance, and enforcement of significant research ethics.

IRB approval is sought after one successfully defends a proposal. IRB approval requires that the researcher obtain proof of certification for the use of human subjects in research. This certification is obtained by completing an online course offered by the Collaborative Institutional Training Initiative (CITI) Program for most institutions. This online course is tailored to the research being proposed. The researcher is strongly advised to review his or her college's policy on IRB certification for the use of human subjects in research to determine the required modules of the online course that must be completed for certification at his or her institution.

Undergoing and successfully completing an IRB certification and approval accomplishes two key tasks: First, the student benefits from the advice of several academics who are trained to detect any potential flaws in terms of research design and methodology that could pose a threat to participants. Second, IRB approval is a stamp of credibility backed by a legitimate academic institution. This credibility is valuable both for the researcher and for the research participants.

The application for IRB approval requires detailed information regarding the researcher, the proposed study, the subject population, any projected funding, any requests for protocol review, and a description of the protocol. Our experience working with doctoral students has revealed that many have found some items on the application document challenging. One such item is the request for protocol review. Students are required to identify the research review section from the following: exempt and expedited (both constitute no more than minimal risk involving the use of human subjects), and full committee review, implemented when a project does not fall under any categories of the exempt or expedited review sections. A further section of the IRB form that needs highlighting is the protocol description. This section requires a detailed description of the subject recruitment process, confidentiality procedures, any potential research risks and benefits to the subjects, informed consent procedures, and the location of the research site, if applicable. An IRB guidebook, published by the U.S. Department of Health and Human Services (Penslar, 1993), explicitly makes note of the difficulties confronting qualitative researchers where informed consent is concerned:

> Fieldwork or ethnographic research involves observation or interaction with the persons or group being studied in the group's own environment, often for long periods of time. Since fieldwork is a research process that gains shape and substance as the study progresses, it is difficult, if not impossible, to specify detailed contents and objectives in a protocol.... Therefore, while the idea of consent is not inapplicable in fieldwork, IRBs and researchers need to adapt prevailing notions of acceptable protocols and consent procedures to the realities of fieldwork.

Submitting the IRB form to the college's IRB office for approval requires inclusion of the following supplementary documents: an informed consent form, interview transcripts, data collection and analysis tools, recruitment materials and permission letters as appropriate, a certificate or proof of having undergone human subject research training as described earlier, and a research site approval letter, if necessary. The following key considerations can help facilitate the application process:

1. Become familiar with the IRB guidelines of your academic institution by obtaining relevant documentation from the IRB office or the office of doctoral studies and also visiting the appropriate website. Where possible, attend relevant workshops or seminars.

2. Describe your research in simple terms, clarifying all technical terminology where applicable. You cannot assume that your application will necessarily be reviewed by somebody wholly familiar with qualitative research.

3. Prior to submitting your application, contact the IRB office for clarification regarding informed consent procedures. In some instances, as mentioned, research may be exempt from the requirement of written informed consent.

4. In your application, be very clear and transparent regarding how you intend to address privacy issues, as well as any issues concerning potential harm to research participants.

5. Expect some delay with the IRB approval process. The application may take an extended period of time, particularly in those studies that propose the use of children or marginalized populations. It is quite standard that you are asked to revise and resubmit your initial application several times before your research complies with IRB standards and procedures.

6. It is important to note that data collection involving human subjects generally cannot begin until final IRB approval of the proposal is issued. In some instances, data collection begins inadvertently such as with pilot studies. Incorporation of such data in the research study needs to be clearly explained and outlined in your IRB application process. In some cases, modification of IRB stipulations is acceptable.

Annotated Bibliography

American Psychological Association. (2010). *Publication manual of the American Psychological Association* (6th ed.). Washington, DC: Author.

This is the style manual of choice for writers, editors, students, educators, and professionals in psychology, sociology, business, economics, nursing, social work, justice administration, and other disciplines in which effective communication with words and data is fundamental. In addition to providing clear guidance on grammar, the mechanics of writing, and APA style, the manual offers an authoritative and easy-to-use reference and citation system and comprehensive coverage of the treatment of numbers, metrication, statistical and mathematical data, tables, and figures for use in writing, reports, or presentations.

American Psychological Association. (2010). *Concise rules of APA style* (6th ed.). Washington, DC: Author.

Compiled from the 6th edition of the *Publication Manual of the American Psychological Association*, this pocket guide includes information on punctuation (for those who confuse slashes with hyphens), capitalization (for those who confuse newtons and watts with Newton and Watt), spelling (for all of us), italicizing, and abbreviating, as well as advice on presenting statistics, tables, figures, quotations, citations, footnotes and appendices (it prefers "appendixes"). It also provides very helpful reference examples, including those from electronic and audiovisual media, a cross-reference to the publication manual, and a checklist for manuscript.

Hacker, D. (2014). *A writer's reference* (8th ed.). Boston: Bedford/St. Martin's.

Rather than providing a set of grammar lessons, this book should be consulted as needed to master the academic style of scholarly writing. The author provides details pertaining to word choice, grammar, sentence style, and punctuation. The author also discusses the most commonly used academic writing styles (APA, MLA, and CMS), as well as various online resources (search engines and databases) that can be accessed through library portals.

Pellegrino, V. C. (2003). *A writer's guide to powerful paragraphs.* Wailuku, HI: Maui'ar Thoughts Company.

Writing is best when it is concise, meaningful, and easily understood, and this book is written with these objectives in mind. The book is designed for writers who seek to improve their writing by providing everything one needs to know about structuring and writing effective paragraphs—the essential element of good writing. As the author aptly points out, a paragraph should be considered a unit of thought, expressing a single idea, communicated through related sentences. The author provides clear and concise explanations of different types of paragraphs and offers practical examples and suggestions. This book can assist writers in learning how to plan their writing by breaking down their ideas into understandable segments and then organizing and combining these segments to produce a logical, flowing, coherent whole.

Schwandt, T. A. (2015). *The Sage dictionary of qualitative inquiry* (4th ed.). Thousand Oaks, CA: Sage.

This up-to-date guide includes current and seminal terms and phrases that have and continue to shape the origins, purposes, rationales, logic, meaning, and methods of the practices that characterize the broad field of qualitative inquiry. Together, these entries constitute a guide to the overall methodological and epistemological concepts and theoretical orientations of qualitative inquiry. Individually, these entries are useful descriptors and explanations that are often required at some point in the research and writing process by both novice and experienced researchers. Right upfront, you need to begin familiarizing yourself with the very fabric of qualitative inquiry, and this book provides the threads of this fabric in a usable and accessible manner.

Schwartz, B. M., Landrum, R. E., & Guring, R. A. (2012). *An easyguide to APA style.* Thousand Oaks, CA: Sage.

Written by respected members of APA's teaching of psychology division, this is a guide to APA writing requirements and might be of use in conjunction with the APA style manual. A clear distinction is provided between style and format, and all the basic fundamentals of academic writing are dealt with in a comprehensive manner. Chapter 5, titled "Thou Shalt Not Steal or Be Lazy," deals with plagiarism (in its many forms), and Chapter 6 discusses the use of biased language (with a particular focus on gender bias), offering ways to go about avoiding common pitfalls and errors in this area. The authors provide helpful advice, tips, and visual representations of how to use APA style, with a particular focus on the whats, hows, and whys related to the use of references and citations. Chapter 10, titled "Everybody Needs References," is particularly useful in this regard. Numerous samples are included throughout the book, and a chapter dealing with common errors constitutes a useful reference for correctly using APA guidelines. Written in clear, conversational, and sometimes humorous style, this text includes easy-to-understand explanations and examples regarding academic writing style and format. The book conforms to the *Publication Manual of the American Psychological Association* (6th ed.), thereby making it an accessible, current, and relevant adjunct resource.

Strunk, W., & White, E. B. (2000). *The elements of style* (4th ed.). New York: Longman.

This timeless book is a wonderful companion as you proceed to write your dissertation. It clarifies the rules and principles of grammar and composition, emphasizing the power of words and the clear expression of thoughts and feelings. Published for the first time in 1919 and then again in 1972, this book is a gem and is small enough and important enough to carry around in your pocket!

Part I: Summary and Discussion

Taking Charge of Yourself and Your Work

Part I of this book addresses the initial and preliminary stages of the dissertation process, and we offer suggestions regarding the various activities involved.

Preparing Yourself and Managing Your Time

- Understanding up front the elements that will constitute each section of your dissertation is a necessary first step. Become familiar with the relationships between and among the multiple components that constitute a dissertation including the technical (micro), practical (macro), and conceptual (meta) levels of thinking that constitute the complex dissertation process.
- Overcome your anxieties and frustrations by viewing and tackling your work in increments—piece by piece, step by step. Action leads to progress, and progress leads to increasing levels of confidence.
- As a resourceful doctoral candidate, create a dissertation support system that contributes to your success by providing emotional and academic support.
- There are many people who have the potential to promote your progress, and the graduate student network is a particularly valuable resource. It is to your advantage to reach out to graduates and other professionals and colleagues who you believe might be helpful to you in this regard.

Organizing Your Work

- Develop your own system to organize and manage the ongoing accumulation of data. This will help you feel in control and less overwhelmed.
- Right from the beginning, be vigilant in saving information. Losing material, even pieces of it, can be a devastating setback in the dissertation process.
- Make use of a journal to capture your thoughts, ideas, and strategies. Recording your thinking means that you will accumulate material that can be revisited and drawn on, and that can form a substantial part of the methodology and analysis chapters of your dissertation. Keeping careful records implies an open-minded and critical approach, and provides ideas for future directions of your work, as well as an "audit trail," which is useful for making validity claims for your study.
- Familiarize yourself with data sources that you will need throughout the process (e.g., library resources, computer databases, and relevant texts).

- Plan your time thoughtfully. The time commitment involved in doing your dissertation is substantial given the volume of work.
- A timetable for your work may or may not formally be required by your committee, but it is an effective way to manage your time and keep you on track. Create a system whereby you work on parts that contribute to the whole—chapter by chapter or even one part of a chapter at a time. The dissertation journey is essentially about achieving milestones one step at a time.

Working With Your Advisor and Committee

- Find a suitable advisement team. This is one of the most important tasks of a doctoral candidate. Each university has a different system in this regard, and you need to make sure of your institution and/or program's policies and procedures.
- Understand that students and faculty are partner stakeholders in the dissertation process. Be aware of student and faculty expectations and responsibilities. This is a necessary element in the dissertation process that many students are not clear on, and hence they have unfulfilled expectations and make unnecessary demands.

Developing Your Study

- Realize that the starting point for any research project involves coming to some decision about a sound, doable topic. The topic is the subject of inquiry around a particular research problem that your study will address. Determine what you want to research and what you want to learn. To identify a researchable topic, begin by looking at a broad area—one you know something about or in which you have a general interest. Although you do not necessarily have to be passionate about your topic, you should like the subject matter because your interest will sustain you and keep you going.
- Once you have identified a general area of interest, narrow your topic. The process of developing a researchable topic is a process of idea generation—the movement from a general interest "out there" toward a more clearly refined idea around a researchable problem. Fashion a narrowly defined problem statement from your topic to control the scope of your research.
- Develop a working title that can serve as a guide and focus. The working title should remain flexible so that it can be refined and re-refined as your study progresses. Keeping notes about how and why your title changes over time is a useful exercise.
- Select a research approach based on the nature of your research problem and your study's purpose and research questions. There are various genres or traditions in qualitative research: case study, ethnography, phenomenology, grounded theory, narrative inquiry/biography, hermeneutics, action research, and postmodernism/poststructuralism. Having decided, you will proceed to design your study within the framework of one of the traditions, with the components of the design process reflecting the principles and features that characterize that tradition.

- Draft a proposal that consists of the first three chapters of what will become your dissertation—introduction, literature review, and methodology. Your proposal in effect is your proposed plan to carry out a particular piece of research. It is brought forth to a hearing by a committee for endorsement and approval to proceed. As such, completing your proposal and holding the proposal meeting is a major step on the road to completing your dissertation.
- Keep in mind that the proposal also requires a review by your university's IRB. Check on institutional and/or program-related requirements with regard to dissertation proposal requirements.
- Make multiple drafts of a proposal as you refine your ideas and become more precise about what will happen in your study.

Guidelines for Academic Writing

- Considering that your audience is primarily the academic community, use formal, scholarly writing. Such writing requires command of basic writing skills, such as good sentence and paragraph construction, logical organization, and appropriate transitions.
- Use outlines to plan and present your writing.
- Read your work aloud to check for syntax, flow, and any unwarranted assumptions and unsupported statements that you may have made.
- Develop the habit of writing defensively. This approach not only ensures clarity but also helps to ensure that what you are writing does not provoke questions in the mind of the readers. Questions can unnecessarily bring into suspect the totality of your argument.
- Ensure that format and style adhere to your specific institution and program's requirements.
- Avoid plagiarism and other forms of academic dishonesty, which are serious matters with serious consequences. Be aware of strategies for avoiding plagiarism, including accidental plagiarism.
- Proofread and edit your work consistently. The goal of proofreading is to enable you to find and correct your own errors in thought and organization. The quality of your work is also a reflection of your respect for the reader.

CONTENT
AND PROCESS

A Chapter-by-Chapter Road Map

PART II

P art II is about writing up your study. Each chapter in Part II mirrors the respective chapter of an actual dissertation. Chapters 5 through 7 set up the study and constitute the study's framework. As pointed out in Part I, these three chapters form your proposal. Chapters 8 through 10 discuss how you actually deal with the data that you collect.

The problem identified in Part I, which addresses why people who have completed all the course work do not go on to complete the research and write their dissertations, is used throughout each chapter in Part II. In this way, you can follow the same idea as it threads through all the different sections that constitute a dissertation. Each chapter in Part II is presented in two sections. Section I provides instructions regarding the specific content of each chapter and how that content is developed. Section II is the application that demonstrates what a written-up chapter would look like based on the content developed. In the "Instruction" section of each chapter of Part II, we offer various road maps—in the form of tables and figures—to guide and plan your thinking. Appendices include completed examples of such road maps based on the "Application" section in each chapter.

Although the objective in each "Application" section is to illustrate the content of an actual dissertation, what we present is not a full-blown dissertation chapter, but a representation or model of what the chapter should look like. As such, bear in mind that in a real dissertation the discussion would need to be extensively more elaborated and expanded. The intent of the "Application" sections is that you will develop a clear grasp of the content, understand the process, and thereby be able to apply what you learn here to your own dissertation. In addition, we stress throughout that requirements vary among institutions and programs, and so with all components of the dissertation, you will need to check with your advisor and/or department regarding planning, preparing, and presentation.

We are careful to point out at the outset and throughout the chapters of this book that while most institutions will approach the proposal and dissertation in common ways, at the same time there are differences in terms of the organization and presentation of the proposal and dissertation, page limits and/or expectations for each chapter, and distinct differences in terms of what and how qualitative language and terminology are used. This book presents information as guidelines that are meant to be flexible per institutional expectations and requirements and subject to modification depending on your institution, department, and program.

Table II.1 provides an overview of the contents of an entire dissertation. It is a prelude to the steps involved in each of the chapters that are described and demonstrated in Part II.

TABLE II.1 ● Overview of Dissertation Content

Chapter 1: Introduction to Research Problem	Chapter 2: Literature Review	Chapter 3: Research Methodology	Chapter 4: Presentation of Findings	Chapter 5: Analysis and Interpretation of Findings	Chapter 6: Conclusions and Recommendations
• Context • Problem • Purpose • Research Questions • Research Approach • Anticipated Outcomes • Researcher Assumptions • Rationale and Significance • Researcher Perspectives • Definitions of Terminology	• Purpose • Rationale for Topics • Description: Topic I • Description: Topic II • Description: Topic III • Summary • Conceptual Framework • Narrative Description • Graphic Depiction	• Purpose • Introduction • Overview of Information Needed • Overview of Methodology • Demographic Data • Analysis and Synthesis of Data • Issues of Trustworthiness • Limitations • Summary	• Purpose • Description of findings must be *objective*. • Findings are not subject to interpretation by researcher.	• Purpose • Description of meaning tied to each finding is *subjective*. • Analysis relates to research questions and is synthesized with data from other methods and literature.	• Conclusion • Typically each conclusion drawn should be tied to the respective finding and interpretations. • Recommendations • Typically there are recommendations for (a) the organization or institution, (b) people in the particular discipline under study, and (c) further research.

Matrix of Findings Through Recommendations:
"If/Then/Therefore/Thus"

			"If I find this..."	"Then I think this means..."	"Therefore I conclude that..."	"Thus I recommend that..."

Introduction to Your Study

Overview

The first chapter of your dissertation is the most critical, and everything that follows hinges on how well this first chapter is constructed. Chapter 1 of your dissertation begins with the *context,* which introduces the research by providing the background that sets the stage for the *problem* to be investigated. Once you have identified a sound, researchable problem, the next step is to describe the *purpose* of the research— that is, *how* you will go about addressing the problem. To carry out the purpose, three to five *research questions* are developed that, when answered, will shed light on the problem you have identified. Therefore, the problem, purpose, and research questions are the building blocks—the very core—of your study; they are intrinsically tied together and the basis from which everything else develops.

Our objective in this chapter is twofold: to provide you with an understanding of how to think through and identify the critical elements in setting up and carrying out a research study and to provide you with an illustration of a well-constructed introductory chapter. In this chapter, we introduce the research problem on which this book is based, and we continue to use this same problem throughout the succeeding chapters to illustrate each step of the dissertation process.

The first chapter of a dissertation is about defining what is to be studied and why it is worth studying. We begin this chapter by reviewing the key elements involved in setting up a sound qualitative study. Although the requirements vary among programs and/or institutions, some common core elements need to be included in a dissertation's first chapter—namely, problem, purpose, and research questions. Each of these elements is described and illustrated in greater detail in the following section.

Section I: Instruction

Research Problem

The heart of a dissertation is articulation of the research problem. This is the place where most committee members go first to understand and assess the merits of a proposal or a dissertation. The problem statement is a brief discussion of a problem or observation succinctly identifying and documenting the need for and importance of the study. After reading the problem statement, the reader will know why you are doing this study and be convinced of its importance. The reader will not be left with an unanswered "So What?" question at the study's conclusion. A problem that leads to a question that can be answered with "yes" or "no" is not suitable for formal, scholarly research.

Beginning researchers often confuse a topic with a research problem. A *topic* refers to a general area of interest. For example, we may be interested in the issue of change because we are living in a time when rapid and increasing changes are taking place all around us. A *research problem* is more specific. It seeks to understand some aspect of the general topic. For example, given our interest in change, we want to better understand how people learn to master or adapt to change. Thus, our problem focuses on the participants' perceptions with respect to some specific change event. In qualitative research, the problem should be open ended and exploratory in nature.

You will need to clearly describe and document the research problem that prompted the study and include appropriate sources to document the existence of a problem worthy of doctoral level research. The problem indicates the need for the study. In writing up your problem statement, be sure that it refers to an important, authentic, genuine problem that we know little about, but that is significant and therefore worthy of investigation. Ask yourself, "So why is this a problem?" The fact that there may be little in the literature on the subject is *not* a problem. For every problem there has to be a worthwhile reason for the study to be conducted. We do not do research because we are interested in a certain topic or because we have a hunch about something and we want to go and *prove* it, as would be the case with quantitative research.

All qualitative research emerges from a perceived problem, some unsatisfactory situation, condition, or phenomenon that we want to confront. Sometimes the source of research is around a particular scholarly debate, a pressing social issue, or some workplace phenomena we want to better understand.

Identifying a good topic and research problem is one of the most often cited stumbling blocks for students who are just beginning the dissertation journey. All too often, students have grand ideas about conducting big and important research in a particular area of interest to them. And all too often, we remind students that, although every topic should have the potential to make a contribution to a particular field, this should not be the overriding objective. Rather, what is most important is that a topic be so narrowly defined and discrete that it is specific enough to be carried out to its conclusion. In other words, if you have too many aspects associated with your problem statement, which is often the case, you will not be able to properly manage and account for all of those aspects.

The first thing to keep in mind in searching for a problem area to investigate is that the problem must be narrowly focused. Second, a logical place to begin looking for an appropriate research topic and problem is within your own personal and/or professional environment. In this way, you may be able to identify a problem and topic that (a) can sustain your interest—this is important since you will be living with your topic for a while; (b) will enable you to demonstrate to the university that you can conduct and carry out a logical and well-developed research project; and (c) will enable you to make recommendations that may benefit you personally, or benefit a particular situation or some aspect of your workplace. These are the considerations that were taken into account in selecting a topic and problem as an example to illustrate each step in the dissertation process, as outlined in this book.

Basically, the problem statement is the discrepancy between what we already know and what we want to know. A research problem is driven by what Booth, Colomb, and Williams (2008) state is "incomplete knowledge or flawed understanding. You solve it not by changing the world but by understanding it better" (p. 59). The problem statement also illustrates why we care—why this study should be conducted. Since all forms of systematic inquiry may be considered as actions in response to problems, having a well-conceived problem statement is an essential component of your research. The problem statement serves a foundational role in that it communicates what is the formal reason for engaging in the dissertation in the first place (Jacobs, 2013).

A problem statement must elucidate the following:

- Theoretical or practical importance.
- The type of research to be employed.
- The population to be investigated and why this population was chosen.
- The variables or factors involved and how these are related and will be measured.
- Clarity, conciseness, and lucidity.

Your problem statement should pass the *ROC* test. This is, your problem must be researchable (doable), original, and contributory.

Researchable

- Could the problem be answered by collecting and analyzing data?
- Do you have the time, resources, and skills to carry out the research?
- Is the research accessible?
- Will you be able to find an organization that will give you written formal permission to do the research on their site? Or are you able to access data through public sources that require no permission to use the data for research?

Original

- Is this a replication study with new population or passage of time?
- Will this study examine or explore a new issue or different perspective of existing problem?
- This study has not been done previously and creates new knowledge.

Contributory

- Should the problem be studied? In other words, is the study warranted?
- Will this study advance scholarly knowledge?
- Will this study contribute to practice?
- Will this study contribute to society?
- Will this study contribute to your personal purpose for the future?
- Will this study make a difference in your profession?

Table 5.1 is a tool you might find useful in outlining and articulating your problem statement.

The research problem we work with in the application sections of this book is, *Why do some doctoral candidates complete all the course work and yet do not go on to complete the research and write their dissertations?* This problem is narrowly defined and focuses on a specific segment of the population; it is relevant to the reader and, hopefully, will contribute to the reader's ability to complete the research and write the dissertation. Once you have identified your own narrowly defined topic and clear, concise problem statement, you are ready to formulate your purpose statement and research questions that must be addressed and answered to shed light on the problem.

Purpose Statement and Research Questions

The purpose statement is the major objective or intent of the study; it enables the reader to understand the central thrust of the research. Specifically, the purpose refers to *how* you will go about addressing the problem—that is, who will be involved and what perceptions they have that are germane to your problem. Given the importance of the purpose, it is helpful to frame it as a short, crisp, almost "bite-sized" statement that can be retained by the reader and researcher alike. Because the purpose is a critical piece of the entire study, it needs to be given careful attention and must be written in clear and concise language.

Henceforth, we recommend that each succeeding chapter of the dissertation include the purpose statement in the introductory paragraph. This notion is demonstrated in each "Application" section. Please note, however, that inclusion of the purpose statement in this way is a requirement that applies to some programs, but not all. If you choose to include the purpose statement in the opening section of all your chapters, be sure that you word this statement exactly the same throughout so that it can be easily identified. Even if you do not include the purpose statement in each chapter's introductory paragraph, in every instance that you mention your study's purpose, be sure to adhere to the same wording throughout. Accuracy and precision in this respect allow for clarity and help avoid potential confusion. This stage is the time not to be creative, but rather to remain practical!

TABLE 5.1 ● Problem Statement Development Template
1. *What?*
In no more than a few sentences, explain what is the problem that the research will addres. Remember, qualitative research emerges from a perceived problem: some unsatisfactory situation, condition, or phenomenon that you seek to confront. List a few relevant, current, peer-reviewed references that support the presence of the research problem and briefly describe the nature of that support.
2. *How, Where, and When?*
In no more than a few sentences, describe the impact of the problem. How are people or researchers' understanding negatively impacted by the problem? When and where is the problem evident? List a few relevant, current, peer-reviewed references that support the impact of the problem that the research proposes addressing and briefly describe the nature of that support.
3. *Why?*
In no more than a few sentences, identify the conceptual basis for the problem. That is, what does the literature outline as the cause of the problem? Remember, the research problem is driven by incomplete or flawed understanding. You solve the problem not by changing it, but by better understanding its cause and the implications thereof. List a few relevant, current, peer-reviewed references that support the conceptual basis of the problem and briefly describe the nature of that support.
4. **Synthesis**
Can you articulate your problem statement? That is, if somebody were to ask you what you were researching, could you succinctly explain the what, how, where, when, and why? As you think about this more, you may discover further areas in need of improvement.

There is a close relationship between the research tradition and the purpose statement. In all traditions, you are trying to *discover* something. With a case study, ethnography, or phenomenology, you are trying to understand, describe, or explore a phenomenon. In grounded theory studies, you are trying to develop or generate theory. Therefore, you need to be specific about the words that you use to define your purpose statement. In addition, the purpose statement should include terms that refer to the specific tradition of inquiry, the research site, and the research participants.

You will see from Figure 5.1 that the purpose is directly related to and flows from the research problem and that the research questions in turn are related to and flow from the purpose. A good strategy for testing the interconnectedness and logic of your problem, purpose, and research questions is to lay all three of these elements out on one page as illustrated in the following example. It is vital to complete this step before you begin writing Chapter 1 because these three elements are the heart of your study, and you must get them right. This simple exercise helps you achieve clarity around the problem in its simplest form, and it identifies how you will go about shedding light on the problem. This step forces you to implode for clarity before you explode and fully develop the subject matter. In other words, to keep your problem in focus, you need to reduce it to simple terms before you can present it in more scholarly and elegant ways. When you do this, you are less likely to lose sight of exactly what aspects of a particular phenomenon you seek to explore. If you take the time to produce this simple one page, it will greatly facilitate the writing of a well-developed first chapter.

Chapter 1, while one of the shorter chapters in a dissertation, it is arguably the most important because everything that follows is a result of how well the critical elements—problem, purpose, and research questions—have been developed.

As you can see from Figure 5.1, the research questions are directly tied to the purpose. This underscores that you must ask the right questions to shed light on the problem. Drafting good research questions is a process that requires mind work. Research questions are often developed at the start of a project, but in qualitative research, there is an ongoing process of formulating and modifying them. Research questions are general questions about the phenomenon under study—what the researcher wishes to learn or understand about it. Research questions are quite different from the more specific questions asked in interviews: The former provide a framework for understanding a phenomenon, whereas the latter are intended to produce the data for the answers to the research questions.

Good research questions should be clear, specific, and unambiguously stated. They should also be interconnected—that is, related to each other in some meaningful way. As such, the questions should be displayed in a logical order. Mostly, the research questions must be substantively relevant; they must be worthy of the research effort to be expended. Therefore, you need to consider carefully the nature of your research questions and the kind of understanding they may generate. Maxwell (2013) offers a useful categorization of the kinds of understanding that qualitative inquiry can generate by way of the following types of questions:

Descriptive—these ask what is going on in terms of actual observable (or potentially observable) events and behavior;

Interpretive—these seek to explore the meaning of things, situations, and conditions for the people involved; and

Theoretical—these are aimed at examining why certain things happen and how they can be explained.

FIGURE 5.1 ●   Road Map for Developing the Dissertation's First Chapter: Necessary Elements

PROBLEM:

Research indicates that significant numbers of people in doctoral programs complete all the course requirements, yet do not go on to complete the research or produce their dissertations. Hence, despite their significant investment in time and money, these people never receive the doctoral degree they set out to obtain, and thus remain ABD. There is little information as to why this phenomenon occurs.

PURPOSE:

The purpose of this multicase is to explore a sample of doctoral candidates' perceptions regarding why they have not managed to complete their dissertations.

RESEARCH QUESTIONS:

(1) On completion of their course work, to what extent do participants perceive that they were prepared to conduct research and write their dissertations?

(2) What do participants perceive that they needed to learn to complete their dissertations?

(3) How do participants attempt to gain the knowledge, and develop the necessary skills and attitudes, that they perceive are necessary to complete their dissertation?

(4) What factors do participants perceive might help them to complete their dissertations?

(5) What factors do participants perceive have impeded and/or continue to impede their progress in working toward completing their dissertations?

Qualitative research questions usually start with *how* or *in what ways* and *what,* thus conveying an open and emerging design. In developing your research questions, it is important that the questions be open ended to foster exploration and discovery. Therefore, avoid wording your questions in ways that solicit yes or no answers. Your research questions should be nondirectional. They should not imply cause and effect or in any way suggest measurement. Do not use terminology that suggests or infers quantitative research, such as *affect, influence, cause,* or *amount.* Also, be sure that your questions remind the reader, and yourself, that you are focusing essentially on perceptions.

Once you have developed your research questions, it is a good idea to step back and test them. You do this by looking at each and asking yourself, "What kind of information will I likely get in response to this question?" As a matter of fact, your cumulative answers form the story line of your study. Let us explain. If the data collection methods are implemented correctly, we should know why people enrolled, what they thought they needed to be successful, what means they took to get what they needed, and what helped or hindered them along the way. Thus, the responses to the questions should tell us why certain people have been unable to achieve what they set out to do in enrolling in a doctoral program.

It should be obvious that if you are going to ask people questions, you have to be able to categorize their responses in some way. The "conceptual framework," which is used to categorize participants' responses, is described more fully in the literature review chapter (Chapter 6). It is mentioned now because the design of the conceptual framework also is tied directly to the research questions; that is, each research question is identified by an appropriate category and set of subcategories. For example, Research Question 1 would be categorized as motivation and will have subcategories such as the various kinds of intrinsic and extrinsic motivations that emanate from theories of motivation in the literature.

Additional Elements

In addition to the problem, purpose, and research questions, there are other associated elements or subsections that appear in a fully developed Chapter 1. It should be noted, however, that aside from problem, purpose, and research questions, there may be some variations in required subheadings depending on individual programs and/ or universities. Begin this section with one or two brief introductory paragraphs in which you tell the reader what research methodology you have used and mention the site and research sample. In this introduction, you also should lay out the organization of the remainder of the chapter so that the reader has a clear idea of this up front. After this brief introduction, you are ready to discuss the context. Following is an outline of typical subheadings that comprise Chapter 1. These headings appear in sequential order:

Context—This is the beginning of the dissertation; it is the stage setting leading up to and introducing the problem to be addressed in the study. The context provides the history, background, and issues germane to the problem. It gives the reader an understanding of circumstances that may have precipitated the problem, the current state of the situation surrounding the problem, and the primary reasons that an exploration of the problem is warranted. It is important to embed your discussion of the context in the ongoing dialogue in the literature. This is not a formal review of the literature, as is done in Chapter 2 of the dissertation; rather, it helps you to build the case for why your research should be undertaken and to convince the reader of the study's need and value. It is in this way that you set up the legitimacy of the problem. The context can usually be covered effectively in five to seven pages.

> **Problem**—*as described previously*
>
> **Purpose**—*as described previously*
>
> **Research Questions**—*as described previously*

Research Design Overview—This section briefly describes the kind of study you are conducting, identifying which among the different qualitative traditions you will be choosing. In this section, you also describe the site and research participants, the data collection methods that you use, and the type of data that you are collecting, as well as the strategies you use for data analysis. This discussion should not be more than a page or two because more explicit information regarding your research approach is provided in Chapter 3.

Rationale and Significance—This discussion is presented in two well-thought-out paragraphs that provide the rationale for the study and its significance. The rationale is the justification for the study presented as a logical argument. It describes the genesis of the study and why it is important to carry it out. This is distinct from the significance of the study, which addresses the benefits that may be derived from doing the study. The significance addresses questions regarding your study such as "So what?" or "What difference does it make?" Therefore, the issue of significance reaffirms the research purpose and is a more detailed explanation of the implications of your study—that is, what benefits will be derived from the study. In other words, in attempting to establish the significance of your research, you should think about the various ways in which your study is likely to contribute to (a) theory (by adding to research and literature), (b) potential practical application, and/or (c) ways in which the study might improve policy.

The Researcher—This section informs the reader what you—as the researcher—bring to the study. Begin by describing your background, education, and professional experience that lends itself to your interest in and knowledge about the subject of your inquiry. You also can share your unique perspectives and interests as they relate to and inform the study. In this way, the reader develops some idea as to why you are prepared (*qualified* is too strong a word) to carry out your research.

Assumptions—These statements reflect what you hold to be true as you go into the study and from which you believe you will be able to draw some conclusions. Your assumptions are based on certain premises that may either hold up or be shown to be unwarranted. The researcher usually identifies four or five assumptions. These are the important issues around your topic that you believe to be true as you begin your research. Later on, at the end of your research (in the analysis chapter), you will revisit and reflect on your initial assumptions.

Definitions of Key Terminology—This section provides the definitions of terminology used in the study that do not have a common meaning or those terms that have the possibility of being misunderstood. These terms should be operationally defined or explained; that is, you must clarify how these terms are used in *your* study. If you use the definitions of others, be sure to include the authoritative sources to support these definitions. Which terms to define and clarify is a matter of judgment. Generally these are the terms that are central to your study and that are used throughout. Making terms explicit adds precision and ensures clarity of understanding.

Chapter Summary Discussion

This chapter described the critical components that set in place a research study: problem, purpose, and research questions. It stressed the interconnectedness of each of these components and underscored that they are at the core of the research and that everything that follows hinges on how well these components are constructed and aligned. In addition to these major components, the chapter also described and illustrated all the other elements that comprise a well-developed introductory chapter, including research approach, researcher assumptions and perspectives, rationale and significance, and definitions of key terminology.

Quality Assessment Chapter Checklist

Problem	✓ Is the background of the problem clearly presented?
	✓ Is adequate background information presented for an understanding of the problem?
	✓ Is the problem appropriate for qualitative inquiry?
	✓ Is the problem sufficiently narrow in scope? That is, can you differentiate the problem from your broader topic?
	✓ Is the problem clearly and logically articulated?
	✓ Does the discussion move from the general to the specific?
	✓ Is the problem clearly situated within the literature; that is, does the literature serve to place the problem in context?
	✓ Is there a logical segue that leads directly to the purpose statement?
Purpose	✓ Is the purpose clearly, succinctly, and unambiguously stated?
	✓ Is it clear as to how the research purpose will address the problem?
	✓ Is your purpose relevant to your chosen research tradition?
Research Questions	✓ Are the research questions clearly focused?
	✓ Are research questions open ended so that they will foster exploration and discovery?

	✓ Would answers to research questions shed light on the problem? ✓ Are all your research questions interconnected; that is, is there a natural relationship among them? ✓ Is there alignment among problem, purpose, and research questions?
Research Approach	✓ Is your research approach appropriate and feasible as a means of qualitative inquiry? ✓ Is your research methodology appropriate and feasible for a qualitative research design?
Researcher Perspectives	✓ Does this section inform the reader what the researcher brings to the study? ✓ Do you discuss how researcher experience and/or perspective are related to the problem?
Researcher Assumptions	✓ Are researcher assumptions and biases revealed and explained?
Rationale and Significance	✓ Is there a well-thought-out rationale that provides justification for this study? ✓ Is a convincing argument explicitly or implicitly made for the importance or significance of this research? ✓ Is it clear how this research will contribute to the knowledge base and/or practice and/or policy?
Definition of Terms	✓ Does the chapter conclude with definitions and/or explanations of key terminology that might not have a commonly understood meaning? ✓ If you include definitions, have you properly cited all relevant authoritative sources?
And...	✓ Have you checked for institutional and/or programmatic requirements regarding the content and structure of Chapter 1? ✓ Have you checked for institutional and/or programmatic requirements regarding appropriate use of qualitative language and terminology? ✓ Is the writing throughout clear and readable? Refer to Chapter 4 "Guidelines for Academic Writing."

Section II: Application

Now that we have reviewed and explained the essential elements required to construct a research study and introduce it in Chapter 1, we are ready to see what an actual written-up first chapter of a dissertation would look like using the problem previously identified.

CHAPTER 1 OF THE DISSERTATION

Introduction

This study seeks to explore the phenomenon of why some people who enter doctoral programs complete all the course work, but do not go on to complete their dissertations. The purpose of this multicase study is to explore with a sample of doctoral candidates their perceptions of why they have not managed to complete their dissertations. It was anticipated that the knowledge generated from this inquiry would afford new insights and so inform higher education practice. This research employed qualitative multicase study methodology to illustrate the phenomenon under examination. Participants of this study included a purposefully selected group consisting of 20 doctoral candidates who had completed the course work but not yet completed their dissertations.

This chapter begins with an overview of the context and background that frames the study. Following this is the problem statement, the statement of purpose, and accompanying research questions. Also included in this chapter is discussion around the research approach, the researchers' perspectives, and the researchers' assumptions. The chapter concludes with a discussion of the proposed rationale and significance of this research study and definitions of some of the key terminology used.

Background and Context

Although there has been a proliferation in the number of doctoral degrees granted in the last two decades, there also has been an increase in attrition rates in doctoral programs. The status of "all but dissertation" (ABD) has been a critical one in graduate education since the 1960s, and its poignancy—and its permanency—has been growing (Sternberg, 1981). That doctoral candidates struggle, stall, and ultimately fail to complete their doctorates still remains one of the central issues in doctoral education in the United States in the 21st century.

It is estimated that around 50% of students who enter doctoral programs leave without graduating (Bair & Haworth, 1999; Berg, 2007; Bowen & Rudenstein, 1992; Dunn, 2014; Lovitts, 1996, 2001; Lovitts & Nelson, 2000). As Bowen and Rudenstein (1992) state, "The percentage of students who never earn PhDs in spite of having achieved ABD status has risen . . . the absolute numbers are high enough to be grounds for serious concern" (p. 253). These authors further report that, for many of those who eventually receive the degree, it takes between 6 and 12 years to do so. Failure to complete doctoral programs not only represents a personal setback to the individual in pursuit of the degree, but also is wasteful in terms of resources, time, and money for institutions and academic departments (Katz, 1995; Lenz, 1995).

More recently, Dunn (2014) reports that the Council of Graduate Schools confirmed this phenomenon with its PhD Completion Project, which tracked 9000 doctoral students among 30 institutions from the early 1990s through 2004. Findings indicated that 57% of students who started doctoral programs completed within 10 years, and that roughly 30% dropped out altogether. Key to these findings is that attrition rate spikes when students begin their dissertations.

The completion of a doctoral dissertation is usually the most taxing and difficult academic requirement a student will face during her or his term of graduate education (Brause, 2004; Dunn, 2014; Meloy, 1992, 1994; Rudestam & Newton, 2001; Sternberg, 1981). The journey through the required research and writing processes is a challenging one, pushing the student intellectually, philosophically, emotionally, and financially. Many studies have been conducted to understand the reasons for students' attrition in doctoral programs (Bair & Haworth, 1999; Dunn, 2014; Green & Kluever, 1996, 1997; Heinrich, 1991; Lovitts, 1996; Meloy, 1994; Miller, 1995). The studies of Heinrich (1991) and Meloy (1992), for example, indicate the significant role the advisement relationship plays. Lovitts (1996) identifies lack of institutional support as a major contributing factor; this support could be in the form of information about the program or in relationships between students and faculty. Dunn (2014) identified mentoring and advising as key contributing factors.

It appears that many students in doctoral programs proceed through the steps with only a vague understanding of the process of writing a dissertation. They are not fully prepared for the complexity and intensity inherent in the doctoral process. They lack the necessary knowledge and skills, and hence find themselves floundering. Although one can speculate as to what knowledge, skills, and attitudes are needed to successfully complete a dissertation, and although existing literature provides a multitude of perspectives regarding what it takes to successfully complete a dissertation, there seems to be little conclusive agreement. Therefore, this study seeks to shed light on why some people who enroll in doctoral programs complete all the course requirements, but do not complete their dissertations and obtain the degree they sought. It is this problem that this study seeks to address.

Problem Statement

Research indicates that significant numbers of people in doctoral programs complete all the course requirements, yet they do not go on to complete the research and produce the dissertation. Hence, despite their significant investment in time and money, these people never receive the doctoral degree that they set out to obtain and thus, remain ABD. There is little information as to why this phenomenon occurs.

Statement of Purpose and Research Questions

The purpose of this multicase study was to explore with 20 doctoral candidates their perceptions of why they have not completed their dissertations. It is anticipated that, through a better understanding of the motivation and needs of doctoral candidates, the issues and challenges they face, and the availability of academic resources, more informed decisions can be made by both prospective and current doctoral candidates as well as academic institutions. To shed light on the problem, the following research questions are addressed:

1. On completion of their course work, to what extent do participants perceive they were prepared to conduct research and write the dissertation?
2. What do participants perceive they need to learn to complete their dissertation?
3. How do participants attempt to develop the knowledge, skills, and attitudes they perceive are necessary to complete the dissertation?
4. What factors do participants perceive might help them to complete the dissertation?
5. What factors do participants perceive have impeded and/or continue to impede their progress in working toward completing their dissertation?

Research Approach

With the approval of the university's institutional review board (IRB), the researchers studied the experiences and perceptions of 20 doctoral candidates. These participants had completed all the required course work, yet had not been able to complete their dissertations. This investigation represented a multicase study using qualitative research methods. Case study seemed most suited as a research methodology, with its features and characteristics fitting well with the present study. This research explores a bounded social phenomenon through in-depth data collection methods, involving multiple data sources. This case study involves a detailed description of a context and its participants, accompanied by an analysis of the data for themes, patterns, and issues. As is typical of case study methodology, analysis is not for the purpose of generalizing beyond the case, but rather for rich description of the case in order to understand the complexity thereof.

In-depth interviews were the primary method of data collection. The interview process began with the researchers conducting two pilot interviews. The information obtained through 20 individual interviews subsequently formed the basis for the overall findings of this study. Each interviewee was identified by a pseudonym, and all interviews were tape recorded and transcribed verbatim. To support the findings emanating from the in-depth interviews, participants completed critical incident reports.

Although the nature of this study prevented the researchers from achieving triangulation of data, a comprehensive review of the relevant literature and pilot tests shaped and refined the two data collection methods used. Coding categories were thus developed and refined on an ongoing basis, guided by the study's conceptual framework. In addition, various strategies were employed, including the search for discrepant evidence, inter-rater reliability in the coding process, and peer review at different stages as the study progressed.

Assumptions

Based on the researchers' experience and background as academic advisors, three primary assumptions were made regarding this study. First, course work does not prepare doctoral candidates to conduct research and write their dissertations. This assumption is based on the premise that the attrition rate in doctoral programs is high—estimated at 50%. Second, because doctoral students are mature adults, they will be sufficiently self-reliant and self- directed, and that will enable them to conduct research and write the dissertation. This assumption is guided by a predominant adult learning principle that says adults have a preference for planning and directing their own learning. Third, because students have successfully completed all their course requirements, they should be able to carry out a research project and write a dissertation. This assumption is based on the premise that past success is likely to be a predictor of future success. Fourth, doctoral candidates do not always receive the direction and guidance they need from their advisors, and hence will learn informally to obtain what they need to successfully complete their work. This assumption is based on the experience that we have had as dissertation advisors. Fifth and finally, people who enroll in doctoral programs are strongly motivated to obtain the doctoral degree. This assumption is premised on the notion that people would not make the significant investment in time and money to enroll in a doctoral program without a strong desire to achieve the goal of obtaining the degree.

The Researchers

At the time of conducting this study, both researchers were employed as faculty members in a doctoral program as teachers and academic advisors. Thus, the researchers bring to the inquiry process practical experience as working professionals in a doctoral program, having both knowledge and understanding of the environmental context.

The researchers acknowledge that the same experiences that are so valuable in providing insight could serve as a liability, biasing their judgment regarding research design and the interpretation of findings. In addition to their assumptions and theoretical orientation being made explicit at the outset of the study, the researchers remained committed to engage in ongoing critical self-reflection by way of journaling and dialogue with professional colleagues and advisors. Moreover, to address their subjectivity and strengthen the credibility of the research, various procedural safeguards were taken, such as triangulation of data sources, triangulation of methods, and inter-rater reliability checks with professional colleagues.

Rationale and Significance

The rationale for this study emanates from the researchers' desire to uncover ways to encourage and help students complete their dissertations. These students may be prospective doctoral students, candidates stalled at some stage of the process, or those who may have decided to abandon their work altogether.

Increased understanding of the research process and development of the skills needed to write and complete the dissertation may not only reduce the number of ABDs, but also increase the potential for a greater number of students to attain a doctoral degree. A terminal degree not only may afford the recipients more career options and personal gratification, but also has the potential to benefit society at large.

Definitions of Key Terminology Used in This Study

ABD—An acronym that refers to those people who have enrolled in a doctoral program and have completed all the course work, but who have not gone on to complete their dissertation and graduate with a doctoral degree.

Dissertation—A doctoral research project that presents a problem for investigation, employs methods to collect data on the problem, reports and analyzes findings emanating from the data collection, draws conclusions, and makes recommendations based on the findings.

Doctoral Student—A student enrolled in a doctoral program who has not yet taken the mandated certification exam, but who is active in some phase of the required course work.

Doctoral Candidate—A student who has completed all the course work and passed the certification exam and is either working on the proposal development or involved in some stage of dissertation research.

Proposal—The point at which a student presents and justifies his or her research ideas in order to gain approval from a faculty committee to proceed with the study. Only when a student's proposal has been approved can he or she embark on the research. The proposal consists of the first three chapters of a student's dissertation.

Annotated Bibliography

Booth, W. C., Colomb, G. G., & Williams, J. M. (2008). *The craft of research* (3rd ed.). Chicago: University of Chicago Press.

This book offers clear, helpful, and systematic guidelines on how to conduct qualitative research and report it effectively. Especially helpful are Chapters 3 and 4, which offer informed instruction on how to move from an interest to a topic and then how to shape the topic into a more clearly defined and researchable problem replete with purpose and associated research questions. Chapter 15 offers useful suggestions for how to communicate and present evidence visually. Throughout the book, the authors emphasize the importance of clarity and precision in designing a viable, cogent study.

Creswell, J. W. (2013). *Qualitative inquiry and research design: Choosing among five traditions* (3rd ed.). Thousand Oaks, CA: Sage.

A classic in qualitative research methods, this text provides a comprehensive summary of the major qualitative traditions or genres including narrative research, phenomenology, grounded theory, ethnography, and case study. Going beyond the philosophical assumptions, perspectives, and theories, in Chapter 6 the focus turns to the introduction of a qualitative study, the key elements involved in developing the study's introduction, and maintaining alignment and integration among the elements: stating and developing the problem, formulating the purpose statement, and generating central research questions and subquestions. Consistent with Creswell's view throughout the book is the emphasis on how these three elements relate to the particular chosen qualitative genre or tradition of inquiry, and how this evolves through what he calls "encoding" specific terms and words, and "foreshadowing" ideas that are to be developed later. The author illustrates how this might be accomplished by providing several useful exercises as well as illustrative examples from qualitative studies in the social sciences.

Creswell, J. W. (2014). *Research design: Qualitative, quantitative, and mixed methods approaches* (4th ed.). Thousand Oaks, CA: Sage.

This book is accessible, readable, and useful in terms of providing clear guidelines for designing qualitative research, with an emphasis on underlying philosophical assumptions, a review of the literature, an assessment of the use of theory in the different research approaches, and reflections regarding the importance of ethics in scholarly inquiry. Part II of this book deals with the necessary components of a research proposal. Chapters 5 through 7 focus on the mechanics of composing and writing a scholarly introduction, explaining in great detail how to go about developing a researchable problem, setting the problem within an appropriate context by reviewing relevant literature, identifying and articulating a qualitative purpose statement, and asking viable research questions. There is also discussion around writing the abstract, as well as articulating limitations, delimitations, and the significance of a study. A five-part introduction is presented as a model or template of a qualitative study introduction. To illustrate his model, Creswell presents and analyzes a complete introduction to a published research study. Writing exercises conclude each chapter, allowing readers to practice the principles they learn.

Maxwell, J. (2013). *Qualitative research design: An interactive approach* (3rd ed.). Thousand Oaks, CA: Sage.

Joseph Maxwell, one of the leading authors of qualitative research, presents and justifies the purpose of a qualitative study proposal. In so doing, he makes clear the various elements that constitute qualitative research design, and provides a clear strategy for creating workable relationships among these design components and the proposal argument. As he explains, the design, logic, and coherence of a research study are crucial, and throughout the planning process, there are various issues to deal with. Maxwell clearly describes the considerations that inform your decisions about these issues. These design issues include clarifying the purpose of your study, creating a theoretical context for your research, formulating strong research questions, and conducting the study. In Chapter 6 he discusses in detail the controversial concept of validity in qualitative research, and clearly explains validity threats (bias and reactivity), and ways to check for these. Chapter 7 includes a model for proposal structure. Appendices include sample qualitative proposals.

Richards, L., & Morse, J. M. (2013). *Readme first for a user's guide to qualitative methods* (3rd ed.). Thousand Oaks, CA: Sage.

This book is designed for advanced undergraduate or graduate students in the social sciences, with the intent of developing a deeper understanding of the language of qualitative inquiry, or as the authors put it "to start thinking qualitatively." This text explores the fit of research question, data gathering, and analysis across five traditions: ethnography, grounded theory, phenomenology, discourse analysis, and case study. The reader is taken through all key steps involved in research design, from software choice and use, data making, coding, and abstracting, to presentation and publication of findings. The authors emphasize the variety of methodological choices, and as such provide a "map" of methods with tables explaining how and why different research questions, sorts of data, approaches to analysis, and outcomes are associated with and fit best with different methods. Suggestions are offered for how best to go about identifying and selecting the most appropriate choice of inquiry tradition, with a strong focus on the researcher reflexivity, as well as the integrity of qualitative methods; that is, matching research questions with appropriate methods. Included are useful bibliographic references for each of the major qualitative research traditions.

Saldana, J. (2015). *Thinking qualitatively: Methods of mind.* Thousand Oaks, CA: Sage.

This book acknowledges the challenge of teaching students not just how to collect and analyze data, but how to actively *think* about them. Rather than a "how-to" manual, the chapters of this book constitute an epistemological exercise in understanding and reflecting on qualitative methods, thereby encouraging the development of the core analytical skills and interpretive frames needed for the approaching the qualitative research endeavor. As the author emphasizes, qualitative research is as much about mindset as it is about technique. Each chapter of the book presents one "method of mind": thinking analytically, realistically, symbolically, ethically, multidisciplinarily, artistically, summarily, interpretively, and narratively. The reader is provided with various applications, including a vignette or story related to the thinking modality at hand, as well as practice exercises. Designed to help researchers "rise above the data," the book encourages meta-thinking (thinking about thinking) by exploring how qualitative research designs, methods of data collection and data analysis, and qualitative research write-ups can be enriched and enhanced through different lenses, filters, and perspectives on social life.

Schram, T. H. (2003). *Conceptualizing qualitative inquiry: Mindwork for fieldwork in education and the social sciences.* Upper Saddle River, NJ: Merrill Prentice Hall.

This book aptly conveys the iterative and interconnected processes involved in the design of qualitative research. The focus is on the practical issues involved in conceiving of and connecting the ideas that prompt and guide a thoughtful and coherent research study. Most useful is the detailed description of the interplay among the various components involved in conceptualizing and designing the study: developing and situating a researchable problem, generating a research purpose, forming research questions, and clarifying researcher perspectives.

Developing and Presenting
Your Literature Review

Chapter 6 Objectives

Section I: Instruction

- Provide an understanding of the function and purpose of a literature review (the "what").

- Describe the role of a research-based critical literature review in a dissertation (the "why").

- Outline the skills related to the various steps involved in conducting and presenting a thorough and systematic review of the literature, including identifying and retrieving relevant material and sources, as well as analyzing, evaluating, and synthesizing ideas found in the literature (the "how").

- Offer a thorough appreciation of the role, structure, and function of a conceptual framework, and explain its development and application based on qualitative research principles.

Section II: Application

- Present a completed literature review chapter for your dissertation.

Overview

This chapter provides a guide to what some see as one of the most daunting tasks involved in writing a dissertation—that of reviewing topic-specific literature. A dissertation demonstrates your ability to write a coherent volume of intellectually demanding work. A key part of the dissertation that illustrates your scholarship is the way in which you have analyzed, organized, and reported the relevant literature. With thoughtful preparation, careful planning of your work and time, and helpful guidelines, this *is* a manageable task.

In conducting a literature review, you are forced to think critically and consider the role of argument in research. Thus, reviewing the literature is research in and of itself. Because a dissertation is really about demonstrating your ability to conduct and carry out a research project, our intent throughout this book is to help you understand what it means to be a researcher. With regard to the literature review chapter, an underlying assumption is that if you can understand the ideas and master the techniques and methods inherent in the literature review, this will be helpful to you in your own research.

Often students put off doing their literature review because they do not fully understand its purpose and function or they are unsure of the procedures to follow in conducting a literature search. In this chapter, we attempt to address both of these issues. We also address the conceptual framework as an integral element of the research process, and provide detailed explanation regarding how to develop a conceptual or theoretical framework, where it would be introduced in the dissertation, and how it functions in analysis. Once you have completed your literature review, you may want to refer to Appendix B: Rubric for Evaluating a Literature Review.

This chapter is divided into two sections. Section I, "Instruction," discusses the purpose and function of the literature review; the role the literature review plays in a dissertation, pointing out possible differences with respect to the different qualitative traditions; and the actual steps involved in conducting and presenting a thorough and systematic literature review. The section also includes discussion around structure and function of the conceptual framework. Section II, "Application," demonstrates how to organize and write an actual literature review chapter. Here we focus on the specific problem as outlined in Chapter 1, and using this as an example, we explain and illustrate how to develop the associated literature review and conceptual framework.

Section I: Instruction

Function and Purpose of the Literature Review

The review of related literature involves the systematic identification, location, and analysis of material related to the research problem. This material can include books, book chapters, articles, abstracts, reviews, monographs, dissertations, research reports, and electronic media. A key objective of the literature review is to provide a clear and balanced picture of current leading concepts, theories, and data relevant to your topic or subject of study. The material, although consisting of what has been searched, located, obtained, and read, is not merely a simplistic summative description of the contents of articles and books, nor is it a series of isolated summaries of previous studies. Your readers are being asked to view this literature review as representing the sum of the current knowledge on the topic, as well as your ability to think critically about it.

Areas of inquiry within disciplines exist as ongoing conversations among authors and theorists. By way of your literature review, you join the conversation—first by listening to what is being said and then by formulating a comment designed to advance the dialogue. The literature review thus involves locating and assimilating what is already known and then entering the conversation from a critical and creative standpoint. As Torraco (2005) defines it, "The integrative literature review is a form of research that reviews, critiques, and synthesizes representative literature on a topic in an integrated way such that new frameworks and perspectives on the topic are generated" (p. 356). Ultimately, your review "tells a story" by critically analyzing the literature and arriving at specific conclusions about it.

A literature review requires a technical form of writing in which facts must be documented and opinions substantiated. Producing a good literature review requires time and intellectual effort. It is a test of your ability to manage the relevant texts and materials, analytically interpret ideas, and integrate and synthesize ideas and data with existing knowledge. One of the ways to improve your writing is to read as widely as possible. Look for examples of good and bad writing. Try to identify ways in which other authors have structured and built their arguments, as well as the methods and techniques they have used to express their ideas.

Role and Scope of the Literature Review in the Dissertation

The major purpose of reviewing the literature is to determine what has already been done that relates to your topic. This knowledge not only prevents you from unintentionally duplicating research that has already been conducted, but it also affords you the understanding and insight needed to situate your topic within an existing framework. As Boote and Beile (2005) explain,

> A substantive, thorough, sophisticated literature review is a precondition for doing substantive, thorough, sophisticated research. "Good" research is good because it advances our collective understanding. To advance our collective understanding, a researcher or scholar needs to understand what has been done before, the strengths and weaknesses of existing studies, and what they might mean. (p. 3)

A review of the literature enables you to acquire a full understanding of your topic; what has been already said about it; how ideas related to your topic have been researched, applied, and developed; the key issues surrounding your topic; and the main criticisms that have been made regarding work on your topic. Therefore, a thorough search and reading of related literature is, in a very real sense, part of your own academic development—part of becoming an "expert" in your chosen field of inquiry.

As Hart (2005) explains, "A literature review forms the foundation for the research proper" (p. 26). It is incumbent on you, as the researcher, to find out what already exists in the area in which you propose to do research before doing the research. You need to know about the contributions that others have made relative to your topic because this prior work, as well as current research and debate, will provide you with the framework for your own work. In reviewing the literature, areas of concentrated interest, as well as areas of relative neglect, will become apparent, and so you will begin to identify a "space" for your own work. You also will gain a deeper understanding of the interrelationships and intersections between the subject under consideration and other subject areas. Therefore, a review of the literature allows you to get a grip on what is known and to learn where the "holes" are in the current body of knowledge. A review of the literature also enables you to recognize previously reported concepts or patterns, refer to already established explanations or theories, and recognize any variations between what was previously discovered and what you are now finding as a result of your study.

Qualitative researchers use existing literature to guide their studies in various ways depending on the type of study being conducted. Depending on the research tradition you have adopted, there are subtle differences in the interplay between prior knowledge and discovery. As such, there are differences regarding the purpose and process for planning the research design and presenting the review of the literature with respect to each of the research traditions. There are some general guidelines regarding whether the literature is referred to *before* asking questions and data collection or *after* data collection and data analysis (Creswell, 2014). For example, in a phenomenological study, the literature is reviewed primarily following data collection so that the information in the literature does not preclude the researcher from being able to "bracket" or suspend preconceptions. If conducting a grounded theory study, some literature review is conducted initially to place the study in context and to inform the researcher of what has been done in the field. The main literature review is conducted *during* concept development, however, because the literature is used to define the concepts and further define and clarify the relationships in the theory developed from the empirical data. In grounded theory, the literature becomes a source for data (Corbin & Strauss, 2015). When categories have been found, the researcher trawls the literature for confirmation or refutation of these categories. The objective is to ascertain what other researchers have found and whether there are any links to existing theories. In conducting an ethnographic study, the literature is reviewed before data are collected, serving as a background for the research question and informing the researcher as to what will be studied and how it will be studied. With narrative inquiry and case study, both "before" and "after" approaches are employed: An initial review is conducted after the development of the research question to shape the direction of the study, and the literature also is reviewed on an ongoing basis throughout the study to compare and contrast with the data that have emerged and the study's conceptual framework.

No matter which qualitative tradition or genre you have adopted, the review of related literature is more than just a stage to be undertaken and a hurdle to be overcome. Right from the beginning, literature review is an essential, integral, and ongoing part of the research process. Aside from the formal review of related and relevant literature of Chapter 2 of the dissertation, which demonstrates that you show command of your subject area and an understanding of the research problem, you will more generally need to conduct reviews of the literature at various stages of the dissertation process.

At the initial stages, a preliminary search and analysis of the literature is usually necessary to focus on a researchable topic and evaluate its relevance. It is the progressive honing of the topic, by way of the literature review, that makes most research a practical consideration. Having done that and having developed a narrowly defined problem statement, you then set or situate your problem within a context. To do this, it is important to consult the literature to see whether the study's problem has been addressed and how and to what extent the issues surrounding the problem have been addressed.

Besides providing a foundation—a theoretical framework for the problem to be investigated—the literature review can demonstrate how the present study advances, refines, or revises what is already known. Knowledge of previous studies offers a point of reference for discussing the contribution that your study will make in advancing the knowledge base. As such, the literature review is a conscious attempt to keep in mind that the dissertation research emerges from and is contained within a larger context of educational inquiry. The literature that describes the context frames the problem; it provides a useful backdrop for the problem or issue that has led to the need for the study. The literature review also can assist you in refining your research questions. Furthermore, previous studies can provide the rationale for your research problem, and indications of what needs to be done can help you justify the significance of your study.

It is important to realize that the literature review does not formally end once you have written your introductory and literature review chapters, but carries over into subsequent chapters as well.

As a qualitative researcher, you must demonstrate the ability to assess the methodologies that you will be using in your research. This type of assessment is necessary to display a clear and critical understanding of how you will be conducting your study and why you have chosen to conduct it that way. The aim of the methodology chapter is to indicate the appropriateness of the various design features of your research, including your research approach and the specific methodology employed. In this regard, relevant references from the literature are necessary to illustrate the respective strengths and weaknesses of each of the data collection methods you intend to employ.

Being familiar with previous research also facilitates interpretation of your study's findings because the latter will need to be discussed in terms of whether and how they relate to the findings of previous studies. If your findings contradict previous findings, you can describe the differences between your study and the others, providing a rationale for the discrepancies. However, if your findings are consistent with other findings, your report could include suggestions for future research to shed light on the relevant issues.

You might be asking, "What is the scope of a literature review?" Just how much literature you will need to cover is a difficult question to answer. As a rule of thumb, a literature review should represent the most current work undertaken in a subject area, and usually a 5-year span from the present is a tentative limit of coverage. For historical overviews, however, you might reach beyond the 5-year span. However, there is no formula that can be applied. Base your decision on your own judgment and the advice of your advisor. The following general guidelines can assist you:

- Avoid the temptation to include everything. Bigger does not necessarily mean better. A concise, well-organized literature review that contains relevant information is preferable to a review containing many studies that are only peripherally related to your research problem.
- When investigating a heavily researched and well-developed area, review only those works that are directly related to your specific research problem.
- When investigating a new or little-researched problem area, gather enough information to develop and establish a logical framework for your study. Therefore, review all studies related in some meaningful way to your research problem.

As you continue reviewing the relevant and appropriate literature, you will know when you have reached a saturation point when you begin to encounter the same references and can no longer find any new sources. Generally speaking, a literature chapter is usually between 30 and 50 pages. However, this number depends, to a large extent, on the complexity of your study and the preferences of your advisor. Therefore, take time to clarify this with her or him prior to writing the review.

Remember, because you are attempting to provide a comprehensive and up-to-date review of your selected areas, it is important to revisit the literature review toward the end of your study to make sure no new research has been overlooked. This step is especially important if much time has passed since you wrote the original literature review for your proposal. Thus, as your study comes to a close, it may be necessary to conduct a new literature search to make sure that all new studies conducted since you wrote the original literature review are included. Moreover, as we remind you in Part III of this book, the literature review is an important early task. Once you complete your study, you need to reread your literature review and ensure that everything therein is directly relevant to your study. Based on your findings and the analysis and interpretation of those findings, whatever is deemed irrelevant should be eliminated. Equally important, if a section of literature review is missing, it will need to be added.

Preparing for the Literature Review

Finding relevant material for a comprehensive literature review involves multiple strategies and a wide variety of sources. First, it is important to become familiar with your institution's library. You should check on what services your library provides, how to access these services, and the regulations and procedures regarding the use of library services and materials. In this regard, university libraries usually offer short informative seminars or courses.

Materials other than books, such as journals and conference papers, are generally obtainable through your library databases. This step is where your university library becomes an especially useful and efficient resource. Through their subscription to these databases, libraries have become gateways to information, and technological advancements have opened up a range of new possibilities to researchers. Some of the more commonly used electronic library databases for the social sciences are presented as Appendix C.

There are a few hundred databases that can link you to the relevant scholarly publications. Each database has its own unique features; familiarizing yourself with these features will enable you to access and conduct electronic searches. Once accessed, you can search according to your topic of interest and obtain either abstracts or full-text articles. Search processes are not necessarily the same across all databases. The art of database searching involves learning how to input terms that will connect you with the material most related to your topic. Because database formats change frequently, you should check with librarians for recent information regarding new tools or strategies included in the latest versions of the databases.

Aside from online searches, you also should spend time in the library getting used to call numbers related to your topic in order to find the appropriate sections. To produce a comprehensive literature review, you have to be thorough. Many sources that are needed for review are not available online. Conducting a literature search using only online sources might mean that you miss some critical information.

Retrieval and review have their own set of requisite technical skills. A comprehensive literature search on a topic involves managing databases, references, and records. A common thread running through the discussion of the various stages involved in conducting a literature review is how to manage and organize information, materials, and ideas. Table 6.1 shows the various steps involved in constructing a well-developed literature review. Following is a more detailed explanation of each of the steps involved.

Step 1: Identify and Retrieve Literature

The literature review involves locating and assimilating what is already known. To do this, the writer must experience what Fanger (1985) describes as "immersion in the subject" by reading extensively in areas that either directly or indirectly relate to the topic under study. To begin, you need to select available documents, published and unpublished, on the topic. Through your search, you will begin to identify the relevant classic works and landmark studies, as well as the most current work available.

Primary source documents contain the original work of researchers and authors. These sources contain first-hand information, meaning that you are reading the author's own account of a specific topic. Examples include scholarly research articles, books, diaries, speeches, manuscripts, interviews, records, and audio and video sources. Secondary sources describe, summarize, or discuss information or details that are originally presented in another source. Secondary sources are written by authors who *interpret* the work of others, including abstracts, indexes, reviews, encyclopedias, magazine articles, almanacs, popular journal articles, commentaries, and textbooks. Also included among secondary sources are wikis and websites. Secondary sources are useful because they combine knowledge from many primary sources and provide a quick way to obtain an overview of a field or topic. They also are a useful resource for obtaining other sources of information related to your research topic. At the same time, secondary sources cannot always be considered completely reliable, and this is something you will need to determine. As such, as a serious graduate researcher, you should not rely solely on these, but should base your review on primary sources as much as possible.

Remember, too, that seminal works are integral to your research. Sometimes referred to as pivotal or landmark studies, seminal works present an idea of great importance or significance, and so they are cited and referred to time and time again in the research. Seminal work may emerge naturally as you progress in your search. But identification of seminal work also relies on your own thoroughness in the examination and synthesis of scholarly literature. It is important to keep in mind that seminal studies may have been published quite some time ago. Therefore, limiting a database search to the past 5 years, for example, may exclude seminal studies from your results. To avoid overlooking pivotal research that may have occurred in years past, it is recommended that you not use a date limiter in your literature search. As you proceed in your search, note which authors are making significant contributions to increasing the knowledge base with regard to your chosen topic. In addition to seeking primary material, you might want to revisit the earlier studies of these writers to note the development of their theory or ideas.

A Comprehensive Search Process The retrieval effort consists of a series of stages:

Stage 1: Use keywords and combinations of keywords (descriptors) to identify potential sources: Using various combinations of keywords maximizes the possibility of locating articles relevant to your planned study. Seek and make records of citations that seem to be relevant to your topic.

Stage 2: Skim and screen the sources: Assess each piece of literature to ascertain whether the content is relevant to your study.

Stage 3: Acquisition: Print documents that are available electronically. In some cases, only an abstract is available. In those cases where the material seems relevant, you need to obtain the full-text document. Check out books; copy articles from journals and chapters from books; and if material is unavailable through your own library, order interlibrary loans.

A comprehensive literature search on a topic that covers all the necessary sources and resources is a demanding and rigorous process. It is seldom possible to find all

TABLE 6.1 ● Road Map for Conducting the Literature Review

1: Identify and Retrieve Literature

- Search library catalogues/library stacks.
- Familiarize yourself with online databases, and identify those that are relevant for your field of study.
- Develop parameters that will yield focused results by selecting pertinent keywords or descriptors and specifying a limited range of publication dates (go back 5–10 years).
- Try out general descriptors and various combinations of subdescriptors. In this way, your search is refined, and all possible yields are covered.
- Search the Internet for relevant information and resources.
- From all the sources that you use, try to obtain both theoretical and empirical (research-based) literature.
- Make sure to include primary as well as secondary sources.
- Identify and include the relevant classic works and landmark studies related to your topic.
- Also seek review articles that provide "state of the art" scholarship on a particular topic. In other words, review as much up-to-date work as possible.
- In collecting literature, be prepared to refine your topic more narrowly.
- Keep control: From the beginning, develop a system for recording and managing material.
- At the end of the study, revisit online databases to check for any new literature that may have emerged.

2: Review and Analyze the Literature

- Look for essential components in the literature.
- Extract and record information by asking systematic questions of the literature.
- Develop an analytic format and use it consistently.
- Write a short overview report on each piece of literature reviewed, including specific detailed information.
- For research articles, extract technical elements and establish tables or matrices.
- While analyzing the specifics, be on the lookout for broader themes and issues.

3: Synthesis: Write the Review

- Organize separate elements as one integrated, creative whole.
- Determine the patterns that have emerged, such as trends, similarities, and contradictions/contrasts.
- Identify themes and translate them into corresponding headings and subheadings.
- Write a first draft.
- Ensure that your argument flows logically and coherently, that it is written clearly, and that it is well supported by citations.
- Test the draft by inviting/soliciting feedback from colleagues and advisors.
- Edit, revise, and refine, incorporating feedback from others.

4: Develop the Conceptual Framework

- Develop the conceptual framework as an integral part of your study. It is a repository for the findings as well as a tool for analysis. As such, careful development is essential.
- Establish categories that are directly tied to the research questions.
- Develop descriptors for each category that are based on the literature, pilot study findings, and personal "hunches."
- Be prepared to refine and revise your conceptual framework as the study progresses.

Source: This chart first appeared in Bloomberg, L. D. (2007). *Understanding qualitative inquiry: Content and process* (Part I). Unpublished manuscript.

the information required within the space of a few weeks. Often initial search strategies may not reveal what you are looking for; therefore, you will need to search more widely in the databases and also make use of more complex combinations of words and phrases. Proceed with persistence, flexibility, and tenacity. Persistence means being thorough in your search and keeping detailed records of how you have managed your search activities.

Following are some organizing strategies to assist you in the identification and retrieval process:

1. Because you will return to the library databases time and again to continue your review, it would be wise to develop a system of keeping track of keywords (descriptors) and combinations of keywords you have used. In the dissertation, you will have to report on how the literature was selected and what procedures were used to select the material, so keeping a record of this information is important.

2. It is also important to keep track of each book or document that you consult. In this regard, you should keep diligent bibliographic citations. You will save much time by writing each reference in its proper form initially. There are various software programs available such as EndNote (www.endnote.com), RefWorks (www.refworks.com), Zotero (www.zotero.org), and ProCite (www.procite.com) that enable you to create a list of bibliographic references. These online research management, writing, and collaboration tools are designed to help researchers easily gather, manage, store, and share all types of information, as well as generate citations and bibliographies. Endnote integrates well with most library search engines. Zotero automatically creates references from uploaded PDF files, which means you are storing the references and research in the same place, which is convenient and useful.

3. You may prefer to maintain an ongoing alphabetically arranged, accurate record by way of a Word document; many times, this way is the easiest and most efficient. We suggest that you prepare a typed list of each piece of literature reviewed, making sure that all details (authors, titles, dates, volume numbers, page numbers, etc.) are correct. This list then becomes a working draft of your references. To avoid the frustration of having to search for information at a later stage (and possibly not being able to track it down), keep a close check on this list, making sure not to inadvertently omit any details as you go along. If the reference is a book, be sure to include the library call number because you may need to return to it later. This list will encompass all materials that you have retrieved and thus will have some bearing on your study. In the final version of your dissertation, you will include only a reference list, not a bibliography—that is, not all the reading you may have done, but only a list of those texts that are cited in the body of the manuscript.

4. Collecting literature is an ongoing process. You need to develop some system for classifying sources into those that have a direct bearing on your topic and those

that are more peripherally related to your topic. You need to be selective in choosing material most relevant to your study. Always keep in mind the problem that your study is addressing. As you gather and sort material, ask yourself how and in what ways the material relates to your research problem. You might categorize each piece of material as *very important, moderately important,* or *mildly important.* After locating pertinent material for review, you should store these files, especially those that are central to your topic and that you think you might cite. When possible, you should save material electronically to allow for efficient and easy retrieval.

Exploring and Evaluating Web Resources Although not scholarly, the Internet will more than likely be your initial starting point for topic ideas and information. Start by searching for some of the keywords related to your area of interest to begin a very broad scan of the range of topics and information sources. Use keywords such as trending news or trending topics, recent research, controversial issues, policy debates, and other relevant terms to locate recent news. With the tremendous amount of information available via electronic media, it is crucial that you learn to access this information. However, anyone anywhere can put information on the web, so any information from the Internet should be cited with caution. Remember that using the Internet to find academic information takes a lot of hard work to carefully evaluate and determine if a web resource is a reliable, authoritative, or even scholarly.

The Internet has made it possible for anyone to publish web pages. Most websites have not undergone a review process for inclusion in a collection. For these reasons, you should closely evaluate any Internet resources you find to ensure they contain balanced, factual information. One of the key purposes of evaluating online is to judge how trustworthy or reliable a source they are if you intend to use and cite them. A second purpose is to identify the sort of information which is immediately obvious in print publication; that is, information about the publisher and author. Reliable Internet resources may include peer-reviewed journal articles, government reports, conference papers, industry and professional standards, scientific papers, news reports, and quick facts and figures. However, keep in mind that just because a website is well presented does not mean that it contains accurate information. Following are a few things you can look for in Internet resources to determine whether or not they are reliable sources of information.

1. Can you identify the author of an Internet resource? Is it clear who is responsible for the document? If so, is there any information about the person or organization responsible for the document? Authority means knowing about this author's education, work history, affiliations, additional publications, etc.
2. Who published the Internet resource? Was the web page published by a business, university, government organization, or professional association?
3. Can you find the date the Internet resource was last updated or published? Currency means knowing the date when the document was produced or last updated, and being able to identify the historical context for the document.

4. Does the Internet resource cite the work of others? Are sources clearly listed so they can be verified? Is there editorial input? Is spelling and grammar correct?

5. Does the content of the resource seem balanced and scholarly, or is it biased? Are biases and affiliations clearly stated? The aspiration to be objective, however difficult it might be to achieve, is a traditional value of academic research.

6. What is the intended audience for the Internet resource? Is it appropriate for university level research? Or is it geared toward secondary education or a more general audience?

7. What is the domain of the Internet resource? If it ends in .org, .gov, or .edu it is more likely to be a scholarly source. If it ends in .com or .net it is less likely to be a scholarly source.

Blogs can also be a valuable source for information on trending issues, current events, recent research, debates and more. Scholars, associations, executives, innovative researchers, every day practitioners, and students are just some of the people who write blogs. Knowing about and reading blogs that are written by experts in the field, or relevant associations, may be an important step in identifying current studies and trends in a subject area. The website ResearchBlogging.org aggregates blog posts regarding recent peer-reviewed research and publications. Most online popular and news magazines have blog sections. *Psychology Today* offers a large index of their blogs with a guide to their blogging experts' credentials. Harvard Business Review Blog Network features entries written by top executives and business leaders.

The ease of access of web-based articles makes these sources of materials highly attractive. Remember, if you cannot determine the author of information or the date it was produced, however, it has no place in academic research. Although many websites for government agencies, professional organizations, and educational institutions provide useful information, you should always evaluate information obtained from a website for currency, legitimacy, accuracy, and potential bias.

Step 2: Review and Critically Analyze the Literature

Once you have undertaken a comprehensive literature search, you will need to critically assess each piece of material to analyze its content. In other words, you read with the goal of producing a product—an analytical evaluation. Toward this end, you need to put yourself in the role of researcher and prepare a systematic and comprehensive method of critical analysis.

Analysis is the job of systematically breaking down something into its constituent parts to describe how they relate to one another. Analysis should be viewed not as a random dissection, but as a methodological examination. Although there is a degree of exploration involved in analysis, you should aim to be systematic, rigorous, and consistent. In this way, the identification of the individual and similar elements in a range of materials can be compared and contrasted. Analysis lays the foundation for critique. Critique identifies the strengths and key contributions of the literature as well as any deficiencies, omissions, inaccuracies, or inconsistencies. By highlighting the strengths and identifying the deficiencies in the existing literature, critical analysis is a necessary step toward adding to the knowledge base. When writing the literature review, you will need most of this information in order to put together a synthesized, analyzed, and evaluated product. You are practicing dissecting literature for the important specific pieces of information needed. You are condensing the amount of information that you will need to refresh your memory later. And you are developing a way to document, compare, and contrast what has been researched, what has been found, what has worked, what has not, and what has been recommended. All of these are the essential skills you will need to have in your toolbox for the dissertation journey. Right now you cannot know just how extremely important these skills are as you are collecting your sources.

Analysis consists of two main stages:

Skim and Read

1. Skim the book or article first, noting its topic, structure, general reasoning, data, and bibliographical references.
2. Go back and skim the preface and introduction, trying to identify the main ideas contained in the work.
3. Identify key parts of the article, or if a book, identify key chapters. Read these parts or chapters, as well as the final chapter or conclusion.

Highlight and Extract Key Elements What you are trying to do is understand the historical context and state of the art relevant to your topic. You are looking at what has been covered in the literature, but you are also looking for gaps and anomalies. Although there will be considerable variation among the different pieces of literature, it is imperative to develop a format and use it consistently. A consistent format will pay off when you begin to synthesize your material and actually write the review. Begin by asking specific questions of the literature. These questions will help you think through your topic and provide you with some idea of how to structure your synthesis discussion.

- What are the origins and definitions of the topic?
- What are the key theories, concepts, and ideas?
- What are the major debates, arguments, and issues surrounding the topic?
- What are the key questions and problems that have been addressed to date?
- Are there any important issues that have been insufficiently addressed or not addressed at all?

In analyzing research studies, you need to identify and extract some of the more technical elements common to all research studies, such as problem, purpose, research questions, sample, methodology, key findings, conclusions, and recommendations. The purpose of reading analytically is to identify and extract these pertinent components in the literature. However, as you read and analyze, you should be on the lookout for the broader themes, issues, and commonalities among the various authors. Also be aware of "outliers" (i.e., points of divergence and difference). Regarding research articles reviewed, make notes of major trends, patterns, or inconsistencies in the results reported. Also try to identify relationships between studies. These findings will all be important to mention in the final synthesis, which aims to integrate all the literature reviewed. As you continue to read and analyze the literature, also begin to think about what other information you might need so you can refine your search accordingly.

Following are some organizing strategies to assist you in analyzing your material:

1. Read your "very important" documents first. Highlight, make notations in the margins, or write memos on sticky notes of inconsistencies, similarities, questions, concerns, and possible omissions as you go along.
2. Develop a computerized filing system of Word documents for your literature review. For every piece of material that you read, write a brief summary that covers the essential points: major issues, arguments, and theoretical models. Include conclusions that you can draw, and note any inferences that you can make regarding your own study.
3. As you read, be sure to jot down any pertinent comments or quotations that you think might be useful in the presentation of your review. In so doing, be careful to copy quotations accurately. Make sure to use quotation marks when extracting material directly, so as to avoid inadvertently plagiarizing others' ideas and/or words. Direct quotations also require page numbers, and it will save you considerable time and energy later in the process if you have noted these page numbers accurately.

Annotated Bibliographies

Using annotated bibliographies is one key means to begin organizing literature for later synthesis and inclusion. Whereas a bibliography is a list of sources (books, journals, websites, periodicals, etc.) that one has used for researching a topic, an annotated bibliography is essentially a summary, evaluation, and reflection of each of your sources:

- **Summarize**: Ask yourself: What are the main arguments? What is the point of this book or article? What topics are covered? If this is a research article, what is the thesis and scope of the study, the findings (including any unexpected findings), and the conclusion? Essentially, if somebody asked you what this book or article was about, what would you say?
- **Assess**: After summarizing a source it is helpful to evaluate it. Ask yourself: Is it a useful source? How does it compare with other sources in my bibliography? Is the information credible and/or reliable? Is this source biased or objective? What is the goal or objective of this source? Do I think the author of this source has achieved this goal or objective? Why or why not? If this is a research article, what

is your determination with regard how this study fits with other related studies, and why does the researcher think the findings are important or significant?

- **Reflect**: Once you have summarized and assessed a source, you need to ask how, if at all, it fits with your research. Ask yourself: Was this source helpful to me? How, and in what ways does it help me shape my argument? How, if at all, can I use this source in my research? Has this source changed the way I think about my topic or research problem? If so, how and in what ways?

When you write annotations for each source that you read, you are not just *collecting* information; you are being forced to read each source more carefully and much more critically. At the professional level, annotated bibliographies allow you to see what has been done in the literature and *where and how your own research and scholarship can fit*. Writing an annotated bibliography also helps you gain a good perspective on relevant bodies of literature, and what is being said about your topic. You will begin to develop a good understanding of the issues in your field (current and/or historic), and what others are debating or discussing. Remember, you want your annotations to be useful and meaningful to you, so adding a note that places the material in the context of something else that you've read or in relation to your own research projects will serve to make the annotation more valuable and persuasive. Mostly, this exercise helps you develop your own point of view, a critical element of a good literature review.

Digesting Scholarly Sources

Digesting scholarly sources can be very challenging, and the more you read, the harder it becomes to remember key information. It is therefore essential to be extremely detail oriented so that you do not miss anything. Various other tools, in addition to annotated bibliographies, may be useful at this point in the process. Regarding primary research-based sources, consider preparing a summary sheet that compares important characteristics across all the studies that you have reviewed. A template for the analysis and critique of research-based literature is provided as Table 6.2. A template for the analysis and critique of theoretical literature is provided as Table 6.3. These are both useful analytical tools for methodological analysis of the articles prior to beginning the review by conveying the results of your analysis, noting similarities and differences among research studies and/or theories. These tools act as a quick reference and serve as a record of your literature search. In addition, as you fill out each section for each resource, you begin to visualize and internalize the patterns of systematic research efforts. You may see certain links between concepts, gaps in terms of methodology, or recommendations for future research efforts that might suggest a feasible and worthy topic area for your study. Use the sections in each table to help you review, critique, and summarize *each* piece of literature. Remember, you do not need to complete every section, as some might not always apply. The sections are listed as a means to help you generate ideas as you work on reviewing and critically analyzing the literature. Tables such as these can appear in the appendix of your dissertation. Alternatively, they can be included in the body of the literature review chapter to augment and clarify the narrative discussion.

When you first start writing analyses and evaluations of the literature, these may be fairly long (both winded and lengthwise). This is somewhat useful because it means that when you need to use them, you will be reminded of the article or book, and you will be able to pick and choose what you need. As you become focused more on what it was that you would be writing about, your analyses and evaluations would most likely became shorter. With practice, you can more concisely capture all of the required elements of an analysis. Remember, just like you would not build a home without a sturdy and solid foundation, if you want to make steady progress, scholarly work cannot proceed without the necessary foundation of the comprehensive analysis of the literature that support or contradict the concepts, theories, and statements that you need to make.

When you have finished reviewing and critically analyzing all the scholarly sources you have collected, be sure to revisit your entire (and rapidly growing) bibliography to make certain that it is complete and up to date.

You now have a complete record of what the literature states about key variables, ideas, and concepts related to your study. Reading through your summaries will serve to highlight important themes, issues, commonalities, and differences—in effect, these are the answers to your critical questions. The resulting insights will give you a sense of the forest as well as the trees. This sense will prepare you to integrate the material you are reading and proceed with writing a coherent and logical synthesis of the literature.

As mentioned, one component of becoming an independent scholar is learning how to provide an evaluative critique of the work of other scholars. A critique of scholarly work requires your ability to use high-level critical thinking skills. In addition, you must be able to write constructively and communicate your ideas well, with clear and focused writing. To do so, first you need to demonstrate your ability to clearly and precisely summarize and critically evaluate specific information. Second, you need to demonstrate your ability to clearly present that evaluative information in writing that meets academic and professional expectations. These skills will be invaluable as you go on to develop your literature review and proceed on your journey to become an independent scholar.

Step 3: Synthesis: Write the Review

Once you have analyzed each of your scholarly sources, you can start synthesizing the information you have collected. In other words, the next step is to integrate or combine your resources and determine what conclusions can be drawn from the resources as a group. In terms of preparing to write a dissertation, the conclusions should lead the reader to why your study should be conducted as the next logical step in adding to the literature on the topic area.

TABLE 6.2 ● Template for Analysis and Critique of Research-Based Literature

Study Title: _____

Author/Researcher: _____

Date of Study: _____

Publication: _____

Methodological Approach/ Research Design/ Sampling Methods/ Methods of Analysis	
Bodies of Literature Reviewed	
Conceptual/Theoretical Framework	
Research Sample/ Participants	
Research Site	
Research Problem	
Research Purpose	
Research Question	
Subquestions	
Data Collection Instruments	
Key Findings	
Research Study Limitations	
Conclusions	
Recommendations/ Implications for Practice, Policy, Research, Theory	

Overall Impressions/Notes to Self: Value/Relevance for Current Dissertation/Call for Further Research:

Source: A version of this chart first appeared in Bloomberg, L. D. (2007b). *Understanding Qualitative Inquiry: Content and Process* (Part I). Unpublished manuscript.

TABLE 6.3 ● Template for Analysis and Critique of Theoretical Literature

Study Title: _____

Author/Researcher: _____

Date of Study: _____

Publication: _____

Overview of Theory	
Key Premise/s	
Reasoning Evidence is provided that clearly supports the claim/s. Opposing claims are recognized and addressed.	
Relevance Extent to which the information directly supports your topic and is useful to your study. What are the implications for your current research?	
Overall Impressions/ Evaluation Does the author suggest the findings can be applied in theory and/or practice? How useful does this work seem to you with regard to theoretical and/or practical applications?	
Synthesis Synthesize the pieces of your critique to emphasize your own main points about the author's work; its relevance and/or application to other theories you have reviewed and to your own study.	

Source: A version of this chart first appeared in Bloomberg, L. D. (2007b). *Understanding Qualitative Inquiry: Content and Process* (Part II). Unpublished manuscript.

Summary and Synthesis: A Comparative Overview After you select the literature and organize your thoughts in terms of critically analyzing the literature into discrete parts, you need to arrange and structure a clear and coherent argument. To do this, you need to create and present a synthesis—reorganizing and reassembling all the separate pieces and details so that the discussion constitutes one integrated whole. This synthesis builds a knowledge base and extends new lines of thinking.

Whereas analysis involves systematically breaking down the relevant literature into its constituent parts, synthesis is the act of making connections between those parts identified in the analysis. Synthesis is not about simply reassembling the parts. Rather, it is about recasting the information into a new and different arrangement— one that is coherent, logical, and explicit. This process might mean bringing new insights to an existing body of knowledge. The intent is to make others think more deeply about and possibly reevaluate what may hitherto have been taken for granted.

Summarizing and synthesizing information are both strategies that are used in reading, review, and research. Both are important skills or techniques in making sense of what one is reading. However, it is important to remember that they are different activities. Each has a different purpose, process, and outcome. Table 6.4 highlights the key differences between summarizing and synthesizing information.

TABLE 6.4 ● Comparison: Synthesis and Summary

Synthesis	Summary
An advanced reading technique or skill that requires critical analysis, creativity, and insight.	A basic or intermediary reading technique.
Combines and contrasts information and ideas from different sources.	Information is collated, reiterated, and restated.
Information from different sources is integrated to highlight important points of connection and relatedness, to address similarities and differences, and to draw conclusions.	Information is pulled together and listed to highlight important or key points.
Combines parts and elements from a variety of sources into one unified or integrated entity.	Addresses distinct sets of information. Each piece of information or source remains distinct and separate.
Focuses on deeper ideas and details.	Presents a cursory overview.
The final product reflects the author's knowledge about the sources, but also creates new insights or perspectives that add value to the intellectual discussion.	The final product indicates and describes what the sources stated.
Synthesis extends the literal meaning of a text to the inferential level. The final product achieves new ways of thinking and understanding about a body of literature.	A summary captures the literal meaning of texts. The final product demonstrates an understanding of the overall body of literature that was summarized.

The good news is that you are already experienced in synthesizing information. You infer relationships among sources probably on a daily basis, including between a story you heard on the news and something you read in a newspaper. Similarly, to synthesize the literature you have collected, you will look to find relationships between your scholarly sources. The first step is digesting the material and understanding what the sources say. The second step is critically analyzing the sources. The third step is going beyond your critique to determine the relationship among your sources. For example, you might find in your readings that certain themes emerged, such as Theme A, B, and C. You might group information from your sources by theme and then compare and contrast. Another scenario could be that your critical analysis revealed that there was one seminal study done that all other researchers expanded upon. Are there overall themes or patterns in the literature? Based on whatever patterns or themes you find, what can you infer beyond what the sources say? What do you believe the patterns or themes suggest? Do they suggest future areas of inquiry? May they suggest a direction for your own research efforts?

A key element that makes for good synthesis is integration, which is about making connections between and among ideas and concepts. It is about applying what you are researching within a larger framework, thereby providing a new way of looking at a phenomenon. Your literature review is a demonstration of how your research problem is situated within the larger conversation and/or part of a broader theoretical scheme. To achieve a well-integrated literature review, you must be sure to emphasize relatedness and organize the material in a well-reasoned and meaningful way.

Synthesis is not a data dump; it is a creative activity. In discussing the literature review, Hart (2005) refers to the "research imagination." An imaginative approach to searching and reviewing the literature includes having a broad view of the topic; being open to new ideas, methods, and arguments; "playing" with different ideas to see whether you can make new linkages; and following ideas to see where they might lead. We see the literature review as somewhat of a sculpture—a work of art that, in its molding, requires dedication, creativity, and flexibility.

It is important to continue to point out that although the writing process as described might seem somewhat linear, in actuality, the writing process is more cyclical or iterative. As you are writing, you might find you need additional resources. This means going back to searching the literature, analyzing the information, and integrating the information into your work. Similarly, you should work to stay current with research in your field, which may also lead you to incorporating additional sources. It cannot be stressed enough that synthesis is an iterative and recursive process where drafts are refined, revised, and reworked until a final best version is crafted.

Presenting the Review

A literature review must be based on a well-thought-out design or plan that integrates the material discussed. The results of your analysis can provide you with ideas for the structure of your review. To present a coherent and logical review, it is important to create a detailed outline prior to writing. You cannot begin without this. An outline will save you time and effort in the long run and will increase your probability of having an organized review. Don't be surprised, however, if the outline changes as you write. In fact, this is quite often the case, as you will need to arrange and then rearrange to maintain a logical flow of thought.

To create the outline, you need to determine how various theorists define the topic and the themes and/or patterns that have emerged. Themes and patterns translate into headings and subheadings. Differentiating each major heading into logical subheadings gives structure to the review as a whole, helping to advance the argument and clarifying the relationships among sections. Headings and subheadings also enable the reader to see at a glance what is covered in the review. With a completed outline, you can begin to sort your references under their appropriate headings, and so begin to present your discussion. Following are some important guidelines for writing.

Be Selective A comprehensive literature review need not include every piece of material that you have located and/or read. Include only material that is directly relevant to your research problem and the purpose of your study. Although all the material that you reviewed was necessary to help you to situate your own study, not every citation with respect to an issue need be included. The use of too many or nonselective references is an indication of poor scholarship and an inability to separate the central from the peripheral.

Provide Integration and Critique It is your task as a writer to integrate, rather than just report on, the material you have read. Comment on the major issues that you have discovered. Never present a chain of isolated summaries of previous studies. We have stressed throughout this book that you will need to demonstrate an analytical and critically evaluative stance. Once you have pulled together all of the salient perspectives of other authors vis-à-vis your topics, you need to stand back and provide critique. However, providing a critique in an academic work does not mean you make a personal attack on the work of others. When it comes to writing a critical evaluation, you must treat that work with due respect.

Maintain Legitimacy In using the literature on a topic, you are using the ideas, concepts, and theories of others. Therefore, it is your responsibility to cite sources correctly and comply with academic and legal conventions. This means being scrupulous in your record keeping and ensuring that all details of referenced works are accurately and fully cited. This includes work obtained via electronic media such as the Internet, although copyright protection for data on the Internet is currently in a state of flux.

Limit Use of Quotations As stated in the writing section of Section I, try to limit the use of direct quotations and quote only materials that are stated skillfully and are a clear reflection of a particular point of view. The practice of liberally sprinkling the literature review with quoted material—particularly lengthy quotations—is self-defeating; unessential quotations are a distraction from the line of thought being presented. Mostly, you should paraphrase rather than quote directly. However remember that any ideas whatsoever that you borrow from others require proper citation or acknowledgment.

Follow Academic Style There are various conventions in academic writing, including such things as the use of certain words and phrases. Some words that might be common in everyday language and conversation are inappropriate for use in a dissertation. For example, "it is obvious," "it is a fact," "everyone will agree," and "normally" are assumptions and presuppositions and as such, are often imprecise. In addition, be sure to guard against using discriminatory language. Bear in mind at all times you are writing not an editorial column, but a piece of scholarly research to be read by the academic community. You can benefit from seeking feedback from others. It often takes a critical, objective eye to point out gaps, flaws, and inconsistencies in one's writing.

Revise, Revise, and Revise A first draft should be just that—a preliminary, tentative outline of what you want to say based on a planned structure. Every writer goes through a series of drafts, gradually working toward something with which he or she can be satisfied. Often what is helpful is to distance yourself from your review and then go back and revisit. Time away for thinking and reflection tends to create "aha moments" and fresh insights. The final draft should be as accurate as possible in terms of both content and structure.

Step 4: Develop the Conceptual Framework

The review and critique of existing literature should build a logical framework for the research, justify the study by identifying gaps in the literature, and demonstrate how the study will contribute to knowledge development. Development of a conceptual framework, which follows the literature review, posits new relationships and perspectives vis-à-vis the literature reviewed, thereby providing the conceptual link between the research problem, the literature, and the methodology selected for your research. In this way, the conceptual framework becomes the scaffolding of the study. Most important, it becomes a *working tool* consisting of categories that emanate from the literature. These categories become the repository for reporting the findings and guiding data analysis and interpretation.

Doctoral students are expected to raise their level of thinking from micro (content) to meta (process) levels of conceptualization. Melding the conceptual framework explicitly within the dissertation displays scholarly maturity—that is, increased capacity to think about the conceptual background and context of the research. Engaging with conceptual frameworks is an essential prerequisite for doctoral students. This is the means through which students, as researchers, are able to articulate the wider theoretical significance of their research, their chosen research design, the conceptual significance of their study's findings, and how their study makes a contribution to knowledge.

As research practitioners, we recognize the significance of seeking intellectual rigor, and the role of conceptual frameworks in achieving this. We have also observed how students encounter difficulties in conceptualizing their research. In our experience, graduate students seem to lack an understanding of the nature and role of the conceptual framework—what it is, what its purpose is, where it is derived from, how it is developed, how it is used, and what effect it has on research; as such, they find themselves at a loss in the process of developing a conceptual framework. Moreover, oftentimes experienced researchers and advisors themselves encounter challenges in guiding candidates as to what constitutes a rigorous and meaningful conceptual framework (Anfara & Mertz, 2015; Ravitch & Riggan, 2012). These respective difficulties result in large part from research methodology texts lacking a common language regarding the nature of conceptual frameworks. This confusion is compounded by disagreement regarding how both theory and literature are intended to inform and structure research (Ravitch & Riggan, 2012). In researching this topic ourselves, we certainly appreciate how our doctoral students struggle to comprehend the nature of the conceptual framework.

The reason for this knowledge gap is that the term is somewhat an abstract notion, conjuring up a "model" or "diagram" of some sort. Moreover, there does not appear to be a uniform and consistent definition, and discussions in the literature around conceptual frameworks are not clear or precise. As we reviewed the qualitative research literature, it became increasingly clear that those writers who do attempt to explain the notion of conceptual frameworks do not do so conclusively, and therefore oftentimes offer only vague or insufficient guidance to students in terms of understanding the actual role and place of the conceptual framework in the dissertation. As such, the structure and function of a conceptual framework continues to mystify and frustrate. Questions about conceptual frameworks that students regularly ask include the following:

- What is a conceptual or theoretical framework?
- Why should I include a conceptual framework in my dissertation? That is, what purpose does it serve in the research process? And what are its role, function, and application in the dissertation?
- How can the conceptual or theoretical framework strengthen my study? In other words, what is its value?
- What might be the limitations of a conceptual or theoretical framework in my study?
- How do I create my study's conceptual framework, and where would I place it in the dissertation?
- Each of these key questions is addressed below.

The Conceptual Framework: An Overview Merriam (1998) argues that the conceptual framework affects every aspect of the study, from determining how to frame the problem and purpose to how the data are collected. As Ravitch and Riggan (2012) explain, a conceptual framework enables researchers to make reasoned defensible choices, match research questions with those choices, align analytic tools with research questions, and thereby guide data collection, analysis, and interpretation. Similarly, others contend that without some conceptual framework, there would be no way to make reasoned decisions in the research process (Marshall & Rossman, 2015; Maxwell, 2013; Miles & Huberman, 1994; Miles, Huberman, & Saldana, 2014; Schram, 2003).

Some view the conceptual framework as a "map" of theories and issues relating to the research topic. Theories are formulated to explain, predict, and understand phenomena and, in many cases, to challenge and extend existing knowledge, within the limits of critical bounding assumptions. The theoretical framework is the structure that can hold or support a theory of a research study. K. F. Punch (2000) explains a conceptual framework as representing "the conceptual status of the things being studied and their relationship to each other" (p. 54). Maxwell (2013) views it this way:

> A concept map of a theory is a visual display of that theory—a picture of what the theory says is going on with the phenomenon you're studying . . . Concept mapping is a tool for developing and presenting the conceptual framework for your design. (p. 54)

Blaxter, Hughes, and Tight (1996) explain the components of conceptual frameworks as follows:

> Defining the key concepts and contexts of your research project should also assist you in focusing your work. . . . They define the territory for your research, indicate the literature that you need to consult and suggest the methods and theories you might apply. (pp. 36–37)

As Bernard and Ryan (2010) point out, there are generally three steps in building models: (1) Identify key concepts to be included; (2) show linkages among constructs— that is, identify how and in what ways the constructs are related; and (3) test those relationships. These steps are not always sequential. You will find yourself going back and forth among them throughout the research and writing process. It is important to remember that thinking about your conceptual framework and actually building it is an iterative process. As such, an initial conceptual framework can—and most likely will—be revised, reflecting emergent findings and new insights (Maxwell, 2012; Ravitch & Riggan, 2012). Miles, Huberman, and Saldana (2014) define a conceptual framework as "the current version of the researcher's map of the territory being investigated" (p. 20). Implicit in this view is that conceptual frameworks evolve as research evolves. This notion accommodates purpose (boundaries) with flexibility (evolution) and coherence of the research (plan/analysis/conclusion), which all stem from conceptual frameworks. Of interest is that Weaver-Hart (1988) argues that conceptual frameworks contain an inherent dilemma, recognizing that the term itself is a contradiction because concepts are abstract whereas frameworks are concrete. As a consequence, she views the conceptual framework as "a structure for organizing and supporting ideas; a mechanism for systematically arranging abstractions; sometimes revolutionary or original, and usually rigid" (Weaver-Hart, 1988, p. 11). We contend strongly that the conceptual framework, while guiding research, evolves and unfolds both generatively and recursively as the research process progresses, and as such should be construed as including both rigor and fluidity in its iterative development and refinement.

We tend to agree that the conceptual framework plays an extremely central role throughout the entire research process, and, most important, in the final analysis, and that without conceptual development and refinement and a clear relationship to research design and implementation, a study could remain weakly conceptualized, undertheorized, and less generative of quality data. The conceptual framework of your study is like the frame of a house. It holds up and supports your study, the same way in which a house frame holds up the house. This means that the problem you are trying to investigate, the research questions you pose, the research design and methodology you choose, and the actual research methods you employ to gather and analyze your data *all have to be tied to the framework*. Thus, in our view, because it is so central a component of your dissertation, and because its scope is far reaching throughout the subsequent chapters of a dissertation, development of the conceptual framework requires careful, logical, and thoughtful explication.

A conceptual framework draws essentially on theory, research, and experience, and as such it is the structure, heuristic device, or model that guides your research. You may be thinking that this still sounds very abstract, and with good reason. While the conceptual framework is alluded to in most serious texts on research, it is described in some, and only fully explained in very few. As such, the conceptual framework is often the missing link in student scholarship. In reviewing the literature, it becomes apparent that the notion of the conceptual framework is explained and presented *quite differently* by different authors. Competing conceptualizations of the relationship between theory and qualitative research, as well as divergent definitions of what a theoretical or conceptual framework is and why and how it is used, certainly add to the frustration and confusion!

Role, Function, and Application of the Conceptual Framework It should be noted that the terms *conceptual framework* and *theoretical framework* are often used interchangeably, and rarely is a clear differentiation made. A theory is a relationship among related concepts, assumptions, and generalizations. By virtue of its application nature, good theory in the social sciences is of value precisely because it fulfills one primary purpose: to explain the meaning, nature, and challenges of a phenomenon, often experienced but unexplained in the world in which we live, so that we may use that knowledge and understanding to act in more informed and effective ways. Concepts are defined as interrelated ideas. As Cohen, Lawrence, and Morrison (2000) point out, concepts enable us to impose some sort of meaning on the world; through them reality is given sense, order, and coherence. (That is, concepts are the means by which we are able to come to terms with our experience.) This idea suggests conceptualization as "meaning making" in research. The implication is that a conceptual framework is more than just a set of theories and issues related to the research topic.

What is key is the *cyclical role* for conceptual frameworks in providing coherence for research. A well-conceived conceptual framework *is influenced by and at the same time influences* the research process at all levels and at all stages. Developing a conceptual framework compels researchers to be explicit about what they think they are doing, and also helps them to be selective—to decide which are the important features of the research, which relationships are likely to be of importance or meaning, and hence what data they are going to go ahead and collect and analyze (Blaxter et al., 1996; Bryman, 2001; Maxwell, 2013; Ravitch & Riggan, 2012).

It becomes clear then that the *relationships* between theoretical variables, constructs, or concepts are an essential component of high-quality research and are expressed explicitly through conceptualizations and frameworks. The conceptual framework itself gives meaning to the relationship between variables by illustrating that theories have the potential to provide insight and understanding regarding research topics; it is the device that makes sense of data. In this way, the conceptual framework becomes the lens through which your research problem is viewed, providing a theoretical overview of intended research as well as some sort of methodological order within that process.

A well-defined conceptual framework contributes toward thinking more acutely about your research: It frames and grounds your entire study. It helps define the research problem and purpose, as well as selection of appropriate bodies of literature for review. It serves as a filter for developing appropriate research questions. And it acts as a guide for data collection, and analysis and interpretation of findings. This way of viewing the conceptual framework locates it as fulfilling an integrating function between highlighting theories that offer explanations of the issues under investigation, and providing a scaffold within which strategies for the research design can be determined, and fieldwork undertaken. This view of the conceptual framework thus locates it as *giving coherence* to the research act through providing traceable connections between theoretical perspectives, research strategy and design, fieldwork, and the conceptual significance of the evidence. A framework is simply the structure of the research idea or concept and how it is put together. The conceptual framework is therefore essentially a bridge between *paradigms that explain* the research issue and the *actual practice* of investigating that issue.

Viewed this way, then, the conceptual framework fulfills two distinct roles: First, it provides a theoretical clarification of what researchers intend to investigate, and enables readers to be clear about what the research seeks to achieve and how that will be achieved. Second, the conceptual framework forms the theoretical and methodological bases for development of the study and analysis of the findings. Students often do not realize how critical the conceptual framework is in guiding the analysis of the data that have been collected. We stress that the conceptual framework is a practical working tool for guiding the analysis of the data collected, and it becomes the foundation for what will become the coding legend or coding scheme.

The Value of the Conceptual Framework The conceptual or theoretical framework strengthens your study in the following ways:

1. Has the ability to organize and focus a study. Qualitative researchers can feel overwhelmed by the mountain of data that confronts them. First, by serving as a "sieve" or "lens," the framework assists the researcher in the process of sorting through the data, and knowing how the pieces drawn from the various data relate to each other and where they "fit" in the larger picture. Second, the conceptual framework "frames" every aspect of the study in terms of both the process and the product, including design, sampling, research questions, literature review, data collection, data analysis, and interpretation of findings.

2. An explicit statement of theoretical assumptions permits the reader to evaluate them critically.

3. The framework situates the research within a scholarly conversation, and connects the researcher to the existing body of knowledge. Guided by relevant theory and concepts, you are given a basis for your assumptions, research approach, and choice of research methods. The framework also provides you with labels and categories that help explain and develop descriptions and analysis.

4. Articulating the theoretical assumptions of a research study forces you to address questions of "why" and "how." It permits you to move from simply describing a phenomenon observed to generalizing about various aspects of that phenomenon.

5. Having a theory and conceptual structure helps you to identify the limits to those generalizations. A conceptual or theoretical framework specifies which key variables or factors influence a phenomenon of interest. It alerts you to examine how those key variables or factors might differ and under what circumstances.

6. The conceptual framework becomes the means by which new research data can be interpreted and coded for future use, as well as a means to guide and inform future research efforts and improve professional practice.

Limitations of the Conceptual Framework While the conceptual or theoretical framework has a role and function in the dissertation process, there are some critiques that are worthy of mention and that should be taken into consideration:

Anfara and Mertz (2015) make an important statement about the role and function of the conceptual framework in qualitative research. In acknowledging that the term does not have a clear and consistent definition, they also point out very clearly that a framework allows the researcher to "see" and understand certain aspects of the phenomenon being studied while hiding other aspects. A theoretical framework can reveal and/or conceal meaning and understanding. They can allow us to see familiar phenomena in novel ways, but they can also blind us to certain aspects of the phenomena or distort the phenomena being studied by filtering out critical pieces of data. As such, it is important to bear in mind that while your framework provides a meaningful way of seeing, thinking, and understanding, no theoretical or conceptual framework provides one perfect or complete explanation of what is being studied, an important consideration in your research process in terms of the effects of your framework on your research (including data collection as well as data analysis). Indeed, as exemplified in Anfara and Mertz (2015), using different frameworks on the same data can broaden and deepen the understanding derived. Moreover, "a framework can potentially disrupt the dominant narrative in the field, and even what counts as knowledge about a phenomenon" (Anfara & Mertz, 2015, p. 229).

Anfara and Mertz (2015) also point out two other potential additional limitations of conceptual or theoretical frameworks: First, while the framework certainly has the ability to organize and focus a study, the framework could be too reductionistic, stripping the phenomenon of its complexity and interest. Second, the framework could be too detereministic, forcing the researcher to "fit" the data into predetermined categories.

In the following section, we describe how a conceptual framework is developed, how it is used as a coding legend to sort and analyze the data, and how it can subsequently be logically simplified and presented graphically as a model that represents the overall design of a given research project.

Creating Your Conceptual Framework The conceptual framework is not something that is found readily available in the literature. You will have to review pertinent research literature for theories and analytic models that are relevant to the research problem you are investigating. The selection of theories should depend on appropriateness, ease of application, and explanatory power. *Below are some strategies for developing the conceptual framework:*

1. Examine your study title and research problem. The research problem anchors your entire study and forms the basis from which you construct your theoretical framework.
2. Brainstorm on what you consider to be the key constructs or concepts in your research. Answer the question, what factors contribute to the presumed effect?
3. Review all related literature to find answers to your research question.
4. List the constructs and concepts that might be relevant to your study.
5. Review the key social science theories that are related to your study, and choose the theory or theories that can best explain the relationships between key constructs and concepts.
6. Discuss the assumptions or propositions of the relevant theories, and point out their relevance to your research.

Although presented in a step-wise fashion, please remember that the above process is not linear, but rather cyclical and iterative. It requires deep thinking and critical analysis on your part. It also requires creativity and innovation, since your framework will become the basis for understanding, analyzing, and designing ways to investigate relationships within the social system you are studying. Remember, too, that it is quite usual to develop and discard several potential conceptual frameworks until one is finally chosen. Again, this is part of the iterative qualitative research process. A review of the literature for studies similar to yours will reveal what types of theoretical or conceptual frameworks other researchers have utilized. We encourage you to read through the theoretical framework chapters or sections of dissertations and journal articles related to your study because in this way, you will begin to see how this is approached by other scholars.

Presenting Your Conceptual Framework The review and critique of existing literature culminates in a conceptual framework. The conceptual framework is described in detailed narrative form and can also be summarized and displayed as a schematic diagram—that is, a visual device that represents the overall design of a research project including key concepts and their relationships. Thinking and reflective inquiry require that you create structures that will enable you to examine your own assumptions and ask deep questions of your research. In this regard, diagrams of various kinds become useful and relevant.

Diagrams may include mind maps, flowcharts, tree diagrams, and so on. A concept map (Cañas & Novak, 2005; Kane & Trochim, 2006; Maxwell, 2013; Miles & Huberman, 1994; Miles et al., 2014; Novak, 1998; Wheeldon & Ahlberg, 2012) is one type of diagram that lays out key ideas related to your area of research and indicates relationships between these areas. Concept mapping (sometimes referred to as "mental mapping" or "concept webbing") entails plotting the conceptual "space" of your research and is a useful medium for thinking about information and visualizing relationships in different ways, developing and testing ideas, and containing the study by indicating and highlighting connections, gaps, and/or contradictions. Concept maps can also assist in data analysis in a number of ways, assisting researchers in the development of deeper insights by recognizing explicit and implicit meanings and assumptions (Wheeldon & Ahlberg, 2012). Concepts are usually presented as boxes or circles, and are connected to each other (or not) with lines, arrows, or symbols, indicating some type of relationship among them. For a thematic analysis, boxes typically represent concepts such as themes identified in the data (i.e., codes) or higher-level conceptual themes the researcher generates. Current qualitative software packages are becoming increasingly sophisticated in terms of concept-mapping functions that depict complex conceptual relationships. Concept maps can be developed collaboratively with colleagues or advisors and as such can engender the high-level conversation and dialogue that is necessary to promote, stimulate, and expand reflective inquiry.

A diagram is more than just a repository of thought; it is a working and living document that arises from analysis. As such, the diagram becomes an important analytic tool in your qualitative research process. As Corbin and Strauss (2015) explain, diagrams "begin as rudimentary representations of thought, and grow in complexity, density, clarity, and accuracy as the research progresses" (p. 117). Ravitch and Riggan (2012) explain this well when they say,

The conceptual framework is more than just a passive artifact or academic hoop to jump through and more than a static graphic of literatures read or key concepts in a vacuum. Rather, it is a dynamic meeting place of theory and method. (p. 141)

It is important that while you may choose to present your conceptual framework in diagrammatic or pictorial form, you should be prepared to explain, describe, and articulate that diagram in great detail, including all major constructs or concepts as well as relationships among all the key elements.

Remember that there is no single way to go about developing, using, articulating, and presenting a conceptual framework. A useful starting point is to engage in a process of critical inquiry and self-examination, and to continue this critical stance throughout the research process. Identification of your own personal and professional motivation for engaging in your chosen research topic or phenomenon is a useful beginning. Ask yourself why you have engaged in your research, what about it interests you, how your motivation might impact your research approach, what are your underlying assumptions and hunches, and what informs these assumptions and hunches. Next, proceed to ask yourself questions that relate to the broader intellectual conversations in your field as these constitute the context and background for your research: Ask yourself what some of the key arguments are, what your stance is vis-à-vis these arguments, what are the key critical questions that you have vis-à-vis conversations in the field, how you conceptualize your research in relation to these conversations, and what you hope your study will contribute to the overall intellectual conversation.

In Section II of this chapter, we explain the development of the conceptual framework and illustrate its application. An example of a completed conceptual framework is also included as Appendix E. The intent is that with new insights and knowledge regarding the role and function of a conceptual framework, you will be able to craft one that is distinctively yours and unique to your own study. How the conceptual framework functions specifically with regard to data analysis is elaborated upon in Chapter 8 ("Analyzing Data and Reporting Findings").

Chapter Summary Discussion

Broadly speaking, a literature review is a narrative that integrates, synthesizes, and critiques the research and thinking around a particular topic. It sets the broad context of the study, clearly demarcates what is and is not within the scope of the investigation, and justifies those decisions. A literature review should not only report the claims made in the existing literature, but also examine it critically. Such an examination of the literature enables the reader to distinguish what has been and still needs to be learned and accomplished in the area of study. Moreover, in a good review, the researcher not only summarizes the existing literature, but also synthesizes it in a way that permits a new perspective. Thus, a good literature review is the basis of both theoretical and methodological sophistication, thereby improving the quality and usefulness of subsequent research. As the foundation of the research project, a comprehensive review of the literature in a dissertation should accomplish several distinct objectives:

- Frame the research problem by setting it within a larger context.
- Focus the purpose of your study more precisely.
- Lead to the refinement of research questions.
- Form the basis for determining the rationale and significance of your study.
- Enable you to convey your understanding of your research approach, as well as the specific data collection methods employed.
- Link your findings to previous studies.
- Place research within a historical context to show familiarity with state-of-the-art developments.
- Enable you to justify, support, and substantiate your study's findings.
- Contribute to analysis and interpretation of your study's findings.
- Enable you to develop a conceptual framework that can be used to guide your research.

It should be apparent to you that the literature review is a sophisticated form of research in its own right that requires a great deal of research skill and insight. You are expected to identify appropriate topics or issues, justify why these are the appropriate choice for addressing the research problem, search for and retrieve the appropriate literature, analyze and critique the literature, create new understandings of the topic through synthesis, and develop a conceptual framework that will provide the underlying structure for your study. Your conceptual or theoretical framework emanates from your literature review and is used to limit the scope of the relevant data by focusing on specific concepts and theories, and defining the specific viewpoint (framework) that you as the researcher will take in analyzing and interpreting the data to be gathered. Your conceptual framework will also provide the basis for understanding the essence of your study and building knowledge by confirming or challenging theoretical assumptions.

Thinking about the entire literature review process may initially be overwhelming and intimidating. Instead of viewing it as one big whole, think of it as a series of steps—and steps within those steps. Tackle each topic one by one and set small achievable goals within each topic area. Be sure to subdivide your work into manageable sections, taking on and refining each section one at a time. The important point, and one that we stress throughout, is that you should proceed in stages. Like the skier traversing the terrain, the best way to be successful is to divide and conquer!

Quality Assessment Chapter Checklist

Preparing the Literature Review	✓ Are you clear about the role and scope of the literature review vis-à-vis your chosen qualitative research tradition? ✓ Are you familiar with all available resources including library indexing systems and electronic databases? ✓ Have you set up your own systems for identifying, retrieving, organizing, and storing your information? ✓ Have you made sure that all information is securely saved by way of electronic storage and backup systems?
Writing the Literature Review	✓ Do you have a clear introduction to this chapter that includes your purpose statement (if required), as well as an explanation of how the chapter will be organized? ✓ Does your review show a clear understanding and critique of each topic? ✓ Do you write with authority and develop a critical perspective in discussing the work of others? ✓ Is the review comprehensive? Does it cover the major issues and thinking around each topic? ✓ Have you included historical as well as current and most up-to-date coverage? ✓ Does the path of your argument flow logically? ✓ Is the review analytical and critical and not merely summative and descriptive? Do you include opposing points of view? ✓ Is the review well organized and systematically presented? ✓ Do you include an introductory paragraph that outlines the way you organize the different bodies of literature? ✓ Are the methods for conducting the literature review sufficiently described? ✓ Does the order of headings and subheadings seem logical? ✓ Do you include logical segues between sections? ✓ Do you make use of transitions to link and integrate paragraphs? ✓ Do you include summary paragraphs at the end of each major section, as well as an overall summary at the end of the chapter? ✓ Is the writing throughout clear and readable? Refer to Chapter 4 "Guidelines for Academic Writing." ✓ Have you checked that you have not used somebody's words without appropriate quotation marks or stated the ideas of others as if they were your own, thereby constituting plagiarism? ✓ Have you avoided too much paraphrasing and too many direct quotations that detract from the readability of the chapter? ✓ Are all authors who make the same point combined in a citation?
	✓ Are all citations included in the reference list? ✓ Have all citations that you have not included been eliminated from the reference list? ✓ Are the majority of your references published in the past 5 years? ✓ Have you checked your recommended style manual for format, punctuation, grammar, and correct use of each and every citation? ✓ Have you edited and reedited your work?
Developing the Conceptual Framework	✓ Does your conceptual framework draw on theory, research, and experience? ✓ Does your conceptual framework depict the overall "territory" of your research? ✓ Does your framework provide theoretical clarification of what you intend to investigate? ✓ Does your framework illuminate the relationships among theoretical variables? ✓ Does your framework enable a reader to understand *what* your study seeks to achieve and *how* that will be achieved? ✓ If you have developed a diagrammatic model, is this clearly and accurately presented? In other words, does it make sense and have meaning?

✓ If you have developed a diagrammatic model, is this accompanied by comprehensive descriptive narrative?
✓ If you have developed conceptual categories, are these directly tied to the research questions?
✓ Do you have at least one conceptual category per research question?
✓ Have you included descriptors that are based on the literature, pilot studies, and your own hunches?
✓ Do these descriptors make sense?
✓ Are there any other descriptors that you may have forgotten to include?
✓ Does your conceptual framework add value to the way you and others understand your research?
✓ Does your conceptual framework enhance the conceptual quality of your dissertation?

Section II: Application

Having discussed the purpose and function of the literature review and resulting conceptual framework, as well as the various steps involved, we are now ready to introduce what a completed literature review chapter should look like. In this application section, we focus on the specific research problem as outlined in the introductory chapter of the dissertation and explain how to develop and present the associated literature review and conceptual framework.

Please note that because of the nature of the literature review, it would be impractical to present here a full-blown literature review on our topic. Rather, we have identified each of the actual steps that should be followed in completing your literature review and provided illustrative examples in outline or skeleton form. The intent of presenting the application piece in this way is that you could use these steps as a template and present your own literature review in the same order. These steps include the following:

1. Provide a statement of purpose.
2. Identify the topics or bodies of literature.
3. Provide the rationale for topics selected.
4. Describe your literature review process, report all your literature sources, and identify the keywords used to search the literature.
5. Present the review of each topic.
6. Present your conceptual framework.
7. Provide a brief chapter summary of the literature review and its implications for your study.

Steps 1 through 4 constitute all that is necessary to introduce the literature review to the reader. Steps 5 and 6 constitute the "meat" of the review. Step 7 is intended to highlight the main points, thereby providing some closure for the chapter. In the following pages, we put each of these steps into play and provide an illustration of Chapter 2, the literature review of a dissertation. Bear in mind that the application section that follows is a skeleton view of a literature review chapter. Were each section to be more completely and fully developed, as would be required in an actual dissertation, such a chapter would obviously be much more extensive.

CHAPTER 2 OF THE DISSERTATION

Literature Review

Overview

The purpose of this multicase study was to explore with 20 doctoral candidates their perceptions of why they have not managed to complete their dissertations. Specifically, the researchers sought to understand how the experiences of these individuals may have inhibited their progress in conducting and carrying out research. To carry out this study, it was necessary to complete a critical review of current literature. This review was ongoing throughout the data collection, data analysis, and synthesis phases of the study.

This critical review explores the interconnectedness of the experiences of participants and the resources that they perceived were available to them. In light of this, two major areas of literature were critically reviewed: (a) higher education and doctoral programs and (b) adult learning theory. A review of the literature on higher education and doctoral programs provides an understanding of the context, history, structure, rules, and regulations under which candidates must work to obtain doctoral degrees. Adult learning theory is reviewed to provide a context for understanding what knowledge, skills, and attitudes were perceived as needed by the participants and how they attempted to learn what they perceived they needed.

In providing a rationale for your choice of topics, in some instances you might want to include an explicit assertion, a contention, or a proposition that relates to the research problem and that is substantiated by supporting literature. The assertion or contention should be broad and is based on the overall judgments you have formed thus far based on an analysis of the literature.

To conduct this selected literature review, the researchers used multiple information sources, including books, dissertations, Internet resources, professional journals, and periodicals. These sources were accessed through ERIC, ProQuest, eduCAT, and CLIO. No specific delimiting time frame was used around which to conduct this search. Because of the nature of the three bodies of literature reviewed, the historical development, for example, of higher education and doctoral programs was considered significant and therefore an arbitrary criterion, such as a time frame, might preclude the inclusion of substantial relevant material.

Throughout the review, the researchers attempted to point out important gaps and omissions in particular segments of the literature as and when they became apparent. In addition, relevant contested areas or issues are identified and discussed. Each section of the literature review closes with a synthesis that focuses on research implications. The interpretive summary that concludes the chapter illustrates how the literature has informed the researchers' understanding of the material and how the material contributes to the ongoing development of the study's conceptual framework.

The prior section included how the literature was selected, how information was accessed, what if any time delimitations were employed, what keywords and procedures were used to search the literature, what databases were used, and if appropriate, what criteria were used for retaining or discarding the literature. You also may choose to explain the main ideas and themes from the literature that you identified and by which you carried out your analysis.

Topics Reviewed

Having introduced the reader to your review, go on to present your topics in the order in which you have introduced them in the prior section. For each topic, establish an outline for yourself.

Typically, the outline is made up of three interrelated sections: (a) introduction, (b) discussion, and (c) summary, conclusions, and implications that relate to the discussion.

For each topic, start off by putting the reader in the picture so that she or he understands where you are going with your review of a particular topic or subject and how you intend to tackle it. This becomes your introduction to the topic. Give the reader a rationale for the topic and a brief overview of how you have organized the discussion. You also should preview the main points that you will make in the body of the discussion.

The introduction is followed by a systematic review of the material and is subdivided by headings and subheadings based on your analysis and synthesis of the literature. Think carefully about how you would like to organize the discussion. Usually you would start with general material to provide the reader with a comprehensive perspective. You would then proceed to discuss the material that is closely related to your own particular study. Thus, in planning how you will write, arrange your headings and subheadings accordingly because these will allow the reader to follow your train of thought. When appropriate, and especially with research-based literature, you also might employ the summary tables that you constructed when analyzing the literature because these tables reflect the variables or themes inherent in your discussion. At the end of the discussion of each topic, you should offer a concise and cohesive summary that highlights and clarifies the salient points discussed.

Summary

To provide some form of clarity and closure for the reader, you also need a final concluding summary at the end of the discussion that identifies all the key points mentioned in the review. This final summary should make reference to the line of argumentation that was specified in the introduction and pull the entire discussion together. The point of all the summaries—both those at the end of each topic and the final chapter—is to tell the reader what your review yielded in terms of informing your study.

Conceptual Framework

The review and critique of the literature, combined with the researchers' own experience and insights, has contributed to developing a conceptual framework for the design and conduct of this study. The conceptual framework developed for this study helps to focus and shape the research process, informing the methodological design and influencing the data collection instruments to be used. The conceptual framework also becomes the repository for the data that were collected, providing the basis for and informing various iterations of a coding scheme. As such, this framework provides an organizing structure both for reporting this study's findings and for the analysis, interpretation, and synthesis of these findings. In this way, the conceptual framework is essentially a "working tool."

Each category of the conceptual framework is directly derived from the study's research questions as outlined in Chapter 1. The first research question seeks to determine the extent to which participants perceived they were prepared to conduct research and write the dissertation following the completion of their course work. Therefore, the logical conceptual category to capture responses to this question is "Preparedness for Dissertation Process." The second research question seeks to identify what candidates perceive they need to learn to carry out the dissertation process. The category titled "KSA" is all-encompassing and thus appropriate. The third research question is intended to uncover how candidates go about acquiring the knowledge, skills, and abilities they perceive they need. Hence, the appropriate categorization is "How They Learn." The fourth and fifth research questions attempted to get at the factors that either help or hinder people's progress in the dissertation process; thus, "Facilitators" and "Barriers" are appropriate categories. To further explain each of the categories, the researchers drew on the literature, pilot test data, and their own educated guesses about potential responses to the research questions, which resulted in the various bulleted descriptors under each of the respective categories. During the course of data collection and analysis, some of the descriptors within each of the major categories were added, some were deleted, and others were collapsed. The conceptual framework was thus continually revised and refined.

As you may note, the prior narrative introduces your conceptual framework and describes what you mean by a conceptual framework, how you have developed it, and how it will be used in your study—that is, its nature, role, and function vis-à-vis your own particular study. You should be aware, like so many aspects of the dissertation, that the conceptual framework takes time to develop. As with the literature review, you will go through various iterations until you finally arrive at a workable, tight conceptual framework for your study. A completed conceptual framework, based on the example used in this book, is included as Appendix E.

Annotated Bibliography

Anfara, V. A., & Mertz, N. T. (Eds.). (2015). *Theoretical frameworks in qualitative research* (2nd ed.). Thousand Oaks, CA: Sage.

Recognizing a lack of understanding of the role of the theoretical framework in qualitative research, the purpose of this edited text is to explain through discussion and example what a theoretical framework is, how it is used in qualitative research, and the impact it has on the research process. The book is essentially a "reflective thinking tool": It is presented in the format of a multiplistic conversation about how theory is used in actual qualitative studies. The editors offer a brief summary of the definitions of theory and theoretical frameworks particularly in relation to methodology, and a wide variety of distinctive, sometimes unusual, theoretical frameworks drawn from a number of disciplines are included. The subsequent chapters present examples of studies by some of today's leading qualitative researchers, all of whom are advocates for further discussion regarding the role and function of theoretical frameworks in qualitative research. In-depth reflections on the use of a range of frameworks employed in accessible published studies help readers learn to use and understand theory. In addition, in Chapter 12, a sample of former doctoral students show how they arrived at the frameworks used in their dissertations, and thus offer interesting insights. Both novice and experienced qualitative researchers will be able to learn first-hand from various contributors as they reflect on the process and decisions involved in completing their study. The book also provides background for beginning researchers about the nature of theoretical frameworks and their importance in qualitative research; about differences in perspective about the role of theoretical frameworks; and about how to find and use a theoretical framework. In light of the inadequate and often confusing discussion of theoretical frameworks, which is notably problematic to novice as well as experienced researchers, this text offers extensive and practical coverage of conflicting conceptions and discrepancies. In addition to providing guidance regarding integration of theoretical frameworks into solid research designs, this book aptly initiates a thought-provoking discussion about the complexities involved, and as such is a very useful text in this regard.

Boote, D. N., & Beile, P. (2005). Scholars before researchers: On the centrality of the dissertation literature review in research preparation. *Educational Researcher, 34*(6), 3–15.

These authors posit that acquiring the skills and knowledge to analyze and synthesize the research in a field of specialization should be the focal, integrative activity of predissertation doctoral education. Moreover, they argue that a thorough, sophisticated literature review is the foundation for substantial research. Indeed, the academic community should be able to assume that a dissertation literature review indicates a doctoral candidate's ability to locate and evaluate scholarly information and synthesize research in his or her field. Yet as these authors indicate, despite the assumption that dissertation literature reviews are comprehensive and up to date, in many instances, literature reviews are poorly conceptualized and written. This article discusses in detail the various functions of the dissertation literature review and suggests criteria for evaluating the quality of dissertation literature reviews.

Booth, W. G., Colomb, G. G., & Williams, J. M. (2008). *The craft of research* (3rd ed.). Chicago: University of Chicago Press.

This book includes useful guidelines regarding how to locate printed and recorded sources, as well as sources found on the Internet; how to gather data directly from people; how to assess the reliability of sources; how to read and take notes accurately; and how to make arguments and claims and how to support them.

Cooper, H. (2010). *Research synthesis and meta-analysis* (4th ed.). Thousand Oaks, C: Sage.

This text discusses the complex issues in conducting a literature review with a particular focus on research synthesis in the social and behavioral sciences. Presenting a trustworthy and convincing integration of the research literature is a task that has profound implications for the accumulation of knowledge. State-of-the-art research synthesis has indeed been impacted by the growth in the amount of research, and the rapid advances in computerized research retrieval systems. Access to social science scholarship has changed dramatically. Developing a list of trustworthy research articles on a topic of interest involves lengthy and tedious scrutiny of available items. The focus of this book is on the basic tenets of sound data gathering with the task of producing a comprehensive integration of past research on a topic. The author highlights critical questions pertaining to gathering information from studies, evaluating the quality of studies, analyzing and interpreting the outcome of studies, and synthesizing information. Techniques are provided for searching the literature with an emphasis on new technologies and the Internet. Included are basic procedures as well as more complex meta-analysis procedures and how these are applied, ways of presenting synthesized data, and threats to the validity of research synthesis conclusions.

Fink, A. (2014). *Conducting research literature reviews* (4th ed.). Thousand Oaks, CA: Sage.

The final outcome of a research review is the synthesis of the contents of the literature and an evaluation of its quality. This book provides an answer to the question, "Now that I have conducted a literature review, what should I do with it?" This book provides readers with an understanding of how to engage with the literature by synthesizing research, justifying the need for and significance of research, and explaining findings of studies. Key features include the use of Boolean operators for simple and advanced literature searches, the use of bibliographic software, and the systematic organization of literature. Included are numerous examples and references from the social, behavioral, and health sciences, as well as PowerPoint slides linked to each of the chapters.

Galvan, J. L. (2014). *Writing literature reviews: A guide for students in the social and behavioral sciences* (6th ed.). Glendale, CA: Pyrczak.

This book offers instruction on how to plan and implement the various stages involved in completing a major writing assignment such as the literature review chapter of a dissertation.

Useful information is provided on how to search databases for reports of original research and related theoretical literature, critically analyze these types of literature, and synthesize them into a cohesive narrative. Included are detailed, step-by-step instructions, and these are illustrated with examples from a wide range of academic journals.

Hart, C. (2005). *Doing a literature review*. Thousand Oaks, CA: Sage.

This book is a practical and detailed guide to researching, preparing, and writing a literature review at the doctoral level. This accessible text offers advice on good practices with regard to searching for existing knowledge on a topic, understanding arguments, analyzing and synthesizing ideas, managing information, and writing up and producing a well-crafted, critical, and creative review.

O'Dochartaigh, N. (2012). *Internet research skills* (3rd ed.). Thousand Oaks, CA: Sage.

This is a concise guide to effective online research for the social sciences and humanities. The first section of the book deals with online publications, devoting separate chapters to academic articles, official publications, and news sources, which form the core secondary sources for social science research. The second section of the book deals with the Internet, a vast, complex, and confusing realm of materials, many of which have no direct print counterpart. The author explains newly developed approaches to using online materials, and offers suggestions for organizing research and Internet research methods. Included is also discussion regarding the use of social networks for research, as well as various illustrations and exercises to apply practically.

Ravitch, S. M., & Riggan, M. (2012). *Reason and rigor*. Thousand Oaks, CA: Sage.

This book provides a fresh perspective on understanding the "why" of conceptual frameworks—that is, the functional role of conceptual frameworks in organizing data and guiding empirical research. The authors illustrate how developing a conceptual framework is part of the process through which researchers identify questions and key lines of inquiry, develop appropriate data collection strategies for pursuing these questions, and monitor and critically reflect on their own thinking and understanding. The book provides direction regarding making use of existing knowledge (theory, methods, and empirical research) in combination with emergent observation and experience in an endeavor to ask deeper questions, develop robust and justifiable strategies for exploring those questions, present and contextualize research findings, and explain the significance and limitations thereof. Included are examples from research studies of prominent researchers and scholars from different fields and disciplines. These examples, paired with the authors' insight and reflections on the research process, vividly illustrate how conceptual frameworks inform research design, data, collection, analysis, interpretation, and write-up of the study.

Wallace, M., & Wray, A. (2011). *Critical reading and writing for postgraduates* (2nd ed.). London: Sage.

Each aspect of a dissertation merits its own critical literature review. You should expect to critically engage with literature in justifying your investigation of the substantive topic, your choice of theoretical orientation to frame your research, the methodological approach and detailed methods through which you gather your data, and the interpretation of your findings. Reference to this literature is made at various points during your investigation, and within your written account. As these authors explain, critical literature reviews reflect the intellect of the reviewer, who has decided the focus, selected texts for review, engaged critically with and interpreted the evidence they offer, synthesized what was found, and written the final account.

Overall, this is a very useful text that clearly signposts a route through the pathways involved in critiquing not only research sources in your field of study, but also the "right" sources. The book delivers this in two ways: First, it develops an ability to critically ask questions of a chosen research source in order to help the reader determine its suitability, rigor, validity, level of authority of findings, and conclusions; second, it develops a reflective and self-critical approach to the reader's own research and writing in order to produce a strong research paper or proposal that meets the required standards. The volume is carefully structured so as to enable students to apply ideas suggested in the progressive development of their skills of critical analysis and appreciation, while providing several illustrative example critiques of texts that encompass disciplinary areas including linguistics, education, business and management. Chapter 13 explores what makes for a high-quality written account of a dissertation, highlighting the importance of critical literature reviews and pointing out how the researcher's account should be logically sequenced, developing a convincing overall argument. Chapter 14 offers various tools to help with developing an overall argument throughout the research process. These tools relate directly to the discussion in Chapter 13. First, the authors offer a means for you (and your advisor) to keep track of the development of your overall argument as you plan your investigation and write your dissertation. Second, the authors describe an outline structure for a dissertation reflecting six steps for integrating critical literature reviews into the development of an overall argument. Finally, the authors suggest a way of applying a simple test to your written account, in order to check for flaws in the logic of your argument and for any material that may be irrelevant. At some point, you may want to write about your research for an academic journal or present it at a conference or seminar, and that is the focus of Chapter 15. Here the authors provide valuable input and tips regard presenting your research to the wider scholarly community. The book is written in a clear and straightforward fashion that is guaranteed to make you think, as well as encouraging constructive and engaging modes of writing. The companion website contains several useful exercises and templates.

Wheeldon, J., & Ahlberg, M. K. (2012). *Visualizing social science research: Maps, methods, and meaning.* Thousand Oaks, CA: Sage.

This introductory text presents basic principles of conceptualizing social science research that have applicability to various stages of the research process, including qualitative, quantitative, and mixed methods approaches. Visualizing social science research refers to the processes, techniques, and tools that contribute to framing and understanding the inquiry process. The authors present a variety of graphic illustrations (maps of various types, graphs, and diagrams) to illuminate processes including clarification of research design, data collection, methodology, exploration of measurement, analysis strategies, and presentation of findings. The text includes research examples that are drawn from a number of disciplines, reflective activity to review key concepts, and suggested additional readings.

Presenting Methodology and Research Approach

Chapter 7 Objectives

Section I: Instruction

- Identify the key components of the methodology chapter: (a) introduction and overview, (b) research sample, (c) overview of information needed, (d) research design, (e) methods of data collection, (f) methods for data analysis and synthesis, (g) ethical considerations, (h) issues of trustworthiness, (i) limitations and delimitations of the study, and (j) chapter summary.

- Provide an explanation of how each component of the research methodology must be developed and presented.

- Show that you understand how all of the components combined form a logical, interconnected sequence and contribute to the overall methodological integrity of the study.

Section II: Application

- Present a completed methodology chapter for your dissertation.

Overview

Chapter 3 of the dissertation presents the research design and the specific procedures used in conducting your study. A research design includes various interrelated elements that reflect its sequential nature. This chapter is intended to show the reader that you have an understanding of the methodological implications of the choices you have made and in particular, that you have thought carefully about the linkages between your study's purpose and research questions and the research approach and research methods that you have selected.

Note that in the proposal's Chapter 3, you project *what you will do* based on what you know about the particular methods used in qualitative research, in general, and in your tradition or genre, in particular; hence, it is written in future tense. In the dissertation's Chapter 3, you report on *what you have already done.* You write after the fact; hence, you write in past tense. As such, many of the sections of Chapter 3 can be written only after you have actually conducted your study (i.e., collected, analyzed, and synthesized your data).

To write this chapter, you need to conduct a series of literature reviews pertaining to the methodological issues involved in qualitative research design. You need to show the reader that you (a) have knowledge of the current issues and discourse and (b) can relate your study to those issues and discourse. In this regard, you need to explain how you have gone about designing and conducting your study while making sure that you *draw supporting evidence from the literature* for the decisions and choices that you have made.

This chapter is usually one of the dissertation's lengthiest because of the amount of material involved, but remember that institutional requirements vary greatly, so be sure to check on what is expected of you. The literature review chapter is essentially a *discussion* in which you explain the course and logic of your decision making throughout the research process. In practice, this means describing the following:

- The rationale for your research approach
- The research sample and the population from which it was drawn
- The type of information you needed
- How you designed the study and the methods that you used to gather your data
- The theoretical basis of the data collection methods you used and why you chose these
- How you have analyzed and synthesized your data
- Ethical considerations involved in your study
- Issues of trustworthiness and how you dealt with these
- Limitations and delimitations of the study and your attempt to address these

As has been pointed out throughout, please be aware that while most institutions will approach the dissertation in common ways, at the same time there are differences in terms of the organization and presentation and distinct differences in terms of what and how qualitative language and terminology are used. This book presents information as guidelines that are meant to be flexible per institutional expectations and requirements and subject to modification depending on your institution, department, and program.

Following are the two sections that make up this chapter. Section I offers instruction on how to develop each section of Chapter 3. Section II illustrates application by way of the example used throughout this book and gives you some idea of what a complete Chapter 3 could look like, depending on your institution's particular requirements and stipulations. Note that Section I includes various "how-to" matrices, charts, and figures. Although not all of these may make their way into the main body of your final dissertation, they can and often do appear as "working tools" in the dissertation's appendix.

Section I: Instruction

The dissertation's third chapter—the methodology chapter—covers a lot of ground. In this chapter, you document each step that you have taken in designing and conducting the study. The format that we present for this chapter covers all the necessary components of a comprehensive methodology chapter. Universities generally have their own fixed structural requirements, so we recommend that before proceeding to write, you discuss with your advisor how to structure the chapter as well as the preferred order of the sections and how long each section should be. Most important, make sure (a) your sections are in a logical sequence, and (b) what you write is comprehensive, clear, precise, and sufficiently detailed so that others will be able to adequately judge the soundness of your study. Table 7.1 is a road map intended to illustrate the necessary elements that constitute a sound methodology chapter and a suggested sequence for including these elements.

As pointed out previously, although qualitative research as an overall approach is based on certain central assumptions, it is characterized by an ongoing discourse regarding the appropriate and acceptable use of terminology. Current thinking over the years has caused some qualitative researchers to develop their own terminology to more effectively reflect the nature and distinction of qualitative research, whereas others still borrow terminology from quantitative research. Throughout this chapter, we point out instances in which you should be aware of these differences so that you can make an informed choice.

Introduction and Overview

The chapter begins with an opening paragraph in which you restate the study's purpose and research questions and then go on to explain the chapter's organization. You then proceed to discuss how your research lends itself to a qualitative approach and why this approach is most appropriate to your inquiry. Critical to a well-planned study is the consideration of whether a qualitative approach is suited to the purpose and nature of your study. To convey this notion to the reader, it is necessary to provide a rationale for the qualitative research approach, as well as your reasons for choosing a particular qualitative tradition—namely, case study or multiple case study, ethnography, phenomenology, biography, grounded theory, action research, or postmodernism/poststructuralism.

In your discussion, you begin by defining *qualitative inquiry* as distinct from quantitative research. Then you go on to discuss the values and benefits derived from using

TABLE 7.1 ● Road Map for Developing a Methodology Chapter: Necessary Elements

1: Introduction and Overview

Begin by stating purpose and research questions. Go on to explain how the chapter is organized. Then provide a rationale for using a qualitative research approach (i.e., why qualitative research is appropriate for your particular study), as well as a rationale for the particular qualitative tradition/genre you have chosen. Provide a brief overview of your study.

2: Research Sample

Describe the research sample and the population from which that sample was drawn. Define and discuss the sampling strategy used (purposeful, purposive, or criterion sampling), as well as your criteria for sample selection. Depending on the qualitative research tradition, a sample can include people, texts, artifacts, or cultural phenomena. In this section, describe the research site if appropriate (i.e., program, institution, or organization).

3: Overview of Information Needed

Describe the kinds of information you will need to answer your research questions. Be specific about exactly what kind of information you will be collecting. Four general areas of information are needed for most qualitative studies: contextual, perceptual, demographic, and theoretical information.

4: Research Design

This section outlines your overall research design/methodology. It includes the list of steps in carrying out your research from data collection through data analysis. The two sections that follow elaborate in greater detail on the methods of data collection and the process of data analysis. The narrative in this section is often augmented by a flowchart or diagram that provides an illustration of the various steps involved.

5: Data Collection Methods

Explain that a selected literature review preceded data collection; although this informs the study, indicate that the literature is not data to be collected. Identify and present all the data collection methods you used, and clearly explain the steps taken to carry out each method. Include in the discussion any field tests or pilot studies you may have undertaken. To show that you have done a critical reading of the literature, you may be required to discuss the strengths and weaknesses of each method of data collection used. In this regard, either you may include in this section what the literature says about each of the methods you will be using, or the literature on methods may be a separate section.

6: Data Analysis and Synthesis

Report on how you managed, organized, and analyzed your data in preparation to report your findings (Chapter 4) and then how you went on to analyze and interpret your findings (Chapter 5). It is important to note that this section of Chapter 3 can thus be written only after you have written up the findings and analysis chapters of your dissertation.

7: Ethical Considerations

This section should inform the reader that you have considered the ethical issues that might arise vis-à-vis your study and that you have taken the necessary steps to address these issues.

8: Issues of Trustworthiness

This section discusses the criteria for evaluating the trustworthiness of qualitative research—credibility, dependability, and transferability. Moreover, you should indicate to the reader that you have a clear understanding of the implications thereof vis-à-vis your own study and the strategies you employed to ensure and enhance trustworthiness.

9: Limitations and Delimitations

Limitations and delimitations identify potential weaknesses inherent in the study and the scope of the study. You need to cite all potential limitations and your means to address these limitations. The discussion should include problems inherent in qualitative research generally, as well as limitations that are specific to your particular study. Regardless of how carefully you plan a study, there will always be some limitations, and you need to explicitly acknowledge these. Note that generalizability is not considered a limitation as this is not the goal of qualitative research; rather, the focus is on transferability—that is, the ability to apply findings in similar contexts or settings. Limitations are external conditions that restrict or constrain the study's scope or may affect its outcome. Delimitations, on the other hand, are conditions or parameters that you as the researcher intentionally impose in order to limit the scope of your study (e.g., using participants of certain ages, genders, or groups; conducting the research in a single setting).

10: Chapter Summary

A final culminating summary ties together all the elements that you have presented in this chapter. Make sure that you highlight all the important points. Keep your concluding discussion concise and precise.

---

a qualitative approach—in other words, its strengths. You would not talk about its weaknesses here; you will do that in the last section of the methodology chapter called "Limitations and Delimitations." Make sure that this first section flows logically and that you structure your discussion well by using appropriate headings and subheadings. Once the overall approach and supporting rationale have been presented, you can move on to explain who the research participants are, the sampling strategies you used to select the participants, what kind of data were needed to inform your study, and the specific data collection and data analysis strategies employed.

Research Sample

In this section, you need to identify and describe in detail the methods used to select the research sample. This provides the reader with some sense of the scope of your study. In addition, your study's credibility relies on the quality of procedures you have used to select the research participants. Note that some qualitative researchers object to the use of the word *sample* in qualitative research, preferring terms such as *research participants* or *selected participants*. This is another example of the discourse among qualitative researchers that was mentioned previously.

Some research is site-specific, and the study is defined by and intimately linked to one or more locations. If you are working with a particular site, be it a particular place, region, organization, or program, the reader needs some detail regarding the setting. Although it is typically mentioned briefly in the beginning pages of Chapter 1 of your dissertation (the introduction), in this section of Chapter 3, you need to talk more specifically about how and why the site was selected.

After discussing the site, if applicable, you proceed to tell the reader about the research sample—the participants of your study. You also need to explain in some detail how the sample was selected and the pool from which it was drawn. This discussion should include the criteria used for inclusion in the sample, how participants were identified, how they were contacted, the number of individuals contacted, and the percentage of those who agreed to participate (i.e., the response rate). You also need to discuss why the specific method of sample selection used was considered most appropriate.

In qualitative research, selection of the research sample is purposeful (Patton, 1990, 2015). This type of sampling is sometimes referred to as *purposive sampling* (Merriam, 1998, 2009) or *judgment sampling* (Gay, Mills, & Airasian, 2006). Theoretical sampling, in contrast, is used in grounded theory studies. Theoretical sampling is set to work to generate theory through the investigation of the empirical social world (Emel, 2013).

The logic of purposeful sampling lies in selecting information-rich cases, with the objective of yielding insight and understanding of the phenomenon under investigation. This method is in contrast to the random sampling procedures that characterize quantitative research, which is based on statistical probability theory. Random sampling controls for selection bias and enables generalization from the sample to a larger population—a key feature of quantitative research. Remember, one of the basic tenets of qualitative research is that each research setting is unique in its own mix of people and contextual factors. The researcher's intent is to describe a particular context in depth, not to generalize to another context or population. Representativeness in qualitative research, and extrapolating from the particular to the general, is secondary to the participants' ability to provide information about themselves and their setting.

As its name suggests, a qualitative researcher has reasons (purposes) for selecting specific participants, events, and processes. As Reybold, Lammert, and Stribling (2013) point out, in qualitative research, the logic of selection is grounded in the value of information-rich cases and emergent, in-depth understanding not available through random sampling. From this perspective, purposeful selection is a strategy for accessing appropriate data that fit the purpose of the study, the resources available, the questions being asked, and the constraints and challenges being faced. Purposeful selection is more than a technique to access data; our selection choices frame who and what matters as data. Moreover, these selection choices interface the other methods in a study to ultimately become the stories that are told, an extremely important consideration for researchers.

The purposeful selection of research participants thus represents a key decision in qualitative research. Thus, in this section, you need to identify and provide a brief rationale for your sampling strategy. The strategy that you choose depends on the purpose of your study, and you need to make that clear in your discussion. For example, in a phenomenological study, you might employ "criterion-based sampling." Criterion sampling works well when all the individuals studied represent people who have experienced the same phenomenon. In a grounded theory study, you would choose the strategy known as *theoretical sampling* (or *theory-based sampling*), which means that you examine individuals who can contribute to the evolving theory. In a case study, you might use the strategy of *maximum variation* to represent diverse cases to fully display multiple perspectives about the cases. Appendix F presents an overview of the variety of purposeful sampling strategies used in qualitative research.

Once you have offered a rationale for your sampling strategy, you need to go on to discuss the nature and makeup of your particular sample. Describe who these individuals are, disclose how many individuals constitute the sample, and provide any relevant descriptive characteristics. It is also helpful to include charts to augment and complement the narrative discussion. Providing information regarding selection procedures and research participants will aid others in understanding the findings. Having provided a description of the research sample and the setting, you are now ready to proceed to explain exactly what types of information you will need from the participants.

Overview of Information Needed

This section briefly describes the kinds of information you need to answer your research questions and thus shed light on the problem you are investigating. Four areas of information are typically needed for most qualitative studies: contextual, perceptual, demographic, and theoretical. The following sections define the content and the specific relevancy of each of these areas.

Contextual Information Contextual information refers to the context within which the participants reside or work. It is information that describes the culture and environment of the setting, be it an organization or an institution. It is essential information to collect when doing a case study set in a particular site or multiple similar sites because elements within the environment or culture may, as Lewin (1935) reminds us, influence behavior. Lewin's fundamental proposition is that human behavior is a function of the interaction of the person and the environment. This theory is particularly relevant when one is trying to understand the learning behaviors of a discrete segment of a population in a particular organizational or institutional setting.

Given the nature of contextual information, such a review would provide knowledge about an organization's history, vision, objectives, products or services, operating principles, and business strategy. In addition, information on an organization or institution's leaders and its structure, organizational chart, systems, staff, roles, rules, and procedures would be included in this area of information. The primary method of collecting contextual information is through an extensive review of organization or institutional internal documents, as well as a review of relevant external documents that refer in some way to the organization or institution. Documentation can be of a descriptive and/or evaluative nature. Refer to Appendix Q for a document summary form template.

Demographic Information Demographic information is participant profile information that describes who the participants in your study are—where they come from, some of their history and/or background, their education, and other personal information such as age, gender, occupation, and ethnicity. Relevant demographic information is needed to help explain what may be underlying an individual's perceptions, as well as the similarities and differences in perceptions among participants. In other words, a particular data point (e.g., age) may explain a certain finding that emerged in the study.

Demographic information is typically collected by asking participants to complete a personal data sheet either before or after the interview or other data collection methods have taken place. The information is then arrayed on a matrix that shows participants by pseudonym on the vertical axis and the demographic data points (age, gender, education, etc.) on the horizontal axis, as illustrated in Table 7.2. This demographic matrix, which is usually presented in the prior section, in which you discuss your research sample, can also later be used in conjunction with frequency charts. The latter, to be explained further on, table the findings to help you with cross-case analysis, which is required later in the dissertation process. A sample completed participant demographics matrix appears as Appendix G.

Perceptual Information Perceptual information refers to participants' perceptions related to the particular subject of your inquiry. Particularly in qualitative research when interviews are often the primary method of data collection, perceptual information is the most critical of the kinds of information needed. Perceptual information relies, to a great extent, on interviews to uncover participants' descriptions of their experiences related to such things as how experiences influenced the decisions they made, whether participants had a change of mind or a shift in attitude, whether they described more of a constancy of purpose, what elements relative to their objectives participants perceived as important, and to what extent those objectives were met.

It should be remembered that perceptions are just that—they are not facts—they are what people perceive as facts. They are rooted in long-held assumptions and one's own view of the world or frame of reference. As such, they are neither right nor wrong; they tell the story of what participants believe to be true. Refer to Appendix R for a participant summary form template.

TABLE 7.2 ● **Template for Participant Demographics Matrix**

Participant Code	Pseudonym	Years Enrolled	Program Concentration/ Discipline	Gender	Age
TOTAL N = X				F = X (X%) M = X (X%)	

Theoretical Information Theoretical information includes information researched and collected from the various literature sources to assess what is already known regarding your topic of inquiry. Theoretical information serves to

- Support and give evidence for your methodological approach;
- Provide theories related to your research questions that form the development and ongoing refinement of your conceptual framework;
- Provide support for your interpretation, analysis, and synthesis; and
- Provide support for conclusions you draw and recommendations you suggest.

It is recommended that you create a matrix that aligns your research questions with the information you assess and the methods that you will use to collect that information. Creating this type of alignment ensures that the information you intend to collect is directly related to the research questions, therefore providing answers to the respective research questions. For planning purposes, the alignment indicates the particular methods you will use to collect the information. It is useful to array a table similar to Table 7.3, which illustrates how you might go about setting up such a matrix. A completed sample overview of information needed is presented as Appendix H.

Research Design

Once you are clear about the information you need and the methods you will use to obtain those data, you are ready to develop and present your research design. The research design is the *plan for conducting the study.* There is no agreed upon structure for how to design a qualitative study, however, and in fact, books on qualitative research vary greatly in their suggestions regarding research design. Engaging in research involves choosing a study design that corresponds with your study's problem, purpose, research questions, choice of site, and research sample. This calls to the fore the concept of methodological congruence (Richards & Morse, 2013), whereby all the study's components are interconnected and interrelated so that the study itself is a cohesive whole rather than the sum of fragmented, isolated, disparate parts. You will also need to consider whether the design is a comfortable match with your worldview and your skills. It is thus important to understand the philosophical foundations underlying different types of qualitative research so that you can make informed decisions as to the choices available to you in designing and implementing a research study. Remember, although all of qualitative research holds a number of characteristics and assumptions in common, there are key variations in the disciplinary base that a qualitative study may draw from, what the intent of the study may be, and hence in how a qualitative study may be designed and implemented. Thus a narrative life history study would be differentiated in terms of design and implantation from a case study that seeks to investigate participants' experiences in a particular bounded context, from an ethnographic study that focuses on culture, and from a grounded theory study that is designed to build a substantial theory. Other considerations regarding choice of research design have to do with identifying a theoretical or conceptual framework that forms the scaffolding or underlying structure of the study.

Once you are clear about the information you need and the methods you will use to obtain those data, you are ready to develop your research design. Whatever combination of methods you choose to use, there is a need for a systematic approach to your data. The main objective of this section of the methodology chapter is to identify and present the data collection methods and explain clearly the process you undertook to carry out each method. Be sure to include in your discussion any field tests or pilot studies you may have undertaken to determine the usefulness of any instruments you have developed. Because the research design in qualitative research is flexible, you should also mention any modifications and changes you might have made to your design along the way. That is, describe all the steps that you took as you moved through the study to collect and analyze your data. Indicate the order in which these steps occurred, as well as how each step informed the next. The narrative can be accompanied by a flowchart or diagram that illustrates the steps involved. A sample research design flowchart appears in Appendix I. Various formats of a flowchart can be used; however, be careful to keep it as simple and as informative as possible. "Pretty," elaborate flowchart designs often miss the point. Simplicity and logic are key.

TABLE 7.3 ● Template for Overview of Information Needed

Research Questions	Type of Information Needed (a) Contextual (context/background) (b) Demographic (c) Perceptual	Information Yielded (a) Background, History, Culture, Mission, Site Description, etc. (b) Age, Gender, Ethnicity, Discipline, etc. (c) Participants' Attitudes, Perceptions, Ideas, Thoughts, etc.	Method of Data Collection
1. Research Question 1			
2. Research Question 2			
3. Research Question 3			
4. Research Question 4			
5. Research Question 5			

*Lists of documents and instruments for all data collection methods should appear as appendices.

Appropriate methods are derived from having done your analysis of the kinds of information you need to answer your research questions. A brief statement concerning your literature review precedes the discussion of methods and process. The purpose of this brief predata collection literature review statement is to underscore (a) the theoretical grounding for the study, (b) that the review of the literature was ongoing and related research was continually updated, and (c) that the conceptual framework developed from the literature review was used to guide the data analysis, interpretation, and synthesis phases of the research. This literature review statement comes before the identification and description of methods because although the literature review is ongoing, generating new information and supporting evidence, it is not a data collection method per se. You are now ready to discuss the methods you will use in your study.

Methods of Data Collection

Extensive engagement with participants, data, and setting is an essential feature of all qualitative research, whatever modes of data gathering are used. Engagement with participants in their social worlds is essential to understanding subjective meanings, and it is important that the study's findings are informed by the data rather than the researcher's own preconceptions. This requires reflexivity, that is, a deep awareness on the part of researchers of their own preconceptions and assumptions and reflection on their roles and emerging understandings while engaged in the research process. Based on the research questions, specific data collection methods are chosen to gather the required information in the most appropriate and meaningful way. It should be noted that a solid rationale for the choice of methods used is crucial, as this indicates *methodological congruence* and illustrates that the choice of methods is grounded in the study's conceptual framework and overall research design. Information gathered during data collection needs to be recorded in a manner that enables the researcher to analyze and meaningfully report the data.

It is critical that you clearly and accurately explain *how* you obtained your findings for the following reasons:

1. Readers need to know how the data was obtained because the method or methods you chose affects the findings and by extension, how you likely interpreted them.
2. In most cases, there are a variety of different methods you can choose to investigate a research problem. The methodology section of your paper should therefore clearly articulate the reasons *why* you chose a particular procedure or technique.
3. The reader will want to know that the data was collected or generated in a way that is consistent with accepted practice in the field of study. Unreliable method produces unreliable results and as a consequence, undermines the value of your interpretations of the findings.

4. In the social and behavioral sciences, it is important to provide sufficient information to allow other researchers to adopt or replicate your methods. This is particularly important when a new method has been developed or an innovative use of an existing method is utilized.

A common pitfall in writing this section is the tendency to describe the data collection methods chosen as if they exist in a vacuum without explaining the logical connections among the methods you have chosen, your research questions, and your research approach. Following are the sequential steps that must be covered in this section. Be specific and precise in your discussion as you proceed:

1. Describe each data collection method you used.
2. Provide a rationale for each of the methods selected.
3. Provide complete information about how you used each method.
4. Describe how you developed each of your instruments.
5. Describe how you field-tested your instruments.
6. Describe how you recorded and safeguarded your data.
7. Describe the steps you took to preserve confidentiality and anonymity of data.

Qualitative researchers are concerned about the validity of their communication. To reduce the likelihood of misinterpretation, we employ various procedures, including redundancy of data gathering and procedural challenges to explanation. These procedures, called *triangulation,* are considered a process of using multiple perceptions to clarify meaning. Keep in mind that the use of multiple methods of data collection to achieve triangulation is important to obtain an in-depth understanding of the phenomenon under study. There are several methods used in qualitative research to choose from: interviews (often the primary method), summative focus groups, document review, observation, and critical incident reports. A variety of combinations of methods can be employed. Surveys and questionnaires, which are traditionally quantitative instruments, also can be used in conjunction with qualitative methods to provide corroboration and/or supportive evidence. Appendix J provides a summary overview of the qualitative data collection methods from which to choose. Appendix K provides a sample interview schedule. Appendix P provides a sample critical incident instrument. Following is a brief summary and critical overview of each of the most common qualitative data collections tools:

Interviews In any qualitative study, interviews may be the overall strategy or only one of several methods employed. The interview is often selected as the primary method for data collection because it has the potential to elicit rich, thick descriptions. Further, this method offers researchers an opportunity to clarify statements and probe for additional information. Creswell (2013), Denzin and Lincoln (2013a, 2013b), and Marshall and Rossman (2015) state that a major benefit of collecting data through individual, in-depth interviews is that they offer the potential to capture a person's perspective of an event or experience.

Interviews can range in structure from a list of predetermined questions to a totally free-ranging interview in which there is no structure set ahead of time. Typically interviews for qualitative research are in-depth in order to capture perceptions, attitudes, and emotions of the interview participant. Interviews aim to elicit participants' views of their lives, as portrayed in their stories, and so gain access to their experiences, feelings, and social worlds. Interviews can be unstructured or semistructured. The former are usually conducted in everyday conversational style. Semistructured interviews are used to facilitate more focused exploration of a specific topic, using an interview guide. The success of an interview depends on the nature of the interaction between the interviewer and the research participant, and on the interviewer's skill in asking good questions. Indeed the generativity of the interview depends on both partners and their willingness to engage in a deep discussion about the topic of interest. As Brinkman and Kvale (2015) note, an interview is an "inter-view," that is, an exchange of views between two persons.

Although interviews have inherent strengths, there are various limitations associated with interviewing. First, not all people are equally cooperative, articulate, and perceptive. Second, interviews require researcher skill. Third, interviews are not neutral tools of data gathering; they are the result of the interaction between the interviewer and the interviewee and the context in which they take place (Fontana & Frey, 2003; Rubin & Rubin, 2012; Seidman, 2012).

Observation   Observation is a central and fundamental method in qualitative inquiry and is used to discover and explain complex interactions in natural social settings. In the early stages of qualitative research the emphasis is on discovery. The researcher may enter the setting with broad areas of interest, but without predetermined categories or strict observational checklists. Through this type of open-ended entry, the researcher is potentially able to discover recurring patterns of behavior, interactions, and relationships. After these patterns are identified and described through early analysis of field notes, checklists might become more appropriate and context-sensitive. Focused observation may then be used at later stages of the study, for example to see if analytic themes explain behavior and relationships over a period of time or in a variety of settings. The term "participant observation," as its name suggests, explains the researcher as both a participant and an observer through immersion in the setting in order experience reality as the research participants do. This method of gathering data raises the issue of "positionality," that is, the researcher's relationship with participants, the nature of that involvement, how much of the study's purpose will be revealed to participants, and how ethical dilemmas will be managed.

Observation differs from interviews in that the researcher obtains a first-hand account of the phenomenon of interest rather than relying on someone else's interpretation or perspective. There are texts that describe what and how to observe, the interdependent relationship between the observer and the observed, how to record observations in the form of field notes, and how to analyze and interpret observation data.

Focus Group Focus groups, or group interviews, are facilitated group discussions and possess elements of both participant observation and individual interviews, while also maintaining their own uniqueness as a distinctive research method (Liamputtong, 2011). Participants are usually selected because of shared social or cultural experience, or shared concerns related to the study's focus. A focus group is essentially a group discussion focused on a single theme (Kreuger & Casey, 2015; Stewart & Shamdasani, 2015).

One strength of focus groups is that this method is socially oriented, studying participants in an atmosphere that is often more natural and relaxed than a one-to-one interview. As with other types of interviews, the format allows the facilitator the flexibility to explore often-unanticipated issues as they arise in the discussion. The goal is to create a candid conversation that addresses, in depth, the selected topic. The underlying assumption of focus groups is that, within a permissive atmosphere that fosters a range of opinions, a more complete and revealing understanding of the issues will be obtained. Focus groups are planned and structured, but are also flexible tools (Liamputtong, 2011). Kreuger and Casey (2015) list various uses of focus groups: (a) elicit a range of feelings, opinions, and ideas; (b) understand differences in perspectives; (c) uncover and provide insight into specific factors that influence opinions; and (d) seek ideas that emerge from the group.

It must be acknowledged that focus groups, while serving a useful function, are not without disadvantages, including issues of power dynamics (some views held by a minority of participants could be minimized) or groupthink (there might be a tendency for participants to agree with others and reflect the collective views of group members). Furthermore, logistical difficulties might arise from the need to manage conversation while attempting to extract data, requiring strong facilitation skills. As such, should researchers choose to use this method they will need to develop strong facilitation skills (Fontana & Frey, 2003).

Critical Incidents Critical incident reports are a data collection method first formulated by Flanagan (1954), useful because qualitative research methodology emphasizes process and is based on a descriptive and inductive approach to data collection. Qualitative researchers often select critical incident instruments with the intention of corroborating interview data and further, to allow the uncovering of perceptions that might not have been revealed through interviews. Of particular importance is that written critical incident reports probe assumptions, allowing time for reflection.

Although there is support in the literature for the use of the critical incident as an effective technique for enhancing data collection, researchers should be mindful of Brookfield's (1991, 2005) repeated caution that critical incidents cannot be the sole technique for collecting data. Critical incidents are too abbreviated to provide the rich descriptions that can be obtained in interviews and observations. A further concern regarding the use of critical incident reports has to do with the accuracy of data because this technique relies solely on the respondents' recall. A related concern is that, although reporting information that respondents perceive is important, the researcher may fail to report salient incremental data and the information, as such, may be incomplete.

Survey Surveys, while typically a quantitative data collection method, can be used as an adjunct to many of the methods described above. An advantage of survey methodology is that it is relatively unobtrusive and relatively easily administered and managed (Fink, 2013; Fowler, 2014). It must be acknowledged, however, that surveys alone can be of limited value for examining complex social relationships or intricate patterns of interaction. In keeping with the qualitative research tradition, surveys often include some open-ended questions that seek to tap into personal experiences and shed light on participants' perceptions.

Document Review Another primary source of qualitative data is document review. The term *document* is broadly defined to cover an assortment of written records, visual data, artifacts, and even archival data. Although some documents may be developed at the researcher's request, most are produced independently of the research study, and thus offer a valuable resource for confirming insights gained through other methods of data collection. Researchers often supplement participant observation, interviewing, and observation with gathering and analyzing documents produced in the course of everyday events. As such, the analysis of documents is potentially rich in portraying the values and beliefs of participants in the setting. As with other methodological decisions, the decision to gather and analyze documents should be linked to the study's research design and will indicate the need for seeking corroboration of the meaning of the documents through other data collection methods. There are many useful texts that cover the various kinds of documents, their use in qualitative research, ethical issues involved, and the various strengths and limitations associated with documents as sources of data.

Remember that multiple data gathering techniques are frequently used in qualitative studies as a deliberate strategy to develop a more complex understanding of the phenomena being studied. This goes back to the importance of triangulation for enhancing the quality of data from multiple sources (e.g., people, events), in multiple ways (e.g., interviews, observations, document review), with the idea that this practice will illuminate different facets of situations and experiences and help portray them in their entirety and complexity.

A note of clarification: *Methodology* refers to how research proceeds and encompasses a range of logistical, relational, ethical, and credibility issues. The term *methods* commonly denotes specific techniques, procedures, or tools used by the researcher to generate and analyze data. Unlike the overview of methodology discussed earlier, which reflects an overall research strategy, this section describes what the literature says about each of the methods you used in your study. In other words, you discuss how the instruments you have chosen are appropriate to your study, making use of the literature to support each of your choices.

To show that you have done a critical reading of the literature and to acknowledge that data collection methods, although certainly useful, are not without some disadvantages, the discussion should include some detail regarding the strengths and weaknesses of each method. In your discussion, present the methods of data collection in the order in which you use them and be sure to structure the discussion well by having a separate heading for each method.

Based on the research questions, specific data collection methods are chosen to gather the required information in the most appropriate and meaningful way. Remember too that triangulation strengthens your study by combining methods. Having presented the methods that you have used to gather data, you are ready to go on and explain how the data have been recorded and managed, as well as your strategies for data analysis.

Because interviews are, in most cases, the primary method of data collection, it is useful at this point to explain how interview questions are developed. To carry out the purpose of your study, all the research questions must be satisfied. Therefore, designing the right interview questions is critical. To ensure that the interview questions are directly tied to the research questions, type out in bold font each of your research questions and then underneath each brainstorm three or four questions that will get at that research question. When you have done this for each of your research questions, you should have a list of 12 to 15 interview questions. To do a preliminary test of your interview questions, think about all probable responses you might get from each interview question, and reframe the questions until you are satisfied they will engender the kind of responses that refer directly to the research questions. A sample of a completed interview schedule or interview protocol based on research questions is presented as Appendix K.

Constructing a matrix that lists the research questions along the horizontal axis and the interview questions down the vertical axis can further indicate the extent to which your interview questions have achieved the necessary coverage of your research questions. Table 7.4 is an illustration of this approach. This type of matrix, which allows a visual overview of the required coverage of the research questions via the interview schedule, in conjunction with pilot interviews, can help you further refine your interview questions.

Data Analysis and Synthesis

In this section, you report on how you managed, organized, and analyzed your data in preparation to write up and present your findings (Chapter 8) and then how you went on to analyze and interpret your findings (Chapter 9). Thus, it is important to note that this section of Chapter 3 of your dissertation (the methodology) can be written only *after* you have written up the findings and analysis chapters of your dissertation.

One of the most common shortfalls in presenting qualitative research (and hence one of the most common critiques of published qualitative research methodology) is what Guest, MacQueen, and Namey (2012) refer to as the "black box approach to data analysis"—that is, inadequate description of analytic procedures and reasoning. Oftentimes, researchers simply state that they conducted thematic analysis in the belief that this constitutes sufficient information. Appropriate methods of data analysis depend on the research purpose and nature of data collected, but certain fundamental steps must be taken to constitute a comprehensive (reliable and valid) account of the analytic process. Describing decisions taken for arriving at certain judgments during data analysis—that is, an "audit trail" (Lincoln & Guba, 1985; Miles & Huberman, 1994; Miles, Huberman, & Saldana, 2014)—enhances transparency and is an indication of good methodological practice. This would include details such as how codes were developed and applied to the data, code definitions (and any changes and/or redefinitions that might have occurred in the process), methods used to address coding reliability, and methods of assessing intercoder agreement (in cases where multiple coders are involved). If qualitative data software is used, the name and version of the program should be provided along with the reporting functions used in the analysis. As a further indication of validity, where possible, researchers should document feedback on their interpretation of data from study participants—that is, "member checks."

The process of data analysis begins with putting in place a plan to manage the large volume of data you collected and reducing it in a meaningful way. You complete this process to identify significant patterns and construct a framework for communicating the essence of what the data revealed given the purpose of your study. Here your conceptual framework becomes the centerpiece in managing the data. The categories that comprise your conceptual framework become the repositories of your data. Thus, as you look at your raw data, categorize them within the construct of your conceptual framework and assign initial codes to relevant quotes. This iterative process of open coding leads to the ongoing refinement of what will become your final coding schema. Generally, include your coding schema or coding legend as an appendix. Appendix L is a completed coding scheme sample. In addition, it is useful to show the reader how your coding scheme developed. Appendix M offers such an illustration.

TABLE 7.4 ● Template for Research Questions/Interview Questions Matrix

Interview Questions	Research Questions			
	1:	2:	3:	4:
1.				
2.				
3.				
4.				
5.				

Therefore, the process of analysis is both deductive and inductive. The initial categories of your conceptual framework were deductively obtained from the literature. From your own experience and the data as they emerged from pilot tests, you begin to see patterns and themes. In this way, coding occurs inductively. As the coding schema continues to emerge, you must obtain inter-rater reliability by requesting colleagues, usually three, to read one of your interview transcripts to test your codes. Any discrepancies that result from the independent review by your colleagues must be discussed and reconciled with each of them. Such discrepancies may result in additional exploration of the data. Exploration of such discrepancies in which further clarification is needed will help you as the researcher to refine how you state your findings, as well as subsequent analysis and recommendations (Creswell, 2013). You also can have these same colleagues act as "devil's advocates" or peer reviewers throughout data collection, analysis, and interpretation.

Computer software programs can be useful in both managing and analyzing your data. Various programs enable the researcher to store, categorize, retrieve, and compare data (see Appendix Z). At the same time, there are other researchers who prefer to manage and analyze their data manually—to see visual displays of the data as they move through the analysis process. These researchers also are concerned with what they perceive as a limitation related to mechanical handling of data (Merriam, 2009), and so they may feel more comfortable using flip charts, tables, charts, and matrices. We are not suggesting one approach over the other because the method you select to manage and analyze your data is a matter of personal preference and depends on what you are most comfortable with and/or institutional requirements.

Whether you use a computer-based system or a manual one, the development of visuals—tables and/or figures—can be useful in helping you organize your thinking in preparation for writing. Aside from helping you develop your own thinking, visuals also are useful for displaying your data so your readers can better understand them. Various types of charts can be constructed, and you can indeed be quite creative in devising these charts. For presenting and analyzing findings, we have found three charts to be particularly effective: data summary tables, the analysis outline tool, and consistency charts.

Data summary tables, discussed in greater detail in Chapter 8 ("Analyzing Data and Reporting Findings"), can help you in preparing to present the findings from the data. These tables are used for recording the number and types of participant responses, tracking the frequency of participant responses against the categories on your conceptual framework, and formulating overall finding statements with respect to each of your research questions. Sample data summary tables are presented as Appendices T through Y.

To further help in the analysis and interpretation of findings, we suggest using what we call an interpretation outline tool. This tool, discussed in more detail in Chapter 9 ("Analyzing and Interpreting Findings"), prompts you to probe beneath the surface of your findings to uncover the deeper meanings that lie beneath them. A sample interpretation outline tool appears as Appendix CC. Consistency charts, discussed further in Chapter 10 ("Drawing Trustworthy Conclusions and Presenting Actionable Recommendations"), help align your thinking with respect to how each finding can generate suitable conclusions and recommendations. A sample completed consistency chart is presented in Appendix EE.

Because qualitative research is, by its nature, flexible and because there are no strict guidelines and standards for qualitative analysis, every qualitative researcher will approach the analytic process somewhat differently. Therefore, it is necessary to (a) provide a detailed description of how you went about analyzing your data, (b) refer to the matrices that you used to display your data, and (c) identify the coding processes used to convert the raw data into themes for analysis. Your description should include specific details about how you managed the large amount of data. Include information about the computer software, sticky notes, index cards, flip charts, or other processes that you used. This list helps the reader clearly understand how and in what ways you reduced or transformed your data.

As a last point in this section, it is important that researchers understand what is meant by *synthesis of the data*. Whereas analysis splits data apart, synthesis is the process of pulling everything together: (a) how the research questions are answered by the findings, (b) how the findings from interviews are supported from all other data collection methods, (c) how findings relate to the literature, and (d) how findings relate to the researcher's going-in assumptions about the study. This process is not linear; rather, you describe your findings, interpret and attach meaning to them, and synthesize throughout your discussion.

Ethical Considerations

As researchers, we are morally bound to conduct our research in a manner that minimizes potential harm to those involved in the study. We should be as concerned with producing an ethical research design as we are an intellectually coherent and compelling one.

Colleges, universities, and other institutions that conduct research have institutional review boards (IRBs) whose members review research proposals to assess ethical issues. Although all studies must be approved by your institution's IRB committee, there are some unique ethical considerations surrounding qualitative research because of its emergent and flexible design. Ethical issues can indeed arise in all phases of the research process: data collection, data analysis and interpretation, and dissemination of the research findings. For the most part, issues of ethics focus on establishing safeguards that will protect the rights of participants and include informed consent, protecting participants from harm, and ensuring confidentiality. As a qualitative researcher, you need to remain attentive throughout your study to the researcher–participant relationship, which is determined by roles, status, and cultural norms.

In this section of Chapter 3 of your dissertation, you need to show the reader that you have considered the ethical issues that might arise vis-à-vis your own study, you are sensitive to these issues, and you have taken the necessary steps to address these issues. In most instances, you will be talking in generalities; the potential issues that could arise apply to any qualitative research study and are usually not specific to your own. Because protection of human subjects is such an important issue in social science research, the main point is that you acknowledge and convey to the reader that you have considered and taken heed of the issues involved. Remember, informed consent is central to research ethics. It is the principle that seeks to ensure that all human subjects retain autonomy and the ability to judge for themselves what risks are worth taking for the purpose of furthering scientific knowledge. In this regard, it is important that you include in your appendix a copy of the consent form that you used in your study. A sample research consent form appears in Appendix N.

Issues of Trustworthiness

In quantitative research, the standards that are most frequently used for good and convincing research are validity and reliability. If research is valid, it clearly reflects the world being described. If work is reliable, then two researchers studying the same phenomenon will come up with compatible observations. Criteria for evaluating qualitative research differ from those used in quantitative research in that the focus is on how well the researcher has provided evidence that her or his descriptions and analysis represent the reality of the situations and persons studied. In this section of Chapter 3 of your dissertation, you need to clarify to the reader how you have accounted for trustworthiness regarding your own study.

As mentioned previously, qualitative research is characterized by an ongoing discourse regarding the appropriate and acceptable use of terminology. Current thinking has led some qualitative researchers to develop alternative terminology to better reflect the nature and distinction of qualitative research, whereas others still feel comfortable borrowing terminology from quantitative research. Some qualitative researchers argue for a return to terminology for ensuring rigor, and refer to various "validation strategies" (Creswell, 2013; Maxwell, 2013; Morse, Barrett, Mayan, Olson, & Spiers, 2002). Others object to the use of traditional terms such as *validity* and *reliability*, preferring instead *credibility* and *dependability*. This contrast is a matter of institutional and/or personal preference, and we recommend that you check with your advisor or committee in this regard. Lincoln and Guba (1985) originally made the argument for the importance of *trustworthiness* in qualitative research as a means for reassuring the reader that a study was of significance and value. Lincoln and Guba (1985, 2000), among others, belong to the latter camp, proposing various criteria for evaluating the trustworthiness of qualitative research:

1. **Credibility**: This criterion refers to whether the participants' perceptions match up with the researcher's portrayal of them. In other words, has the researcher accurately represented what the participants think, feel, and do? Credibility parallels the criterion of validity (including both validity of measures and internal validity) in quantitative research. Evidence in support of credibility can take several forms:

a. Clarify up front the bias that you, as the researcher, bring to the study. This self-reflection creates an open and honest attitude that will resonate well with readers. You should continually monitor their own subjective perspectives and biases by recording reflective field notes or keeping a journal throughout the research process.

b. Discuss how you engaged in repeated and substantial involvement in the field. Prolonged involvement in the field facilitates a more in-depth understanding of the phenomenon under study, conveying detail about the site and the participants that lends credibility to your account.

c. Check on whether your interpretation of the processes and interactions in the setting is valid. Typically, qualitative researchers collect multiple sources of data. The information provided by these different sources should be compared through triangulation to corroborate the researcher's conclusions.

d. Use multiple methods to corroborate the evidence that you have obtained via different means. Triangulation of data collection methods also lends credibility.

e. Present negative instances or discrepant findings. Searching for variation in the understanding of the phenomenon entails seeking instances that might disconfirm or challenge the researcher's expectations or emergent findings. Because real life is composed of different perspectives that do not always coalesce, discussing contrary information adds to the credibility of your account.

f. To ensure that the researcher's own biases do not influence how participants' perspectives are portrayed and to determine the accuracy of the findings, make use of "member checks," which entails sending the transcribed interviews or summaries of the researcher's conclusions to participants for review.

g. Use "peer debriefing" to enhance the accuracy of your account. This process involves asking a colleague to examine your field notes and then ask you questions that will help you examine your assumptions and/or consider alternative ways of looking at the data.

2. **Dependability**: This criterion parallels reliability, although it is not assessed through statistical procedures. Dependability refers to whether one can track the processes and procedures used to collect and interpret the data:

a. Provide detailed and thorough explanations of how the data were collected and analyzed, providing what is known as an "audit trail." Although it is not possible to include all of your data in the findings chapter, many qualitative researchers make it known that their data are available for review by other researchers.

b. Ask colleagues to code several interviews, thereby establishing inter-rater reliability. This process of checking on the consistency between raters reduces the potential bias of a single researcher collecting and analyzing the data.

3. **Transferability**: Although qualitative researchers do not expect their findings to be generalizable to all other settings, it is likely that the lessons learned in one setting might be useful to others. Transferability is not whether the study includes a representative sample. Rather, it is about how well the study has made it possible for readers to decide whether similar processes will be at work in their own settings and communities by understanding in depth how they occur at the research site. Thus, transferability refers to the fit or match between the research context and other contexts as judged by the reader. As a criterion of trustworthiness, transferability is assessed by the following factors:

   a. The richness of the descriptions included in the study give the discussion an element of shared or vicarious experience. Qualitative research is indeed characterized generally by "thick description" (Denzin, 2001). Ethnographer and anthropologist Clifford Geertz (1973) coined the term "thick description" with an emphasis on the need to understand and elaborate the symbolic import of what is observed and systematically documented during fieldwork. Thick description is the vehicle for communicating to the reader a holistic and realistic picture.

   b. The amount of detailed information that the researcher provides regarding the context and/or background also offers an element of shared experience.

This section of the dissertation's Chapter 3 addresses this central question: How do we know that the qualitative study is believable, accurate, and plausible? To answer this question, one must have some knowledge of the criteria of trustworthiness in qualitative research and the approaches to addressing these criteria. You need to discuss the criteria for evaluating the trustworthiness of qualitative research and to indicate to the reader that you have a clear understanding of the implications thereof vis-à-vis your own study. As the researcher, you are expected to display sensibility and sensitivity to *be* the research instrument. Begin this section by discussing what validity and reliability in qualitative research involve, using references from the literature to support your statements. Then go on to talk about the strategies that you have employed to enhance the trustworthiness of your own study vis-à-vis validity (credibility), reliability (dependability), and generalizability (transferability).

Limitations and Delimitations of the Study

Confusion sometimes exists around the terms *limitations* and *delimitations,* and this issue deserves some clarification.

Limitations of the study are those characteristics of design or methodology that impacted or influenced the interpretation of the findings from your research. These are the constraints regarding transferability, applications to practice, and/or utility of findings that are the result of the ways in which you chose to design the study. *Limitations* of the study expose the conditions that may weaken the study (Locke, Spirduso, & Silverman, 2000; Rossman & Rallis, 2012).

- Always acknowledge a study's limitations. It is far better for you to identify and acknowledge your study's limitations than to have them pointed out because you appear to have ignored them.
- Keep in mind that acknowledgment of your study's limitations is an opportunity to make suggestions for further research. If you do connect your study's limitations to suggestions for further research, be sure to explain the ways in which these unanswered questions may become more focused because of your study.
- Acknowledgment of your study's limitations also provides you with an opportunity to demonstrate that you have thought critically about the research problem, understood the relevant literature, and correctly assessed the methods chosen for studying the problem. A key objective of the research process is not only to discover new knowledge, but also to confront assumptions and explore the unknown.
- Claiming limitations is a subjective process because you must evaluate the impact of those limitations. Don't just list key weaknesses and the magnitude of a study's limitations. Limitations require a critical, overall appraisal and interpretation of their impact. You should answer the question: Do these problems with errors, methods, trustworthiness, etc. eventually matter and if so, to what extent?

Delimitations refer to the initial choices made about the broader, overall design of your study and should not be confused with documenting the limitations of your study that were discovered after the research has been completed. Delimitations are those characteristics that define and clarify the conceptual boundaries of your research. They are a way to indicate to the reader how you narrowed the scope of your study. As the researcher, you control the delimitations, and you should make this clear, by stating the conscious exclusionary and inclusionary decisions you make about how to investigate the research problem. In other words, not only should you tell the reader what it is you are studying and why, but you must also acknowledge why you rejected alternative approaches that could have been used. The point is not to document every possible delimiting factor, but to highlight why obvious issues related to the research problem were not addressed. Examples of some typical delimitating choices would include:

- The key aims and objectives of your study
- The research questions that you address
- The various factors and features of the phenomenon being studied
- The method(s) of investigation
- The time period your study covers
- Location of the study
- The sample selected
- Any relevant alternative theoretical frameworks that could have been adopted.

Review each of these research decisions. Not only do you need to clearly establish what you intend to accomplish in your research, but also you should also include a declaration of what the study does not intend to cover. Do not view delimiting statements as admitting to an inherent failing or shortcoming in your research. Delimitations are an accepted element of academic writing intended to keep the reader focused on the research problem by explicitly defining the conceptual boundaries and scope of your study. Acknowledging delimitations addresses any critical questions in the reader's mind of, "Why did the author not examine this?"

In this section of Chapter 3 of your dissertation, you cite potential limitations and your means of addressing and guarding against these limitations. Regardless of how carefully you plan a study, there are always some limitations, and you need to explicitly acknowledge these. This section describes the problems inherent in qualitative research and how you can control for these limitations to the extent possible. In most instances, you can control for limitations by acknowledging them. Limitations arise from, among other things, restricted sample size, sample selection, reliance on certain techniques for gathering data, and issues of researcher bias and participant reactivity. Discussing limitations is intended to show the reader that you understand that no research project is without limitations and that you have anticipated and given some thought to the shortcomings of your research. Stating the limitations also reminds the reader that your study is situated within a specific context, and the reader can make decisions about its usefulness for other settings.

Chapter Summary

The purpose of a final culminating summary is to tie together everything that you have presented in this chapter. Provide a short summary overview, making sure to cover all the sections of this chapter, recapping and highlighting all the important points. Keep the discussion concise and precise.

The application section that follows is a skeleton view of a methodology chapter. The methodology chapter, as evidenced from the prior instructions, is lengthy, and much detail is required in each section. In an actual dissertation, each section of this chapter would be more thoroughly elaborated, and hence would require a much more extensive discussion.

Chapter Summary Discussion

Writing the methodology chapter of your dissertation requires time, mind work, and a great deal of reflection about the nature of your inquiry. You most certainly want to present well-reasoned research that will illustrate the integrity of your study. Be sure to give careful thought to how you present the discussion, and, as always, remember to work from an outline. Your headings and subheadings in this chapter are contingent on your particular university's requirements. How well you present this chapter illustrates to the reader that you have carefully designed and produced a sound study based on the principles of qualitative research.

Quality Assessment Chapter Checklist

Introduction	✓ Do you restate the research purpose? ✓ Does the introduction describe the general organization of the chapter?
Research Sample	✓ Do you provide a comprehensive description of your research sample and the population from which it was drawn? ✓ Do you discuss and explain the research site (organization/program/institution)? ✓ Do you discuss in detail your sampling strategy/strategies, citing appropriate literature? ✓ Are the criteria for sampling selection stated and explained? ✓ Are the details and characteristics pertaining to the sample adequately discussed? ✓ Have you discussed issues of access and consent?
Information Needed	✓ Is the information that is needed to conduct the study clearly and specifically outlined? (This should include demographic, perceptual, and contextual information.) ✓ Are you clear how and from whom the necessary information will be obtained? ✓ Do you provide a logical connection between the type of information needed and the methods you have selected to obtain that information?
Research Design Overview	✓ Do you describe qualitative research as your chosen research paradigm, citing appropriate literature? ✓ Do you offer a convincing argument for choosing qualitative research? ✓ Do you provide a convincing argument for the particular qualitative tradition or genre (or combination of traditions) that you have chosen? ✓ Do you describe your chosen qualitative research methods including rationale for suitability regarding addressing the research questions? ✓ Have you cited appropriate methodological literature? ✓ Do you list all the steps entailed in carrying out data collection? ✓ Do you list all the steps entailed in carrying out data analysis? ✓ Are all your methodological steps reported in sufficient detail so that the study could be replicated? ✓ Do you include explanation of any field tests or pilot studies, including administration and description of findings (if appropriate)? ✓ Do you include a timeline? If so, have you described in chronological order each step taken in conducting the study? ✓ Are all charts and/or figures that you have included comprehensive and relevant?
Data Collection	✓ Are the data collection methods sufficiently described? The description of each instrument should relate to the function of the instrument in the study and what the instrument is intended to measure. ✓ Do you provide a rationale for the selection of instruments used? ✓ Have you provided a comprehensive literature review of the data collection methods used and included details regarding the strengths and limitations of each method? ✓ If an instrument was developed specifically for this study, have you described procedures involved in its development, validation, and administration? ✓ Do you describe how, when, where, and by whom data were collected? ✓ Are the data collection methods congruent with the problem being investigated and the specific qualitative tradition employed? ✓ Has triangulation of data collection methods been achieved?

(Continued)

(Continued)

Data Analysis and Synthesis	✓ Do you report on how you have managed and organized your data? ✓ Do you report in detail on how you coded and analyzed your data in order to report on the study's findings (Chapter 4)? ✓ Do you report in detail on how you analyzed and interpreted your findings (Chapter 5)? ✓ Are your methods of data analysis congruent with the principles of qualitative research? ✓ Are all themes and patterns adequately described? ✓ Are all charts and/or figures that you have included comprehensive and relevant?
Ethical Considerations	✓ Do you discuss all relevant ethical issues? ✓ Do you explain how you have addressed all relevant ethical issues? ✓ Do you include how you have satisfied IRB requirements?
Issues of Trustworthiness	✓ Do you articulate the criteria for evaluating trustworthiness in qualitative research, citing appropriate literature? ✓ Is all the terminology you include appropriate for qualitative research? ✓ Do you discuss how you have addressed issues of credibility and the various strategies you have employed? ✓ Do you discuss how you have addressed issues of dependability, and the strategies you have employed? ✓ Do you explain the issue of transferability in relation to your study?
Limitations and Delimitations	✓ Do you clearly delineate all limitations pertaining to your study and your means to address these? ✓ Do you articulate all appropriate and relevant delimitations pertaining to your study?
Summary	✓ Does your culminating summary integrate all the elements presented in this chapter? ✓ Do you include all key points? ✓ Is your summary comprehensive and focused?
And...	✓ Does the discussion illustrate that you have a good understanding of the assumptions and principles of qualitative research? ✓ Does the discussion have a logical flow? ✓ Are headings and subheadings used effectively to structure and present the discussion? ✓ Does the discussion in each section flow logically? ✓ Are transitions from one section of the chapter to another clear and logical? Have you made use of effective segues? ✓ Are all tables, figures, and appendices used effectively and appropriately? ✓ Do all tables and figures follow the format specified by your required style manual? ✓ Are columns and rows of each table labelled correctly? ✓ Does the title of each table and/or figure indicate exactly (clearly and concisely) what the table or figure is intended to represent? ✓ Have you checked for institutional and/or program-related differences regarding the content and structure of Chapter 3? ✓ Have you checked for institutional and/or program-related differences regarding the appropriate use of qualitative language and terminology? ✓ Is the writing throughout clear and readable? Refer to Chapter 4 "Guidelines for Academic Writing."

As emphasized throughout this book, writing a dissertation is not a linear process. Rather, it is an iterative and recursive one that requires much back and forth, reminder notes to yourself, and memos to change, revise, and update what you have already written. Chapter 3 is one of those chapters that must remain flexible and open to change right up to the very end. Frustration is inevitable, but don't despair! This is all part and parcel of managing and organizing the research and writing process.

Section II: Application

Now that we have reviewed and explained the essential elements required to conceptualize and systematically develop your methodology chapter, we are ready to see what an actual written-up third chapter of a dissertation would look like using the research problem and purpose previously identified. The application section that follows is a skeleton view of a methodology chapter. Were each section to be more completely and fully developed, as would be required in an actual dissertation, such a chapter would be more extensive. In addition, as emphasized throughout this book, there are many options with regard to qualitative research presentation, and requirements vary among institutions and programs. Therefore, as with other components of the dissertation, you will need to check with your advisor and/or department about the content and presentation of your study's methodology chapter.

CHAPTER 3 OF THE DISSERTATION

Methodology

Introduction

The purpose of this multicase study was to explore with a sample of doctoral candidates their perceptions of why they have not managed to complete their dissertations. The researchers believed that a better understanding of this phenomenon would allow educators to proceed from a more informed perspective in terms of design and facilitation of doctoral programs. In seeking to understand this phenomenon, the study addressed five research questions: (a) On completion of their course work, to what extent did participants perceive they were prepared to conduct research and write the dissertation? (b) What did participants perceive they needed to learn to complete their dissertation? (c) How did participants attempt to develop the knowledge, skills, and attitudes they perceived are necessary to complete the dissertation? (d) What factors did participants perceive might help them to complete the dissertation? (e) What factors did participants perceive have impeded and/or continue to impede their progress in working toward completing their dissertation?

This chapter describes the study's research methodology and includes discussions around the following areas: (a) rationale for research approach, (b) description of the research sample, (c) summary of information needed, (d) overview of research design, (e) methods of data collection, (f) analysis and synthesis of data, (g) ethical considerations, (h) issues of trustworthiness, and (i) limitations of the study. The chapter culminates with a brief concluding summary.

Rationale for Qualitative Research Design

Qualitative research is grounded in an essentially constructivist philosophical position, in the sense that it is concerned with how the complexities of the sociocultural world are experienced, interpreted, and understood in a particular context and at a particular point in time. The intent of qualitative research is to examine a social situation or interaction by allowing the researcher to enter the world of others and attempt to achieve a holistic rather than a reductionist understanding (Bogdan & Biklen, 2007; Locke et al., 2000; Maxwell, 2013; Merriam, 1998, 2009; Patton, 1990; Schram, 2003; Schwandt, 2000). Qualitative methodology implies an emphasis on discovery and description, and the objectives are generally focused on extracting and interpreting the meaning of experience (Bogdan & Biklen, 2007; Denzin & Lincoln, 2013a, 2013b, 2013c; Merriam, 1998, 2009). These objectives are contrasted with those of quantitative research, where the testing of hypotheses to establish facts and to designate and distinguish relationships between variables is usually the intent.

It was the researchers' contention that purely quantitative methods were unlikely to elicit the rich data necessary to address the proposed research purposes. In the researchers' view, the fundamental assumptions and key features that distinguish what it means to proceed from a qualitative stance fit well with this study. These features include (a) understanding the processes by which events and actions take place, (b) developing contextual understanding, (c) facilitating interactivity between researcher and participants, (d) adopting an interpretive stance, and (e) maintaining design flexibility.

Rationale for Case Study Methodology

Within the framework of a qualitative approach, the study was most suited for a case study design. As a form of research methodology, case study is an intensive description and analysis of a phenomenon, social unit, or system bounded by time or place (Creswell, 2013; Merriam, 1998; Miles & Huberman, 1994; Stake, 1995, 2000, 2001). As Merriam (1998) indicates, qualitative case study is an ideal design for understanding and interpreting educational phenomena. As she describes it,

> A case study design is employed to gain an in depth understanding of the situation and meaning for those involved. The interest is in process rather than outcomes, in context rather than a specific variable, in discovery rather than confirmation. Insights gleaned from case studies can directly influence policy, practice, and future research. (Merriam, 1998, p. 19)

The present research fit well with Merriam's criteria because it sought to better understand why certain people who complete the course work do not go on to complete the dissertation and hence do not graduate with a doctoral degree.

The Research Sample

A purposeful sampling procedure was used to select this study's sample. To yield the most information about the phenomenon under study, purposeful sampling is a method that is typical of case study methodology (Patton, 1990; Silverman, 2011, 2013; Silverman & Marvasti, 2008). The researchers sought to locate individuals at a variety of universities. Thus, a snowball sampling strategy, sometimes referred to as network or chain sampling (Miles & Huberman, 1994; Patton, 2015), was employed, whereby participants were asked to refer other individuals whom they knew to be ABD (all but dissertation). The criteria for selection of participants were as follows:

- All participants were enrolled in a doctoral program for at least 3 years.
- All participants completed the course work and passed the certification examination.

A delimiting time frame of 3 years was decided on by the researchers to ensure adequate experience in a doctoral program. Purposeful sampling allowed for sampling across various locations in the United States. The research sample included 20 individuals. Included in the sample were individuals from doctoral programs at nine universities, including Columbia University, Wayne State University, University of Massachusetts, University of Georgia, University of Southern California, University of Michigan, Rutgers University, Fordham University, and Northwestern University. Purposeful selection also was based on variation across certain distinguishing characteristics. Although participants were all ABD doctoral candidates, there were differences among them along the following parameters: length of time spent in doctoral program, university and discipline, gender, age, and occupation.

Information Needed to Conduct the Study

This multicase study focused on 20 doctoral candidates from nine universities located in different regions of the United States. In seeking to understand why these doctoral candidates have not obtained doctoral degrees, five research questions were explored to gather the information needed. The information needed to answer these research questions was determined by the conceptual framework and fell into three categories: (a) perceptual, (b) demographic, and (c) theoretical. This information included

- doctoral candidates' perceptions of what they needed to know and how they went about obtaining what they needed to conduct their research and complete their dissertations;
- demographic information pertaining to participants, including years in program, doctoral program concentration/discipline, age, gender, and ethnicity; and
- an ongoing review of the literature providing the theoretical grounding for the study.

Overview of Research Design

The following list summarizes the steps used to carry out this research. Following this list is a more in-depth discussion of each step.

1. Preceding the actual collection of data, a selected review of the literature was conducted to study the contributions of other researchers and writers in the broad areas of higher educational programs and adult learning theory.
2. Following the proposal defense, the researchers acquired approval from the IRB to proceed with the research. The IRB approval process involved outlining all procedures and processes needed to ensure adherence to standards put forth for the study of human subjects, including participants' confidentiality and informed consent.
3. Potential research participants were contacted by telephone, and those who agreed to participate were sent a questionnaire by mail. The survey was designed to collect demographic as well as perceptual data.
4. Semistructured, in-depth interviews were conducted with 20 ABD doctoral candidates in nine universities located across the United States.
5. Interview data responses were analyzed within and between groups of interviewees.
6. Critical incident instruments were given to participants at the end of each interview to check data collected through other means. Of the 20 participants, 12 responded.
7. A focus group was conducted with six ABDs who were drawn from the pool of participants identified for this study to cross-check data from that group with the data collected through interviews.

Literature Review

An ongoing and selective review of literature was conducted to inform this study. Two topics of literature were identified: higher education doctoral programs and adult learning theory. The focus of the review was to gain a better understanding of what prompted participants to enroll in doctoral programs, the requirements and challenges inherent in these programs, and the effect on participants and the means they took to meet the requirements and overcome the challenges they faced.

IRB Approval

Following the literature review, the researchers developed and successfully defended a proposal for this study that included the background/context, problem statement, purpose statement, and research questions outlined in Chapter 1; the literature review included in Chapter 2; and the proposed methodological approach as outlined in Chapter 3.

Data Collection Methods

The use of multiple methods and triangulation is critical in attempting to obtain an in-depth understanding of the phenomenon under study. This strategy adds rigor, breadth, and depth to the study and provides corroborative evidence of the data obtained (Creswell, 2013; Denzin & Lincoln, 2011). Therefore, this study employed a number of different data collection methods, including a survey, interviews, critical incident reports, and a focus group.

Phase I: Survey

Potential participants were contacted. Of those who were contacted to participate, three individuals declined. The 20 individuals who agreed to participate were sent a questionnaire by mail and were asked to return the completed forms by way of a self-addressed envelope. The questionnaire was designed to collect profile data and also asked participants their purposes for enrolling in a doctoral program. The survey appears as Appendix O.

An advantage of survey methodology is that it is relatively unobtrusive and relatively easily administered (Fink, 2013; Fowler, 2014). It must be acknowledged, however, that surveys can be of limited value for examining complex social relationships or intricate patterns of interaction. In keeping with the qualitative research tradition, the survey used in the present study included some open-ended questions that sought to tap into personal experiences and shed light on participants' perceptions. For the purposes of the present study, the survey had a distinct place in the study's methodological design and served as a useful complement or adjunct to other data collection methods.

Phase II: Interviews

The interview was selected as the primary method for data collection in this research. The interview method was felt to be of the most use in the study because it has the potential to elicit rich, thick descriptions. Further, it gave the researchers an opportunity to clarify statements and probe for additional information. Creswell (2013), Denzin and Lincoln (2013a, 2013b), and Marshall and Rossman (2015) state that a major benefit of collecting data through individual, in-depth interviews is that they offer the potential to capture a person's perspective of an event or experience.

The interview is a fundamental tool in qualitative research (Brinkmann & Kvale, 2015; Seidman, 2012). Brinkmann and Kvale (2015) describe the qualitative research interview as an "attempt to understand the world from the subject's point of view, to unfold the meaning of the subject's experiences, to uncover their lived world" (p. 1). As Patton (1990) similarly claims, "qualitative interviewing begins with the assumption that the perspective of others is meaningful, knowable, and able to be made explicit" (p. 278). The researchers' logic for using this data collection method was that a legitimate way to generate data is to interact with people (i.e., talk to and listen to them), thereby capturing the meaning of their experience in their own words.

Although interviews have certain strengths, there are various limitations associated with interviewing. First, not all people are equally cooperative, articulate, and perceptive. Second, interviews require researcher skill. Third, interviews are not neutral tools of data gathering; they are the result of the interaction between the interviewer and the interviewee and the context in which they take place (Fontana & Frey, 2003; Rubin & Rubin, 2012; Seidman, 2012).

Interview Schedule and Pilot Interviews. With guidance from their advisor, the researchers used the study's five research questions as the framework to develop the interview questions. Matrices were constructed to illustrate the relationship between this study's research questions and the interview questions as they were being developed. Three doctoral colleagues were then asked to review and provide feedback to the researchers. Their comments were incorporated, and the researchers resubmitted the schedule of questions to their advisor. With the advisor's approval, two pilot interviews were conducted by phone. The preliminary themes that emerged from the pilot interviews revolved around reasons that individuals enroll in doctoral programs and their learning during the process. From the pilot interviews, a series of open-ended questions was developed, which enabled the researchers to allow new directions to emerge during the interview. The final interview schedule is included as Appendix I.

Interview Process. The researcher sent individual e-mails to prospective participants describing the purpose of the study, inviting their participation, and requesting a convenient date and time for a telephone interview. The researcher sent confirming e-mails to the 20 individuals who agreed to be interviewed. The interviews took place between August and October 2006. Before each interview commenced, the interviewee was asked to review and sign a university consent form required for participation in this study (see Appendix N). All interviews were conducted telephonically and were tape-recorded in their entirety. At the end of each interview, the interviewee was asked to complete and return by e-mail the critical incident instrument, which had been prepared by the researchers. On completion of the interview, the audiotape was transcribed verbatim.

Phase III: Critical Incidents

The researchers selected critical incident instruments with the intention of corroborating interview data and further, to allow the uncovering of perceptions that might not have been revealed through the interviews. Critical incident reports, a data collection method first formulated by Flanagan (1954), are useful because qualitative research methodology emphasizes process and is based on a descriptive and inductive approach to data collection (Bogdan & Biklen, 2007). Of particular importance is that written critical incident reports probe assumptions, allowing time for reflection (Brookfield, 1991; Marshall & Rossman, 2015).

Although there is support in the literature for the use of the critical incident as an effective technique for enhancing data collection, with several authors noting its advantages (Bogdan & Biklen, 2007; Brookfield, 1991; Flanagan, 1954), the researchers were mindful of Brookfield's repeated caution that critical incidents cannot be the sole technique for collecting data. Critical incidents are too abbreviated to provide the rich descriptions that can be obtained in interviews and observations. A further concern regarding the use of critical incident reports has to do with the accuracy of data because this technique relies solely on the respondents' recall. A related concern is that, although reporting information that respondents perceive is important, the researcher may fail to report salient incremental data and the information, as such, may be incomplete.

The critical incident instrument was developed by the researchers and further refined by their advisor. The instrument was field tested in conjunction with the pilot interviews. The results of the field test called for minor revisions, and these were incorporated into a final critical incident form/instrument. This instrument is included as Appendix P. The researchers subsequently gave the critical incident instrument to the 20 participants in this study at the end of each interview. The instrument asked respondents to think about a specific time when they felt ill prepared to conduct some part of the dissertation process. Specifically, participants were asked to briefly describe the incident, indicating who was involved, what they learned, and how they thought their learning would influence how they would handle similar situations in the future. Participants were given a self-addressed envelope and were requested at the end of the interview to return completed critical incidents to the researchers as soon as possible. The researchers received 12 completed critical incidents from among the 20 participants. Although the researchers had hoped for a greater response, when analyzed, the returned critical incidents served as a "validity check" on some aspects of the data uncovered in the interviews.

Phase IV: Focus Group

Focus groups, or group interviews, possess elements of both participant observation and individual interviews, while also maintaining their own uniqueness as a distinctive research method (Liamputtong, 2011). A focus group is essentially a group discussion focused on a single theme (Kreuger & Casey, 2015; Stewart & Shamdasani, 2015). The goal is to create a candid conversation that addresses, in depth, the selected topic. The underlying assumption of focus groups is that, within a permissive atmosphere that fosters a range of opinions, a more complete and revealing understanding of the issues will be obtained. Focus groups are planned and structured, but are also flexible tools (Liamputtong, 2011). Kreuger and Casey (2015) list various uses of focus groups, many of which fit well with this study's purpose. These are to (a) elicit a range of feelings, opinions, and ideas; (b) understand differences in perspectives; (c) uncover and provide insight into specific factors that influence opinions; and (d) seek ideas that emerge from the group.

It must be acknowledged that focus groups, while serving a useful function, are not without disadvantages. Among these disadvantages is groupthink as a possible outcome (Fontana & Frey, 2003). Furthermore, logistical difficulties might arise from the need to manage conversation while attempting to extract data, thus requiring strong facilitation skills.

One 1½-hour formative focus group was convened with six participants who were not part of the study sample. These participants were purposefully selected based on the established criteria. The purpose of this focus group interview was twofold: (a) to augment the information obtained and (b) to provide additional data to ensure trustworthiness and credibility. In the open-ended format that was used, the researchers asked the group to explore two issues. First, what did they feel helped them the most in the research process? Second, what challenges and obstacles did they encounter that impeded their progress?

The researchers contacted the 20 study participants seeking their interest in joining a focus group discussion. The study participants were advised of the purpose and were told that the discussion would be held over an Internet conference call system and would be audiotaped. Eleven of the 20 participants responded that they would be willing to join the discussion, and the first 6 respondents were selected. A general e-mail was sent by the researchers thanking the participants who had expressed interest. Following that, the researchers contacted each of the focus group members to schedule a convenient time to hold the discussion.

Methods for Data Analysis and Synthesis

The challenge throughout data collection and analysis was to make sense of large amounts of data, reduce the volume of information, identify significant patterns, and construct a framework. In this regard, Merriam (1998, 2009) cautions researchers to make data analysis and data collection a simultaneous activity to avoid the risk of repetitious, unfocused, and overwhelming data.

The formal process of data analysis began by assigning alphanumeric codes according to the categories and descriptors of the study's conceptual framework. The researchers prepared large flip chart sheets. These sheets were color coded and taped on the wall. Each sheet identified the descriptors under the respective categories of the conceptual frame-work. As the process of coding the transcripts proceeded, new flip chart sheets were pre-pared to capture other themes as they emerged.

Before cutting and pasting coded participant quotations, the researchers shared samples of coded interviews with two colleagues. Discussion with both colleagues confirmed the research-ers' designations. The researchers also prepared written narratives on each of the sheets after all the data had been assigned. These narratives were helpful in cross-checking the data and served as a secondary analysis.

As a final step, to see whether there were any variables that would account for similari-ties or differences among participants, the researchers tested the coded data on the sheets against the frequency charts prepared for each finding and the numerically coded profile data on the participants. This step aided the researchers in their cross-case analysis of the data, which is described more fully later.

The coding process fragments the interview into separate categories, forcing one to look at each detail, whereas synthesis involves piecing these fragments together to reconstruct a holistic and integrated explanation. Overall, the researchers' approach was to come up with a number of clusters, patterns, or themes that were linked together, either similarly or diver-gently, and that collectively described or analyzed the research arena. Toward this end, the researchers essentially followed a three-layered process in thinking about the data. First, they examined and compared threads and patterns within categories. Second, they compared connecting threads and patterns across categories. Third, the current work was situated with respect to prior research and was compared and contrasted with issues that had been raised by the broader literature. These three layers were not separate, but were interlocked and iterative throughout the synthesizing process.

Based on analysis and synthesis, the researchers were able to move forward and think about the broader implications of this research. Toward this end, they formulated several conclusions and developed various practical and research-related recommendations.

Ethical Considerations

In any research study, ethical issues relating to protection of the participants are of vital concern (Marshall & Rossman, 2015; Merriam, 1998, 2009; Pring, 2000; Schram, 2003). A social science researcher is responsible for both informing and protecting respondents. The research process involves enlisting voluntary cooperation, and it is a basic premise that par-ticipants are informed about the study's purpose. The central issue with respect to protecting participants is the ways in which the information is treated. Although it was anticipated that no serious ethical threats were posed to any of the participants or their well-being, this study employed various safeguards to ensure the protection and rights of participants.

First, informed consent remained a priority throughout the study. Written consent to voluntarily proceed with the study was received from each participant. Second, participants' rights and interests were considered of primary importance when choices were made regarding the reporting and dissemination of data. The researchers were committed to keeping the names and/or other significant identity characteristics of the sample organizations confidential. Cautionary measures were taken to secure the storage of research-related records and data, and nobody other than the researchers had access to this material.

Issues of Trustworthiness

In qualitative research, trustworthiness features consist of any efforts by the researcher to address the more traditional quantitative issues of validity (the degree to which something measures what it purports to measure) and reliability (the consistency with which it measures it over time). In seeking to establish the trustworthiness of a qualitative study, Lincoln and Guba (2000) use the terms *credibility, dependability, confirmability,* and *transferability,* arguing that the trustworthiness of qualitative research should be assessed differently from quantitative research. Regardless of the terminology used, qualitative researchers must continue to seek to control for potential biases that might be present throughout the design, implementation, and analysis of the study.

Credibility

The criterion of credibility (or validity) suggests whether the findings are accurate and credible from the standpoint of the researcher, the participants, and the reader. This criterion becomes a key component of the research design (Creswell, 2014; Marshall & Rossman, 2015; Maxwell, 2013; Merriam, 1998, 2009; Miles & Huberman, 1994; Miles, Huberman, & Saldana, 2014). Seeking not to *verify* conclusions, but rather to *test the validity* of conclusions reached, entails a concern with both methodological and interpretive validity (Mason, 1996).

Methodological validity involves asking how well matched the logic of the method is to the kinds of research questions that are being posed and the kind of explanation that the researcher is attempting to develop. Dealing with this type of validity involves consideration of the interrelationship between the research design components—the study's purpose, conceptual framework, research questions, and methods. Interpretative validity involves asking how valid the data analysis is and the interpretation on which it is based. Although this step is somewhat dependent on methodological validity, it goes further in that it directs attention to the quality and rigor with which the researcher interprets and analyzes data in relation to the research design (Mason, 1996).

To enhance the methodological validity of the study, the researchers triangulated data sources as well as data collection methods. Gathering data from multiple sources and by multiplemethods yields a fuller and richer picture of the phenomenon under review. To enhance the interpretive validity of this study, the researchers employed various strategies. First, they clarified their assumptions up front, and the steps through which interpretations were made also were charted through journal writing. Second, the researchers used various participatory and collaborative modes of research, including the search for discrepant evidence and peer review, which has been discussed at length by Lincoln and Guba (2000). This entails looking for variation in the understanding of the phenomenon and seeking instances that might challenge the researcher's expectations or emergent findings. Reviewing and discussing findings with professional colleagues was a further way of ensuring that the reality of the participants was adequately reflected in the findings.

Dependability

Reliability in the traditional sense refers to the extent that research findings can be replicated by other similar studies. Qualitative research usually does not cover enough of an expanse of subjects and experiences to provide a reasonable degree of reliability. As argued by Lincoln and Guba (2000), the more important question becomes one of whether the findings are consistent and dependable with the data collected. As the researchers understood it, in qualitative research the goal is not to eliminate inconsistencies but to ensure that the researcher understands when they occur. Thus, it becomes incumbent on the researcher to document her procedures and demonstrate that coding schemes and categories have been used consistently.

Toward this end, inter-rater reliability (Miles & Huberman, 1994) was established by asking colleagues to code several interviews. Although coding was generally found to be consistent, there were certain instances where the raters made some inferences that could not be fully supported by the data. In these cases, the researchers reviewed the data and reconciled differences in interpretations. In addition, the researchers maintained an audit trail (Lincoln & Guba, 1985) that chronicled the evolution of their thinking and documented the rationale for all choices and decisions made during the research process. This trail, which Merriam (1998) describes as offering "transparency of method," depended on the researchers keeping a journal as well as a record of memos that included detailed accounts of how all the data were analyzed and interpreted.

Confirmability

The concept of *confirmability* corresponds to the notion of objectivity in quantitative research. The implication is that the findings are the result of the research, rather than an outcome of the biases and subjectivity of the researcher. To achieve this end, a researcher needs to identify and uncover the decision trail for public judgment. Although qualitative researchers realize the futility of attempting to achieve objectivity, they must nevertheless be reflexive and illustrate how their data can be traced back to its origins. As such, the audit trail (Lincoln & Guba, 2000) used to demonstrate dependability, including ongoing reflection by way of journaling and memo, as well as a record of field notes and transcripts, serves to offer the reader an opportunity to assess the findings of this study.

Transferability

Although generalizability is not the intended goal of this study, what was addressed was the issue of *transferability* (Lincoln & Guba, 2000)—that is, the ways in which the reader determines whether and to what extent this particular phenomenon in this particular context can transfer to another particular context. With regard to transferability, Patton (1990) promotes thinking of "context-bound extrapolations" (p. 491), which he defines as "speculations on the likely applicability of findings to other situations under similar, but not identical, conditions" (p. 489). Toward this end, the researchers attempted to address the issue of transferability by way of thick, rich description of the participants and the context. Depth, richness, and detailed description provide the basis for a qualitative account's claim to relevance in some broader context (Schram, 2003).

Limitations of the Study

This study contains certain limiting conditions, some of which are related to the common critiques of qualitative research methodology in general and some of which are inherent in this study's research design. Careful thought has been given to ways of accounting for these limitations and to ways of minimizing their impact. Unique features of qualitative research methodology present potential limitations in its usage.

Because analysis ultimately rests with the thinking and choices of the researcher, qualitative studies in general are limited by researcher subjectivity. Therefore, an overriding concern is that of researcher bias, framing as it does assumptions, interests, perceptions, and needs. One of the key limitations of this study is the issue of subjectivity and potential bias regarding the researchers' own participation in a doctoral program first as students and currently as faculty members.

A related limitation was that interviewees may have had difficulty adjusting to the researchers taking on the role of interviewers, a phenomenon referred to by Maxwell (2013) as *participant reactivity.* Because a few of the participants knew the researchers, their responses may have been influenced or affected. They may have tried overly hard to cooperate with the researchers by offering them the responses they perceived the researchers were seeking or might be helpful to them. Alternatively, because of familiarity with the researchers, these few participants might have been guarded and therefore less candid in their responses.

Recognizing these limitations, the researchers took the following measures. First, they acknowledged their research agenda and stated their assumptions up front. Coding schemes were scrutinized by advisors and through peer review, as were coded documents and transcripts. To reduce the limitation of potential bias during data analysis, the researchers removed all participant names and coded all interview transcripts blindly so as not to associate any material or data with any particular individual. To address the problem of participant reactivity, the researchers continued to reflect on how and in what ways they might be influencing participants. Furthermore, they made a conscious attempt to create an environment that was conducive to honest and open dialogue. Experience as interviewers, as well as prior research experience, was helpful in this regard.

Aside from issues pertaining to bias and reactivity, a further major limitation of this study was that the research sample was restricted. Therefore, a critique of this research might be the limited possibility of generalizing this study to other groups and other programs. Although generalizability was not the intended goal of this study, what the researchers addressed is the issue of transferability (Lincoln & Guba, 2000). By way of thick, rich description, as well as detailed information regarding the context and background of the study, it was anticipated that knowledge could be assessed for its applicability and applied appropriately in other contexts.

Chapter Summary

In summary, this chapter provided a detailed description of this study's research methodology. Qualitative case study methodology was employed to illustrate the phenomenon of why some people who complete all the doctoral course work do not go on to complete the dissertation, never obtain the doctoral degree, and hence remain ABD. The participant sample was made up of 20 purposefully selected individuals. Three data collection methods were employed, including individual interviews, critical incidents, and a focus group. The data were reviewed against literature as well as emergent themes. Credibility and dependability were accounted for through various strategies, including source and method triangulation.

A review of the literature was conducted to devise a conceptual framework for the design and analysis of the study. A process analysis enabled the key themes from the findings to be identified. Through a comparison with the literature, interpretations and conclusions were drawn, and recommendations were offered for both educational practice and further research. The intent was that this study would make a contribution to the understanding of doctoral students, current and future, with regard to their completing a dissertation. In addition, it is hoped that this study will be of value to those educators who are responsible for doctoral programs.

Annotated Bibliography

Brinkmann, S., & Kvale, S. (2015). *Interviews: Learning the craft of qualitative research interviewing* (4th ed.). Thousand Oaks, CA: Sage.

Interviewing is an essential tool in the repertoire of any qualitative researcher, yet the "hows" and "whys" of the interview process are not always easily understood. Geared for researchers and graduate students in the social sciences, this book does a good job of explaining the theoretical underpinnings and the practical aspects of the interview process. After examining the role of the interviewer in the research process, the authors consider some of the key epistemological, practical, and ethical issues involved with interviewing. They then take the reader through what they call "the seven stages of the interview investigation," from designing a study to writing it up. Included are discussions around cutting-edge developments in qualitative interviewing, the "craft" of interviewing, and linguistic modes of interview analysis. Practical and conceptual assignments as well as "toolboxes" provide a means to dig deeper into the material gleaned from interviews, and thereby achieve a more meaningful level of understanding. Particularly useful are the chapters on interview transcript analysis (Chapters 11–14); trustworthiness of interview knowledge, including the social construction of validity (Chapter 15); and ways of reporting interview knowledge (Chapter 16). The text includes useful discussion of more recent developments in qualitative interviewing, including narrative, discursive and conversational analyses.

Creswell, J. W. (2013). *Qualitative inquiry and research design: Choosing among five traditions* (3rd ed.). Thousand Oaks, CA: Sage.

Creswell uses the metaphor of a "circle of interrelated activities" to describe a process of engaging in activities that include but go beyond collecting data. In Chapter 7, he introduces each data collection activity, including locating a site, gaining access, and establishing rapport; purposeful sampling strategies to obtain a research sample; collecting different forms of data by way of different methods (interviews, observation, document review, and audiovisual material); recording procedures; exploring field issues; and storing data. Furthermore, he explores how each of these activities varies by genre or tradition of inquiry (narrative research, phenomenology, grounded theory, ethnography, and case study). In Chapter 8, Creswell discusses generally, as well as more specifically for each of the five traditions, the different procedures for data analysis and ideas regarding the representation of data in both narrative and visual form. Creswell summarizes three general approaches to analysis, and presents a data analysis spiral that he uses as a conceptualization for exploring each of the five traditions of inquiry. In addition, this author provides discussion around the use of software analysis for qualitative research, introducing four software programs, including the features of each program and templates for coding data within each of the five qualitative traditions. Chapter 10 discusses the intricacies involved in the issue of trustworthiness: establishing multiple standards for quality validation and evaluation.

Denzin, N. K., & Lincoln, Y. S. (2013b). (Eds.). *Collecting and interpreting qualitative materials* (4th ed.). Thousand Oaks, CA: Sage.

This is Volume III of the three-volume paperback versions of *The Sage Handbook of Qualitative Research*, fourth edition. The comprehensive collection of chapters, written by "experts" in the field, is geared for graduate students in the social sciences and humanities, and covers a variety of qualitative methodological issues related to gathering, analyzing, and interpreting empirical materials. Unlike most of the other books recommended in this section's annotated bibliography, this book is not a "how-to" handbook; rather, it uncovers and examines the philosophical and political implications of qualitative research methodology, addressing issues of equity and social justice. Part I includes discussion around methods of empirical data collection, including interviews, observation, documents and material culture, focus groups, critical arts-based inquiry, oral history, visual methodologies, and autoethnographic methods. The chapters in Part II discuss interpretive adequacy, forms of representation, post-qualitative inquiry, the new information technologies and research, the politics of evidence, writing, and evaluation practices. Also included is a chapter on qualitative research and technology. The book presents a glossary of terms that offers students and researchers a ready resource to help decode the language of qualitative research, as well as a list of recommended readings that provide additional sources on specific topic areas related to one's research.

Dominice, P. (2000). *Learning from our lives: Using educational biographies with adults.* San Francisco: Jossey-Bass.

The life-history method of qualitative research is a rich adjunct to other more traditional empirical methods. Storytelling is a natural part of the human experience, and the adaptation of this essentially human process as a legitimated research method is relatively new. A long-established technique in anthropological research, this method of collecting data is becoming more widely used in the development of oral and local history within the educational, health, and social sciences. There is currently much emphasis on helping individuals find their voice, encouraging diversity, and using narratives to understand learner perspectives. *Learning From Our Lives* richly addresses these issues. This is the first professional guide to using educational biography with adult learners. It offers engaging anecdotes and narratives, insightful interpretations and analyses, and numerous examples of different biographical approaches.

Fink, A. (2013). *How to conduct surveys: A step-by-step guide.* Thousand Oaks, CA: Sage.

This book guides readers through the process of developing their own rigorous surveys and evaluating the credibility thereof, as well as of surveys created by others. Practical guidance centers on choosing and designing the appropriate type of survey, writing survey questions and responses, formatting the survey, sampling strategies for deciding on the characteristics and numbers of respondents to include and how often they should be surveyed, and data analytic methods. Throughout, the author emphasizes the need for careful planning and testing of surveys. Included is discussion around issues pertaining to online and Internet surveys, ways of thinking about reliability and validity, and novel methods of presenting survey findings. The book provides relevant websites and survey reports. Throughout the book are sections called "Making a Decision," the purpose of which is to assist the reader to make informed choices through weighing up advantages and disadvantages at each stage of the process.

Hesse-Biber, S. N., & Leavy, P. (2011). *The practice of qualitative research* (2nd ed.). Thousand Oaks, CA: Sage.

This book is a problem-centric approach to qualitative research, and is presented essentially as a real-world "practice model." The first chapter offers an overview of the dimensions of qualitative research. Subsequent chapters offer a step-by-step approach to designing a qualitative or mixed methods research study, collecting and interpreting data, and writing up findings. Discussions around interviews, focus groups, and sampling are particularly instructive. Ethnographic, case study, and mixed methods research is discussed in comprehensive detail. A comprehensive review of exemplary research studies is included throughout and is designed to engage the reader in hands-on research practice. Ethical considerations and research tips for guiding students through the research process are included in each chapter. The book includes sections on concept mapping, cross-cultural focus groups, and use of computer-assisted technologies for analyzing qualitative data. Glossaries, reflective questions, and access to additional resources are included throughout. A final chapter raises questions and issues regarding future directions of qualitative research including kinds of research, emergent methods and tools, and ethical considerations.

Kim, J. (2015). *Understanding narrative inquiry: The crafting and analysis of stories as research.* Thousand Oaks, CA: Sage.

This comprehensive, thought-provoking review of narrative inquiry in the social and human sciences guides readers through the entire narrative inquiry process—from locating narrative inquiry in the interdisciplinary context, through the philosophical and theoretical underpinnings, to narrative research design, data collection (excavating stories), data analysis and interpretation, and theorizing narrative meaning. Six extracts from exemplary studies, together with questions for discussion, are provided to show how to put theory into practice. Rich in stories from the author's own research endeavors and incorporating chapter-opening vignettes that illustrate a graduate student's research dilemma, the book not only accompanies readers through the complex process of narrative inquiry with ample examples, but also helps raise their consciousness about what it means to be a qualitative researcher and a narrative inquirer in particular. This text offers the historical and philosophical context for narrative research, ample methodological instruction, and robust examples, making this a truly comprehensive text. Particularly impressive is the attention to the different genres of narrative including arts-based and visual-based. Extremely well researched and referenced, this text addresses sophisticated theoretical underpinnings of narrative research, including the rationales and justifications for engaging in both storytelling and the analysis of stories. It also explores a wide variety of helpful strategies for interviewing, fieldwork, and writing. At the same time, it grounds and humanizes its sophisticated scholarship through an inviting, conversational style replete with personal anecdotes, while its many concrete examples of research practice in action further enhances its usefulness for those interested in this rapidly maturing inquiry approach.

Liamputtong, P. (2011). *Focus group methodology: Principles and practice.* Thousand Oaks, CA: Sage.

This book is pertinent to postgraduate students, and offers a basic understanding of how to adopt this methodology to suit the exigencies and circumstances in particular social and cultural settings. The text begins by offering the history and development of the use of focus groups in the health and social sciences, ethical considerations, and key critiques of focus group methodology. The author then proceeds to lead readers through the entire process of designing a focus group study, by providing clear practical advice regarding conducting interviews to managing, analyzing, and making sense of focus group data, and presenting findings. Included too are discussions on the use of cross-cultural and virtual focus groups. Case studies, examples, tutorial activities, and sources for further reading are included throughout.

Madden, R. (2011). *Being ethnographic: A guide to the theory and practice of ethnography*. Thousand Oaks, CA: Sage.

Full of practical "how to" tips for applying theoretical methods, this book also provides anecdotal evidence and advice for new and experienced researchers on how to engage with their own participation in the field, that is, "being ethnographic." The text clearly sets out the important definitions, methods, and applications of field research while reinforcing the infinite variability of the human subject and addressing the challenges presented by ethnographers' own passions, intellectual interests, biases, and ideologies. Classic and personal real-world case studies are used by the author to introduce new researchers to the reality of applying ethnographic theory and practice in the field. Topics include talking to people (negotiations, conversations, and interviews); being with people (participation); looking at people (observations and images); description (writing "down" field notes); analysis to interpretation (writing "out" data); and interpretation to story (writing "up" ethnography). The book is excellent for students new to the field as concepts such as reflexivity, ethics, and research relationships are explored and executed in detail. The book reflects critical engagement with the analysis of ethnographic text discussions around how to code ethnographic transcripts and generate themes, which is often a methodological challenge, and also addresses the challenges of writing notes in the field. Clear, engaging, and informative, this book provides comprehensive guidelines as well as practical tools and study aids for those engaged in ethnographic research.

Marshall, C., & Rossman, G. B. (2015). *Designing qualitative research* (6th ed.). Thousand Oaks, CA: Sage.

This text addresses the complexity and flexibility of qualitative research, and offers comprehensive instruction regarding the challenges involved in the design of a sound qualitative study. Chapter 6 offers useful guidelines regarding the various primary data collection methods including observation, in-depth interviews, life history, narrative inquiry and digital storytelling, document and historical review, and objects and artifacts of material cultures. In Chapter 7 the authors provide stimulating discussion around secondary and specialized methods of data collection and combinations of methods, among them interaction analysis, multimodal approaches, computer applications, and Internet technologies. The focus is on how to design a data collection strategy by way of thoughtfully combining methods so that they build on and complement one another. Chapter 8 deals with recording, managing, analyzing, and interpreting data. This chapter deals with defending the value and logic of qualitative research, and offers some useful insights and background reading around issues of trustworthiness and ethics in qualitative inquiry. The book also includes thoughtful discussion around dealing with time, resources, and political stressors inherent in the research process. Particularly useful are the exhaustive and well-organized bibliographies, lists of key concepts, and notes found at the end of each of these chapters.

McNiff, J. (2014). *Writing and doing action research*. Thousand Oaks, CA: Sage.

This cutting edge text provides a comprehensive and user-friendly guide to the practical aspects of action research methodology and writing for dissemination and publication, specifically at the doctoral level. The author provides guidelines regarding how to carry out an action research project, present findings in the dissertation, and write up the research with an eye to informing policy. In addition there are guidelines for demonstrating the quality of the research and the writing. The author outlines the principles, practices, and methods of action research and explains how to communicate understandings of its nature and uses through text. Not only is this a how-to book, but also it shows what action research means to different people in different research settings and tries to illustrate how all aspects of research and writing can be interwoven into a seamless communicative whole where each informs and strengthens the other. The author claims to be especially interested in the politics of writing, how writing can be used intellectually as a means of rethinking one's ideas and politically as a means of self-empowerment. Included throughout are excerpts taken from action research projects in a wide range of settings and presents exercises to help students develop successful written accounts of their research process. McNiff is one of the leading experts in practitioner research, and this text is an invaluable resource for those contemplating an action research dissertation.

Merriam, S. B. (2009). *Qualitative research: A guide to design and implementation.* San Francisco: Jossey-Bass.

The primary focus of this book is on the characteristics of qualitative research, with applications to case study as a primary emphasis. A key focus is on choice of qualitative research design that is most relevant to one's field of practice. Part I provides the conceptual foundation and lays out some of the choices and decisions involved in conducting a qualitative study including design and sample selection. Part II consists of three chapters that are devoted to data collection techniques: These chapters include how to record and evaluate interview data, how to conduct observations and record observation data in the form of field notes, and the use of documents (including written records, visual data, and artifacts), illustrating inherent strengths and limitations. The application of all three methods of data collection are explained in detail with regard to case study methodology. Chapter 9 of Part III deals with issues of trustworthiness and research ethics likely to arise in qualitative research. The appendix of this book presents a useful template for what goes into a methodology chapter of a qualitative proposal and/or dissertation.

Mertler, C. A. (2012). *Action research: Improving schools and empowering educators* (3rd ed.). Thousand Oaks, CA: Sage.

This is a comprehensive and practical guide to action research for the practicing educator. The text introduces the process of conducting one's own action research project, providing educators with the necessary knowledge and skills to begin thinking about an action research design as well as meaningful and impactful ways of communicating research findings to relevant stakeholders and interested parties. Included are various examples of action research with careful attention to research methods and procedures, coverage of research ethics, templates of complete action research reports, recommendations regarding additional literature and research, and study tools including PowerPoint slides, quizzes, and online links. A unique section encourages educators to develop their own action research communities with a focus on the importance of sharing, reflecting, and dialogue. The book's broad, balanced coverage makes it an ideal resource for those in the educational field interested in action research as a participatory and collaborative approach toward inquiry, including teachers, administrators, lay leaders, counselors, and intervention specialists.

Patton, M. Q. (2015). *Qualitative research and evaluation methods* (4th ed.). Thousand Oaks, CA: Sage.

Patton's classic book brings together theory and practice, offering many useful strategies for designing and conducting qualitative studies. The text engages the multiple philosophical and historical trajectories within a variety of qualitative research traditions while integrating this discussion with the practice of research design, fieldwork strategies, and data analysis. The text illuminates all aspects of qualitative inquiry through examples, stories, and cartoons; summarizing and synthesizing exhibits; and a wide range of highlight sections/sidebars that elaborate on important and emergent issues. Full case studies are included to illustrate extended research and evaluation examples. In addition, each chapter features an extended "rumination" about a core issue of persistent debate and controversy. The rich variety of examples serves to clarify and deepen understanding of the qualitative research process in its many facets. Especially useful are the sections on the defining characteristics of qualitative research, the variety of qualitative research traditions, sampling procedures, methods and techniques of data collection (there are detailed and thorough chapters dealing with observation methods, interviews, and other creative modes of data collection), data analysis and interpretation (including computer-assisted analysis), ethical issues, and criteria for enhancing credibility and addressing transferability. Patton is one of the forebears of qualitative research. This often-quoted book set the standards for the field in the 1980s and 1990s. Recently revised, it brings readers up to date with the variety of current perspectives about (as well as the variety within) qualitative inquiry. In addition, the book includes a student study site with access to full text Sage journal articles that have been selected for each chapter.

Ritchie, J., Lewis, J., Nichols, C., & Ormston, R. (2014). (Eds.). *Qualitative research practice: A guide for social science students and researchers.* Thousand Oaks, CA: Sage.

Written by a team of leading researchers, this edited volume guides students through the process of qualitative research from beginning to end, through design, sampling, data collection, analysis, and reporting. This is a practical account of how to carry out qualitative research that recognizes a range of current approaches and applications. Chapter 3 deals with design issues and includes selection of data collection methods based on chosen research topic and research questions. Chapter 4 deals with ethical considerations in qualitative research and includes guidelines and codes for ethical practice. The chapter discusses key issues such as undue intrusion, informed consent, confidentiality, enabling participation, and protecting researchers from adverse consequences. Chapter 5 discusses the design and selection of samples, including strategies (theoretical, convenience, and purposive sampling), key features of qualitative sampling, and implementation of sample design. Chapters 7 through 9 bring to the fore the complexity of data collection, and the methods most commonly used, namely, in-depth interviews, focus groups, and observation. Each of these methods is explored in detail, and the emphasis is on practical application. This book is an ideal guide for both researchers and practitioners faced with the challenges of conducting qualitative research in both applied and theoretical settings in complex real-life contexts.

Seidman, I. (2012). *Interviewing as qualitative research: A guide for researchers in education and the social sciences* (4th ed.). New York: Teachers College Press.

Most qualitative research employs interviewing as a primary method of data collection. This resource provides clear, step-by-step guidance for new and experienced interviewers to help develop, shape, and reflect on interviewing as a qualitative research method. While proposing a phenomenological approach to in-depth interviewing, the author includes principles and methods that can be adapted to a range of interviewing approaches. Using concrete examples of interviewing techniques to illustrate the issues under discussion, this text helps readers understand the complexities of interviewing and its connections to broader issues of qualitative research. The text provides an introduction to the IRB process in its historical context, including an expanded discussion of informed consent and its inherent complexities. Special attention is paid to the rights of participants in interview research one word as those rights interact with ethical issues. Especially useful are the guidelines for managing, reducing, analyzing, and interpreting interview data. Suggestions are provided regarding transcription and the different ways in which interview data can be displayed. This latest edition has been expanded to include clarification of important phenomenological assumptions that underlie the interviewing approach presented in the book (Chapter 2), discussion around long-distance interviewing and its implications for the relationship between interviewers and participants (Chapter 7), discussion related to the pros and cons of computer-assisted qualitative data analysis software (Chapter 8), and ethics (Chapter 9). References and suggestions for additional reading offer a deeper consideration of methodological, ethical, and philosophical issues.

Stake, R. E. (1995). *The art of case study research*. Thousand Oaks, CA: Sage.

This classic text is a concise and very readable guide to case study methodology. Unique in his approach and style, Stake draws from naturalistic, holistic, ethnographic, phenomeno-logical, and biographic methods to present a disciplined, qualitative exploration of case study methods. In his exploration, Stake uses and annotates an actual case to demonstrate how to address some of the major issues involved in case study research, including how to select the case (or cases) that will maximize learning, how to generalize what is learned from one case to another, and how to interpret what is learned from a case study. Uniquely, this book legitimizes direct interpretation as a case research method. It covers such topics as the differences between quantitative and qualitative approaches to case study, data gathering methods and triangulation of methods, analyzing qualitative data (coding, sorting, and pattern analysis), the roles of the researcher, and ways of reporting a case study. Also provided are end-of-chapter "workshops" that help students focus on new concepts. This text contains a useful bibliography of references and a glossary index. Of particular interest are Chapter 6, which covers the researcher with regard to the researcher as teacher, evaluator, advocate, and more; Chapter 7, which addresses research validity in qualitative research in connection with triangulation and presents triangu-lation protocols as one solution to increasing the validity of case studies; and Chapter 8, which provides the reader with useful ways in which to organize and report case findings. Because of its engaging style, wellspring of examples, suggestions, and practical tips, this book is well suited to researchers seeking to more fully understand the case study approach as perceived by one of the seminal leaders in case study work. This text can also serve as a very short introductory manual to qualitative research in general.

Urquhart, C. (2013). *Grounded theory for qualitative research: A practical guide*. Thousand Oaks, CA: Sage.

This book provides an excellent introduction for social science post-graduate students wanting to know more about the "how to" of grounded theory research. Clearly written, this book cen-ters on three major strands: The first strand (Chapters 1 and 2) traces the historical development and intellectual foundations of grounded theory and examines how this tradition of qualitative research is ever-evolving and transforming so that it remains relevant for current contexts. The second strand (Chapters 3, 4, 5, and 6) provides an overview of the principles involved in grounded theory, including the processes associated with coding and conceptualization in grounded theory. What is most useful about this text is that it introduces the reader to the practicalities of research design, coding, and theory building. The third strand (Chapters 7, 8, and 9) addresses issues of scaling up emergent theory, writing up and presenting the study, and revisiting the strengths of this ever-emergent research tradition. Overall, the book provides the tools and insights to tackle key questions: What is grounded theory? How does one code and theorize using grounded theory? How does one write up a grounded theory study? The concluding chapter deals with contributions of grounded theory as a qualitative research approach and future directions. Each chapter con-cludes with summary, exercises, web resources, further reading suggestions, and frequently asked questions. It is the book's practical application that is most appealing.

Yin, R. K. (2014). *Case study research: Design and methods* (5th ed.). Thousand Oaks, CA: Sage.

This landmark text on case study methodology, revised and updated from the original publi-cation, offers comprehensive coverage of case study as a rigorous research method and how it is applied in practice. At the outset, the author provides an overall graphic of the entire case study research process, which outlines each step in the process. In each of the succeeding chapters, each step is clearly and thoroughly explained, from design to collecting, analyzing, and reporting findings. The text highlights research features of numerous published exemplars, providing methodological insights to illustrate similarities between case studies and other social science methods. This book is distinctive in that it presents the breadth of case study research and its scholarly heritage at a detailed and practical level. Chapter 1 outlines a workable technical definition of the case study as a research method, and its differentiation from other social science research methods. Chapter 2 includes extensive discussion of case study designs. Chapter 5 presents case study analysis techniques. Chapter 6 focuses on reporting and presenting case study findings. Useful in-text learning aids include "tips" that pose key questions and provide answers, practical exercises, endnotes, and a cross-referencing table. The glossary of terms directly related to case study research is useful, too.

Analyzing Data
and Reporting Findings

Chapter 8 Objectives

Section I: Instruction

- Provide a conceptualization of qualitative data analysis.
- Identify the specific strategies involved in analyzing qualitative data.
- Explain how to organize, reduce, and prepare raw data through coding and categorization.
- Explain how to formulate clear and precise findings statements based on analysis of the data.
- Describe how to report and present findings in a clear, comprehensive, and systematic manner.

Section II: Application

- Present a completed findings chapter for your dissertation.

Overview

Analysis is an exciting and challenging aspect of the qualitative research process, requiring a degree of systematic searching and creativity. Although there are stages dedicated to formal analysis, analysis is an inherent and ongoing part of the research and writing process. As Spencer, Richie, and Ormston (2014) explain,

Analysis does not begin when the researchers have finished collecting their data, but is an ongoing and inherent part of the whole process of qualitative research and should infuse all aspects. The analytical part of a researcher's brain should always be alert to the implications of their choices at each stage of the research process. (p. 275)

Once you have collected your data by way of the various data collection methods that you have chosen to use, your next step is to manage, organize, and make sense of all the separate pieces of accumulated information. Qualitative data include excerpts from documentation, interview transcripts, survey comments, focus group transcripts, critical incident forms, field notes from observations, and so on. In addition, you may have collected some quantitative data by way of survey methodology, yielding numbers, frequencies, and percentages. All of these data are called *raw data* because they are as yet untouched by you. Your task is to transform them into something meaningful by analyzing them and making inferences from these discrete pieces of information.

Many students become overwhelmed at this point of the dissertation process, having completed or still being immersed in data collection and faced with mounds and mounds of "stuff" and unsure about what needs to be done first. Frequently, the comment is that they are overloaded with data and drowning. Many students have some notion of *what* they must do, but are uncertain about *how* to really go about doing it. A common problem facing qualitative researchers is the lack of agreed-on approaches for analyzing qualitative material. Although there is some information regarding how and why to use qualitative research methodologies, there is considerably less information on the actual "nuts and bolts" of what to do with the data after the research has been conducted.

Although most research courses and textbooks describe the basic structure of research, few move the student into the areas of data organization and analysis. Much is made of the process of *coding*—assigning an alphanumeric system to segments of transcripts. Less attention is paid, however, to application—that is, how to use coded material. Typically, the results are that students come up with excellent ideas for research, conduct solid literature reviews, produce what sound like viable research designs, and even collect massive amounts of data. The problem arises, however, at this point: What do you do with the collected data? In this chapter, we provide the "what" as well as the "how" regarding transforming raw data into meaningful findings. Section I, "Instruction," describes what needs to be done and explains in a series of steps how to go about this. Section II, "Application," provides an example of a findings chapter. Using the research problem carried throughout this book, we present the actual findings of the research that we conducted.

When you reach this point in the research process, it is essential to keep an open mind, remembering that qualitative research is all about discovery. You need to look carefully at all of your data, seeking to uncover important insights regarding the phenomenon that you are researching. These are your "findings." The procedures you use to accomplish this need to be well thought out, explicitly documented, and directly connected to your research questions. Subsequently, in the following chapter, "Analyzing and Interpreting Findings," you will synthesize all your data sources and insights, creating an interpretation that is holistic and integrated.

There is often confusion around the idea of data analysis in qualitative research and what it actually entails. Qualitative data analysis is the process of bringing order, structure, and meaning to the masses of data collected. Broadly speaking, qualitative data analysis is the researcher's attempt to summarize all the collected data in a dependable and accurate manner. This process is based on induction: The researcher starts with a large set of data and seeks to progressively narrow them into smaller important groups of key data. There are no predefined variables to focus analysis as there are in quantitative research. Qualitative data analysis requires the researcher to be patient and reflective in a process that strives to make sense of multiple data sources. The analytic procedure falls essentially into the following sequential phases: organizing the data, generating categories, identifying patterns and themes, and coding the data.

We want to draw your attention to the fact that, although Chapter 5 of the dissertation deals with analysis and interpretation, it should become evident to you that the process of analysis begins occurring in Chapter 4 by way of organizing and transforming raw data into what are called the "research findings." Essentially, Chapter 4 of the dissertation involves the analysis of data to produce findings. The following chapter, Chapter 5, involves the analysis, interpretation, and synthesis of those findings. Both chapters involve analytic decisions. These two chapters together should convince a reader that you, the researcher, are sufficiently knowledgeable about the interlocking analytic processes that constitute qualitative research.

Section I: Instruction

Organizing and Preparing Data for Analysis

Data Management Strategies The data generated by qualitative methods are voluminous, and the sheer quantity of raw data can indeed be quite daunting. If data are to be thoroughly analyzed, they must be well organized. Understanding the ways in which the data can be organized and managed is hence important. As mentioned in Part I, attention to detail in managing data is important at every stage of the research process. This notion becomes all too clear when it is time to write up the research. Once you are sure that your data are well organized, the analysis can begin in earnest.

Transcribe your interviews as soon as possible, and assign identification codes to each transcript. Bear in mind that you must know your data intimately. Although extremely tedious, transcribing your interviews yourself is one way of immersing yourself in your data and becoming more familiar with it. Remember that doing your own transcriptions, or at least checking them by listening to the tapes as you read them, can be quite different from just working off transcriptions done by somebody else.

Although extremely time consuming, it is imperative that interviews be transcribed verbatim. The exact words of participants must be recorded, along with any aspects of nonverbal communication, such as pauses, laughter, or interruptions. These nonverbal nuances are usually noted within parentheses as they occur. If you are having your transcriptions done by a professional transcriber, you need to make these instructions clear. Also, if computerized data analysis tools are going to be used, the data might have to be converted into a format that is compatible with the software program to be used.

Make sure all your information is complete and legible. Write dates on all transcriptions and field notes. Label all notes according to type (observers' notes, memos, transcriptions, etc.). Be sure to make copies of all your material; from an early stage, find a way to securely store the data in well-labeled computer files so that you know where to locate the different pieces of information. It is prudent—and indeed highly advisable—to back up all your data, putting one master copy away someplace for safekeeping. As mentioned in Part I, it is essential to sort and order your data for easy retrieval. Safely storing the data also ensures that you are honoring the confidentiality of participants—an essential ethical consideration.

If you have collected any quantitative material, you need to summarize the data to illustrate patterns. In a qualitative study, quantitative findings are secondary and are used to supplement and/or augment the primary qualitative findings. We recommend that you "chunk" your data and prepare the quantitative component at the outset prior to embarking on qualitative data analysis. While you analyze quantitative and qualitative data separately and in different ways, as you see later in this chapter, in qualitative research, reporting the findings means that data from all sources are seamlessly woven to provide an overall integrated and holistic presentation.

In a qualitative study, usually simple descriptive statistics will suffice vis-à-vis quantitative data. Measures of central tendency include such things as mean, mode, and/or median. Measures of variability include such things as range and standard deviation. Raw scores must first be converted to percentages, and graphical or mathematical procedures such as tables, graphs, or bar charts (histograms) are then used to depict patterns in the data. The reference in this chapter's annotated bibliography, namely, Huck's (2000) *Reading Statistics and Research*, might be useful in the analysis and presentation of survey results. If you intend to use more sophisticated quantitative measurement procedures, we suggest that you seek professional advice and consult with the appropriate quantitative references.

Inductive, Deductive, and Abductive Analysis Let us interject at this point to offer a very brief outline of three quite general forms of qualitative analysis. The well-known models of reasoning, commonly referred to as induction, deduction, and abduction, illustrate the basic "thinking" behind analysis. Understanding these models thus allows us to make decisions regarding how we will go about *using our data*.

First, induction is data-driven analysis. The idea is that data lead to theory, and in pure form, an inductive approach builds on the idea that data can more or less "speak for themselves" and may offer us a truly "grounded theory." The metaphor driving this model is the metaphor of "collecting" (Brinkmann, 2014). Researchers collect data to form a bouquet that is informative about something more general than any individual flower is capable of. The critique of an inductive approach is that the point of research is not to develop general theories, but to understand particulars.

Second, deduction is a theory-driven analysis. The idea is that theory determines data, in the sense that hypotheses and assumptions are articulated within the background or context of theory, which is then tested in confrontation with the so-called empirical world; that is, raw data. The metaphor for this approach is a "framework" or "paradigm." Qualitative researchers often talk about having a "theoretical framework," "conceptual framework" to guide the entire study from conceptualization through data analysis. This is the general approach to qualitative data analysis (unless one is doing a pure grounded theory study), and the one adopted in this book.

Brinkmann (2014) introduces a third approach to qualitative analysis, which he sees as an alternative to the "inductive collector" and the "deductive framer." He introduces the image of the "abductive tool-user"; the bricoleur or craftsperson. As he explains, unlike induction and deduction, both of which address the relationship between data and theory, abduction is seen as a form of reasoning that is concerned with the relationship between *situation* and *inquiry*. As Brinkmann (2014) explains, "It occurs in situations of breakdown, surprise, bewilderment, and wonder" (p. 722). Abduction is thus a form of reasoning used in situations of uncertainty when we seek an understanding or explanation of why something happens. The goal of the abductive process is not to arrive at fixed or universal knowledge through the collection of data. Rather, the goal is to be able to act in a specific situation. Hence, this approach has its roots in the Pragmatism of Charles S. Peirce. Inquiry is thus the process of trying to understand a situation by "sense-making." The result of sense-making (which may be a concept or a theory) is then tested to see whether the situation is resolved. According to the abductive model, then, we engage in research, inquiry, and analysis for purposes of living, and theories and methods are some of the tools used in the process.

Deciding on an Analytic Approach It must be pointed out at the outset that different qualitative research traditions or genres promote specific strategies for data analysis. Data analysis in the different traditions is similar, but there are some fundamental differences. For example, grounded theory is systematic in its approach: Categories of information are generated (open coding), one of the categories is selected and positioned within a theoretical model (axial coding), and a story is explicated from the interconnection of the categories (selective coding). Coding and categorizing involve the "constant comparison" method that continues throughout the study. As the name implies, this method involves systematically comparing sections of text and noting similarities and differences between these sections. Through the emergence of major categories, theory can evolve. Case study and ethnographic research involve a detailed description of the setting or individuals, followed by analysis of the data for themes, patterns, or issues (Stake, 1995; Wolcott, 1994). Phenomenological research makes use of significant statements, the generation of meaning units, and the development of an "essence" description (Moustakas, 1994). Researchers who use this approach are reluctant to describe specific analytic techniques, fearing that these might be seen as rules and become inflexible (Hycner, 1985). As such, the focus is on attitude and the response to the phenomenon under study. The aim is to achieve an analytic description of the phenomena not affected by prior assumptions.

Whatever tradition or genre one adopts, perhaps the most fundamental underlying operation in the analysis of qualitative data is that of discovering significant classes or sets of things, persons, and events and the properties that characterize them. In qualitative research, we are interested in the language of the participants or texts. We work with the data (words) to identify units of information that contribute to themes or patterns—the study's findings. Therefore, analysis has to do with data reduction and data display.

In qualitative research, interviewing is often the major source of data needed for understanding the phenomenon under study. This process generates an enormous amount of text. To make the data more readily accessible and understandable, the vast array of words, sentences, and paragraphs has to be reduced to what is of most importance and interest and then transformed to draw out themes and patterns. Most important in qualitative research is that the analytic process is an interweaving of inductive and deductive thinking.

Although committed to empathy and multiple realities, the researcher decides what story will be reported. As Stake (2000) puts it, "This is not to dismiss the aim of finding the story that best represents the case, but to remind that the criteria of representation ultimately are decided by the researcher" (p. 441). All researchers enter the field with a certain perspective and certain assumptions, yet the material should not be addressed with a set of hypotheses that you set out to prove or disprove. Rather, you need to approach your transcripts with an open mind, seeking what emerges as significant from the text. As Seidman (2012) writes, "The interviewer must come to the transcript prepared to let the interview breathe and speak for itself" (p. 100). Your assumptions are usually articulated in your conceptual framework. Theories and prior research inform this framework, offering potential categories. At the same time, the conceptual framework remains flexible and open to the unexpected, allowing the analytic direction of the study to emerge.

The following classification of Crabtree and Miller (1992) illustrates one view of how analytic approaches might differ:

1. Quasi-statistical approaches: Use word or phrase frequencies to determine the relative importance of terms and concepts. This approach is typified by content analysis— the process of converting qualitative data into a quantitative format.
2. Template approaches: Key codes are determined either on an a priori basis (i.e., derived from theory or research questions) or from an initial read of the data. These codes serve as a template or "bins," remaining flexible as the data analysis

process proceeds. This approach makes use of matrices, networks, flowcharts, and diagrams that supplement descriptive summaries of the text.

3. Editing approaches: These are more interpretive and flexible than the above. There are no (or few) a priori codes. Codes are emergent. This is typified by the grounded theory approach.

4. Immersion approaches: This approach is the least structured and most interpretive, emphasizing researcher insight, intuition, and creativity. Methods remain fluid and are not systematized.

Although there are some specific analytic differences according to the qualitative tradition or genre that is adopted, qualitative analysis, as we see it, is somewhat of a stepwise procedure that involves a blend of approaches. Our view is that tightly organized and highly structured schemes can filter out the unusual and serendipitous. The approach we adopt in explaining this chapter, as is seen, is essentially a combination of the template and editing approaches. We see this balance as the most readily applicable to the flexibility that characterizes all types of qualitative research.

Remember that whatever approach you choose to use should be based on what you feel most comfortable with and be most suited to the research tradition that you have adopted. In addition, the preference of your advisor and your department will of course need to be taken into consideration. Remember, too, that you are expected to be able to describe in detail your analytic approach and to show that you are able to demonstrate how you got from your data to your conclusions. This step is necessary to enhance both the credibility (validity) and the dependability (reliability) of your study.

A Systematic Procedure for Data Analysis

Although we offer a stepwise procedure to prepare and analyze the data, please bear in mind that we are *not* implying in any way that the interrelationship among these steps is necessarily linear. Each phase in this multistage process leads logically to the next, yet the process is essentially an iterative and somewhat messy one. You will most likely cycle through the phases more than once, looping back and revisiting earlier phases in an ongoing effort to narrow and make sense of what is in the data. The steps that you take will overlap each other as you continue to read and collect data. As you increasingly internalize and reflect on your data, the initial ordered sequence most likely will lose its structure and become more flexible.

Just how long the analytic process lasts is difficult to predict. It depends largely on the nature of the study, the amount of data collected, and the analytic and synthesizing abilities of the researcher. The process can be repetitious, tedious, and time consuming. However, there is no substitute for fully immersing yourself in your data. Take the time to read and reread. Really live with your data. Getting to know intimately what you have collected, and struggling with the nuances, subtleties, caveats, and contradictions, is an integral part of the process. Keep an open mind, and be prepared for the unexpected. Remain patient. Accept that the process in its entirety will take time, and be aware of not making premature judgments. Figure 8.1 includes the iterative steps of the analytic process. Following the figure is a more detailed discussion of the key activities involved in the process.

Review and Explore the Data You will need to examine each piece of information and building on insights and hunches gained during data collection, attempt to make sense of the data as a whole. To achieve this goal, begin by carefully reading over all the data provided by the various data collection sources. Read the transcriptions of your interviews, critical incidents, and/or focus groups. If you have used document review, read over your documentation, too. What you are really doing is reading to get some feel for the "story line," including the major and minor stories that are being told within the data. This initial reading of all the data is done to gain an overall sense of the whole before you break it into its constituent parts.

It is important that you get a good feel for your data—an experience that usually generates emergent insights. In reading over the data, try to make sense of what people are saying. Also try to integrate what different people are saying. The more familiar you are with the details of your data, the better you will be able to present it, and the better your analysis of it will be. In this first go-around, read through each transcript and try to identify the "big ideas." Although the big ideas are likely to become altered or refined, they provide an initial framework for the development of the study's findings.

Qualitative analysis usually results in the identification of recurring patterns or themes that cut through the data (Merriam, 1998, 2009). Saldana (2013) defines a theme as "a *phrase* or *sentence* that identifies what a unit of data is *about* and/or what it *means*" (emphasis in original, p. 139). As Ryan and Bernard (2003) explain, you know you have found a theme when you can answer the question, "What is this expression an example of?" (p. 87). Repetition is the most common theme recognition technique, and is based on the premise that if a concept reoccurs throughout and/or across transcripts, it is likely a theme (Ryan & Bernard, 2003). Data analysis demands a heightened awareness of the data and an open mind to recurring and common threads, some of which may be subtle (Guest, MacQueen, & Namey, 2012). The real purpose of this initial read is to *really* immerse yourself in your data and gain a sense of their possibilities. As you read, make notes of or highlight relevant words and phrases that you think capture important aspects of the data. Remember that these should bear some relationship to the research questions and should not simply be some random words that seem to occur with regular frequency. Ask yourself, "What is this about? What seems to be emerging?" Check these ideas against the categories and descriptors of your conceptual framework.

While we have already discussed this in greater detail in Chapter 6 ("Developing and Presenting the Literature Review"), we return for a moment with a brief reminder of how the conceptual framework functions with regard to data analysis and the role that it plays in terms of organization and presentation of findings:

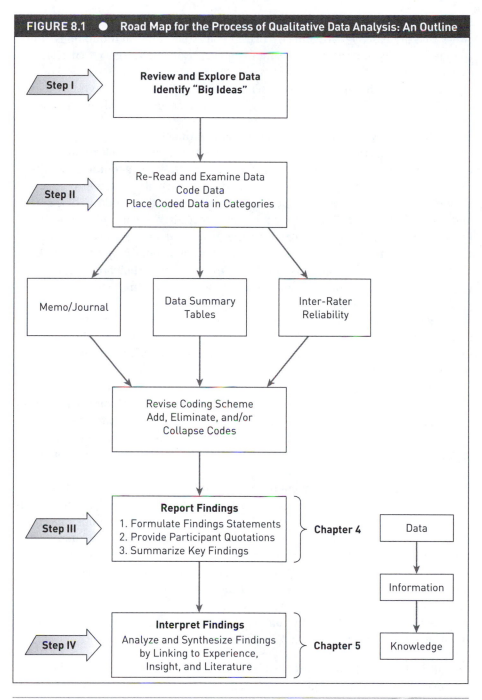

FIGURE 8.1 ● Road Map for the Process of Qualitative Data Analysis: An Outline

Source: This figure first appeared in Bloomberg, L. D. (2007). *Understanding qualitative inquiry: Content and process* (Part I). Unpublished manuscript.

Step 1: Developing Categories   Give careful thought to developing conceptual categories that are based on and directly tied to your study's research questions. To be comprehensive, you need to make sure there is at least one category that relates to each research question. These categories form the backbone of your study. As you will see, they become the repository for presenting your findings. They also translate into analytic categories later on in your study, and so become an essential analytic tool.

Step 2: Developing Descriptors for Each Category   Under each category, you lay out the categories' descriptors. These descriptors reflect what you have learned from the reviewed literature, data from your pilot studies, and your own educated guesses or hunches based on your own experiences and knowledge about how people might respond to each of your research questions. Not all of your descriptors will be useful, and you will certainly refine these as the study proceeds. The conceptual framework remains flexible and emergent. Based on the data you collect, some of the descriptors may remain intact, others may be deleted, or new ones may be added. Each category and descriptor will be assigned a code that maps participants' responses to the research questions, forming categories and subcategories. In the findings chapter of the dissertation, the categories and descriptors become the headings and subheadings for organization and presentation of findings. The conceptual framework is included in the dissertation's appendix. Here the title changes to "Coding Legend" or "Coding Scheme," as you assign symbols (codes) to each main category and each of the respective descriptors.

As you read through your transcripts, in addition to highlighting parts of the text and underlining sections and issues that seem important and relevant, jot down in the margins any ideas, thoughts, reflections, and comments that come to mind. This process will provide you with a record of your initial sense of the data. Later, when you are deeper into the analytic process, you may find that some of these early impressions are useful and hold up throughout.

If your study includes document review, a useful tool to help collate and organize all the information that you are able to glean from documents is a document summary form. With regard to interviews, critical incidents, and focus groups, after reading each transcript carefully, make summary notes for each participant. Summarizing data in this way is important because it creates a profile of each document and/or each individual research participant. Moreover, much of what occurs in later analytical steps requires reducing the data to units. Reduction of data requires a researcher to think about smaller bits of data, and this step runs the risk of missing the forest for the trees. Templates for the document summary form and the participant summary form are included as Appendices Q and R, respectively.

Reread and Code the Data   The first step in the analytic process is to consider the "big ideas" or themes. Saldana (2013) refers to this process as "theming the data" (pp. 175–181). Brinkman and Kvale (2015) call this same process "thematizing" (p. 105). Following this step, the second step is to dissect and classify the data and place sections of material into categories. Although it is important initially to become familiar with your data, you do not want to drown in it. Thus, an important step is to reduce all that you have collected to a manageable database, grouping it in useful ways. This step is essentially what Seidman (2012), Creswell (2013), and Guest et al. (2012) refer to as a "winnowing process." Often you will notice many more potential themes than you actually end up elaborating in a given analysis. Just because something is noticeable does not mean that it is meaningful or noteworthy in terms of your study's analysis. On an initial reading of the text, often certain ideas, phrases, or expressions catch a coder's attention, but these may not be relevant to the analysis at hand. Conversely, the relevance of some themes is not immediately apparent during the analytic process. A good rule of thumb, therefore, is to err on the side of caution. If you are unsure of the significance of a potential theme as you read through your data, flag it for later attention. (All qualitative software analysis programs provide options for doing this.) It is important to recognize that not everybody will perceive exactly the same themes in the same way. Breadth and depth of knowledge and experience with the research setting and topic will influence what a reader perceives. As such, systematic procedures are needed for finding, defining, and coding themes. From your large stacks of papers that contain your raw data, you have to find ways to distill the information into smaller sets of notes that characterize your total data. To do this, you need to develop a systematic and manageable system of classification (i.e., a coding scheme). In essence, analytic objectives keep you focused on the task at hand, and this should help you prioritize which themes to develop in the analysis. This is one of the key functions of the conceptual framework.

The reduction process includes questioning the data, identifying and noting common patterns in the data, creating codes that describe your data patterns, and assigning these coded pieces of information to the categories of your conceptual framework. Your conceptual framework is the centerpiece in managing and reducing the data. A sample conceptual framework is included as Appendix E. The categories that comprise your conceptual framework become the repositories of your data. In effect, you turn your conceptual framework into a coding scheme/legend by assigning codes to each category and each subcategory (or descriptor). That coding scheme is included in your dissertation's appendix. At the same time, the uncoded conceptual framework should remain intact and is usually presented at the end of your literature review chapter. A sample coding scheme is included as Appendix L.

What Is Coding? Much is made about coding as a fundamental skill for qualitative analysis. Although there is really nothing that mysterious about it, the literature on data analysis and coding in particular is voluminous, and the vast amount of information can certainly be overwhelming. There are some cutting-edge texts that offer comprehensive and authoritative accounts of coding, and the different options and variations available to the qualitative researcher. For a more in-depth account of the practical strategies associated with qualitative data analysis, the following texts are highly recommended: Bazeley (2014), Harding (2013), Kuckartz (2014), and Saldana (2013).

Coding is essentially a system of classification—the process of noting what is of interest or significance, identifying different segments of the data, and labeling them to organize the information contained in the data. Coffey and Atkinson (1996) explain coding as "a mixture of data [summation] and data complication . . . breaking the data apart in analytically relevant ways in order to lead toward further questions about the data" (pp. 29–31). Saldana (2013) captures it well, providing a succinct definition of a "code":

> A code in qualitative inquiry is most often a word or short phrase that symbolically assigns a summative, salient, essence-capturing, and/or evocative attribute for a portion of language-based or visual data . . . . In qualitative data analysis, a code is a researcher-generated construct that symbolizes and thus attributes interpreted meaning to each individual datum for later purposes of pattern detection, categorization, theory-building, and other analytic processes. Just as a title represents and captures a book, film, or poem's primary content and essence, so does a code represent and capture a datum's primary content and essence. (pp. 3–4)

Richards (2015) adds a new angle about the term "coding." As this author points out, in common use, coding refers to data reduction, either by a system of symbols or numbers. While quantitative coding *reduces* data, qualitative coding is about data *retention*. Similarly, Bazeley (2014) does not view coding as a mechanistic data reduction process, but rather one designed to stimulate and facilitate analysis by providing a means of access to evidence, for querying data and for testing assumptions and conclusions. The goal of qualitative research is to learn from the data, and to keep revisiting data extracts until you see and understand emergent patterns and explanations. In the same vein, Saldana (2013) refutes the critique that coding in qualitative research is reductionist, stating that "my definition of coding approaches the analytic act as one that assigns rich symbolic meanings through essence-capturing and/or evocative attributes to data. . . . Most of these methods are geared toward discovering a participant's voice, processes, emotions, motivations, values, attitudes, beliefs, judgments, conflicts, microcultures, identities, life course patterns, etc. These are not reductionist outcomes but multidimensional facets about the people we study" (p. 38). Viewed in this way, then, the purpose of coding is *not just to label* all parts of your documents about a topic, but rather to *bring them together* so they can be reviewed, and your thinking about the topic developed. Coding also allows you to return to the data you want to inspect, interrogate, revisit, and interpret. Bear in mind that coding is a cyclical act (Saldana, 2013). Rarely is the first cycle of coding perfect. Subsequent cycles of recoding further filters, focuses, and highlights the salient features of your data, providing the potential for generating and expanding on categories, themes, concepts, and for grasping meaning and/or building theory. Remember, the development of an original theory is not always a necessary outcome for qualitative inquiry. However, it is pre-existing theories that drive the entire research process; hence, the centrality of the conceptual or theoretical framework throughout the research endeavor. Indeed, the integral role played by the conceptual framework is something we try to emphasize throughout this book.

Codes are, in effect, a type of shorthand—the names or identifiers that you attach to chunks or segments of data that you consider relevant to your study. As such, you can use any system that works for you, be it alphanumeric or some form of symbol. Some people find it useful to use highlighting pens to color code their data. Whatever system you choose to use, as you read your material, the codes that you assign signal what you think is going on in a piece of data. Remember, coding is *more than counting.*

Coding Versus Content Analysis A brief word here about content analysis is warranted to establish the differences between this method and qualitative data analysis. Content analysis is a qualitative research method utilized in document or archival research, used to determine the presence of certain words or concepts within texts or sets of texts (Cozby & Bates, 2012; Leedy & Ormrod, 2013). Researchers quantify and analyze the presence, meanings, and relationships of words and concepts, and make inferences about the messages within the texts, the writer(s), the audience, and even the culture and time of which these are a part. This approach can be highly systematized or more loosely organized and can be used for examining thematic similarities and interpreting the findings of multiple studies (Finfgeld-Connett, 2014). Content analysis can also be combined with quantitative analysis in a mixed methods study.

The key component of content analysis is the coding of the material to be investigated, and this can be approached inductively or deductively (Finfgeld-Connett, 2014). If approached inductively, the researcher begins the research with a brief list of themes, and identifies more as the coding and research process occurs. In the deductive approach, the researcher begins with a list of themes, and codes the material according to the predetermined list (although the researcher does typically allow for adaptability if the material suggests other themes). Regardless of the approach, the researcher must create a coding scheme that places the content of the text into systematic categories that can be related back to the research questions (Cozby & Bates, 2012; Finfgeld-Connett, 2014). To conduct a content analysis on any text, the text is coded; that is, broken down, into manageable categories on a variety of levels—word, word sense, phrase, sentence, or theme—and then examined using one of content analysis' basic methods: conceptual analysis or relational analysis. *Conceptual analysis* establishes the existence and frequency of concepts most often represented by words of phrases in a text. *Relational analysis* goes one step further by examining the relationships among concepts in a text. Content analysis helps to construct research questions by defining the categories to be applied, defining and developing the coding process, and analyzing the results of the coding process (Cozby & Bates, 2012). Content analysis allows closeness to the text, which can alternate between specific categories and relationships and also statistically analyzes the coded form of the text. While content analysis offers researchers a flexible, systematic method for developing and extending knowledge, this analysis of existing documents can help quantify information already gathered to answer questions that are newly proposed or have been previously proposed with limited information gathered. Disadvantages are that the method is inherently reductive, particularly when dealing with complex texts, that it tends often to simply consist of word counts, and that it often disregards the context that produced the text.

In traditional content analysis studies, therefore, counting the number of times a particular set of codes occurs is indeed an important measure in assessing the frequency of items or phenomena. However, in the qualitative analysis process, frequency of occurrence is not necessarily an indicator of significance. As Saldana (2013) describes it,

> The analytic approaches for most of these coding methods do not ask you to count; they ask you to ponder, to scrutinize, to interrogate, to experiment, to feel, to empathize, to sympathize, to speculate, to assess, to organize, to pattern, to categorize, to connect, to integrate, to synthesize, to reflect, to hypothesize, to assert, to conceptualize, to abstract, and—if you are really good—to theorize. Counting is easy; thinking is hard work. (p. 39)

Coding *well* requires that you reflect deeply on the meanings of each and every piece of data. And coding *well* requires that you read and reread as you code and recode. Coding *well* leads to total immersion in and closeness with your data, and becoming intimately familiar with its details, nuances, and subtleties. Coding is a first step to really *rethinking* your data. As such, coding should be regarded as having a purpose, rather than an end in itself. Some of the many purposes of qualitative coding include

- A method of discovery to stimulate deeper thinking about the data you have collected;
- To reflect on what the coded segments tell you about the category and its meanings;
- Enables you to organize and group similarly coded data into categories or "families" based on shared characteristics;
- To ask questions about how the category relates to other ideas that develop from the data;
- To create further finer categories from discovering different dimensions in the data gathered in the first round of coding;
- To search for blends or combinations of categories, and to compare different categories;
- To note how categories that are consolidated in various ways begin to transcend the "reality" of the data, and progress toward the thematic, conceptual, and theoretical levels; and
- To compare how different researchers interpret data.

Beginning the Coding Process As you read your material, reference segments or units of text by highlighting or bracketing them. These segments can be single words, phrases, sentences, or even whole paragraphs. Codes can be written in the margins or alongside the appropriate segments of text. A sample coded interview transcript segment is presented as Appendix S. As with all aspects of the research process, precision is key. It is of the utmost importance to know who said what. Therefore, do not forget to include participant identification with each unit of information. In addition, label each passage with a notation system that will designate its position in the original transcript. Later, when considering an excerpt taken from its original context, you may want to check the accuracy of the text, perhaps going back to the audiotape. Specific labeling of each excerpt allows for such retracing.

At this point in the reading, marking, and labeling process, it is important to keep labels tentative. As you read and mark units or sections from the material, one way is to begin to label them using terms based on the actual language of the participants— known in the language of grounded theory as an *in vivo* term. This process is called *open coding*, a grounded theory concept where the descriptors emerge from the data and is essentially the same as what Patton (1990, 2015) refers to as *inductive analysis*. While using in vivo labels, note whether there is something in the data that might fit one of the descriptors of your conceptual framework. The procedure of using predetermined coding categories and seeking to fit the data into such categories is against the spirit of pure grounded theory. Although we make use of some concepts from grounded theory, please note that the approach we adopt in this book is not a pure grounded theory approach.

If you use predetermined categories, you run the risk of analyzing data by coding text units according to what you expect to find. Your conceptual framework must remain flexible and open to change throughout the entire analytic process. Remember, the reason you have spent so much time and energy talking to participants is to find out what *their* experience is and to endeavor to understand it from *their* perspective. In the process of working with excerpts and seeking connections among them, be aware that not all your data will fit your predetermined categories. Rather than trying to force data into categories, you will most likely have to create some new, emergent descriptors and/or collapse and/or eliminate some of them. As you go along, you will see that some categories may contain clusters of coded data that merits further refinement into subcategories. You will see too that some coded excerpts might fit under more than one category. For now, place them wherever seems most appropriate. Instead, you might choose to place the same excerpt of text under more than one category. When making tentative placements, make notes. Later on you will proceed to sort coded text more specifically.

At this stage of the process, you, as the researcher, are exercising judgment as to what you think is significant in each interview transcript. Some passages stand out because they are striking to you in some way. Others stand out because they are contradictory and seem inconsistent with your conceptual framework. Although it may be tempting to put those aside, you should exercise caution and not submit to researcher bias. In this regard, you must be vigilant in not seeking only material that supports your own opinions and remaining open to the unexpected.

As you will come to realize, too, any given segment of data might be viewed differently by two different researchers or even coded using more than one label by one researcher. There is no single "correct" way to organize and analyze the data. Moreover, rarely will anyone get coding "right" the first time. Therefore, it is necessary that you read, reread, and reexamine all of your data to make sure that you have not missed something or coded something in a way that is inappropriate given the experience of participants. At this point, inter-rater reliability is also required. Have a colleague review your work to see whether your codes are appropriate and relevant to your research questions. Alternatively, have a colleague code some of the same transcripts that you have been working on to check for consistency. Compare and discuss similarities and differences. There are many reasons that different researchers would view and interpret the data in different ways, including researcher bias, personal interests, style, and interpretive focus. As Saldana (2013) stresses, intercoding agreement is not about trying to be objective, but rather about achieving similar results between two or more people. Assigning symbolic meanings (i.e., a code) to qualitative data is a subjective act. And naturally, since each of us perceives the social world differently, we analyze it differently, and therefore, code it differently. As such, you would not expect consistency of qualitative coding between colleagues, and so inconsistency is not a cause for concern (Richards, 2015). Indeed, exploring reasons for inconsistency is a worthwhile exercise as important insights can emerge from the different ways in which people look at the same set of data. Moreover, as Guest et al. (2012) put it, "Recoding is not a sign you have done things wrong, it is simply part of doing things well" (p. 76). And remember, because coding is a cyclical act, recoding usually occurs with a more attuned perspective.

As you read, sort, and code, two other processes should be occurring simultaneously: (a) preparing data summary charts and (b) writing memos and/or journaling.

The first thing you need to do is fill out data summary tables—one for each research question. These tables are tools that help you compile what participants have said about each of the categories in the conceptual framework and record how many participants' comments fall under the same categories. These tables are a way to summarize participant data. They provide a way to highlight the evidence to support what the researcher says she or he has found. In the absence of such a summary, identification of pervasive themes and findings is up to either the discretion of the researcher or the interpretation of the reader.

To accurately report and analyze the findings of your research, you have to be rigorous about recording participant responses. Toward this end, get in the habit of filling out data summary tables as you code. Perform the two activities in tandem so that no information is lost. It is useful to array data summary tables as outlined in Table 8.1. These tables are essentially matrices in which the participants (under pseudonyms) are listed down the vertical axis, with the descriptors (the different aspects of each category) being listed along the horizontal axis. These descriptors should be

TABLE 8.1 ● Template for Data Summary Table

	Descriptor 1	Descriptor 2	Descriptor 3	Descriptor 4	Descriptor 5	Descriptor 6	Descriptor 7
Pseudonym1							
Pseudonym2							
Pseudonym3							
Pseudonym4							
Pseudonym5							
Pseudonym6							
$N = X$	# = x %	# = x %	# = x %	# = x %	# = x %	# = x %	# = x %

listed exactly as they appear under each category of your conceptual framework. How each participant responds to each of the descriptors on the horizontal axis is then checked off, and tallies (raw frequencies as well as percentages) are noted at the bottom of each column. A data summary table should be developed in this same format for each category of the conceptual framework. In this way, you have a consistent record of findings regarding all your participants' responses across all of your categories. The categories are directly tied to your research questions. Samples of completed data summary tables are presented as Appendices T through Z.

Although qualitative research is not essentially about quantifying data, and although the intent is not to reduce the data to numeric representations (as in the case of quantitative research), tallies and frequencies in qualitative research are acceptable and are essentially a supplement to the narrative. Data summary tables are working tools that create a record of who said what and how many times a particular response occurs. As such, these tables are an essential precursor to interpretation, where you will need to look closely at both individual participants and the overall group of participants—that is, cross-case analysis.

As you read through your data, different ideas come into your mind. These ideas might be the basis for interpretations or even conclusions and recommendations later on. Therefore, you need to record all these thoughts so that you do not lose them. You might consider keeping a journal and/or some system of memo as to what is going on with the data. *Memoing*, a concept originally referred to by Strauss (1987), involves recording and writing notes about certain occurrences or sentences that seem of vital interest. Memos can trigger thinking processes and as Strauss explains, are the written versions of an internal dialogue going on during the research. By recording what you think is going on, you can capture new descriptors as they emerge through your reading and coding, which descriptors seem to overlap, and which descriptors are not appearing, thus needing to be eliminated. In this way, your notes serve to inform your coding scheme and become the basis for a coding scheme development chart (see Appendix M). The notes that you jot down, either in the form of memos or as part of a research journal, also can form the basis for an interpretation outline tool (see Appendix CC), an analytic category development tool (see Appendix DD), and a consistency chart of findings, interpretations, and conclusions (see Appendix EE). These charts are working tools that help guide and clarify your thinking and, as such, can be included in the appendix of your dissertation. These charts also form part of your audit trail—a necessary element for establishing your study's validity.

Sort and Categorize Quotations Once you have coded your material, you are ready to copy and paste or cut out and place the quotes in their appropriate analytic categories (i.e., categorize your units of information). In categorizing material, some people prefer pasting quotes to index cards and stacking these in piles. Others prefer cutting out quotes and placing these in manila envelopes marked with the category name. We promote the idea of flip charts—either actual or electronic—because they are visual. Whatever system you choose, make sure that, before you begin cutting (literally or figuratively), you have copied or scanned your original data and that these are safely stored.

If you decide to use the method of flip charts, you need to create a separate flip chart for each category. On each flip chart, list the category name and underneath that the category's descriptors. Bear in mind that the categories of your conceptual framework are the superordinate headings that provide the organization for the units of data. The descriptors within each category become the subordinate headings. Actual flip charts can be pasted to your walls, and the quotes can be pasted to these. "Electronic flip charts" are essentially a computerized version, whereby the charts are Word documents on your computer, and quotes from your transcripts are copied and pasted electronically. Whichever mode you choose to use—be it actual or electronic—is a matter of personal preference. In either case, what is useful about the chart approach is that it enables you to visualize your data, live with it, and think about it.

As you paste quotations in the appropriate categories, look for any units of information that do not fit any of your existing descriptors. Keep these in a pile marked "Miscellaneous." Once you have finished going through all your transcripts, revisit these and see where they should fit or alternatively, create a new place for them under emergent descriptors. When you identify passages that are important, but you are unsure of which category in which they should fall, write a memo about those passages. In writing about them, their properties might become clearer, leading you to discover what it is you find important in them both individually and relatively. This step becomes important for interpretation.

Once all the units of information have been placed under categories, review the descriptors for any overlap. Sometimes descriptors have similar characteristics or properties; that is, they really mean one and the same thing. Splitting two descriptors is sometimes arbitrary, and they can be better collapsed into one. At other times, a descriptor may be too broad or too nuanced and would make more sense if it were subdivided into more than one.

Reread your miscellaneous units of information and reconsider them in the light of the newly revised categories. First, if any can be appropriately placed under any of the new descriptors, do so. Second, it is possible that some units of information are still simply not relevant, and in these cases, discard them. Third, some units provide relevant information that contributes to understanding of the research problem but still do not fit with any of the existing categories. These information units do not warrant being discarded. Rather, they might become categories of their own. In other words, to accommodate your findings, it is imperative that your coding scheme and conceptual framework remain flexible throughout.

Using Computer Software for Data Analysis

As you can see, the approach used in this book for data analysis is a manual one. We have explained the process of data analysis as it is done traditionally to intentionally highlight the thinking and the mechanics involved. While computer assisted qualitative data analysis (CAQDAS) has become more prevalent over the last few years, you need to be aware that although various different types of software programs for qualitative research are available, the principles of the analytic process are the same whether one is doing it manually or with the assistance of software. Silver and Lewins (2014) provide a thorough overview of the most commonly used analytic software packages currently available, describing key features, discussing practical relevance vis-à-vis the various qualitative genres, and offering some useful insights regarding the strengths and limitations of adopting computer software for qualitative data analysis.

Appendix Z presents a brief overview of currently available qualitative data analysis software resources.

Be aware that the software *does not* code the data for you. That task is still always your responsibility as the researcher. Software can indeed be of great assistance in classifying, sorting, filing, storing, and reconfiguring data to enable analytic reflection. The programs currently available are useful in mechanically organizing data and performing a number of analytic operations. With the use of these programs, for instance, you can create shorthand versions of themes or categories. After you sort your data, how many times a theme has been placed in a given category can be done automatically, and some programs can make connections among the categories to develop higher-order conceptual structures.

In addition, as mentioned previously, qualitative analysis software provides various options for tagging text for later review. Included in software programs are functions whereby footnotes, comments, and highlights from different readings of a particular document can be merged into a master document, as well as techniques for tagging generic "unique" codes to apply to segments of text that might be of importance with regard to fitting with the bigger analytic picture.

Software analytical packages are essentially a tool that can make the numerous tasks of the analytic process efficient and are certainly useful in assembling and locating information. However, there are various limitations involved with this method that you should be aware of. Software cannot interpret the emotional tone that is often critical to understanding the findings and therefore neglects to take into account the contextual basis of information. In our experience, we have found that in searching out and producing every coded item each time these appear, the software tends to produce data—mostly in the form of discrete words and phrases—in the absence of their surrounding context. In so doing, although precise and concise, some of the richness of the data can become lost in the process. Moreover, with so many instances of discrete items, this method can produce a data glut, which can be overwhelming to the researcher. A further caveat regarding the use of computer-aided analysis is that, although books for learning the programs are widely available, qualitative software programs require time and skill to learn and employ effectively. As Weitzman and Miles (1995) point out, when contemplating the use of software, you should consider how computer literate you are, how at ease you are with the prospect of exploring and learning new software, and what kind of analysis you intend to do. As many authors point out, it is impractical to prescribe which software program is "best." In addition, what worked for somebody else, might not work for you or your particular study. As the researcher, you are the best judge of your needs and your personal preferences, so it would be wise to explore several of the available programs to make an informed decision. Be aware of the options, and be careful to select your tools wisely so that they help rather than hinder your analysis efforts.

The method you select to manage and analyze your data is ultimately a matter of personal preference and depends on what you are most comfortable with and/or institutional requirements. Therefore, we do not advocate one way over another. If you are choosing software, it is important that you differentiate between programs that manage data and programs that actually perform data analysis. The former allows the researcher to store, index, sort, and retrieve data, whereas the latter actually does content analysis. Information regarding the different types of available software and associated features is offered by various other authors (Creswell, 2014; Merriam, 2009; Silverman, 2013; Silverman & Marvasti, 2008).

Presenting Research Findings

Overview You, the researcher, are the storyteller. Your goal is to tell a story that should be vivid and interesting while also accurate and credible. In your report, the events, the people, and their words and actions are made explicit so that readers can experience the situation as real in a similar way to the researcher and experience the world of the participants. It must be remembered that the reader cannot always see the hard work that has gone into the development of the story or the complexity of strategies and procedure that produced it.

Qualitative analysis is a creative and ongoing process that requires thoughtful judgments about what is significant and meaningful in the data. Your study is only as good as the data you have to analyze and the care that you take in analyzing the data. What you have done up until now is transform your raw data into some format that will facilitate your analysis. Through coding, you have reduced your data and created groupings and subgroupings of information. Reducing is the first step toward presenting your data. Having reduced your data, you now have to shape it into a form in which it can be shared or displayed (Miles & Huberman, 1994; Miles, Huberman, & Saldana, 2014). What you share and display are essentially the multiple perspectives supported by the different quotations that your research yields. The goal is to provide rich descriptions, often referred to as "thick description" (Denzin, 2001)—an essential aspect of qualitative research. Exemplary studies indeed make readers feel as if they are *living* the experiences described. This is the real power of qualitative research.

As a general rule, findings should be represented as objectively as possible and without speculation—that is, free from researcher bias. Presentation of findings also is extremely important. Your presentation will hopefully lead your readers to understand your findings as clearly as you do. Therefore, the way you set up and structure this chapter must be neat and precise. Moreover, if your findings chapter is well organized, the analysis chapter that follows will be much more easily accomplished.

In qualitative research, interviewing is usually the major source of the data needed for understanding the phenomenon under study. The findings of qualitative research are typically reported in a narrative manner. Reports of qualitative studies usually include extensive samples of quotations from participants. These quotations provide the detail and substantiate the story that you are telling. By using the participants' own words, the researcher aims to build the reader's confidence that the reality of the participants and the situation studied is accurately represented. In a qualitative study, quantitative findings, if there are any, are secondary and are used to supplement and/or augment the qualitative findings. The quantitative material should therefore be seamlessly woven into the discussion, either in narrative form (where you would state explicitly how the quantitative results either support or refute the qualitative findings) or in graphic form (tables and charts can be used to augment the discussion by way of clear visual depictions).

Be aware that findings are often written up in different ways depending on the research tradition or genre adopted. If you have used a pure approach, we suggest that you consult with your advisor and the relevant literature regarding appropriate and distinctive forms of presentation.

The narrative can be presented by way of several different formats, and various authors have offered suggestions as to how qualitative research findings might be presented (Guest et al., 2012; Henderson & Segal, 2013; Rubin & Rubin, 2012; Seidman, 2012). One way to present your findings is to develop and craft participant profiles or vignettes of individual participants and to group these into categories. Miles and Huberman (1994) and Miles, Huberman, and Saldana (2014) describe a vignette as "a concrete focused story" (p. 83). Van Maanen (1988, 1995) recommends presenting ethnographic research through different styles of "tales" as a way of presenting truthful cultural portraits. Yet another approach to presentation—one that is often used in case study research—is to mark individual passages or excerpts from the transcripts and group these in thematically connected categories. The latter is the more conventional and commonly used way of presenting qualitative findings. Because it is a flexible format that fits a wide range of topics, we describe this approach in some detail as follows:

Presentation of Findings as Quotation Categories Begin with an introductory paragraph or two in which you restate the purpose of your study (if required) and tell the reader how the chapter will be organized. Provide the reader with an outline that illustrates the way in which you will go about discussing your findings. This outline enables the reader to create a mental map of your presentation and then find that information as he or she peruses your text. If you have used computer software to aid your data analysis, you need to identify the program that you used and the steps you undertook in its use. You will tell the reader what your intention was in choosing the software and what it accomplished.

If you have a bounded case study, that is, if your research takes place at a particular site or location or if it is tied to a particular institution, organization, or program, you need to offer the reader a detailed description of the physical setting. In some cases, where appropriate, an entire chapter is devoted to describing the setting. In others, a section of several pages in the findings chapter is set aside for this; usually this precedes a presentation of the themed participant responses classified by way of coded categories. In some instances, the identity of the research setting is required to remain anonymous. In the interest of confidentiality, you need to account for anonymity by assigning the research setting a pseudonym.

Description of the setting is drawn primarily from the review of available documents. Documents can be of a public or private nature and can include descriptive and/or evaluative information pertaining to the research context. A review of the available documents provides descriptions and factual evidence regarding the context and its culture, and it also uncovers environmental factors and issues that may impact participants' perceptions about this context. Following a review of each document, you should summarize the relevant findings and record these systematically. A template of a document summary form is included as Appendix Q. An examination of all the summaries of all your documents will provide the information you need to write this section of your findings chapter.

Description of the setting should incorporate all the important aspects of the context and environment in which the study takes place, including such things as descriptions of the organizational structure, background and history, mission, vision, policies and procedures, culture and environment, and the population from which the research sample was drawn. In describing the setting, be sure to clarify what is unique about it, as well as what characteristics of the setting are compelling and/or unusual. Thus, discussion of the setting serves to situate your study within a context. In addition, in your analysis, data revealed from the document review can be used to confirm or disconfirm data collected by other methods.

The most common means of organizing a findings chapter, and the approach that we use in this book, is through a discussion of the research questions one by one and the evidence you have from the data about how they might be answered. As you prepare to present your findings, remember that you should have at least one finding per research question. Because you are seeking to shed light on your problem, no research question should be left unanswered. All research questions must be answered. Formulating strong comprehensive finding statements requires that you study your data summary tables. Look at what each participant says in terms of each of the aspects of each finding, and ask yourself: What do I see here? What do I now understand is the answer to each research question?

An overwhelming question facing any researcher embarking on the write-up of the research report is "Where do I begin to tell my story?" Data are complex, particularly thematic data that involve crosscutting and hierarchical themes. Adding multiple sites and/or populations increases this complexity exponentially. Complexity can be represented in many ways, each potentially as valid and informative as the next. The first step in presenting findings, therefore, is what Guest et al. (2012) refer to as "finding your anchor." In other words, what will you lead your story with? What is the primary finding or set of findings you wish to highlight in your findings section? What are your most significant or robust data as they relate to your research problem and purpose? Once you have established this "anchor" or meta-theme, the rest of your findings should follow logically.

To plan and lay out the discussion that should follow each of your findings statements, we suggest doing an outline or what we call a "findings road map." A sample findings road map is presented as Appendix BB. This tool is constructed from the conceptual framework in conjunction with your data summary tables. The overall intent is not to quantify qualitative data; tallies and frequencies are essentially a supplement to the narrative. What *is* important to report is the concentration of individual responses and the concentration of responses across individuals.

The headings and subheadings on the findings road map provide the organizational structure for the discussion. In constructing your road map, keep in mind that nobody wants to read pages and pages of findings. The tension is this: When reporting findings, the idea is to be concise. Yet the idea is also not to split hairs too finely. Therefore, look for any headings that overlap and can be collapsed.

In qualitative research, you as the researcher are telling the story of what you learned from participants. As such, participants' quotes are used to illustrate the points that you are making. In other words, you are telling the story of your research as you see it; as you make your points, you are giving "clues" to the reader about what people said. It is important to mention this because those clues or lead-in sentences are the very points that you are making. You cannot leave it to the reader to decide what the point is; you have to tell the reader the gist of what the research participant is saying that supports the points in your story. If you took the quotes out of your findings chapter, however, one would still have to be able to see the story. Remember that, although the quotes are your support and your evidence, if you had to remove all your quotes, your clues should be able to stand alone and "tell the story." Therefore, make sure that all your lead-in sentences are, in each case, specific. Your careful choice of words will reflect your clear understanding of your findings. If you mislead the reader or cause readers to "do the work" themselves, you jeopardize your study, introducing the possibility of it being misinterpreted or worse still, rejected.

With short quotes (those that are no longer than a sentence or two), lead in with the participant's name (pseudonym) and be sure that the quoted material is placed within quotation marks. With longer quotes (those that are 40 words or more), use block indentation rather than quotation marks, and place the participant's name at the end of the quote. Then if you have two strong quotes, indent each with respective names at the end of the quotes. Two strong quotes can and should be presented one after the other with no sentence in between. Your lead-in sentence makes your point, and it represents what some of the participants said. In effect, therefore, the two (or three) quotes that you use are representative of what has been said by some others as well. In reporting the findings, what you should be doing is not reporting what every individual said, but rather reporting how various individuals, even though they are expressing it in a slightly different way, are making the same point.

Following are some further useful pointers in planning your discussion:

- Under each findings statement, report your findings from the highest to the lowest frequency. That is, talk first about those aspects of the finding that are most prominent and continue to report on findings in descending order.
- Make sure that percentages and words that you use match (100% would translate to "all," 95% would be an "overwhelming majority," 75% would be "a majority," 30% would be "some," 10% would be "a few," etc.).
- Be selective in your choice of quotes. Remember, the function of quotes is not to illustrate the perceptions or experiences of just one single individual, but rather to be representative of a group of people who share the same sentiment. That is, quotes are intended essentially to demonstrate and give examples of patterns that have emerged in the research. In selecting quotes, therefore, aim for richness and precision. Use only the strongest quotes that clearly show evidence of the points you are trying to make.
- Make sure that all the quotes you use are focused on the point you are trying to make. Quotes should clearly illustrate the concept being discussed. Be concise. Get to "the meat of the quote"—the essence that refers to and supports the point you are making—by eliminating redundancy, wordiness, and repetition. Use ellipses (. . .) to connect supportive phrases that you want to use. Only tell the reader that which she or he needs to know—only that which is directly related to the points you are making. Although there is usually a lot of interesting information, and although much of it might be tempting to include, be sure to include only that which is relevant in terms of providing answers to your research questions.
- Begin looking for and flagging "good" quotes as soon as you start reviewing your data. Be sure to tag these quotes so that you can easily find them when it comes to writing up your findings chapter.
- Keep in mind that quotations never stand on their own, but are linked to the context in which they occur and the claim that the researcher wishes to make. This way, they provide evidence for their assertions. As such, great care should be taken not to take quotes out of context or to mislead the reader about their meaning.
- Exercise skill in dissecting quotes in the right places. Be careful not to change or distort the quote in any way, but rather to pick out those phrases that highlight or stress the main point/idea you are making.
- Always use participants' words verbatim, including errors of speech and repetition. Irrelevant sentences and comments can be removed, and this is indicated by ellipses within the quotation.
- Indicate laughter, coughing, pauses, facial expressions, or any other gestures or emotions by way of including these instances within parentheses when these occur within the quote. Use italics where a word or phrase is emphasized.
- If you make the determination that adding an explanatory word and/or phrase will assist the reader in better understanding the quote, use square brackets.

The same applies for localized colloquial expressions with which readers may be unfamiliar.

- Provide a label for each quote that indicates which type of participant is speaking. The label is provided in parentheses following the quote and can indicate participant identity by way of age, sex, occupation, and/or participant pseudonym. Be sure never to use actual names in your report.
- Do not repeat the same quotes.
- Try not to over- or underquote any one individual. That is, make sure there is fair representation among participants. It should not appear that your findings are based on information from only a few sources.
- Don't overuse quotes. Doing so makes the manuscript read like one long transcript.

When you reach the end of the presentation of your findings, which is usually extremely detailed, you owe it to the readers to tie the whole chapter together, reminding them of what they have learned in the preceding pages. Write a concluding paragraph, in which you briefly explain what you have found. Explain in summary form what the chapter has identified, and prepare the reader for the chapters to follow by offering some foreshadowing as to the intent and content of the final two chapters of your dissertation.

Thematic Presentation of Findings While the standard form of presenting quotes in qualitative research is to weave them into your narrative, this is not the only form. Quotes can also be presented according to themes as part of tables, figures, or charts. Be creative. The overall goal is to convey the story line of your research in an engaging, meaningful, and credible manner.

The challenge throughout data collection and analysis is to reduce the volume of information, identify significant patterns or categories, and construct a meaningful and workable framework for communicating the data. One way of presenting categories of findings on a macro level is to crystallize the narrative by theme or phenomenon, and present this in chart form. As can be seen in Table 8.2, provide the reader with (a) an overview description of each emergent theme (phenomenon or issue) with keywords derived from a factor or other type of analysis; (b) an outline of findings that contribute to the theme; (c) a comparative summary of the range of key points made by individual participants or groups of participants supported by brief, direct quotations; and (d) an action step—that is, key associated questions for further discussion and consideration. A separate chart should be compiled for each theme that emanates from your findings. Sample thematic charts are presented as Appendix Y.

Chapter Summary Discussion

Qualitative data analysis is an attempt to summarize the data collected from multiple data sources in a dependable and accurate manner. When analyzing qualitative data, you need to challenge yourself to explore every possible angle to find patterns and relationships among the data. The amount of data that need to be transcribed, organized,

TABLE 8.2 ● Template for Thematic Chart

THEME A
Name the theme or phenomenon.
List keywords that describe the theme. These words can be gleaned from supporting quotations and from the literature.
OVERVIEW
Explain and describe the theme or phenomenon.
FINDINGS/OUTCOMES
List studies' findings that contribute to and are evidence of your stated theme.
PARTICIPANT PERSPECTIVES
To address perspective discrepancy, support your theme by providing a comprehensive range of participant views that explain and illustrate the findings. List a range of appropriate verbatim quotations.
MOVING FROM FINDINGS TO ACTION
List key questions that will stimulate further discussion and critical reflection. These questions serve as a springboard into analysis and interpretation for the next chapter. Questions should be open ended so as to elicit deep responses. In addition to "What?" and "How?" ask: "Why?" "Why not?" "What if?" "What if not?" "What else?" "How else?" "In what way/s?"

Source: This figure first appeared in Bloomberg, L. D. (2011). *Understanding qualitative inquiry: Content and process* (Part III). Unpublished manuscript.

and reduced can indeed be overwhelming. This chapter explains how to go about organizing and preparing the data for analysis and includes discussion around data reduction and data display. Organizing, preparing, and presenting the findings of your research is, as described in this chapter, a somewhat objective exercise; the researcher is, in this instance, a reporter of information.

Although the mechanics of data analysis vary greatly and are undertaken differently depending on genre and theoretical framework, some general guidelines can be useful. Although the guidelines we provide describe the analytic process as if it were a series of separate sequential steps, it must be remembered that qualitative data analysis is an interactive and recursive process, rather than a linear one. The steps are repeated several times until the researcher feels that there has been sufficient immersion in the data, that sufficient information has been extracted from the data, and that the research questions have been adequately addressed. It is important to recognize that in qualitative research, data collection and data analysis are intimately interconnected processes. Having said that, our view is that for purposes of a dissertation, although it might seem a little contrived, it is most effective to present the findings (an objective exercise) and the analysis of those findings (a subjective exercise) as two separate chapters.

Qualitative research is typically reported in a narrative manner. Although the overall intent is not to quantify qualitative data, tallies and frequencies in qualitative research are essentially a supplement to the narrative. Essentially, you are forming a record of frequently occurring phenomena or patterns of behavior. Once you have established patterns, these need to be explained. You have to consult the literature and consider your pattern findings in light of previous research and existing theory. Do your findings confirm similar research? Do they contradict previous studies? How can you explain these differences or similarities? As you begin to consider answers to these sorts of questions and provide convincing explanations, you are interpreting and synthesizing. This is the stuff of Chapter 9.

Quality Assessment Chapter Checklist

Introduction	✓ Do you have a clear introduction that includes your purpose statement (if required)? ✓ Does your introduction inform the reader as to how the chapter is organized? ✓ Are your data analysis steps clearly identified? ✓ Is it evident how you have managed and organized your data for analysis? ✓ Is your coding process adequately described?
Presentation of Findings	✓ Are your findings statements clearly and precisely stated? ✓ Are the findings presented in relation to the research questions? ✓ Are the findings presented in a logical sequence? ✓ Are the findings clearly organized and easy to follow? ✓ Are the findings directly responsive to the problem raised by the study? That is, do the findings provide an answer to the research questions? ✓ Do the data presented in support of the findings (interview and/or focus group quotations, incidents from field notes, material from documents, etc.) provide adequate and convincing evidence for the findings? ✓ Is this chapter free from interpretation? That is, are your findings reported accurately and objectively? ✓ Are there appropriate lead-in sentences and clues? ✓ Have you selected the strongest and most appropriate quotations to support your point(s)? ✓ Have you trimmed your quotations, eliminating all unnecessary wording? ✓ If you have made use of a road map, is this clear and precise? ✓ Do the headings of your road map correspond with the headings in your narrative?
Summary	✓ Do you include a culminating summary of key findings? ✓ Does your summary paragraph offer some logical link to the next chapter?
And . . .	✓ Did you fill in frequency charts as you were coding so that no information was missed? ✓ If tables and figures are used, are these well organized, self-explanatory, and easy to understand? ✓ Are the data presented in each table described in the text that either follows or precedes it? ✓ Have you tightened up your writing, looking for how to make short, crisp sentences? ✓ Have you refined and revised your initial drafts of this chapter to produce a polished final version? ✓ Have you checked for institutional and/or program-related differences regarding the content and structure of this chapter? ✓ Have you checked for institutional and/or program-related differences regarding the appropriate use of qualitative language and terminology? ✓ Is the writing throughout clear and readable? Refer to Chapter 4 "Guidelines for Academic Writing."

SECTION II: APPLICATION

The application section that follows is a skeleton view of a findings chapter. Essentially, our intention is to provide you with only a "snapshot" of a findings chapter. Were it to be more completely and fully developed, as would be required in an actual dissertation, such a chapter would usually be 40 to 60 pages. As emphasized throughout this book, there are many options with regard to qualitative research presentation. Moreover, requirements vary among institutions and programs, and so, as with other components of the dissertation, you will need to check with your advisor and/or department about presentation of your study's findings.

CHAPTER 4 OF THE DISSERTATION

Presenting Findings

Introduction

The purpose of this multicase study was to explore with a sample of doctoral candidates their perceptions of why they have not managed to complete their dissertations. The researchers believed that a better understanding of this phenomenon would allow educators to proceed from a more informed perspective in terms of design and facilitation of doctoral programs. This chapter presents the key findings obtained from 20 in-depth interviews and seven critical incidents, as well as from a focus group conducted with six additional participants who were not part of the study sample. Five major findings emerged from this study:

1. The overwhelming majority of the participants indicated that the course work did not prepare them to conduct research and write their dissertations.
2. All 20 participants expressed the need to know the content and understand the process involved in conducting research and writing their dissertations.
3. The majority of participants attempted to learn what they needed to know by reaching out in dialogue with colleagues and others, rather than through more formal means.
4. The majority of participants indicated that they relied on their own personal characteristics to facilitate their progress. More than half of these same participants also said colleagues were instrumental in helping.
5. The majority of participants cited lack of good, timely, and consistent advisement as a major barrier standing in the way of their progress.

Following is a discussion of the findings with details that support and explain each finding. By way of "thick description" (Denzin, 2001), the researchers set out to document a broad range of experiences, and thereby provide an opportunity for the reader to enter into this study and better understand the reality of the research participants. The emphasis throughout is on letting participants speak for themselves. Illustrative quotations taken from interview transcripts attempt to portray multiple participant perspectives and capture some of the richness and complexity of the subject matter. Where appropriate, critical incident data are woven in with interview data to augment and solidify the discussion. Following is a further discussion that includes the focus group data.

Finding 1: *An overwhelming majority (19 of 20 [95%]) of the participants indicated that the course work did not prepare them to conduct research or write their dissertations.*

The primary and overriding finding of this study is that the course work did not prepare participants to conduct research or write their dissertations. This finding is highly significant in terms of the overwhelming number of participants (19 of 20 [95%]) who found the course work ineffective in preparing them for the dissertation process. Based on participant descriptions, there appeared to be a lack of connection between the first part of the doctoral program—the course work—and the second part—actually conducting research and writing and presenting it in a completed dissertation. Participants expressed this disconnect in the following ways:

> The dissertation and the course work are two totally different ball games. And so success in one does not make for success in another. The course work gives you knowledge of the field, it gives you the theory, but it doesn't prepare you to write the dissertation. And it doesn't really prepare you to analyze the research you conduct. And I think anyone going in to it needs to understand what a dissertation looks like. How big (emphasis) it is! And consider the other parts of it—not just writing it, but defending it, revising it, editing it—the whole process—you don't really know—no one tells you. (Debbie)

> The course work was confined. The dissertation process didn't have a structure built into it—it wasn't explained, and you find out it is much bigger, and more unwieldy. The process of actually doing it is much more time consuming—and that's if you know what you're doing—which in my case was less than half the time. It is a shame that the course work is not more directed. Ultimately, everything is indirectly associated with the dissertation, and so I think there could have been a better job done explaining what to expect, what you would have to know and be able to do by the end of the course work, and you don't get that, so it is like you've fallen off a cliff. (Fay)

> During the course work, I got only an inkling of what a dissertation represents. But the sheer magnitude of it—it's mind-boggling, really, in terms of research. And nothing prepared you for that. Knowing what I know now, I probably would not have gone into it at all in the first place! (Laughs) (Angela)

All 19 participants described their perception of the ineffectiveness of the course work. Among the comments cited were those by Hank, who said: "The course work did not prepare me for what I had to do in this dissertation; it didn't prepare me for the process that lay ahead," and those by Morris, who commented, "I didn't get the practical information during the course work, and when it was given, it was so poorly explained and so unnecessarily complex as to what we were to do, I just got lost—I never got it."

Most of the participants also spoke unfavorably about the research courses. Anthony recalled, "The course work was not in any way related to the dissertation. I took some research courses, but they were not helpful; they were not related to my dissertation." Another participant said specifically of the research courses: "They never gave us the formula in those classes; you couldn't see it or understand it as a step-by-step process—something I found out the hard way" (Anne). Another participant commented: "Even in those (research) classes intended to explain the process, it was conveyed in a way by complex language, you know, and that kept it shrouded in some kind of mystery" (Frank). Only 1 participant of the 20, while acknowledging that it did not fully prepare her, described the research courses as being somewhat helpful. She said,

> I took the research courses, and I learned a lot. It was difficult. And while I got something out of those courses, I didn't really know how I was going to go about actually doing the research, and I was very apprehensive. You know, the steps in the process were still unclear to me. So when I started out it was scary, almost debilitating. (Lin)

Although most participants appreciated the theoretical foundation the course work provided, they also expressed the need for more focus on the practical aspects of conducting research. Two participants conveyed this view when they said:

> The academic work was certainly expected, and I had to grapple with some difficult theoretical concepts, and it was hard, but it was also stimulating. But what was missing is seeing the whole picture—I didn't understand how I was going to be able to apply those concepts to my research—they didn't really focus on that; they didn't make that clear. (Mollie)

> You can't do this work if you don't have a solid basis, a theoretical foundation, but you also need to know how to use theory to frame your research, and they don't really focus on that. They didn't really teach the "how-to." They said, like, "You have to have a conceptual framework"; well, what is that? How will I know it when I see it? You know, what do I have to do to make one? So while there is certainly a lot to be said for knowing the theories, I think more of the "how-tos" would have been helpful. (Julia)

Finding 2: *All 20 participants (100%) expressed a need to know the content and understand the process involved in conducting research and writing their dissertations.*

The order of magnitude in terms of the number of participants who raised the issue of the course work not having prepared them not only is surprising, but also may account for subsequent participant perceptions regarding what they needed to successfully carry out their work. This notion can be seen specifically in the finding that all 20 of the participants (100%) described that they needed knowledge and understanding of the content and/or the process required to conduct research and write the dissertation.

A few participants (3 of 20 [15%]) described the difficulty they had, and are having, in selecting a good, researchable problem. On this point, Anthony commented, "What I'm finding most difficult is to pinpoint exactly what I want to research—the research problem." As another student put it:

> I have never given up when it comes to education, and I really do not understand why I am having such a tough time finding the right topic and thinking clearly about it. You see they don't help you develop the topic, but when you bring one forward, they're ready to tell you all the reasons why it won't work. I know if I could develop a narrowly defined topic, I could collect the data, analyze it, and write it up, but I just can't seem to get off the ground, and this has been very distressing and depressing for me. (Shana)

Other participants (4 of 20 [20%]) spoke more poignantly about needing help in developing their proposal:

> The problem really was and still is how to develop a problem and purpose and research questions that are concrete. I'm also not sure what will get me over this impasse and what is at the source of it. I know I need help. (Mollie)

I just cannot seem to get my proposal done. Every time I hand in a section, there seem to be so many revisions especially with the methodology. I never realized the proposal was such a hurdle. . . . This has been going on too long, and part of it is my own fault because I just don't seem to be able to stay with it. If I could just get past the proposal, I could probably move on. (Brent)

There were some students (2 of 20 [10%]) who had completed their proposals and found themselves stuck in the beginning stages of the research process:

Looking back to the long process of the dissertation research, one critical stage for me started after my proposal defense when I had the pilot data and wanted more guidance for how to code it so as to pave the way for may later data analysis. I tried myself and coded every line of the pilot interviews based on my initial conceptual framework, which was not very effective. I felt totally lost until another colleague was able to explain in language I understood what a conceptual framework really was and how to use it. If it weren't for him, I would still be stuck. (Sally)

I was doing life history interviews, and they had no structure—none! And so when I went to analyze the data I was having a very, very difficult time identifying emerging categories because I had over twelve hundred pages of script that had to be analyzed and I didn't know where to begin, how to get started. And I was so stuck that I thought about giving up, but somehow I just kept at it. But I can tell you it was nerve-wracking. (Doris)

Other participants (3 of 20 [15%]) said they knew what they were supposed to do with regard to the research, but were not sure about how to carry it out. Following are some of the ways these participants expressed their frustrations in not knowing the process they needed to follow:

I feel like I'm in limbo. The process and what is required is not clear. Basically, once you pass the certification exam, you get a letter of congratulations, and then—boom—that's it! You are alone. I was alone. I feel very alone. (Lin)

The method of doing a dissertation really stood in my way—the method—how to do it. I mean, you know something from the theory, and you've got all those books, but you still don't know *how*. You know a lot of *what*, but you still don't know how. And who is going to show you how? (Jane)

I wish I knew what I needed to do sooner. Then I would have been much further along than I am. But I guess everybody has to have the experience of the process of searching, of exploring *how*. And while you are trying very hard, it is important to have somebody direct you. Especially because you will have a lot—and I mean a lot—of data. I was lucky to have found someone who helped me. (Carin)

In addition to needing to understand the process, two students also spoke about the need to be assertive. In this regard, Lin said: "I learned there is help out there. Nobody tells you where the help is—you have to go and look for it." In this same vein, Angela said, "I have learned not to wait for professors but to seek them out, make appointments with them, and ask questions, and go after what you need to know."

A few of the participants (3 of 20 [15%]) talked about learning to carry out the research process on their own or, as several said, "the hard way." This idea is best illustrated by the comment of one participant who said:

When I started out, I went to the doctoral office, and I picked up some brochures, and the manual helped me understand the process as far as what was required. Then I started reading other dissertations and sort of took them apart to figure out what others had done, and I pieced it together, piece by piece. Nobody told me—I had to find that all out by myself. I learned about the research process in a really hard way. (Brad)

A few of the inactive students (3 of 20 [15%]) reflected on their past experience in trying to understand the process and offered some insights into the complexities involved:

The truth is that I feel that people get engaged in dissertation work without being really absolutely clear as to what it would take in terms of research, in terms of the support we were going to get, in terms of the type of writing we were going to have to do, the time frame as to how long it was going to take. There were so many unknowns. (Angela)

A master's degree is very structured. You know exactly what you are supposed to do and how you are supposed to do it. But when you are in a doctoral program, all of a sudden you are expected to be very independent. And while people may like to be independent there still needs to be some kind of structure. Doctoral students need clear instructions in terms of the presentation of their subject matter but also in terms of how to do the actual data collection, analysis, and the rest. Advisors should plan with students more and guide the students more. They should start exploring topics and the literature review early on—it would make it all so much better, so much less confusing, so much less agonizing. (Julia)

Finding 3: *The majority of participants (15 of 20 [75%]) attempted to learn what they needed to know by reaching out in dialogue with colleagues, rather than through more formal means.*

The overriding finding that the course work did not prepare participants to carry out the practical aspects of conducting research and writing their dissertations was further reflected by the informal, rather than formal, ways by which the majority of students went about trying to get the help and guidance they needed. Half of all participants (50%) spoke of their experiences reaching out to other students. Connie described the value of interacting with colleagues: "The colleagues I met along the way were so helpful; we were supportive of one another. I was so lucky to be part of a cohesive and collaborative group, and we continue to help each other figure things out." Other participants were even more explicit in describing their positive interaction with colleagues:

After the course work, I looked to some of my classmates for help, especially those who were further along than I was, and that helped me a lot. It wasn't that they were experts, but they knew more about the process than I did. They already had approved proposals, and they were collecting data, and I wasn't nearly there yet, and they filled in some gaps for me. And I continue to keep in touch with them, and sometimes I am able to help them, and you know, they understand, because it's like we're all in this together. (Anne)

Everybody is very busy. In every program they enroll too many students, and the professors don't have the time to give the students enough attention. So, in our department the doctoral students get together, and we help each other. We shouldn't really have to do that! But we're all frustrated. (Lin)

In addition to reaching out to others, a number of participants (6 of 20 [33%]) also described how they went about learning informally in self-directed ways. Brad described his strategy in this way: "I spent a lot of my time doing research; I was either in the library or on the Internet, and I just kept digging until I found what I needed." Similarly, another participant said:

> I did an awful lot of reading on my own. I read so many dissertations, I can't even tell you how many, particularly those related to my topic, and that was helpful to me to understand what others had done, how they went about their research. So by reading I had some mental models I could follow. (Anthony)

Fewer participants (5 of 20 [25%]) said they found the post–course work dissertation seminars offered at their universities of help in understanding the practical aspects of doing research. One of these participants described the benefits of these seminars in this way:

> I found the dissertation seminar very helpful. I went regularly, and I learned a lot, and it gave me a very clear outline of how to proceed. Finally, I understood how everything fits together, how the research questions are related to the purpose and how they must fit with your conceptual framework. I finally understood it because we had a faculty person who had a very pragmatic approach—she was so clear in her explanations. I think just about everyone in the seminar felt that way. (Sally)

Only 4 of the 20 participants (25%) mentioned that they got the direction they needed from their advisors. At the same time, these participants also said it was not always easy to get an appointment with their advisors. One of these participants described it in this way:

> It seemed I was always tracking my advisor down when she was on campus. Almost every other week, I tried to contact her. And when I did reach her, and when she had time, she would sit down with me and talk, and every time after talking with her, I clarified a lot of stuff. I would tell someone to start as early as possible to build up a collegiate relationship with their advisor—it's so important. (Jane)

Only 1 of the 20 participants (5%) indicated that the course work was somewhat helpful to her. She said: "The course work helped me to some extent but not enough—it points you in the right direction, but it doesn't fill in the missing pieces" (Lin).

To deal with her frustration, one participant (5%) reached out to other experts in her field. In this regard, she described how she reached out to a faculty person outside her university:

> I was fortunate. I met a professor (in another city) at a conference, and I took it upon myself to e-mail her, and she was kind enough to write back—as a matter of fact we had countless e-mails going back and forth, and she helped me form some initial ideas about how to develop the problem and how to carry out the research. And she didn't have to do that—she didn't know me all that well. I'm just grateful because I don't know what I would have done if I hadn't found her. (Jane)

Finding 4: *The majority of participants (15 of 20 [75%]) indicated that they relied on themselves to facilitate their progress. More than half of these same participants (8 of 15 [53%]) also said that colleagues were instrumental in helping them.*

It was not surprising that, in the absence of formal guidance during course work and because of inconsistent advisement, a majority of participants relied on themselves and their colleagues to help facilitate their progress. Participants framed the need to be self-reliant as follows:

> You need to have perseverance, patience, and basically a very independent spirit, someone who really pretty much knows how to go about finding out what they need to know and doesn't feel disheartened by lack of support and caring. (Angela)

> What helped me was my single-mindedness. I was and am determined—you know, relentless. I think that's how one has to be. You can't sit back and wait for someone to come along to help you—it doesn't work that way—you have to rely on yourself mostly. (Connie)

Many students expressed the need to reach out to colleagues. On this point, Brent commented: "When I'm really stuck I call on some of my classmates. . . . And even if they don't have the answers, they provide moral support." Similarly, another participant said:

> You have to have faith in yourself, you have to believe in yourself, you have to have confidence, and it's about having a positive attitude—you know, one that says I can do this. Sometimes, when I hit a roadblock and my confidence dips, that's when I call on my colleagues, and they give me support and encouragement, and I hope I do that for them when they need it. (Brad)

A few participants (3 of 20 [15%]) said they received help from faculty other than their advisors. This notion was illustrated by one participant who went outside her department for help:

> I went to Professor X when I had questions. And she was great because she's very structured and she had examples of the way to do things. And you could sit with her. She would go over things. She took the time. I believe that to really make this work you have to have advisors who like to advise, who have the skills to advise, and they have to have patience with people. And they need to be trained. It's almost as if they need to be counselors. I didn't have that in my department, with my advisor, so I had to go outside. (Debbie)

Only two participants (10%) described the guidance and direction they received from their advisors in positive ways. In his description of his relationship with his advisor, Dexter said: "I have a very good rapport with my advisor—he's always willing to go over things with me, and he tries to find the time for me, and I know that is not the case with all advisors, so I really appreciate him." Jane corroborated these sentiments when she said: "I developed a very positive relationship and rapport with my advisor, and this was a big plus for me."

Finding 5: *The majority of participants (14 of 20 [70%]) cited lack of good, timely, and consistent advisement as a major barrier standing in the way of their progress.*

Given that only two participants described the guidance and direction they received from their advisors in positive terms, it is not surprising that the majority of participants described the quality, access, and availability of advisors as a major impediment to their progress. (It should be noted that four participants did not share their perceptions of the advisement that they received.) The negative view of advisement is illustrated by the following participant comments:

> Most of them (advisors) don't put much into it because they're not really interested in what their students are doing. If they can't share in getting the credit for it to bolster their tenure . . . I have a kind of jaded view of advisors at this point! I think it's the university structure and the bureaucracy. You know they have to publish or perish. And also I don't know if advisors come into it with the skills, the people skills. I think you really have to be able to work with the student, to understand their frustrations, their issues, the things that block

them, and to help them to be able to overcome those things. In a lot of ways it's a mentoring relationship. And so you have to be authentic. (Debbie)

He (my advisor) really didn't help me at all. Every time I went in to see him, he would say to me, "I'm here to help you." I was yelling silently, "Help me, help me, tell me what to do!" In the end I was so frustrated. I wanted him to give me some specific work. I didn't know what I was supposed to do, instead of just reading the literature. That went on for a long, long time, about 3 to 4 years. (Lin)

I couldn't get anywhere with my first advisor. And I did three proposals with an advisor who kept saying, "Well, that's not it yet. I'll know it when I see it." So it was that kind of response. I think when he said he'd know it when he saw it, he really didn't have a clue himself. He did well with advisees who could find a different way of dealing with that. I really needed some help and more structure or framework in which to get it done, and that wasn't forthcoming. (Anne)

Related to the disappointment that participants expressed concerning advisement, eight of the participants (40%) also cited other faculty and administration and the rigidity of the process. Some of the ways participants summed up their experiences were as follows:

Nobody was really clear, not the faculty, not the administration. The really annoying thing from my perspective is that nobody is really there to give you guidelines. This is a very difficult process, a very lengthy one, and while it is so rigid, so many things are so vague. Most of the time, the feeling is one of loneliness. Hanging out in the wind—it was so over-whelming. (Angela)

It was the constantly changing expectation among the committee members about what I was expected to do and how I was expected to do it. I was writing various chapters, and I had constant and conflicting messages about what I was supposed to write and how I was supposed to write it. That was very frustrating. . . . It seemed like a useless exercise in control. (Hank)

I understand now, which I did not at the beginning, that writing a dissertation is an exercise whose value does not lie in its creative expression or revelation of new knowledge, but [lies] merely in its approved execution in accordance with a particular set of rules. (Morris)

In addition to describing structural impediments, such as ineffective advisement, lack of faculty and administration support, and the rigidity of the process, participants described personal factors that impeded their progress. Among these were professional work demands, personal and family issues, financial constraints, and lack of confidence in ability.

Ten of the 20 participants (50%) talked about the stress and challenges involved in managing their jobs and the time required to work on their dissertations. Following are illustrations of participants' comments regarding professional and work demands:

I found that having a demanding full-time position and a commute on top of it, I just couldn't fit it in. So I don't know if I lost the drive along the way, or if it was just that some other things became more of a priority. I mean, I had to work—that was the priority. So, I would say that people need to really think it through and dedicate the time to do it. (Doris)

Losing my job—that was a huge distracter. And the job that I took was a job that didn't pay me enough. I took it out of necessity, so there was a lot of financial strain imposed. Another thing about losing my job was that I lost the context of where I was thinking of doing my research. So I lost focus on what I actually was going to be doing, and I felt overwhelmed with trying to find something else. (Frank)

Six of the 20 participants (30%) focused on family issues and described these as impeding their progress. As Julia said, "Just when I felt I was beginning to make progress my mother died, and that really set me back." Various other comments illustrate the difficulties involved in managing family commitments:

My wife and I both work, and we have three kids. There's always something going on, you know. Juggling all our schedules, managing everybody's plans and all the family issues, is difficult. There's a lot of pressure. (Carin)

My job changed, and I adopted children. And the combination of these two things meant that I just couldn't do it (the dissertation), and there wasn't anything anybody could do to help me with it at that point in time. (Debbie)

A few other participants (5 of 20 [25%]) expressed concern around funding their doctoral work:

I'm always running around and worrying about how I'm going to pay next semester's tuition. There's little scholarship money available, and I'm digging myself deeper in a hole every year. This has gone on for 9 years. If I didn't have this worry maybe I would have finished. (Doris)

Some participants (5 of 20 [25%]) indicated that they struggled with the lack of confidence they had in their ability to do the work. Shana expressed her self-doubt by saying, "I would tell someone not to be afraid of it (the dissertation) like I was; I spent too much time being afraid." Another participant was even more explicit in explaining her doubts about being able to do the work:

I think it's [the dissertation] a terrifying process—I really do. And I worried so much about whether I could actually do this kind of work; I had a hard time shaking off those self-doubting negative thoughts when they took hold of me. And I don't know that faculty really wants to disarm anybody of what it's all about because it may take away the mystique. (Anne)

Findings From the Focus Group Interview

A focus group interview was held for approximately 1½ hours with six doctoral candidates who were not part of the study sample, but who met all of the criteria for participation. The focus group participants were assured that all of their comments would be held in strict confidence and that each would be identified by a pseudonym. Prior to the session, the researchers contacted the six participants individually by phone to schedule a convenient time to hold the session. Following that conversation, the six participants were sent the same consent form given to all interviewees and were asked to sign and return it in an enclosed stamped and self-addressed envelope to the researchers. Before the session began, the participants were told that the session would be audio recorded and subsequently transcribed by the researchers.

The researchers described their role as facilitators, monitoring the process and advising that the discussion would largely be in control of the participants. Participants were told that there would be two parts to the discussion. In the first part, they were asked to think about their experience in the research process and share with one another their perceptions of factors that helped them during that process. The facilitators indicted they would let the participants know when to turn their attention to the second part of the discussion. In the last part of the discussion, participants were asked to share with one another those factors they perceived might have stood in the way of their progress. Specifically, what, if any, obstacles and challenges did participants face that they believe may have impeded their ability to move forward in their research, and what, if any, action did they take to overcome those challenges and/or obstacles?

It was interesting to see how the discussion by the six focus group participants parallels the findings that emanated from the interviews. All six participants indicated that they relied largely on themselves and a few classmates to help them when they got stuck. Michele said, "I really wanted to get through this process, and I was determined to find out what I needed, no matter what. As an extravert, I wasn't shy about asking my classmates for help or advice; heck, they were in the same boat, so I didn't have to impress them." Jacob followed up quickly by adding, "I was the opposite, Michele—I was and still am a real introvert—you know, I like to figure things out on my own—but this process is so beyond that—so beyond my experience. I had no choice. I had to learn to become more like you, an extravert, not afraid to ask for help, and I mostly went to my peers because my advisor was, let us say, not often available!"

Jacob's comments precipitated a discussion of the access and availability of advisors. Two other members, Kent and Lauren, were almost talking over each other in recounting their experiences with advisement. The following captures a part of what Kent said, "I mustn't have been one of her favorites. I had to wait so long for feedback—it was frustrating as hell—it made me feel disregarded." Lauren added, "I know what you mean about waiting and waiting for feedback, and then when you finally get something, it was, let's say, vague—to be kind. I really needed more direction." Another member, Julia, chimed in: "Yeah, at a time like this who wants to be self-directed?" The group laughed. Much like the descriptions from the interviews, the discussion continued, mostly centering on the frustration the six members had with the accessibility and timeliness of the advisement they received. Only one participant tied lack of advisement to financial difficulties. Beth said, "The tuition we pay—at least at my university—is outrageous and goes up every semester, it seems, and to think you are paying these exorbitant sums in tuition, and you're not getting your money's worth—something is wrong." Nods of acknowledgment led to the close of the discussion.

Both parts of the focus group discussion confirm perceptions of lack of advisement as an impediment to their moving more quickly through the process. The six members' discussions of what they perceived helped them also were consistent with data from the interviews. The focus group members indicated that they largely relied on themselves and their own resourcefulness while seeking the help of their colleagues and peers.

Chapter Summary

This chapter presented the five findings uncovered by this study. Findings were organized according to the research questions. Data from individual interviews, critical incidents, and a focus group revealed research participants' perceptions vis-à-vis their experiences of the dissertation process. As is typical of qualitative research, extensive samples of quotations from participants are included in the report. By using participants' own words, the researchers aim to build the confidence of readers by accurately representing the reality of the persons and situations studied.

The primary finding of this study is that the course work did not prepare participants to conduct research or write the dissertations. This finding emanated from the expressed descriptions of 95% of the participants as they discussed their perceptions of what they needed to successfully conduct research and write their dissertations. In discussing why they felt unprepared after they completed the course work, several participants talked about the lack of connection between the course work and conducting and writing up the research. Although most participants appreciated the theoretical foundation the course work provided, they expressed the need for more focus on the practical aspects of conducting research. A few said they knew what they were supposed to do with regard to the research, but were not sure about how to carry it out.

The second finding was that all 20 participants expressed the need to know the content and understand the process involved in conducting research and writing their dissertations. Some participants described the difficulty they had, and are having, in selecting a good, researchable problem. Others spoke about needing help in developing their proposal. Some had completed their proposals, but found themselves stuck in the beginning stages of the research process. In addition to needing to understand the process, two students spoke about the need to be assertive, and a few others talked about learning to carry out the research process on their own or, as several put it, "the hard way."

The third finding was that the majority of participants attempted to learn what they needed to know by reaching out in dialogue with colleagues and others, rather than through more formal means. Half of all participants spoke of their experiences reaching out to other students. In addition to reaching out to others, a number of participants described how they went about learning informally, in self-directed ways, through reading and research. A quarter of all the participants said they found the post–course work dissertation seminars offered at their universities of help in understanding the practical aspects of doing research, and a quarter also mentioned that they got the direction they needed from their advisors.

The fourth finding was that the majority of participants relied on their own personal characteristics to facilitate their progress. More than half of these same participants also said colleagues were instrumental in helping them. A few participants said they received help from faculty other than their advisors.

The fifth finding was that the majority of participants cited lack of good, timely, and consistent advisement as a major barrier standing in the way of their progress. Some also mentioned lack of faculty and administration support and the rigidity of the process. In addition to these structural impediments, participants also described personal factors that impeded their progress, including professional work demands, personal and family issues, financial constraints, and lack of confidence in ability.

Findings from the focus group corroborated the findings from the interviews. All six participants indicated that they relied largely on themselves, and that they called on classmates to help them when they got stuck. Focus group participants discussed their frustration regarding accessibility and timeliness of the advisement they received, confirming interview perceptions of lack of advisement as a major impediment to moving more quickly through the dissertation process.

Annotated Bibliography

Bernard, H. R., & Ryan, G. W. (2010). *Analyzing qualitative data: Systematic approaches.* Thousand Oaks, CA: Sage.

This book introduces the reader to various methods for analyzing qualitative data—a nebulous task for novice researchers. Unlike many other texts, it covers the extensive range of available methods so that readers become aware of the array of techniques beyond their individual disciplines. Great detail is applied to analysis of observation, interviews, focus groups, and life history. Part I provides an overview of the basics involved in analysis: searching for themes, coding data, and developing conceptual models. Part II comprises 11 chapters, each treating a different method for analyzing text. Included in this section are semantic word analysis, discourse analysis, narrative analysis, content analysis, schema analysis, and comparative analysis. Real examples from the literature across the health and social sciences provide invaluable applied understanding.

Boeije, H. (2010). *Analysis in qualitative research*. Thousand Oaks, CA: Sage.

This book is written for students embarking on a qualitative research project, taking the reader through the process of analyzing data from start to finish. The author sets out a model for coding data in order to break it down into manageable parts, and then offers suggestions regarding reassembling data to create a meaningful picture of the phenomenon under study. The book does a good job of guiding the researcher through the final phase of data analysis— that is, integration of data into a coherent analytical format. The author offers useful ideas pertaining to diagramming, matrices and other visual displays, memoing and thinking-aloud analytic strategies, ways of integrating analysis and interpretation, how to incorporate the use of software when appropriate, and writing up of research. This book includes examples covering a wide range of subjects, making it useful for students across a variety of social science disciplines.

Boyatzis, R. E. (1998). *Transforming qualitative information: Thematic analysis and code development*. Thousand Oaks, CA: Sage.

As this author illustrates, thematic analysis—a process for encoding qualitative information—can be thought of as a bridge between qualitative and quantitative research. As such, the discussion in the book confronts the debate between positivist and postmodernist takes on the research act in an innovative and fresh way. More than that, and in a practical sense, however, this book helps the reader understand the concept of thematic analysis and provides clear guidelines about learning to develop techniques to apply to one's own research. This book shows how to sense themes—the first step in analyzing information—as well as how to develop the various types of codes. This book is useful for researchers across a broad spectrum of disciplines.

Creswell, J. W. (2013). *Qualitative inquiry and research design: Choosing among five traditions* (3rd ed.). Thousand Oaks, CA: Sage.

Written in an easy-to-read way, this book examines the five most common traditions or genres in qualitative inquiry—narrative research, phenomenology, grounded theory, ethnography, and case study—at each phase of the research process. Chapter 8 focuses on data analysis and representation, and includes new techniques being discussed in the qualitative research "conversation" for analyzing data in each of the five traditions. Creswell begins with a generic approach to analysis as provided by various leading authors in the field. He then presents a visual model—a data analysis spiral—that affords conceptual understanding of all the steps involved in the data analysis process, including data management, reading, reading and memoing, and describing and classifying data. Using this model, Creswell explores in greater detail each tradition of inquiry, examining the specific data analysis procedures and different ways of interpreting and representing data within each tradition. The chapter concludes with a critical overview of the use of software programs for qualitative research, and the application of computer-aided analysis within each of the research traditions, including both common and unique features, as well as templates for coding data within each of the traditions.

Flick, U. (2013) (Ed.). *The Sage handbook of qualitative data analysis*. Thousand Oaks, CA: Sage.

This handbook provides a state-of-the art overview of the whole field of qualitative data analysis; from general analytic strategies used in qualitative research, to approaches specific to particular types of qualitative data. The volume includes chapters on traditional analytic strategies such as grounded theory, content analysis, hermeneutics, phenomenology and narrative analysis, as well as coverage of newer trends like mixed methods, reanalysis and meta-analysis. Practical aspects such as sampling, transcription, working collaboratively, writing and implementation are given close attention, as are theory and theorization, reflexivity, and ethics. Written by an international team of experts in qualitative research, the handbook is an essential compendium for all qualitative researchers and students across the social sciences. Part II includes details pertaining to issues such as transcription, collaborative analysis, comparative practices, and induction and deduction. Part III covers analytic strategies pertaining to the different qualitative traditions, and issues regarding the use of software in qualitative analysis. Part IV is the meat of the book, dealing with different types of data and ways of analyzing them. Included are interviews, focus groups, conversation analysis, discourse analysis, observation, documents, news media, images, film, videography, and virtual data. Part V focuses on using and assessing qualitative data analysis. Included in these chapters are discussions around ethical issues, meta-analysis, theorization, generalization, and implementation—that is, putting analyses into practice. This handbook is an illuminating new resource for qualitative and mixed methods scholars. These essays are certain to provoke further investigation, discussion, and theorizing, around what once was a neglected area of qualitative research practice.

Gibson, W. J., & Brown, J. (2009). *Working with qualitative data*. Thousand Oaks, CA: Sage.

This is an accessible introduction of how to develop and apply strategies for the analysis of qualitative data in the social, health, and educational sciences. The emphasis of this book is on exploring ways in which analysis is situated within the context of the entire research process. Data analysis is not a procedural issue but an ongoing conceptual one. As these authors put it, "Analysis is a process, not a stage." Important issues regarding the relationship between theory and analysis are discussed, and this relationship is examined in great detail with regard to grounded theory. Useful chapters include those covering categorization and analysis of documents, interviews, observational material, images, and video. The concept of "thematic analysis" and critiques are presented in detail, as are coding procedures. Included is a chapter on using qualitative analysis software, with an emphasis on the concerns and debates around using computer-assisted software. A final chapter focuses on modes of structuring and presenting different forms of analysis. Through the use of practical examples, the book maps out analytic strategies spanning all phases of the research process, and demonstrates the ways in which these strategies can be appropriately applied.

Guest, G., MacQueen, K., & Namey, E. E. (2012). *Applied thematic analysis*. Thousand Oaks, CA: Sage.

This book provides step-by-step guidance on how to systematically and rigorously analyze text generated from in-depth interviews and focus groups, relating predominantly to applied qualitative studies. The authors introduce and outline an inductive approach that draws on established and innovative theme-based techniques suited to the applied research context. Chapters follow the sequence of activities in the analysis process, and include many useful tools and templates. Real-world examples illustrate and reinforce ideas and procedures described, and detailed working exercises offer hands-on practice vis-à-vis techniques presented. The book covers useful discussion pertaining to coding strategies, planning and preparing for data analysis, trustworthiness considerations (credibility and dependability), data reduction techniques, comparison of thematic data, choice of data analysis software, and writing up and presenting thematic analyses.

Huck, S. W. (2000). *Reading statistics and research* (3rd ed.). New York: Longman.

This book is useful for the qualitative researcher whose study includes a quantitative component. It provides the reader with an understanding of statistical terms, the ability to make sense of and set up statistical tables and figures, knowledge of what specific research questions can be answered by each of a variety of statistical procedures, and a better understanding of how to decipher and critically evaluate statistically based findings. Tables, figures, and passages of text from published research reports are used as examples.

Merriam, S. B. (2009). *Qualitative research: A guide to design and implementation*. San Francisco: Jossey-Bass.

Many texts on qualitative research devote much space to theoretical discussions of methodology and data collection, and relatively little to the management and analysis of data once they are collected. This book redresses that imbalance, devoting an intensive chapter to data analysis. Chapter 8 reviews various strategies for analyzing qualitative data, and addresses the increasing role and function of computers in qualitative data management and analysis. The chapter stresses the iterative nature of data collection and data analysis, recommending that these two processes be conducted concurrently. Management of the voluminous data typical of a qualitative study is another topic addressed in this chapter. The heart of the chapter explains the different levels of analysis possible—ranging from developing a descriptive account of the findings to constructing categories and themes, to interpreting the meaning of the data. The chapter also speaks to within-case and cross-case analysis, which is a common feature of case study analysis. This is followed by a discussion of computer-aided software programs in qualitative data analysis.

Miles, M. B., & Huberman, A. M. (1994). *Qualitative data analysis* (2nd ed.). Thousand Oaks, CA: Sage.

The classic on qualitative data analysis, this book takes the reader through a series of steps that illustrate how to approach and conduct the analytic process. The approach of these authors to data analysis is basically a systematic, deductive one, with the authors reflecting a somewhat formal, positivistic approach. Although those with a more interpretive/inductive outlook might be critical, these authors' goal is to make the qualitative research process manageable and doable. They focus on bounding data collection, developing a coding structure, and building a logical chain of evidence to support research conclusions. A useful and concise discussion regarding purposeful sampling procedure is offered on pages 27 to 34. The sections on coding are useful too as the authors provide a variety of ideas for analytical approaches, offering examples and addressing potential pitfalls. Particularly useful for the dissertation writer is the strong visual emphasis throughout this book; there are the many examples of ways of reducing and displaying qualitative data, including tables, charts, matrices, graphs, maps, networks, and figures. As the authors emphasize, graphic representation allows the reader to "see what's happening." Each of more than 60 methods of data display and analysis is described and illustrated in detail, with practical hands-on suggestions for adaptation and use.

Miles, M. B., Huberman, A. M., & Saldana, J. (2014). *Qualitative data analysis: A methods sourcebook* (3rd ed.). Thousand Oaks, CA: Sage.

The third edition of Miles and Huberman's classic research methods text has been updated by Johnny Saldana, author of *The Coding Manual for Qualitative Researchers* (2013). This is an excellent update to the original text, which has long been central to understanding and teaching qualitative research design. Several of the data display strategies from previous editions are presented in re-envisioned and reorganized formats to enhance reader accessibility and comprehension. The third edition's presentation of the fundamentals of research design and data management is followed by five distinct methods of analysis: exploring, describing, ordering, explaining, and predicting. Each methods profile follows a standard format: Description, Applications, Example, Analysis, and Notes. Each method of data display and analysis is described in detail, with practical suggestions for adaptation and use. Vivid examples from a host of education and social science disciplines show the application of qualitative research methods in real-world settings. The book's most celebrated chapter, "Drawing and Verifying Conclusions," is retained and revised, and the chapter on report writing has been greatly expanded, and is now called "Writing About Qualitative Research." Overall, this book is well organized and clear, and replete with practical applications, resources, and examples. Comprehensive and authoritative, *Qualitative Data Analysis* has been revised for a new generation of critical qualitative researchers confronted with ever changing demands in the field. The companion website includes links to related SAGE journals articles. In addition, several display forms, matrices, and templates from the book will be available for downloading.

Richards, L., & Morse, J. M. (2013). *Readme first for a user's guide to qualitative methods* (3rd ed.). Thousand Oaks, CA: Sage.

These authors provide a framework for understanding the decision-making processes that underlie current thinking about the making of data. A key strength of the book is the discussion and presentation of how to think about qualitative research and analysis. Part II, "Inside Analysis," helps a researcher to think more clearly about what qualitative data actually are (and what they are not), how to record and manage appropriate data, and how to prepare data for analysis. Chapter 5 talks about "making data"—the ongoing complex process in which the researchers and participants collaboratively negotiate data through the diversity of qualitative research methods. The authors illustrate what can be considered "good data" and "bad data," and provide details regarding the process of transforming data—the management and preparation of data for analysis. Chapter 6 deals with the coding process, and includes discussion around what coding is; the different ways of storing, managing, and monitoring codes; and tips and common traps. What is useful is the notion of using codes to develop themes or "themeing." Chapter 7, called "Abstracting," deals with the ability to think abstractly in order to transform data, and "methodological toolboxes" are provided that shed light on the interpretive process. Chapter 8 deals with methodological congruence between method and analysis, and offers useful analytic distinctions among phenomenological, ethnographic, case study, discourse analysis, and grounded theory approaches. As the authors rightfully point out, each tradition is sensitive to particular analytic methods and strategies, as such demanding that the researcher think about analysis in a particular way. Researcher reflexivity is stressed throughout.

Rubin, H. J., & Rubin, I. S. (2012). *Qualitative interviewing: The art of hearing data* (2nd ed.). Thousand Oaks, CA: Sage.

Written in user-friendly language and incorporating many useful examples, this book explains in great detail how to obtain rich, detailed, and evocative information through interviews—the primary method of data collection in qualitative research. The book does well in striking a balance among the different qualitative traditions, addressing many of their criteria, issues, and concerns. Aside from the earlier chapters, which take the reader though all the steps involved in interviewing, extremely useful are Chapter 11, "Analyzing Coded Data in the Responsive Interview Model," and Chapter 12, "Sharing the Results." In both of these chapters, the authors offer clear explanations and suggestions regarding different ways to clarify and summarize concepts and themes, group and sort information, search for patterns and linkages, and produce and present a rich, descriptive narrative.

Saldana, J. (2013). *The coding manual for qualitative researchers* (2nd ed.). Thousand Oaks, CA: Sage.

This book focuses exclusively on the function of codes, coding, and analytic memo writing during the qualitative data collection and analytic processes. The manual profiles a selected repertoire of coding methods generally applied in qualitative data analysis. In total, 32 coding methods are profiled that can be applied to a wide range of research traditions or genres including grounded theory, phenomenology, and narrative inquiry. This repertoire of approaches ranges in complexity from fundamental to advanced levels, covering the full range of qualitative data collection methods. For each approach, the author discusses the method's origins in the professional literature, and offers a thorough description of the method itself, recommendations for practical applications, and clearly illustrated examples. The coding manual does not maintain allegiance to any one specific research genre or methodology. Throughout the book you will read a breadth of perspectives on codes and coding, often purposefully juxtaposed to illustrate and highlight the diverse opinions among scholars in the field. As the author states upfront, "No one, including myself, can claim final authority on coding's utility or the best way to analyze qualitative data" (p. 2). Included in the manual is a discussion regarding how the coding process initiates qualitative data analysis, application of qualitative data analysis software, writing of analytic memos, and advice regarding how best to use coding manuals for particular studies. For each of the analytic approaches discussed, Saldana explains the method's origins and practical applications, and illustrates examples with analytic follow-up. Included in the manual are exercises and activities pertaining to coding and qualitative data analytic skill development, useful operational models and diagrams, and a comprehensive glossary of coding methods and analytic recommendations. This coding manual is an invaluable reference for beginning and advanced qualitative researchers in disciplines including education, sociology, communication, anthropology, psychology, and health care.

Silver, C., & Lewins, A. (2014). *Using software in qualitative research: A step-by-step guide*. Thousand Oaks, CA: Sage.

This volume offers extensive coverage of the practice and principles of Computer Assisted Qualitative Data Analysis (CAQDAS) and will enable researchers to choose the most appropriate package for their needs and get the most out of the software package once they're using it. The authors consider a wide range of tasks and processes in the data management and analysis process, and indicate how and in what ways the software can assist at each stage. The authors present three case studies with different forms of data (text, video, and mixed methods data) and illustrate how each step in the analysis process for each project could be supported by the software. This edition is accompanied by an extensive companion website with step-by-step instructions produced by the software developers themselves. Software programs include ATLAS.ti, Dedoose, HyperRESEARCH, MAXQDA, NVivo, QDA Miner, and Transana. This cutting-edge volume is an invaluable reference for newcomers to CAQDAS as well as an essential reference text for the more seasoned qualitative researcher.

Silverman, D. (2013). *Doing qualitative research* (4th ed.). Thousand Oaks, CA: Sage.

Part III presents a very practical guide to analyzing various types of data, including Internet data. As the author writes: "After the first year of research, people have varying degrees of uncertainty about the future. . . . The uncertain one asks: 'I've collected all these data, now what should I do?'" Using various examples, the author offers various strategies for beginning the data analysis process including how to deal with interview transcripts and field notes. He then goes on to explaining in more detail the actual process of analysis, including data reduction (by way of coding procedures), data display (assembling data by way of matrices, graphs, and charts), and drawing conclusions (noting patterns and themes). Chapter 12 discusses the use of computers to analyze qualitative data. The author provides a thorough overview of the most commonly used analytic software packages available, and offers the reader some useful insights regarding the advantages and disadvantages of this method of analysis. The book includes a companion website with student examples and videos.

Silverman, D., & Marvasti, A. (2008). *Doing qualitative research: A comprehensive guide*. Thousand Oaks, CA: Sage.

Designed for graduate students in the social sciences, this text offers a thorough review of the major methods of qualitative research, with explanations of data analysis techniques specific to each method. Particularly useful is Part III of this book, which focuses on the stage when the researcher has begun to gather and analyze data: Chapter 11 outlines what is to be gained by working with early data sets, and Chapter 12 discusses how the early phases of analysis can be more fully developed. The subsequent two chapters consider the utility of software for qualitative data analysis, inherent advantages and limitations, strategies pertaining to deviant case analysis, and related issues of trustworthiness that need to be considered. Explanations include interdisciplinary and real-world examples, case studies, and exercises that speak directly to readers undertaking new research projects and qualitative dissertations in the United States. Chapter 15 provides useful discussion and examples that pertain to key criteria for evaluating qualitative research. Included are criteria such as analytic depth, credibility, and research methodology.

Analyzing and Interpreting Findings

Overview

Qualitative research begins with questions, and its ultimate purpose is learning. To inform the questions, the researcher collects *data*. Data are like building blocks that, when grouped into patterns, become *information*, which in turn, when applied or used, becomes *knowledge* (Rossman & Rallis, 2012). The challenge of qualitative analysis lies in making sense of large amounts of data—reducing raw data, identifying what is significant, and constructing a framework for communicating the essence of what the data reveal. This was the task of Chapter 8, "Analyzing Data and Reporting Findings." The challenge now becomes one of digging into the findings to develop some understanding of what lies beneath them—that is, what information we now have and what this really means. Analysis, in this sense, is about deconstructing the findings—an essentially postmodern concept.

Your goal in conducting analysis is to figure out the deeper meaning of what you have found, and that analysis began when you assigned codes to chunks of raw data. Now that you have a well-laid-out set of findings, you go to a second level. You scrutinize what you have found in the hope of discovering what it means or more precisely, what meaning you can make of it. You are seeking ways to understand what you have found by comparing your findings both within and across groups and by comparing your study's findings with those of other studies.

In qualitative research, we are open to different ways of seeing the world. We make assumptions about how things work. We strive to be open to the reality of others and understand different realities. We must listen before we can understand. Analysis of the findings begins with careful listening to what others have to say. Begin by asking yourself, "Given what I have found, what does this mean? What does this tell me about the phenomenon under study? What is really going on here?" In asking these questions, you are working back and forth between the findings of your research and your own perspectives and understandings to make sense and meaning. Meaning can come from looking at differences and similarities and from inquiring into and interpreting causes, consequences, and relationships.

Data analysis in qualitative research remains somewhat mysterious (Marshall & Rossman, 2015; Merriam, 2009). The problem lies in the fact that there are few agreed-on canons for qualitative analysis in the sense of shared ground rules. There are no formulas for determining the significance of findings or for interpreting them, and there are no ways of perfectly replicating a researcher's analytical thinking. In this chapter, we purport to offer not a recipe, but rather a guideline for navigating the analytical process. Applying guidelines requires judgment, sensibility, and creativity. Because each study is unique, each analytical approach used is unique as well. As Patton (2015) puts it,

> Qualitative analysis transforms data into findings. No formula exists for that transformation. Guidance, yes, but no recipe . . . In this complex and multi-faceted analytical integration of disciplined science, creative artistry, skilled crafting, rigorous sense-making, and personal reflexivity, we mold interviews, observations, documents, and fieldnotes into *findings*. . . . In short, no absolute rules exist except perhaps this: Do your very best with your full intellect to fairly represent the data and communicate what the data reveal given the purpose of the study. (pp. 521–522)

Remember, the human factor is the great strength of qualitative inquiry. But this can also be a fundamental weakness. There may be clear delineated frameworks for analyzing qualitative data, as discussed in Chapter 8 (for example, Miles, Huberman, & Saldana, 2014; Saldana, 2013). But as Patton (2015) emphasizes, guidelines, exemplars, and procedural suggestions are not rules. Each qualitative study is unique, so the analytical approach taken by the researcher will be unique. As such, because qualitative research depends on the skills, training, capabilities, and insights of the researcher, analysis and interpretation ultimately depend on the analytical intellect and style of each individual analyst.

As with all previous chapters, we present two sections: Section I, "Instruction," talks about (a) thinking about, (b) planning, and (c) presenting your analysis. Section II, "Application," presents what an analysis chapter might look like. By using the example carried throughout this book, we analyze and interpret the findings of the research that we have conducted.

It must be stressed that analyzing and interpreting is a highly intuitive process; it is certainly not mechanical or technical. The process of qualitative data analysis and synthesis is an ongoing one, involving continual reflection about the findings and asking analytical questions. Qualitative researchers often, of necessity, learn by doing. As such, there is no clear and accepted single set of conventions for the analysis and interpretation of qualitative data. Indeed, many qualitative researchers would resist this were it to come about, viewing the enterprise as more an art than a science. Therefore, the term *instructions* for this chapter might be somewhat misleading. Reducing the data and presenting findings can be explained in a stepwise and somewhat mechanical fashion. Analysis, synthesis, and interpretation of qualitative data, in contrast, is a far more nebulous endeavor—hence the clear paucity of published literature on how to actually do it (and hence the limited annotated bibliography that we offer for this section). Rather than instructions, what we provide in this chapter are essentially guidelines for how to think about analysis and principles to use in selecting appropriate procedures that will organically unfold and become revealed as you become immersed in your own study.

Please be aware, too, that the guidelines and principles that we provide are essentially generic and can be applicable across a broad range of qualitative genres or traditions. However, analytical approaches are linked to particular forms of data collection, and are underpinned by specific conceptual and philosophical traditions and their inherent grounding assumptions. Methodological congruence implies that there are analytic distinctions among traditions, genres, and approaches. Each tradition is sensitive to particular analytic methods and strategies; as such, each tradition demands that the researcher think about data analysis and representation in a particular way. In essence, the product of each tradition provides a perspective on reality that is specific to that tradition.

For more details and nuances regarding analysis for pure qualitative traditions such as phenomenology, grounded theory, ethnography, and hermeneutics, we suggest that you consult with your advisor and seek the relevant available literature related to your specific tradition. Creswell (2013) and Patton (2015) provide comprehensive outlines regarding data analysis and representation within the current major qualitative traditions or genres, as well as detailed discussion regarding significant differences and similarities among the various approaches.

The previous chapter discussed how to present the findings of your research by organizing data from various sources into categories to produce a readable narrative. The purpose of this chapter is to provide interpretative insights into these findings. This point in the process is where you shift from being an objective reporter to becoming an informed and insightful commentator or storyteller. No one has been closer to the focus of the study, its data, and its progress than you have. You have done the interviewing, studied the transcripts, and read the related literature. You have lived with and wrestled with the data. You now have an opportunity to communicate to others *what you think your findings mean* and integrate your findings with literature, research, and practice. This process requires a good deal of careful thinking and reflection.

Section I: Instruction

Thinking About Your Analysis

Taking time to reflect on your findings and what these might possibly mean requires some serious mind work—so do not try and rush this phase. Spend a few days away from your research, giving careful thought to the findings, trying to put them in perspective in order to gain some deeper insights. To begin facilitating the kind of thinking process required, we have developed what we call an interpretation outline tool—a mechanism that enables you to consider the findings in a deeper way than you have had to do up until now; to "peel back" all the possible reasons regarding how else a finding can be explained, thereby fleshing out the meanings that underlie each finding. Findings should not be taken at face value.

Essentially, this simple but effective tool prompts and prods you to question each of your findings (and all the various aspects of each finding) by asking "Why?" and "Why not?" over and again, allowing you to brainstorm and exhaust all the possibilities that might explain that finding. In effect, those explanations become the basis of your interpretations. This tool propels you to develop and strengthen your critical thinking and reflection on all the issues surrounding your findings. This is essentially "problem posing"—an inductive questioning process rooted in the works of Lindeman, Dewey, and Piaget, who were advocates of an experiential and dialogical education. Freire (1970) and Mezirow (1981) used problem-posing dialogue as a means to develop critical inquiry and understanding of experience.

Figure 9.1 gives some idea of how such a tool can be developed. A sample completed interpretation outline tool is included as Appendix CC. We suggest that a completed version of an interpretation outline be included in your dissertation's appendix to illustrate the logical development and overview of your interpretive thought processes.

Planning Analysis of Your Findings

In thinking about the analysis, you might ask yourself what this chapter is really all about and what it should constitute. How does one go about seeking the deeper meanings behind the findings? How does one get started? What is really involved? We

FIGURE 9.1 ● Interpretation Outline Tool

STEP 1:

State Analytic Category 1: This category directly relates to your research questions.

Describe the corresponding findings.

Ask "Why?" and "Why not?"

Think critically. Brainstorm all possible reasons. Continue to probe "Why?" and "Why not?"

Ask: What is happening, and why it is happening? *How else* can this be explained? What assumptions am I making? What blind spots might I have overlooked? What alternative interpretations or explanations might exist for what I see in the data?

Look (a) within findings, (b) across findings, and (c) across cases/individuals. State all linkages that can be made to the relevant literature.

Ask also: How does my positionality and my identity (social, cultural, political, psychological, institutional) influence the research process? How can I address this? What trustworthiness issues are emerging? How can I address challenges to credibility and validity?

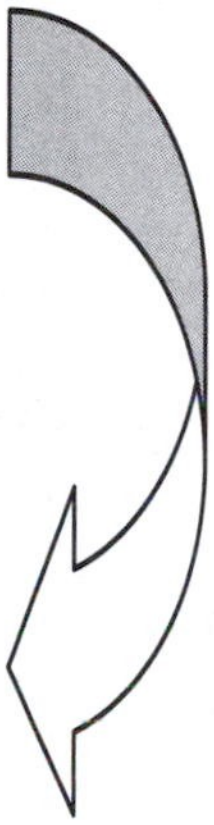

STEP 2:

State Analytic Category 2: This category directly relates to your research questions.

Describe the corresponding findings.

Ask "Why?" and "Why not?"

Think critically. Brainstorm all possible reasons. Continue to probe "Why?" and "Why not?"

Ask: What is happening, and why it is happening? *How else* can this be explained?

What assumptions am I making? What blind spots might I have overlooked? What alternative interpretations or explanations might exist for what I see in the data?

Look (a) within findings, (b) across findings, and (c) across cases/individuals. State all linkages that can be made to the relevant literature.

Ask also: How does my positionality and my identity (social, cultural, political, psychological, institutional) influence the research process? How can I address this? What trustworthiness issues are emerging? How can I address challenges to credibility and validity?

Instruction: Continue in the same manner for each analytic category, exhausting all possible interpretations. In fact, the structured questions in this tool can be asked throughout the research process. In essence, they are a means of checking in with your conceptual framework throughout the process of data collection and analysis of findings.

Source: An initial version of this figure first appeared in Bloomberg, L. D. (2007). *Understanding qualitative inquiry: Content and process* (Part I). Unpublished manuscript. This revised version appears in Bloomberg, L. D. (2011). *Understanding qualitative research: Content and process* (Part III). Unpublished manuscript.

asked ourselves these questions as we set about writing this chapter. We sought the answers by way of structuring our discussion according to three interrelated activities: (a) seeking significant patterns among the findings, (b) making use of description and interpretation, and (c) providing some sort of synthesis or integration.

Think intently about the analytic logic that informs the story you wish to tell. Questions you need to ask yourself include, "What are the key concepts I have used in this study? How do my findings shed light on these concepts and on my broader topic of inquiry? How do the study's findings shed light on the original research problem as set out in the introduction to the dissertation and on related literature and/or theory?" You need to decide the type of story you wish to tell as well as the structure of the chapter. Remember that keeping your findings in context and thinking holistically are among the cardinal principles of qualitative analysis.

Seeking Patterns and Themes Analysis is essentially about searching for patterns and themes—that is, the trends that you see emerging from among your findings. After having spent many hours interviewing (and/or observing) people and contexts, you are likely to come away with some possible explanations of how and why people are saying what they are saying. Having immersed yourself in your data and lived with them for an extended period of time, you have most likely reflected on emergent patterns and themes that run through your findings. You also have probably made conjectures and can offer hypotheses about the significance of certain outcomes, consequences, interconnections, and interrelationships that you see appearing.

Bear in mind that analytical approaches are linked to particular forms of data collection and are underpinned by specific conceptual and philosophical traditions. Each tradition provides a perspective on reality that is specific to that tradition. In this regard, data analysis strategies for case study research include analyzing data through description of the case or cases, including themes and cross-case themes and making use of analytic categories to establish themes or patterns. Ethnography involves analyzing data through description of the culture-sharing group and the themes that emerge about that group. The goal is essentially the analysis and interpretation of cultural themes and patterned regularities. Grounded theory data analysis strategies involve open coding, axial coding, and selective coding, thereby generating theory. In a phenomenological study, the researcher analyzes data for significant statements grouped into "meaning units," with the goal of producing an exhaustive description of the phenomenon by developing themes of meanings. Narrative research strategies analyze data for stories, "re-storying" stories, and developing themes, often employing a chronological dimension.

A few words on significance are necessary at this point. Quantitative researchers utilize statistical tests of significance to research the frequency of responses. Typically these tests of significance are reported with preestablished levels of confidence. Data are numerically analyzed by determining means, modes, medians, rank orderings, and percentages. In qualitative research, we do not seek statistical significance that characterizes quantitative research. In qualitative research, what we mean by significance is that something is important, meaningful, or potentially useful given what we are trying to find out. Qualitative findings are judged by their substantive significance (Patton, 2015). As Patton explains, in determining substantive significance, the qualitative analyst must address certain issues, including the following:

- How solid and consistent are your findings?
- To what extent and in what ways do your findings increase understanding of the phenomenon under study?
- To what extent are your findings consistent with the existing body of knowledge? That is, do they support or confirm what is already known about the phenomenon? Do they refute what is already known? Do they break new ground in discovering or illuminating something?
- To what extent are the findings useful in terms of contributing to building theory, informing policy, or informing practice?

You need to establish some system for representing participants' perspectives on the most significant events or activities by describing the procedures that you have adopted in analyzing your findings. Patterns, as we have come to see them, include both quantitative and qualitative elements. At this point in the process, your data summary tables (see Appendices T through Y for completed examples) and participant demographic charts (discussed in Chapter 7, "Presenting Methodology and Research Approach") become useful for analysis. In the findings chapter, the purpose of the data summary tables was merely to report numbers and percentages of responses. In the analysis chapter, the data summary tables become useful vis-à-vis the significance of your findings. In the analysis of qualitative data, we are interested in the concentration of responses across individuals. Although not really a finding in itself, having a large number of data in a particular area or under a particular descriptor or criterion does suggest where to look for patterns.

Readers need to understand different degrees of significance of your various findings. In this regard, you need to be specific when patterns are clear and strongly supported by the data or when patterns are merely suggestive. Ultimately, readers arrive at their own decisions based on the evidence that you have provided, but your opinions and speculations hold weight and are of interest to the reader because you have obviously struggled with the data and know them more intimately than anybody else.

Looking for emergent patterns among your findings can be considered a first round of analysis. It is important to also look across findings and across dimensions of each finding—the subsets within each finding. This second round of searching for patterns can often generate new insights and usually uncovers patterns that may not immediately have been obvious or apparent in the initial round of analysis. Creating cross-case classification matrices is an exercise in logic. This involves moving back and forth between your findings and crossing one dimension (subset) with another in search of what might be meaningful or significant. Beyond identifying themes and patterns, you now build additional layers of complexity by interconnecting your themes or patterns into a story line. Matrices can certainly push linkages. In creating matrices, however, be careful not to manipulate the data in any way or force the data to make cross-classification fit.

Finding patterns and themes is one result of analysis, whereas finding ambiguities and inconsistencies is another. You certainly want to determine how useful the findings are in illuminating the research questions being explored and how central they are to the story that is unfolding about the phenomenon under study. However, you also should challenge your understanding by searching for discrepancies and negative instances in the patterns. Seek all possible and plausible explanations other than those that are most apparent. Alternative explanations always exist. As is characteristic of qualitative research, you must be willing to tolerate some ambiguity. As such, look at issues from all angles to demonstrate the most plausible explanations. This step enables readers to assess the persuasiveness of your argument.

Once you have established patterns, they need to be explained. In this regard, you need to draw on your own experience and intuition. In addition, you have to once again consult the literature and consider your pattern findings in light of previous research and existing theory. Do your findings confirm similar research? Do your findings contradict previous studies? How can you explain these differences or similarities? As you begin to consider answers to these sorts of questions, you begin to describe and interpret your material.

Description and Interpretation   As Patton (2015) explains:

> Thick, rich description provides the foundation for qualitative analysis and reporting. Good description takes the reader into the setting being described . . . Description forms the bedrock of all qualitative reporting . . . Interpretation involves explaining the findings . . . Interpretation, by definition, goes beyond the descriptive data. (pp. 533–534)

The details in the description are your evidence, your logic; they build your argument. Therefore, description must necessarily precede interpretation. At the same time, the explanation and linkages revealed in the explanation serve to clarify the description and illuminate the details. Description is intended to convey the rich complexity of the research. Interpretation involves attaching significance to what was found; making sense of findings, considering different meanings, extrapolating lessons, making inferences, and offering potential explanations and conclusions. A qualitative report should provide not only sufficient description to allow the reader to understand the basis for an interpretation, but also meaningful interpretation to allow the reader to appreciate the description. Remember, because the data is made meaningful through interpretation (a necessary and vital component of qualitative research!), the very process of meaning-making through interpretive practice and associated researcher reflexivity becomes key. As stressed throughout this book, it is critical that qualitative researchers be explicit about their frame of reference, philosophical standpoint, and their investment in the research (personal, emotional, conceptual, and/or theoretical) because these factors will in one way or another be used to interpret the study's findings.

Just as methodological congruence implies that there are clear analytic distinctions among traditions or genres, demanding that the researcher think about data analysis in a particular way, so are interpretation and representation strategies specific to each tradition. Case study research makes use of deep and complex interpretation and presents an in-depth picture of the case (or cases) using narrative and visual representation (tables, charts, figures, etc.). Ethnographic research conducts interpretation by attempting to make sense of the findings—how and in what ways the culture functions or "works"—and like case study presents narrative and visual description and representation. A grounded theory study engages a series of coding procedures in order to develop a story of propositions, with the goal of presenting a visual model or theory. A phenomenological study develops textural description ("What happened?") and structural description ("How was the phenomenon experienced?"), as well as description of the "essence" of the experience, with narration of the essence being presented by way of discussion and visual representation. Narrative inquiry strives to interpret the larger meaning of the story by focusing on processes, theories, and unique and general features of the story or text. Richards and Morse (2013) provide in-depth discussion regarding analysis and interpretation with regard to the major qualitative genres. Silverman (2011) discusses pragmatics with regard to data analysis and one's chosen research approach. Willig (2014) offers an excellent overview of interpretation in qualitative research, including the origins of interpretation and approaches to interpretation of the major current qualitative traditions or genres.

An interpretive reading of your data involves constructing a version of what you think the data mean or represent or what you think you can infer from the data. You may be wondering why you should even bother with interpretation especially because interpretation involves taking risks and making educated guesses that might be off base. Wolcott (1994) argues for the importance of interpretation in qualitative research not only because interpretation adds a new dimension of understanding, but because the process of interpretation challenges qualitative researchers' taken-for-granted assumptions and beliefs about the processes and phenomena they have investigated—an important aspect of a researcher's personal and professional development.

Interpretation essentially involves reading through or beyond the findings—that is, making sense of the findings. It is about answering the "Why?" and "Why not?" questions around the findings. Interpretation requires more conceptual and integrative thinking than data analysis alone because it involves identifying and abstracting important understandings from the detail and complexity of the findings. Interpretation in effect moves the whole analytic process to a higher level. You (the researcher) arrive at new understandings, finding meaning beyond the specifics of your data. What you have seen in the field and what you have heard participants say all come together into an account that has meaning for the participants, for you, and for the reader. As with qualitative analysis in general, there are no hard-and-fast rules for how to go about the task of interpreting the meaning of the findings. One way to facilitate the process of interpretation is to begin by asking the following questions: What is really going on here? What is the story these findings tell? Why is this important? What can be learned here?

Lincoln and Guba (1985) capture well the essence of interpretation when they ask: What were the lessons learned? Lessons learned are in the form of the researcher's understanding and insight that she or he brings to the study based on her or his personal and/or professional experience, history, and culture. But it is more than this: It is about the meaning derived from a comparison of the findings of your study with information gleaned from the related literature and previous research. Making connections between your study's findings and the relevant literature provides you with a way to share with colleagues the existing knowledge base on a research problem and acknowledge the unique contribution your study has made to understanding the phenomenon studied.

Searching the literature to see whether it corresponds, contradicts, and/or deepens your interpretations thus constitutes a second layer of interpretation. Interpretation, therefore, is not just a conglomeration of personal ideas. It is the subtle combination of your ideas in tandem with what has already been reported in the literature. The findings of your study will either confirm what is already known about the subject area surrounding your research problem or diverge from it. Therefore, it is imperative that you relate your analysis to the available literature on the subject. This transparency, essentially, is what enables a reader to determine whether and to what extent your interpretation is persuasive, plausible, reasonable, and convincing.

Your integrity and credibility as a researcher are given credence by your inclusion of all information, even that which challenges your inferences and assumptions. You are building an argument about what you have learned in the field—an argument that is more compelling than other alternatives. As you put forward your interpretations, you should not forget to challenge the patterns that seem so apparent. Qualitative research is not about uncovering any single interpretive truth. Alternative understandings always exist; to demonstrate the soundness of your interpretation, you should be sure to search for, identify, and describe a variety of plausible explanations.

Remembering that the human factor is both the greatest strength and the fundamental weakness of qualitative inquiry and analysis, the researcher must recognize the subjective nature of the claims made regarding the meaning of the data. One barrier to credible interpretation stems from the suspicion that the analysis has been shaped according to the predispositions, assumptions, and biases of the researcher. Whether this happens unconsciously or inadvertently is not the issue. Rather, the issue is that you counter such a suspicion in the mind of the reader by reporting that you have engaged in a systematic search for alternative patterns and themes and rival or competing explanations and interpretations. This means thinking carefully, and with an open mind, about other logical possibilities and then seeing whether those possibilities can be supported by the findings and the literature. Failure to find strong supporting evidence for contrary explanations helps increase readers' confidence in the interpretations that you have generated.

As you guide the reader through your discussion, you attempt to create a compelling argument for interpreting your data in a specific way. Your reader should have some sense that your interpretations represent an exhaustive search for meaning from all your findings. Your explanations of the meaning drawn from the data should be multidimensional. The reader should get the sense that you have looked at your findings from different angles, that you have taken into account all the information relevant to the analysis, that you have identified and discussed the most important themes, and that your argument is systematically constructed. In the defense, you must be prepared to clarify your interpretations and defend your thinking while listening to alternative perspectives.

Your effort to uncover patterns and themes among your findings, as well as provide a variety of interpretations, involves both creativity and critical thinking. You need to make creative but also careful judgments about what you see as significant and meaningful. In this regard, you rely on your own experience, knowledge, and skills. However, analysis need not be a solitary endeavor—indeed it should not be. Although you are certainly the closest person to your study, discussion, dialogue, and debate with critical colleagues and advisors will certainly be helpful as you look at the findings from a variety of angles and vantage points. Analysis is all about learning what emerges from the findings of your research, and sharing perspectives through dialogue lies at the heart of learning.

Synthesis Qualitative research involves the move from a holistic perspective to individual parts (analysis) and then back to a holistic look at the data (synthesis). Whereas the findings chapter splits apart and separates out pieces and chunks of data to tell the "story of the research," the analysis chapter is an attempt to reconstruct a holistic understanding of your study. Analysis is intended to ultimately depict an integrated picture. What should emerge from your discussion is a layered synthesis. Synthesis is the process of pulling everything together—that is, (a) how the research questions are answered by the findings, (b) to what extent the findings emanating from your data collection methods can be interpreted in the same way, (c) how your findings relate to the literature, and (d) how the findings relate to the researcher's prior assumptions about the study. Synthesis is not, however, a linear process.

As you move toward interpretations about causes, consequences, connections, and relationships, you must be careful to avoid the simplistic linear thinking that characterizes quantitative analysis, which deals with variables that are mechanically linked out of context. Qualitative analysis is about portraying a holistic picture of the phenomenon under study to understand the nature of the phenomenon—which is usually extremely complex—within a given specific context. As such, synthesis becomes key.

Synthesis is ongoing throughout the analytical process. Synthesis is about combining the individual units of analysis into a more integrated whole. You need to account for all the major dimensions that you have studied. From your intimate familiarity with your data, you create a cohesive whole from the isolated bits and pieces. You also need to lead your reader to focus on the larger issues—the broader context. Analysis is ultimately about capturing the meaning or essence of the phenomenon and expressing it so that it fits into a larger picture. One problem that tends to occur is that we become so immersed in a highly specific research topic that we are unable to step back and think about more general and fundamental disciplinary frameworks. Give your research a broader perspective by thinking about how what you have discovered may relate to issues that are broader than your original research topic. Narrowly defined research problems are related to broader social issues. As Coffey and Atkinson (1996) propose:

> Qualitative data, analyzed with close attention to detail, understood in terms of their internal patterns and forms, should be used to develop theoretical ideas about social processes and cultural forms that have relevance beyond these data themselves. (p. 63)

As we have stressed throughout, there is no one "right" way to analyze your findings. You will be judged not on your analysis per se, but rather on your synthesis—that is, the way in which you have organized your discussion around major themes, issues, or topics, and the ways in which you have woven these together. What is of importance is the logic and coherence of your argument, how effectively you have tied your argument to the literature and prior research, and your ability to sweep your discussion into some broad and relevant discourse.

A final word on analysis: Qualitative analysis and interpretation are both an art and a science, and herein lies the tension. Qualitative inquiry draws on a critical as well as a creative attitude. The scientific part demands a systematic, rigorous, and disciplined approach and an intellectually critical perspective. The artistic dimension invites exploration, discovery, insight, innovation, and creativity to generate new possibilities and new ideas. The technical, procedural, and scientific side of analysis is easier to present and teach. Creativity is more difficult to distill and describe. Remember that each analysis is a unique expression of the researcher's skill and creativity. As you approach the analysis of your findings, remain open to new and unexpected possibilities. Be prepared to tolerate ambiguity. Have faith and trust in yourself as a thinker. Spend much time brainstorming. Also take the time to dialogue with others—in depth and critically.

Presenting Your Analysis and Synthesis

Overview In qualitative research, the emphasis is on understanding. You are not seeking to determine any single causal explanation, to predict, or to generalize. Your aim is to tell a richly detailed story that takes into account and respects a context and that connects participants, events, processes, activities, and experiences to larger issues or phenomena. As the researcher, it is your responsibility to explain in great detail what you have found—what you have discovered from your data, the sense you make of it, and what new insights you now have about the phenomenon under discussion. In this chapter, you serve as a guide to your readers, helping them to understand the findings of your study based on your intensive and careful analysis. The chapter is essentially a well-thought-out conversation that integrates your findings with literature, research, and practice.

Just as there is no one correct way to analyze findings, there is no one correct way to organize this chapter. The structure varies depending on your methodology, the findings, and your advisor's preferences. Structure also depends on your research tradition or genre as mentioned previously, with the product of each tradition remaining specific and relevant to that tradition. With the process being a highly intuitive one, and with the real learning taking place in the doing, what we offer is a set of guidelines regarding microstructure of your chapter—that is, a chapter that is well organized, well written, and well argued. These guidelines regarding a way to proceed are based on some strategies that have worked for us in our own research. Our hope is that these guidelines are useful to you in stimulating further thinking and ideas of how you might go about presenting this chapter of your dissertation.

A Set of Guidelines Begin with a brief introductory paragraph that includes your research purpose statement as you have identified it in Chapter 1, as well as a preview of how the chapter is organized so that the reader knows what to expect. Include a summary of the major findings and some explanation of how you have gone about analyzing and synthesizing your data. Exemplary dissertations typically provide sufficient information that enables the reader to envision all the steps that the researcher undertook in preparing and organizing the data. By providing a window into your procedures for analyzing the data, you assure the reader of your attempt to provide an impartial analysis. Moreover, you allow others who might want to follow the same procedures to do so, thereby establishing an audit trail, which contributes to the validity of your study. When professional colleagues are able to follow your line of reasoning, they have a more solid basis for determining the credibility of your study.

To offer this explicit documentation of your analytical procedures, both in the dissertation and at the oral defense, you have to make careful and detailed notes of all the steps you have gone through in the process of analysis, including even the ones that subsequently turned out to be dead ends or unsuccessful. Your explanation of all the decisions and choices that you made along the way conveys a sense of care about how you conducted your research and will promote the credibility of your interpretations.

Once you have introduced your reader to the chapter and given some indication of how the chapter is organized, you need to pull apart all the areas and discuss each one separately. Always remember to make one point at a time and fully flesh it out before moving on to the next point. This rule applies to all writing, especially to writing your analysis. Discuss each point that you make from different perspectives, but stay on target. Avoid redundancy or repetition. Some material might need to be cut, placed in other sections, or saved until later. It is crucial that the reader be able to follow the logic of your argument and grasp what it is that you are trying to communicate.

Do not distract the reader by too many arguments and/or ideas at once. Applying too many concepts at once can make your analysis confusing. Achieving a high-level product requires careful thinking on your part; therefore, revisions and redrafting are to be expected.

Analysis is a multilayered approach. When writing this chapter, keep in mind various key aspects:

- Establish the story line based on your findings. Based on that story, what do you think may really be going on? Think deeper as you go through all of the following levels:

  o Level 1 means looking at each individual finding (i.e., going finding by finding). Ask yourself what each finding means. What are all the possible explanations for what is being said by your participants?

  o Level 2 means looking across your findings. Ask yourself how the findings are related and/or interconnected. To what extent do the findings impact each other?

  o Level 3 means looking across cases (i.e., cross-case analysis). Remember, each person is a "case." Here we look for similarities and differences among participants. You can address these issues by way of your interpretation outline tool (see Appendix AA).

- Structure your discussion by using headings. For example, you may choose to use your research questions or the analytic categories of your conceptual framework. Think carefully of how you can most logically and interestingly set up your discussion.

- When discussing your findings, carefully choose your words. Use qualifiers such as *seems, appears, possible, probable, likely, unlikely,* and so on. In your discussion, you offer ideas, suggest explanations, and/or identify reasons; you do not state facts. You speculate, and therefore you cannot come across as definitive or dogmatic.

- In the course of the discussion, identify any qualifications and/or limitations of factors, such as age, gender, and context, with respect to your findings. Make sure to mention that you have done extensive cross-case analysis, which enables readers to follow your interpretation and judge whether it is plausible. It also enables you to review your own thinking and perhaps find weaknesses or limitations within your discussion, which will then have to be addressed and remedied.

- Remember that analysis is not just a naïve list of findings. In your discussion, you need to weave together the findings from the various data collection methods that you have used. You do this to demonstrate that each method you have used contributes similarly to the same analysis.

- Take responsibility for convincing your readers of the accuracy of your analysis by providing sufficient descriptive information for them to make independent judgments. Be sure to discuss the findings of your study with respect to the literature and prior research. The intent is that the inferences that you are making from your findings in combination with what the literature says will make a compelling argument. Overall, it is important for the reader to know the ways in which your study contributes to the current knowledge base. What are the differences between your study and the findings of previous studies? How do your findings compare with what the literature says? Do your findings help clarify contradictions in the literature? Do your findings go beyond the literature, breaking new ground? Are there any surprises? Surprises are the unanticipated outcomes of your study that may in some way contradict current thinking.

- Aside from including the relevant literature citations, also be sure to weave into your discussion direct participant quotations. The more support you can provide for your discussion, the more likely your readers will be to concur with your analysis.

Your interpretations—that is, your conjectures as to what the findings really mean—should be clear, logical, relevant, and credible:

- *Clear* interpretations are easy to follow. If the reader has difficulty following your train of thought, you run the risk of losing the reader. Information must be presented systematically, and sufficient details must be provided to enable the reader to understand the issues as presented. Information that is presented in tables should always be preceded by the narrative that describes the table.
- Readers will consider your interpretation *logical* if you have presented your discussion in a systematic and thoughtful way. Based on your own understanding of your findings, you should decide which issues need to be addressed first and how the remainder of the discussion will flow naturally from those issues (your interpretation outline tool is your sketch of the order in which you will discuss your findings). Your presentation should lead your readers to understand your findings as clearly as you do.
- Your interpretation must be *relevant*; that is, it must be directly related to the research problem, purpose, and research questions that have guided your research. It also must relate to the literature and/or theoretical base within which your study is situated. Make sure to keep your interpretation tight and focused. Whereas your findings chapter includes a multitude of elements, you now need to focus only on the most important and relevant issues and highlight and address the most prominent findings of your research. Determining the major issues may be viewed as a judgment call on your part. However, you are the person most familiar with your data, and thus you are in a position to help the reader recognize and accept your focus. A good idea is to run your ideas by others, thereby remaining open to different understandings and acknowledging different perspectives.

- Establishing *credibility* in qualitative research means that you have engaged in the systematic search for rival or competing explanations and interpretations. Think carefully about other logical possibilities and see whether those can be supported by the findings and the literature. In doing this, you should not be focused on attempting to disprove alternatives. You are not looking for clear-cut "yes" or "no" answers. Rather, you are searching for the best fit. As such, seek support for alternative ways of seeing things. Also keep track of and report alternative classification systems, patterns/themes, and explanations that you have considered during your analysis, which demonstrates intellectual integrity and lends credibility to your study.
- Give yourself the critical distance necessary to see whether all the parts of your argument are in place. This may require periodic "stepping back" from your research for a time, and/or engaging in critical discussion with colleagues or advisors, and/or journaling.

In thinking carefully about what meaning may lie behind the findings—that is, what is really driving your findings—researchers frequently create visual displays—figures and tables. These displays organize the findings diagrammatically and illustrate the relationships among identified topics, categories, and patterns. Visuals are useful for demonstrating linkages and connections as well as differences within each case, across cases, and across categories, as well as by demographics or other dimensions. The information enables the reader to clearly see and understand issues and concepts discussed in the narrative. In addition to augmenting your discussion, constructing diagrams or charts can help you with your analytical thinking. Displays often help you "see" some aspect of your findings in new ways. Through displays you might notice emergent trends, discover new connections or relationships, or even recognize the significance of certain pieces of information or lack thereof.

The "Analytic Category Development Tool," presented as Figure 9.2, is one example of a visual that gives some idea of how analytic categories can be explained and presented. The tool, a type of flow diagram, traces the logical flow and development of a study's analytic categories from research questions, through findings and outcomes/consequences (the source of the research problem). You need to be mindful in determining the correlation between research questions, findings, and analytic categories, remembering that these are not always simple and linear. A sample completed analytic category development tool is included as Appendix DD. We suggest that a completed version of the tool be included in your dissertation's appendix to illustrate to your readers an overview of the development and emergence of the analytic categories pertaining to your study.

If you choose to include visuals, give careful thought to the most logical place to insert them so as not to interrupt the flow of the discussion. If the diagrams are working tools, they are typically included as appendices. There are different ways

FIGURE 9.2 ● Analytic Category Development Tool			
Research Question	Finding Statement	Outcome/Consequence (Source of Research Problem)	Analytic Category
1.	Finding 1:	⟶	Category 1
2.	Finding 2:		Category 2
3.	Finding 3:	⟶	Category 3
4.	Finding 4:		Category 4

Source: This tool appears in Bloomberg, L. D. (2010). *Understanding qualitative research: Content and process* (Part II). Unpublished manuscript.

of constructing diagrams, charts, and graphs in the analysis of qualitative data. In this regard, Miles, Huberman, and Saldana (2014) and Booth, Colomb, and Williams (2008) offer excellent suggestions. Make sure that all information presented in tables is consistent with information presented in the narrative.

Finally, you will need to tie together the various threads of the discussion. As such, there should be a strong culminating paragraph that provides a concluding summary of the whole chapter. This summary should include the key points made, as well as some form of reflection on the analytic process. You also might choose now to revisit your initial assumptions (stated in your first chapter) and comment on these in light of your findings. The researcher-as-instrument is an inquirer, a writer, an analyst, and an interpreter. We have to leave open the possibility that other researchers might have told a different story given the same set of data. What we learn from our research, how we understand what we find, and how we report it is but one view. Some acknowledgment that there are multiple ways of interpreting data will serve to show that you fully understand the subjective nature of qualitative research. Such an acknowledgment further enhances your study's credibility in the eye of the reader.

There are many subtleties involved in the kind of detailed analysis that is required for a qualitative dissertation. As such, it is unlikely that you will achieve a well-argued, reader-friendly analysis chapter in one go. Writing this chapter takes many hours of thinking and rethinking, and much tightening up is involved to ensure the logic, depth, and breadth of your argument. Based on your advisor's feedback, you usually have to write and rewrite drafts of this chapter, revising and/or expanding sections of it accordingly. In most cases, this step may occur more frequently than you anticipated, as you work toward organizing the sections into a cohesive and powerful chapter that explains your findings. If your interpretation is thoughtful, logical, and reasonable, it is more likely to be compelling to your readers. In addition, it will provide the opportunity for an informed discussion, making a worthwhile contribution to your academic discipline.

Chapter Summary Discussion

As pointed out previously, analysis of data begins to occur before you can present your findings; by coding and sorting, you are in effect analyzing your raw data. Having organized and prepared mounds of raw data so you could present an accurate and objective account of the findings of your research (Chapter 8), you are now ready to move on to the final step of the analytic process: to provide an interpretation and synthesis of those findings. Both in the previous chapter and in this one, we emphasized the distinction between reporting and presenting findings and interpreting them. These are two distinct processes.

We covered some difficult ground in this chapter. Qualitative analysis is not a simple task, and is therefore not simple to explain. Because the concepts of analysis, interpretation, and synthesis are difficult to explicitly articulate, thinking about how to compose a chapter describing these processes is somewhat challenging. Therefore, the suggestions we have made in this chapter should be viewed more in the nature of guides to possible approaches and combinations of approaches, rather than as tight prescriptions.

In the previous chapter, you presented the analysis of your raw data, which were your findings. In this chapter, you presented the analysis, interpretation, and synthesis of your findings. You moved beyond *data* to *information*. In the findings chapter, you stood back and remained objective. Your task was to offer as accurate an account of the findings as possible. In the analysis chapter, you moved from the objective to the subjective. Your voice and opinion, in conjunction with the literature, now take center stage. Findings cannot be taken at face value. Your aim in writing the analysis chapter is to tell a richly detailed story that takes into account a specific context that connects participants, processes, activities, and experiences to larger issues or phenomena.

First, you seek to identify significant patterns or themes. Then you move on to provide some sense of understanding; that is, you attempt to explain these patterns and themes—possibly the most creative part of the dissertation. Findings need careful teasing out. As a researcher, you must ask yourself what you have learned from conducting the research and studying the findings. What connective threads are there among the experiences of your study's participants? How do you understand and explain these connections? What new insights and understanding do you have as a result of conducting your study? What surprises have there been? What confirmation of previous instincts and hunches has there been? Are your findings consistent with the literature? Have they perhaps gone beyond the literature? The answers to these questions add another dimension of understanding to your findings.

Bear in mind that analytical approaches are linked to particular forms of data collection and are underpinned by specific conceptual and philosophical traditions. And just as methodological congruence implies that there are clear analytic distinctions among traditions or genres, demanding that the researcher think about data analysis in a particular way, so are interpretation and representation strategies specific to each tradition. As such, each tradition provides a perspective on reality that is specific to that tradition, and so the way you go about developing themes and presenting interpretations is aligned with your chosen qualitative genre or tradition.

Providing careful step-by-step documentation of your analysis offers other researchers access to your procedures. In this way, your study can become a model for other studies—a contribution to the research community and an implicit affirmation of the value of your work. Readers of dissertations also are drawn to visual representations of information, which typically compare and contrast key findings of the study. Displaying data visually makes things clear and also can facilitate your seeing findings in new and striking ways.

The central requirement in qualitative analysis and interpretation is clear and logical thinking. You need to examine your findings critically so as to produce credible and meaningful interpretations. Interpretation of qualitative data precludes reducing the task to any single defined formula or fixed blueprint. Moreover, we must appreciate that, in dealing with interpretation, we are unavoidably dealing with human subjectivity, and, as such, there are differences in the ways we make meaning. Be sure to acknowledge that there are multiple ways of interpreting findings, that you have sought rival explanations, and that your interpretations are but one perspective. The human as instrument in qualitative inquiry is both its greatest strength and its greatest weakness. Nowhere does this ring more true than in analysis.

Quality Assessment Chapter Checklist

Introduction	✓ Do you have an introductory paragraph that includes a purpose statement (if required) as well as a brief explanation of how you went about analyzing and synthesizing the findings?
Presentation of Analysis and Synthesis	✓ Does your argument flow logically and coherently? ✓ Do you make one point at a time? ✓ Are your interpretations clear, thoughtful, and reasonable? ✓ Are your interpretations relevant to the research problem, purpose, and research questions? ✓ Are the major themes interrelated to show a higher level of analysis and abstraction? ✓ Is your analysis positioned and discussed in terms of the related bodies of literature and previous research? ✓ Have you included relevant participant quotations to support your argument, making sure that these same quotations did not appear in Chapter 4? ✓ Have you made appropriate use of tables and other displays to augment and support the discussion? ✓ Have you made sure that all information presented in tables is consistent with information that is presented in the narrative? ✓ Have you acknowledged that there are multiple ways of interpreting findings and that you remain open to other interpretive possibilities? ✓ If you have chosen to revisit and reflect upon your initial assumptions as stated in your opening chapter, do you flesh these out sufficiently in terms of your study's findings?
Summary	✓ Do you offer a comprehensive and overview summary that integrates all key points?

(Continued)

(Continued)

And . . .	✓ Have you eliminated any needless repetition? ✓ Have you checked for insufficient detail, and areas that are "unfinished"? ✓ Have you checked throughout your discussion for unclear/ambiguous language? ✓ Have you kept track of and reported on alternative classification systems, patterns/themes, and explanations that you have considered during your analysis? ✓ Have you engaged in discussion with critical colleagues throughout the analysis process to hear and acknowledge different perspectives and points of view and to be open to a variety of possible interpretations? ✓ Is the writing throughout clear and readable? Refer to Chapter 4 "Guidelines for Academic Writing."

Section II: Application

Following is the application section, which demonstrates the salient features of an analysis chapter in terms of how it should be structured and the interpretive style it should take on. However, please be aware that what we present in Section II is a sketch of an analysis chapter, rather than a full-blown analysis of the findings. In a real dissertation, the discussion would be elaborated more extensively to achieve deeper and richer levels of analysis and synthesis. As emphasized throughout, there are many options with regard to qualitative analysis and presentation, and requirements vary among institutions and programs. Therefore, as with other components of the dissertation, you will need to check with your advisor and/or department about the content and presentation of your study's analysis chapter.

CHAPTER 5 OF THE DISSERTATION

Analysis, Interpretation, and Synthesis of Findings

The purpose of this multicase study was to explore with a sample group of all-but-dissertation (ABD) students their perceptions of why they had not managed to complete their dissertations. It was hoped that a better understanding of the perceptions of students struggling at various stages of the dissertation process, as well as those students who have become inactive, would provide insight about how to encourage and support other current and future students to successfully conduct their research, write the dissertation, and obtain the desired doctoral degree.

This research used naturalistic inquiry to collect qualitative data by conducting in-depth interviews and collecting supportive data by use of critical incidents and a focus group discussion. Participants in the study included 20 current and former doctoral candidates. The data were coded, analyzed, and organized first by research question and then by categories and subcategories guided by the conceptual framework, as depicted in Chapter 2. The study was based on the following five research questions:

1. Upon completion of the course work, to what extent did participants perceive they were prepared to conduct research and write the dissertations?
2. What did participants perceive they needed to learn to complete their dissertations?
3. How did participants acquire the knowledge, skills, and attitudes they perceived were necessary to complete their dissertations?
4. What factors did participants perceive might help them to complete their dissertations?
5. What factors did participants perceive have impeded and/or continue to impede their progress in working toward completing their dissertations?

Analytic categories are directly aligned with each of this study's research questions. These same analytic categories were used to code the data and present the findings in the previous chapter. In the analysis, the researchers search primarily for connecting patterns within the analytic categories, as well as the connections or themes that may emerge among the various categories. As a secondary level of analysis, the relevant theory and research are tied in, as these themes are compared and contrasted to issues raised by the literature.

The previous chapter presented the findings of this study by organizing data from various sources into categories to produce a readable narrative. The purpose of this chapter is to provide interpretative insights into these findings. Whereas the findings chapter split apart and separated out pieces and chunks of data to tell the "story of the research," this chapter is an attempt to reconstruct a more holistic understanding. Analysis is intended to depict a more integrated picture, and what emerges is a layered synthesis.

The discussion takes into consideration the literature on higher education and doctoral programs and adult learning. The implications of these findings are intended to augment the understanding of the perceptions of why some students are unable to manage completion of their research and the resultant dissertation. The chapter concludes with a reexamination of the researchers' assumptions, which were identified in the first chapter, and a summary that incorporates a note regarding the effect of possible researcher bias in interpreting the findings.

Analytic Category Development

To illustrate the process of developing analytic categories, we revisit the findings from the study conducted in this book. Upon careful analysis of the concentrated responses in our data summary tables, both within individuals and across individuals, themes and patterns emerged. The overriding finding in this study revealed that students perceived the course work did not prepare them for the dissertation process. We named Analytic Category 1 that describes this disconnect "Recognizing the gap between course work and dissertation work." Analytic Category 1 speaks to Findings 1 and 2.

The perceived disconnect between the course work and understanding and knowing how to carry out the research led students to dialogue with colleagues and friends, tapping into their informal networks for a sounding board and assistance. Students relied on their own personal characteristics and self-directed activities to facilitate their progress. We called Analytic Category 2 "Closing the content-process gap." Analytic Category 2 speaks to Findings 3 and 4.

This perceived disconnect between the course work and understanding and knowing how to carry out the research was compounded by the fact that students perceived a lack of timely, consistent, and helpful advisement as a further impediment to their progress. Students encountered various obstacles. Some supports were utilized to overcome barriers to success. We called Analytic Category 3 "Leveraging dissertation support." Analytic Category 3 speaks to Finding 5.

Analytic Category 1: Recognizing the gap between course work and dissertation work.

The first research question sought to determine how well participants understood what they needed to know and what they needed to be able to do to successfully conduct research and write the dissertations once they completed the course work. Participants indicated that there was a disassociation between the first part of the doctoral program, the course work, and what follows as doctoral candidates engaged in the research and dissertation writing process. One of the participants, Morris, reflected this view when he said, "I didn't get the information during the course work. I didn't pick up what I needed to know about actually doing research, and what's worse, I didn't know how to find it out." David Sternberg, author and professor emeritus at John Jay College, gives credence to this perspective:

> The real issues are sociological and structural in the formation, the way the whole doctoral process is shaped. And then linked to that, of course, is that after you have finished your comprehensives, you just fall off the cliff—there is no linkage at all in that sense. You know the dissertation is seen as a trial by fire—you have got to do it yourself. (personal communication, September 14, 2006)

At the same time, casting the onus for not being able to complete the dissertation solely on the design and structure of particular doctoral programs may be misplaced. Such an assertion might be warranted because a number of studies dealing with possible causes of high attrition rates among doctoral students identify not only issues of program design, but factors directly related to students' idiosyncrasies (Bourner, Bowden, & Laing, 2001; Hawley, 2003; Hockey, 1994; Lewis, Ginsberg, Davies, & Smith, 2004).

Let us consider the implications of both perspectives—that of doctoral programs and that of the students enrolled in those programs. It can be argued that the primary purpose of institutions of higher education is to foster critical thinking by exposing students to philosophical and theoretical concepts and to the various bodies of literature that inform theory. Therefore, the focus of doctoral programs is not so much to demonstrate the practical application of theory, but rather to expand and build on existing theory and/or to fill gaps that may exist in the literature.

Hawley (2003) expands on the purpose of doctoral programs as the development of academic scholarship, rather than the training and development of practitioners. The author points out that new psychological and intellectual demands are placed on doctoral students and describes the implications of both demands in this way:

> In most disciplines, the Ph.D. is considered a research degree and means that its primary purpose is not to prepare practitioners, clinicians and teachers but to produce scholars. If you want to be considered a scholar, you must do research. This calls for a major transition in how you think and what you do. (p. 21)

Although attrition in doctoral programs is high, estimated at 50% nationwide (Berg, 2007; Dunn, 2014; Lazerson, 2003; Lovitts & Nelson, 2000; Smallwood, 2004), it also can be said that another 50% of students, exposed to the same course work, are successful in completing their dissertations and subsequently earn their doctoral degrees. This finding suggests that there may be innate or idiosyncratic student characteristics that cause some to succeed in attaining their degrees—despite the fact that course work does not prepare them in the practical application of research—while others remain unable to complete their dissertations.

In addition to possible personal characteristics, there may be environmental factors that contribute to students' success.

Taking on doctoral work can be overwhelming and can place a psychological burden on some students, for which they are unprepared. Karen, one of the participants who commented on this, said, "It (the dissertation) is an overwhelming task, and one doesn't have experience with it, and so it can be very anxiety provoking."

Lovitts (2001) explains the dissertation process as complex, long, and daunting, and one in which students have little or no experience. The author notes

> These are complex processes with which most students have little familiarity or prior experience. Students who reach this stage know (or discover) that they must conduct research that distinguishes them from their peers. Most feel inadequately prepared to do this type of research and find themselves unprepared for the writing in the style required for a dissertation. (Lovitts, 2001, p. 72)

Although lack of experience can lead to confusion and even debilitation, and although the course work has not adequately prepared students, this impasse may only be temporary as students begin learning by doing. Meloy (1994) found that, for novice qualitative researchers, developing a sense of the project's coherence was dictated by the project, rather than any suggested a priori plan or program structure. As she explains,

> One of the most common ways we have of learning to do something is *by doing it*. But "doing research" is becoming more complex and controversial. Although qualitative researchers are making substantial contributions to scholarship by describing not only how research is conceptualized but also how its products are finally presented and understood, there is for novice researchers, and traditionally trained faculty members across the wide array of disciplines, a down side. As the number of methodological options and alternative presentations increases, so does the ambiguity. (Meloy, 1994, p. xi)

In terms of her own research, Meloy (1994) acknowledges that her course work did not fully prepare her to do qualitative research, and she recounts her experience:

> In spite of my coursework, I had no idea of what it felt like to do research. Writing the dissertation was an experience in itself. Adding qualitative research on top of that made for an especially interesting time of learning, reflection, and practice. (p. 2)

Indeed, unlike quantitative research, qualitative research is not structured, systematic, and procedural. As such, course work cannot fully prepare the student for the experience of actually doing it—that is, conducting the research and writing the dissertation. Moreover, aside from the necessary research skills, the level of writing skill required in a dissertation is something that is not easily taught. Thus, it can be reasonably argued that course work cannot be expected to prepare the student for academic writing of a project as intense and complex as a dissertation.

Although some faculty and administrators view lack of progress or even attrition as a function of students' academic ability, motivation, or commitment, Lovitts (2001) and other researchers suggest it is a constellation of psychological and/or personal and structural factors that explains why some students are not able to complete their dissertations while others succeed. Thus, it appears to the researcher that ABD status and attrition rates cannot be placed solely at the doorstep of the institution or squarely on the shoulders of students. Rather, students' progress in doctoral programs might be better understood as the dynamic interaction of students and the institutional context.

Being unprepared may mean, in a sense, that students are unsocialized as to the scope and meaning of a doctoral dissertation (Bauer & Green, 1994; Sternberg, 1981). This notion brings into play the idea of a doctoral dissertation as an institution in itself—that is, the traditional model of a dissertation and all the expectations that go along with it. This theory includes the political aspects involved with faculty, the university system, institutional protocol (ambiguities, nuances, rules, regulations), and working with committee members who often have differing and sometimes even competing requirements. Students often do not have a clear grasp of the policies and procedures involved. The system of dissertation work and the expectations surrounding that system are unfamiliar to them—hence, the general feeling of unpreparedness.

The above notwithstanding, there are still some doctoral faculty who feel the main reason that students do not progress and in some cases even drop out of doctoral programs is because of some aspect of the student's background. Hawley (2003) raises this perspective in her book about the doctoral experiences and feelings of graduating students:

> Standing behind each smiling graduate is the shadow of another person who also expected to be there on the auspicious occasion, but dropped out somewhere along the way. Are these "shadow people" intellectually inferior to those who stayed the course and received their PhD? Is the graduation ceremony portrayed here simply an example of Social Darwinism in which only the fittest (brightest) survive? (p. 3)

To address their perspective, doctoral faculty in some programs have tried to tighten up the admission requirements for enrollment into their programs so as to admit only those students who are able to withstand the pressures of doctoral work (Lovitts, 2001). However, it is interesting to note that more stringent admission requirements in a number of doctoral programs have not affected the dropout rates, which continue to be high (Lovitts & Nelson, 2000). According to Lovitts (2001), those who enter doctoral programs are high achievers in the base case; they are people who have prior academic experience that often includes numerous honors and academic awards, and yet they are among the best and brightest who drop out of doctoral programs. Having taken the onus solely off the students, Lovitts (2001) identifies three reasons for the stagnation and/or dropout rates within doctoral programs, which the author sees more as a function of the interaction of students and the institution. She describes these as follows:

1. It is not the background characteristics that students bring with them to the university that affects their persistence outcomes; it is what happens to them after they arrive.
2. Graduate student attrition is a function of the distribution of structures and opportunities for integration and cognitive map development.
3. The causes of attrition are deeply embedded in the organizational culture of graduate school and the structure and process of graduate education. (p. 2)

Azad and Kohun (2006) attribute feelings of isolation among doctoral students as a major factor affecting their progress. The authors point out that "despite this recognition, the feeling of isolation has yet to be addressed fully in the design of some doctoral programs" (Azad & Kohun, 2006, p. 21). The authors find support from others in the academic community that most doctoral programs are not designed to specifically address the emotional needs, social feelings of estrangement, and/or inadequacy experienced by matriculating doctoral students. In other words, the design of most doctoral programs does not provide a supportive environment for students to successfully complete their dissertations and obtain their degrees (Azad & Kohun, 2006; Berg, 2007; Hawlery, 2003; Lovitts, 2001; Lovitts & Nelson, 2000).

Lack of progress in a doctoral program also may be a function of mutually exclusive expectations on the part of program faculty and the students they enroll. One of the participants in this study wrote the following in his critical incident:

> It was the constantly changing expectations among the committee members themselves about what I was expected to do and how I was expected to do it. (Hank)

As one of the participants who said that her expectations were not met described,

> While I found the course work intellectually stimulating, I was learning a lot—the language, the terminology, the theory. But once I was on my own I had this expectation that I would be given some guidance around actually doing the research, writing the dissertation—and it just wasn't there. Then I started to think it's a matter of learning along the way, and it is up to me to figure it out—but somehow I keep thinking it shouldn't be that way. (Jane)

Brause's (2004) study lends support to the expectations of some doctoral students with regard to the dissertation process and what they believed were the obstacles that stood in their way. One participant in Brause's study described it this way: "I sought assistance in understanding a process which has seemingly been cloaked in 'darkness and secrecy'" (p. 143). Lovitts (1996) also reports that doctoral students understand formal program requirements, but often do not have a good understanding of the informal expectations vis-à-vis carrying out the work. From the perspective of the doctoral program faculty, there may well be an unspoken expectation that the rigors of producing a dissertation require students to be highly self-directed given their view that the doctorate is a terminal degree of intellectual import and of the highest prestige. Hawlery (2003) explains this perception of doctoral faculty in this way:

> It is understandable that academics view the cognitive realm as their primary domain and intellectual accomplishment as their primary mission. Few would argue with this focus. Nevertheless, there are vast differences among faculty in the degree to which they recognize the psychological components implicit in an understanding of this kind. It is subjectively painful experiences that underlie most students' decision to quit, yet many doctoral faculties refuse to concern themselves with that they see as non-cognitive matters. (p. 24)

With regard to the differing expectations, research studies have shown that when students are given timely, relevant information about the program and as important, the doctoral process, they are better able to develop good working relationships and are able to maintain their commitment to the program (Bauer & Green, 1994). This sentiment was expressed by many participants in this study and was best reflected by one, who said,

> I think at the beginning of the course work there needs to be some additional assistance as to how to get people to begin thinking about their dissertation, because indirectly everything is associated, in my opinion, with the dissertation. So I think there could have been a better job done with an overview that keeps getting referred to as one goes through the course work, so as one moves forward in the classes one can see the relevancy. And there should be more about what's expected—you know, what lies ahead. More direction would have been very helpful to me. (Debbie)

In summary, it has been argued in the foregoing that the lack of student progress and even student departure cannot be attributed solely to the fact that course work does not typically prepare students to conduct research and write their dissertations. This view is posited because the intent of course work is primarily to provide a sound theoretical foundation for subsequent research and not to address the practical application of theory. At the same time, there are significant psychological and social aspects that affect students' ability to carry out this work, most notably issues of self-efficacy and feelings of isolation.

In many cases, psychological symptoms and social feelings of estrangement and/or isolation that students experience may be a function of the ambiguity within which the academy portrays the research process during the course work. Participants characterized this phenomenon as "shrouded in mystery." Therefore, it appears there should be opportunities in the design of doctoral programs to demystify the research process without sacrificing the intellectual rigor intended to escalate higher-order thinking among students. The following comments reflect participants' strong reactions when what is expected is not made explicit by the faculty:

> I don't know that faculty really want to disarm anybody of what it's all about because it may take away the mystique. . . . So you are left with this feeling of loneliness—like you are hanging out in the wind—and it's overwhelming. (Anne)

> What I have come to realize as I get further involved in this work is that there is something of a mechanical process to putting this dissertation together. And, you know, if they had explained how these pieces all fit when I was taking classes—it didn't have to be such a mystery, and it doesn't have to be so difficult. And I wonder sometimes if the field—doctoral programs in general—if they just try to make if difficult for students. . . you know, a rite of passage or whatever! (Doris)

The prior comments illustrate the sense of isolation that students experience in the absence of not knowing what is expected and what lies ahead. Research suggests that the more students are informed about the process, the more they are integrated into the academic community, and the more they feel part of its social life, the less likely it is that students will feel isolated and the more likely it is that they will persist in the program (Lovitts, 2001; Tinto, 1993). In light of this notion, it appears that mechanisms need to be put in place to clarify expectations that faculty have of students and what students can reasonably expect of faculty; it is really a question of shared responsibility.

Analytic Category 2: Closing the content-process gap.

The perception of the overwhelming majority of participants in this study that the course work did not prepare them to do research may explain why they also reported they were left to rely on their own resources and the help of colleagues to identify what they needed to learn. The findings revealed that all participants in this study indicated they needed to (a) acquire knowledge about the *content* involved in doing research and/or (b) understand what they actually had to do to carry out the *process* of conducting research.

On the surface, it appears obvious that if students felt the course work did not prepare them to carry out research and write their dissertations, they would seek that information and knowledge elsewhere. However, this may not necessarily be attributed to a failure of the course work. It may likely be that students were more focused on meeting the demands of the course work and not looking beyond to the potential relevancy of the theories to which they were being exposed and how those theories might subsequently inform their future research. Knowles (1980) provides support for this likelihood:

> Adults. . . tend to have a perspective of immediacy of application toward most of their learning. They engage in learning largely in response to pressures they feel from their current life situation. To adults, education is a process of improving their ability to cope with life problems they face now. They tend, therefore, to enter an educational activity in a problem-centered or performance-centered frame of mind. (p. 53)

This may well be the "frame of mind" of many participants in this study, who were focused on the demands of the course work and not the application of what they were learning to subsequent practice. One of the participants expressed it this way:

> As I was going through the course work I was paying a lot of attention to other papers and things. And the research stuff got very much pushed aside for me in my own mind. And it was, well, you know what, I don't have to deal with that right now. I'm going to have to do that at the end of it. But I've really got to get this paper done, and I really have to do well in this class. And I know that when the research stuff was presented, there was something in my unconscious that was saying, "You know what, you can learn this later." (Mollie)

This idea may be further understood in light of what Knowles (1980) describes as having a "readiness to learn" and the associated "timing of the learning." Knowles reminds us that adults must be ready to receive the learning, and this readiness constitutes what he calls a "teachable moment." In other words, presentation of the learning must be timed or in step with a particular stage of development. In this case, development can be understood as students' maturation within the doctoral program.

The majority of participants in this study completed the course work with content knowledge relative to theory, but not content knowledge relative to the practical aspects of what to research and how to conduct the research. The work of Beeler (1991) may provide some further insights. Beeler describes four stages he says students experience as they move through the doctoral journey: (a) unconscious incompetence, (b) conscious incompetence, (c) unconscious competence, and (d) conscious competence. These stages may explain why students in this study were not ready to relate the theories to which they were being exposed to the practical application of research.

The essence of good research is its content; it must be sound, authentic, and researchable. In other words, the subject of inquiry, the problem or phenomenon, must be one that warrants investigation. Several participants in this study described their struggle after the course work to identify a problem about which meaningful research could be conducted. One participant framed the dilemma in this way:

> It's a year later [after the course work] and I am still at this impasse, as the problem really is how to develop a problem and purpose that I can stick with, and I still seem to be having this problem. (Shana)

Participants reported struggling throughout the process to understand *how* they should go about carrying out the research. In reflecting on the process as a whole, Brad, one of the participants, summed up a prevailing view when he said, "If I had more of the *how,* I could have been further along sooner, but I try not to focus on what wasn't but what I have to do now."

Another participant described her struggle and frustration with trying to understand what to do in a critical incident form:

> Looking back to the long process of the dissertation research, one critical stage for me started after my proposal defense when I had the pilot data when I needed guidance on how to code the data so as to pave the way for my later data analysis. When I asked for help, I didn't get the guidance or the direction I was looking for. I was just told—go read the works of so and so, and I struggled a long time with this trying to code every line before I had a breakthrough with the help of a colleague. (Jane)

The struggle of students who lacked the knowledge of what to do and how to do it also is reflected in Brause's (2004) study of the experiences of doctoral students as they engage in the dissertation process:

> The one constant theme was lack of knowledge. There was a clear desire to know as much as possible about the process so that they [students] could predict what was going to happen, allocate time and money wisely, and understand their roles in that process. . . . Explicit information, respondents believed, would make it easier to manage their responsibilities within and beyond their doctoral program, as well as enabling them to feel more knowledgeable about their progress. (p. 149)

In addition to the perception of the majority of participants that the course work did not prepare them to conduct research and write their dissertations, they had little confidence that they would learn what they needed from faculty and/or their advisors post–course work. This perspective is best illustrated by a participant who explained it this way:

> For me, it comes down to how the dissertation process is handled, and how much support you get from faculty once you get to that point because that's where they lost me. I just couldn't get off square one for doing a dissertation. I couldn't get anywhere with my first advisor. And I did three proposals with an advisor who kept saying: "Well, that's not it yet. I'll know it when I see it." (Anne)

Further, it might be that some students were simply unmotivated to move forward with the dissertation work. Having spent many years at this point in the doctoral program, it might simply be that they lacked the necessary energy to continue—that they were, in effect, running out of steam. As one participant stated,

> At this point [following completion of coursework] I was simply exhausted. I had just about come to the end of my tether. . . . Yes, I badly wanted the doctorate—otherwise why would I have enrolled in the first place? But let's face it, I had a life too, and many commitments, including a family who needed me. I weighed the pros and cons and the toll the doctoral work had taken on my life so far, and I started to question whether I really wanted this thing [the doctorate] so badly after all. (Frank)

It cannot be assumed that students who enroll in doctoral program will necessarily be motivated. Motivation is indeed a factor that cannot be taken for granted in terms of adults' participation in learning experiences and in their subsequent learning success (Knowles, 1998; Merriam & Caffarella, 1999; Wlodkowski & Ginsberg, 1995). Knowing why some doctoral students do not progress and what deters their progress is a function of the extent to which intrinsic and/or extrinsic motivating factors are compelling. In the present study, when participants were asked what prompted them to enroll in a doctoral program, almost equal numbers cited extrinsic and intrinsic motivating factors. Therefore, one can surmise that, in this case, motivation was determined not by any one particular motivating factor—either extrinsic or intrinsic—but rather by the *intensity* of the factors at play.

In light of the lack of formal preparation during course work and formal guidance post–course work, as cited earlier, participants went about learning informally by relying primarily on themselves and their colleagues—those others who were, in their view, "in the same boat." This mode of learning is not so much an anomaly, but rather is consistent with the concept in the literature that says adults learn largely through informal means. In fact, it is in the informal domain that most learning occurs. Watkins and Marsick (2009) define informal learning as learning that is predominantly unstructured, experiential, and non-institutional. As such, the authors view informal learning as integral to daily life, asserting that its value comes from the fact that it occurs as people face a challenge, a problem, or an unanticipated need. By its nature, then, informal learning arises spontaneously within the context of real work.

Learning informally requires individuals to engage in self-directed activities, either through interactions with others or independent of others. Candy (1991) characterizes self-directed learners as individuals who take responsibility for their own learning and do not rely on others to tell them what they need to learn. Nor do they rely on structured programs for their learning. Therefore, it was not surprising to see that the participants in this study sought to learn what they needed primarily by engaging in dialogue with colleagues and to a lesser extent, by other solitary activities, such as reading relevant texts and completed dissertations and conducting literature searches for the kinds of information they needed.

Some participants expressed a clear preference for finding things out on their own. For example, in reflecting on the advice she might give to new doctoral students, Debbie commented, "I would tell someone they really need to read, read, read—get a hold of as many dissertations as you can, and examine how they are structured. It helped me a lot, and this was the main way that I figured things out." Other participants, like Lin, talked about "losing themselves for hours in the online library." Angela talked about how invaluable the Internet was in helping her find the information she needed.

The following comment describes the value that most participants in this study placed on having colleagues to talk to and with whom they could brainstorm:

> I started reaching out to some of my peers, and I found they would listen, they understood, and a lot of the time, I would walk away a little bit clearer. You know, you get another perspective, another way of looking at things when you talk it over with someone or with other people. I tried to be there for others when they needed to talk, to discuss ideas or even just listen when they needed to vent; after all they had done that for me. And I don't think I would still be in the program if it weren't for some of my classmates. (Karen)

Many participants maintained consistent communication with colleagues, as one participant, Fay, noted, "After the course work, we formed a small group, and we kept in touch and still do—there's a lot of caring, and we continue to help one another, and we share information." The value that participants in this study placed on their interactions with colleagues finds support generally in the adult learning literature, which places an emphasis on how collaboration, dialogue, and reflection are vehicles for learning (Merriam & Caffarella, 1999; Mezirow, 1991; Mezirow & Associates, 2000; Taylor, Marienau, & Fiddler, 2000). Learning from and with colleagues specifically within the context of doctoral work also finds support in the work of Meloy (1994) and Piantanida and Garman (1999). These researchers found that study groups with colleagues were a strong support factor for students in doctoral programs. Study groups, according to these researchers, were found to encourage scholarly development, generate thought-provoking issues with respect to qualitative research, provide opportunities for dialogue and reflection, and engender emotional support.

Although most participants were involved in self-directed activities to help them learn what they needed to progress in their work, some also mentioned that they received some help in the post–course work seminars they attended. These seminars were described by participants as "less structured than typical course work classes." Although students were provided with contextual material vis-à-vis research, the "discussions were largely informal." Interestingly, participants reported that students who attended these seminars were, in the words of Dexter, "not held accountable for producing work."

Lack of accountability may indeed promote a sense of complacency and allow students unspoken permission to avoid the real work of doing research and writing a dissertation. In contrast, having students set objectives and commit to producing a particular piece of work within a certain given time frame would create momentum for the students' progress. In this regard, lack of accountability may well have contributed to the high "time-to-completion" rate of participants in this study.

A further explanation as to why students did not find these seminars helpful may be due to the fact that they were not involved in setting objectives and planning. Indeed, one of the distinguishing characteristics of many adult learning programs is the shared control of program planning and facilitation (Knowles, 1998). Even when the learning content is, to a large extent, prescribed, sharing control over the learning strategies is believed to make learning more effective. Engaging adult students as collaborative partners satisfies their "need to know," as well as appeals to their self-concept as independent learners.

In summary, although working and learning through others is the primary way that adults learn, in the context of knowing what to do and how to complete research and write a dissertation, it may require the "others" to be informed experts. In other words, although it is important to have empathetic and supportive colleagues, in the absence of some form of formal, structured guidance and/or the accessibility of informed experts, collegial support may well be insufficient and actually slow down the process of completing arduous dissertation work. Further, although a fair amount of self-directed activities is necessary, such as reading other dissertations and searching the literature, time expended on these activities should be content specific—that is, searching out information related specifically to the subject of inquiry at hand.

Analytic Category 3: Leveraging dissertation support.

The perception of participants was that—in the absence of formal help through either course work, faculty, or advisement—they had to rely on themselves and their colleagues to understand and carry out their research. In light of this perception, it is not surprising that participants would cite their own personal attributes or qualities as well as the help of colleagues as primary supports to them in their doctoral work. At the same time, participants cited access and availability of advisors and in some cases, the quality of advisement as the single most significant impediment to their post–course work progress. This perception raises a serious point of contention that warrants closer examination, especially given the pivotal role advisors play in doctoral programs. Lovitts (2001) sheds light on the importance of the advisor in this way:

The advisor influences how the student comes to understand the discipline and roles and responsibilities of academic professionals, their socialization as a teacher and researcher, the selection of a dissertation topic, the quality of the dissertation and subsequent job placement. (p. 131)

Given the importance of advisement in the dissertation process, painting all advisors with the same brush may well be an unfair and unwarranted assumption. As previously mentioned, approximately half of the students who enroll in doctoral programs succeed in obtaining the degree. Thus, in light of the success of roughly half the population of doctoral students, it is likely that those students who completed their dissertations and obtained their doctoral degrees did receive the kind of guidance and support from advisors that is required. However, the fact that more than half of the participants in this study viewed the advisor relationship as an impediment does suggest the advisement that students received may not have been adequate. There may be several reasons that so many students in this study held this perspective. In many cases, the work-load and professional demands placed on faculty can be daunting; hence, they may not always be able to meet students' expectations by providing timely and consistent guidance. Sternberg (1981) sheds light on why faculty members are not always consistently helpful to students:

From a sociological perspective, dissertation advising rates low as a career promoting activity. People are promoted, given tenure, receive more attractive offers from other universities principally in terms of what they publish themselves, certainly not for editing and advising the writing and publications of graduate students. (p. 17)

Consider as well that not all faculty members who provide advisement have the same level of commitment or the same degree of interest in the various research topics of all their advisees. Further, it also is conceivable that advisors can and do become frustrated by the lack of initiative and lack of progress of the part of some students despite the prodding, encouragement, and direction the advisor provides. Given these considerations, one explanation may be that it is easier and even more comfortable for students to blame their lack of progress on their advisors rather than on their own competencies, level of motivation, or even habits of laziness. Another explanation to consider is that conducting research and writing a dissertation is new terrain for most students, one for which most have little or no prior experience on which to draw. As such, it is difficult for students to have the confidence in their ability to carry out such a large-scale scholarly project without the support, encouragement, and direction of advisors who have traversed this terrain and, therefore, are content experts.

At the same time, it should be noted that two participants in this study did comment favorably on their relationship with their advisors. Sally, one of the two, said, "I am a very lucky person; my advisor gives me a lot of feedback, a lot of personal care, and a lot of dedication. I know that is not the case for everyone." Further, that one fourth of the participants did not mention advisement at all—either positively or negatively—may suggest that other personal and overriding issues impeded progress in addition to or beyond the student–advisor relationship.

Doctoral students face all the life issues and demands typical of adulthood. Therefore, it was not surprising that, in addition to lack of support from their advisors, participants cited professional/work demands and personal family issues as significant challenges that stood in the way of their progress. As is the case in most doctoral programs, the participants in this study are working adults who have to manage the demands of both work and school.

In all cases, the participants in this study have to maintain employment to support themselves and their families as well as pay the "not insignificant" tuition. Maintaining balance between work and academic life is not easy; when the demands in one domain increase, productivity in the other may be affected. Maintaining this balance can be stressful, thus producing anxiety and even debilitation that threatens effectiveness in one domain or the other. The level of individual stress placed on students, as with many other adults, is often compounded by concern and worry about other personal, family, and/or health issues.

Because participants in this study perceived that they were not getting the formal help they needed from the course work, the faculty, or their own advisors, they said they had to rely on themselves and their colleagues to get through the research process. Therefore, it is understandable that those participants who persist in the program would describe themselves as being resourceful and used terms such as *dedicated*, *committed*, *motivated*, and *self-directed* as personal characteristics that keep them going. It is likely that the kind of perseverance, and even tenacity, that these characteristics encapsulate are important elements contributing ultimately to a student's ability to successfully complete her or his dissertation.

In summary, why some students do not progress more quickly and others abandon the process altogether is more likely the result of a complex set of factors. In other words, it does not appear to be a function of course work not preparing students, advisors not providing guidance, students not being able to handle the pressures of daily life, or students not being sufficiently motivated or self-directed. Some or all of these factors impinge, to a lesser or greater extent, on the lives of all students. Despite these challenges, some students in doctoral programs persist and prevail, whereas others do not.

Revisiting Assumptions From Chapter 1

It is useful to revisit the five assumptions underlying this study that were stated in Chapter 1. These assumptions were presented at the inception of this study and were based on the researchers' backgrounds and professional experiences. The five basic assumptions identified at the outset are discussed next in light of the analysis of this study's findings.

The first assumption underlying the research was that course work does not prepare doctoral candidates to conduct research and write their dissertations. This assumption held true according to the first finding. The sample of students in this study expressly stated that the course work did not prepare them to carry out the practical aspects of conducting research and writing their dissertations.

A second assumption posited by the researchers was that because doctoral students are mature adults, they will be sufficiently self-reliant and self-directed and that will enable them to carry out research and write their dissertations. This assumption turned out to be partially true. Initially, students appeared to be dependent on the course work and were not prepared to be self-directed. It was only when they had completed the course work and realized they did not know the steps involved or how to proceed that they became self-reliant and were self-directed as they reached out to colleagues for help. This notion was illustrated in the third finding uncovered in this study.

The third assumption was that because students were successful in completing all the course requirements, they would be able to achieve success in doing research. This assumption did not hold to be true. Judging by the slow progress and in some cases, lack of progress of the sample students in this study, past academic success is not always or necessarily a predictor of future academic success.

The fourth assumption is that doctoral candidates do not always receive the direction and guidance they need from their advisors. This assumption held true given that the majority of participants cited the lack of good, timely, and consistent advisement as a major barrier standing in the way of their progress.

The fifth and final assumption is that people who enroll in doctoral programs are strongly motivated to obtain the doctoral degree and are thus likely to complete the dissertation. This assumption did not hold true given that motivation alone is insufficient to carry out doctoral work. This idea was illustrated in Finding 2, which revealed that students needed to understand the content and process involved in research and have the knowledge and skills required to complete their dissertations.

Summary of Interpretation of Findings

This chapter portrayed the dissertation experiences of a sample of doctoral candidates. In summary, the prior discussion illustrates the multifaceted and complex nature of the dissertation experience. The discussion reveals various reasons that students might feel unprepared following course work. It offers an explanation as to what students feel they really need to know to conduct research and write a dissertation, why they then go about learning the way they do, and why certain factors are seen as either supports or barriers to their progress.

The endeavor of analyzing the findings was to produce a nuanced and multitiered, but holistic and integrated, synthesis. The challenge throughout data collection and data analysis, which were not separate but rather interlocking phases of this research, was to make sense of large amounts of data, reduce the volume of information, identify significant patterns, and construct a framework for communicating the essence of what the data reveal given the purpose of the study. In addition, the researchers performed extensive within- and across-case analyses and did not find any significant relationships between any of the demographic factors (age, gender, ethnicity, discipline/field of practice) in explaining the findings one way or another.

Presenting an analysis of the findings uncovered in this study warrants a degree of caution. First, the research sample was small, comprising interview data from only 20 interviews with doctoral students involved in qualitative research. Second, the focus of the study was on those who either are struggling at some stage of the dissertation process or have withdrawn from their doctoral studies entirely. Thus, the perceptions of those students who persist in the process and those who complete the process and obtain the doctorate are not represented. For these reasons, it must be stressed that the implications that can be drawn are specific to the experiences of the sample group under study.

Aside from the potential biases involved in researcher-as-instrument, as is typical of qualitative research, the researchers acknowledge possible additional bias in analyzing the findings because they are faculty members teaching in a doctoral program. Toward this end, and to help minimize this limitation, throughout the process of data collection and data analysis, the researchers engaged in ongoing critical reflection through journaling and discussions with critical colleagues. Remaining open to the possibility that others might have told a different story, this chapter is essentially, and ultimately, a presentation of how *these* researchers understand and make meaning of the material and the connections they see in it.

Annotated Bibliography

Creswell, J. W. (2013). *Qualitative inquiry and research design: Choosing among five traditions* (3rd ed.). Thousand Oaks, CA: Sage.

Following a detailed discussion of data analysis and representation (Chapter 8), Creswell, in Chapter 9, turns his focus to the art of writing and composing the narrative report, which, as he points out, "brings the entire study together." Using the metaphor of architecture, Creswell bases his discussion on four rhetorical issues inherent in the rendering of a qualitative study, regardless of approach: reflexivity and representation, audience, encoding our writing, and using quotes. He then takes each of the five research approaches—narrative research, phenomenology, grounded theory, ethnography, and case study—and assesses and compares two rhetorical structures within each tradition: overall structure (i.e., overall organization of the study) and embedded structure (i.e., specific narrative devices and techniques that the writer uses). In so doing, Creswell highlights the diverse narrative structures for writing a qualitative report and the major differences that exist among the different research traditions. Of particular use is a table (pp. 221–222) that illustrates the diversity of perspectives about writing structural approaches and that clearly reflects different data analysis procedures and discipline affiliations. This key chapter includes additional readings and exercises.

Grbich, C. (2013). *Qualitative data analysis: An introduction* (2nd ed.). Thousand Oaks, CA: Sage.

This is a practical guide to qualitative data analysis and its application with regard to the wide range of different qualitative traditions, including ethnography (autoethnography, ethnodrama, and cyberethnography); grounded theory; phenomenology (existential and hermeneutic); content, narrative, conversation, and discourse analysis; visual interpretation; and semiotic structural and poststructural analyses. Parts I and II cover some of the theoretical and practical issues in qualitative research, which inform decisions regarding research design and analysis. Part III provides an in-depth account of analysis of written and visual documentation, drawing on relevant tools including narrative analysis, conversation analysis, discourse analysis, visual interpretation, and semiotic structural and poststructural analyses. The author provides a response to various epistemological, theoretical, and practical challenges involved in each tradition and ways in which analysis of findings can be appropriately conceptualized, tools developed, and data presented. Part IV is devoted to assembling data into groupings to begin writing up an analysis. This section covers how to theorize from data, how to incorporate data from multiple sources (both qualitative and quantitative), and how to develop a more abstract explanation regarding findings, as well as an exploration of techniques for innovative data presentation, including visual displays, vignettes, and anecdotes. Part VI focuses on interpreting and presenting qualitative data. The book is packed with detailed examples, a glossary, and further reading lists.

Patton, M. Q. (2015). *Qualitative research and evaluation methods* (4th ed.). Thousand Oaks, CA: Sage.

Part III of Patton's book is possibly one of the best texts that we have come across with regard to explaining qualitative analysis, and it is a must-read for those interested in getting a better handle on what is essentially an extremely elusive and ambiguous endeavor. Chapter 8 deals with analysis, interpretation, and reporting of the findings, explaining in great detail the challenges and complexities involved. Especially useful are the sections dealing with thick description, case study analyses, pattern, theme, content analysis, and interpretation of findings. Aside from looking at generic approaches to qualitative analysis, Patton also provides suggestions for what he calls "theory-based analysis approaches." Here he examines the theoretical and philosophical perspectives of phenomenology and grounded theory and offers detailed guidelines for how a qualitative researcher would approach data analysis within each of these traditions. Chapter 9 deals with enhancing the quality and credibility of qualitative analysis. The author details how to determine the criteria for truth and provides insight into some of the current debates about establishing the trustworthiness of qualitative analysis. Written in an engaging style, the author draws the reader into the conversation around core issues of persistent debate and controversy.

Silverman, D. (Ed.). (2011). *Qualitative research* (3rd ed.). Thousand Oaks, CA: Sage.

Part VII of this text, "Qualitative Data Analysis," offers some insights into the complexities underlying some of the routines, procedures, phases, and tactics inherent in qualitative analytic reasoning and practice. Chapter 15 deals with the pragmatics of data analysis, illustrating the routinely cited approaches to qualitative data analysis in order to explore their similarities and differences and describing some of the pragmatic issues that should be considered. Chapter 16 focuses on grounded theory and credibility issues. Chapter 17 deals with narrative inquiry and associated analytical issues such as cases, categories, contexts, and identity construction. Chapter 19 introduces the challenges of "secondary analysis" (i.e., the analysis of data originally collected by another set of researchers) with a particular focus on contextual knowledge or lack thereof. Chapter 20 deals with the validity regarding naturally occurring social interaction (i.e., the interpretation of observations whether or not the inferences that the researcher makes are supported by the data and sensible in relation to earlier research). This chapter includes thought-provoking discussion around issues such as consideration of the truthfulness and transparency of analytic claims, deviant case analysis, generalizability of analytic findings, and use of statistical techniques. Chapter 21 focuses on writing as both process and outcome, and in acknowledging the wide variety of analytic options and representational styles, presents qualitative research as a three-facet framework including the criteria of practice, genre, and audience.

Wertz, F. J., Charmaz, K., McMullen, L. M, Josselson, R., Anderson, R., & McSpadden, E. (2011). *Five ways of doing qualitative analysis: Phenomenological psychology, grounded theory, discourse analysis, narrative research, and intuitive inquiry.* New York: Guilford Press.

This book facilitates a deeper understanding of a variety of qualitative analysis approaches, including phenomenological psychology, grounded theory, discourse analysis, narrative research, and intuitive inquiry. Set as an "adventure" within the field of qualitative research methodology, leading scholars apply their respective analytic lenses and points of view to a narrative account and interview featuring "Teresa," a young opera singer who experienced a career-changing illness. The resulting analyses vividly exemplify what each approach looks like in action. The researchers probe the similarities and differences among their approaches; their distinctive purposes and strengths; the role, style, and subjectivity of the individual researcher; and the scientific and ethical complexities of conducting qualitative research. As an added bonus, the authors present the participant's reaction to the results of the five different analyses and discuss the ethical implications in terms of letting the participant speak for herself, issues of confidentiality, and tensions around interpretation of data. As the authors point out, the goal is to assist seasoned and novice researchers in achieving more rigorous qualitative *praxis*, that is, the reflective application of qualitative analyses. This book clearly illustrates that qualitative analysis is not the mere application of technical procedures, but when properly practiced requires a unique qualitative stance and worldview.

10

Drawing Trustworthy Conclusions and Presenting Actionable Recommendations

> ### Chapter 10 Objectives
>
> *Section I: Instruction*
>
> - Demonstrate how to think about and write sound conclusions.
> - Demonstrate how to think about and write actionable recommendations.
> - Offer ideas for a final reflection statement.
>
> *Section II: Application*
>
> - Present a completed concluding chapter for your dissertation.

Overview

We know how exhausted you are at this point. But you are almost at the end of the process, so keep up the energy for just a short while longer! This final chapter of your dissertation is much more than just a cursory summary of findings. It is your chance to have the last word about your study, and it should help the reader decide what to make of your work. It also should stimulate your readers to think more deeply about the findings of your study and the implications thereof. Please note that some institutions require that the chapter presenting conclusions and recommendations stand alone. In other institutions, conclusions and recommendations are incorporated into the analysis chapter. As we have emphasized throughout this book, in the interests of conforming to structural requirements, we advise that you check with your own program and/or institution. As with all previous chapters, we present this chapter in two sections: Section I, "Instruction," and Section II, "Application."

As you were writing your findings, you may have begun to think about various interpretations and draw tentative conclusions. Remember that interpretation and conclusions in qualitative data analysis are always open to revision. In essence, you are building an argument based on your data and attempting to develop explanations that fit the data—a process of inductive reasoning. This process is unlike quantitative analysis, where you collect data to test a hypothesis, or deductive reasoning.

Section I: Instruction

Let us hearken back for a moment to the Part II table, "Overview of Dissertation Content." The simple but useful matrix in the bottom right corner of the table (reproduced below as Table 10.1) explains the essence of how to think about the conclusions that you will draw from your findings and the actionable recommendations you will be able to make based on those conclusions.

Presenting Trustworthy Conclusions

Thinking About Your Conclusions The interpretation outline tool in the previous chapter (Figure 9.1) was helpful in stimulating critical thinking and reflection about all the potential deeper meanings behind your findings. Findings should not be taken at face value, so you probed and dug deeper beneath the surface of your findings by asking over and again, "Why?" and "Why not?" As such, you were able to brainstorm a number of possible interpretations that explained your findings; that is, you developed some ideas of what you thought the findings really meant.

In thinking about how you were going to interpret your findings, you were in effect saying to yourself, "If I find this . . . then I think this means . . ." In generating conclusions, you need to go back to your findings and interpretations once again and say to yourself, "I found . . . and I think this means . . ."

TABLE 10.1 ● If/Then/Therefore/Thus Matrix

Findings Through Recommendations:			
Findings	**Interpretations**	**Conclusions**	**Recommendations**
"If I find this . . . "	"Then I think this means . . ."	"Therefore I conclude that . . ."	"Thus I recommend that . . ."

Conclusions flow directly from your findings. In effect, the conclusions are assertions based on your findings, and must therefore be warranted by the findings. With respect to each finding, you are asking yourself, "Knowing what I now know, what conclusion can I draw?" Although your conclusions will be backed up by your findings, do not confuse conclusions with findings. Conclusions are not a restatement of your research findings; they represent a higher level of abstraction. Drawing sound and trustworthy conclusions from your findings pushes you to consider broader issues and make new connections among ideas. In effect, by doing this, you are expanding on the significance of your findings.

Just as your conclusions are not the same as findings, neither are conclusions the same as interpretations. Rather, conclusions are essentially conclusive statements of what you now know, having done this research, that you did not know before. As in the case of providing interpretations, writing conclusions draws on your ability to be a critical and, at the same time, creative thinker. In writing up the conclusions, you are in effect evaluating, analyzing, and synthesizing information.

Remember that your study's research questions, right from the beginning, form the backbone of your research. Remember, too, that the findings of your research must provide answers to these questions. To check your thinking and ensure consistency among the research questions and all that follows from them, it is recommended that you develop a matrix—what we refer to as a "consistency chart," presented as Table 10.2. This chart tracks the findings through the interpretations to conclusions, making certain that these components are all aligned. A sample consistency chart is presented as Appendix EE. Note that each finding relates to its same numbered research question so the research question is not repeated in the table.

TABLE 10.2 ● Consistency of Findings, Interpretations, and Conclusions

Findings	Interpretations	Conclusions
Finding Statement 1:	List all possible interpretations in summary form	Identify conclusions you draw from your first finding
Finding Statement 2:	List all possible interpretations in summary form	Identify conclusions you draw from your second finding
Finding Statement 3:	List all possible interpretations in summary form	Identify conclusions you draw from your third finding
Finding Statement 4:	List all possible interpretations in summary form	Identify conclusions you draw from your fourth finding
Finding Statement 5:	List all possible interpretations in summary form	Identify conclusions you draw from your fifth finding

(Continue in the same manner with your other findings.)

It is important to bear in mind, when thinking about and formulating each of your conclusions, that they must be logically tied to one another. That is, there should be some sort of consistency among your conclusions; none of them should be at odds with any of the others. This type of consistency among your conclusions goes without saying; it is a non sequitur. If your study's research questions are tied together or interconnected, as they necessarily should be, and because your findings are the answers to the research questions, then your findings statements also will be interconnected. Hence, your conclusions should logically and meaningfully "fit" with each other and not contradict each other. Your findings, in effect, tell the initial "story of the research." Your interpretations then add another dimension, bringing the story to a deeper level of understanding. Your conclusions become the beginning of a new story. By way of the conclusions, the story of your research is wrapped up, bringing it to its logical finale.

Writing Your Conclusions   As a general rule of thumb, you should provide at least one conclusion for each finding. However, the process is not altogether linear. As such, one conclusion can (but does not always) cut across more than one finding. Each conclusion should be clearly and crisply stated in a few sentences. Following this notion, you need to expand on and amplify your main idea in a paragraph or two. The logic of the argument provides support for your conclusion and enhances its trustworthiness. Because your conclusions must be concise, the discussion should be relevant, organized, and tight. Avoid repetition and ambiguity. Be sure that what you want to say comes across just as you intend.

Presenting Actionable Recommendations

Thinking About Your Recommendations   Recommendations follow your findings and conclusions. In thinking about conclusions, you said to yourself, "I found . . . therefore I know the following to be true . . ." Recommendations are the application of those conclusions. In other words, you are now saying to yourself, "Knowing what I now know to be true, I recommend that . . ." Therefore, recommendations are the final stage of a logical thought process. In your recommendations, your research findings now have a springboard for action.

In Chapter 1 of your dissertation, you discussed the significance of your study. In that discussion, you mentioned who would be likely to benefit from your study, what they would learn from it, and what they would gain from this knowledge. That section in Chapter 1 now becomes the basis for thinking about your recommendations. Be aware that recommendations must move away from the theoretical to the actionable and doable. In other words, what are the *actions* that you would recommend and for whom?

The reasonableness of a recommendation depends on it (a) being logically and clearly derived from the findings, (b) being both content and context specific, and most important, (c) being practical; that is, it is capable of implementation. Whereas your interpretations and conclusions are speculative, and may be the subject of dispute, your recommendations, although a set of opinions, should be firmly grounded in the findings and must be doable.

Recommendations have implications for policy and practice, as well as for further research. Based solidly on your findings, think of all the possible ways that people could and should now do things differently. As a result of your findings, how might practice change? As a result of your findings, what new ideas can now be explored and researched further? How might your study be improved on, and how might future studies in other contexts expand on your study and contribute to the field? In offering practical recommendations, you can and should make recommendations for your own program or organization, as well as for others that are similar. With regard to research recommendations, you might think about implications of your study's limitations and include the appropriate suggestions for further research. In this regard, ask yourself, "In light of what I have learned, what more can be done? What can be done differently now?" Here you might suggest studies designed to replicate your study in other contexts or settings. You might also suggest next-step studies designed to investigate another dimension of your study's research problem.

Writing Your Recommendations Your findings will have implications for both professional practice and further research. You make recommendations based on your own experiences in conducting the research, as well as in any other professional capacity. In writing up your recommendations, it is important that you describe exactly how you envisage each recommendation being implemented. Be specific about identifying who will be responsible for implementation and who will monitor the ongoing implementation.

In offering recommendations, you are free to make a range of suggestions for the usefulness of the findings. Although the liberty to make suggestions is appealing, you should restrict your suggestions to only those that you think will make an important impact and that, to the best of your knowledge, are doable and actionable. Remember that fewer, stronger, and more focused recommendations will make more of an impact than a long list.

Researcher's Final Reflections

Stake (1995) writes,

Qualitative case study is highly personal research. Persons studied are studied in depth. Researchers are encouraged to include their own personal perspectives in the interpretation. . . . The quality and utility of the research is not based on its reproducibility, but on whether or not the meanings generated, by the researcher or the reader, are valued. Thus a personal valuing of the work is expected. (p. 135)

Having come to the close of your study, you might be asking yourself, "How do I personally value my work? How do I personally value the research experience?" In this final section of the final chapter of your dissertation, you have an opportunity (but are not always required) to offer your own thoughts on the experience of conducting the research and writing the dissertation. Here you can describe how you came to your research. You also can reflect on the research experience and what it means to you. What are the lessons learned from conducting the study? What insights and inspirations have you derived from conducting your study? Think about your role as a researcher and what new learning—both personal and professional—you have had as a result of the qualitative research experience. There is cause for celebration! You are now writing your closing paragraphs!

Chapter Summary Discussion

The process of generating solid conclusions and actionable recommendations takes time and should be carefully thought out. In planning how to articulate and present your conclusions and recommendations, you should be sure to discuss provisional ideas with advisors and critical colleagues. Also be sure to complete your own consistency chart because this will help you focus and maintain the necessary alignment between your research questions—the core of your research—and the key elements that follow: findings, interpretations, conclusions, and recommendations. As with other components of the dissertation, you will need to check with your advisor and/or department about the content and presentation of your study's final chapter.

Quality Assessment Chapter Checklist

Conclusions	✓ Are your conclusions clearly derived from your study's findings? In other words, is it clear to the reader that your conclusions are warranted by the findings? ✓ Do you offer at least one conclusion per finding? In other words, even though conclusions can cut across findings, is each finding tied to at least one conclusion? ✓ Are your conclusions logical and clearly explained? ✓ Are you sure that your conclusions are not mere restatements of the findings? ✓ Are you sure that your conclusions are not "interpretations" but rather strong conclusive statements? ✓ Are your conclusions consistent? Do they flow logically and meaningfully from each other and not contradict each other? ✓ Can your conclusions be challenged? If so, play devil's advocate. Can you think of any flaws or limitations in the way in which you have stated and explained each conclusion?
Recommendations	✓ Are all your recommendations justified by the findings? ✓ Are all your recommendations doable and actionable, or are they theoretical and esoteric? ✓ Have you discussed applications for practice? ✓ Have you discussed applications for policy? ✓ Have you offered suggestions for further research? ✓ Have you selected strong recommendations for each of the above sections?

And . . .	✓ Have you made sure whether conclusions and recommendations are required to stand alone as a final chapter or whether these should be incorporated into the analysis chapter? ✓ If this is your dissertation's final chapter, have you included a brief but informative introduction? ✓ If you have included a final reflective piece, does this make a statement regarding your role as a qualitative researcher, and/or your experience in writing the dissertation? ✓ If you step back and review this, your chapter, do you think that it offers the reader a completed picture of your research? ✓ Will your readers be likely to walk away with a good understanding of the study and with a general feeling of finality and closure? ✓ Is the writing throughout clear and readable? Refer to Chapter 4 "Guidelines for Academic Writing."

Section II: Application

CHAPTER 6 OF THE DISSERTATION

Conclusions and Recommendations

The purpose of this multicase study was to explore with a sample of doctoral candidates their perceptions of why they have not managed to complete their dissertations. The conclusions from this study follow the research questions and the findings and therefore address four areas: (a) perceptions that the course work would prepare students to conduct research and write a dissertation; (b) students' uncertainty about what they need to do and how to go about doing what is needed to complete the dissertation; (c) acquiring information, learning the skills, and developing the attitudes needed to complete the dissertation; and (d) what helps or hinders students' learning. Following is a discussion of the major findings and conclusions drawn from this research. This discussion is followed by the researchers' recommendations and a final reflection on this study.

Perceptions That Course Work Would Prepare Students

The first major finding of this research is that the majority of students in this study indicated that the course work did not prepare them to conduct research and write their dissertations. A conclusion to be drawn from this finding is that students who enroll in doctoral programs should not expect that course work alone will or can fully prepare them to conduct research and write their dissertations. Completion of a good dissertation is a content-specific journey taken by the student and as such, becomes a process of discovery. Although research classes during the course work can provide a general understanding of research methods and strategies for conducting research, it may be difficult for students to relate those methods or strategies to some future and often not-yet-identified research problem. In this regard, it also can be concluded that the primary purpose of course work is to provide students with a sound theoretical foundation required for intellectually rigorous research and not to provide the nuts and bolts of application. A further and related conclusion that can be drawn is that, although doctoral programs do include courses on research, in some cases such courses may be inadequate in providing a basic and rudimentary understanding of qualitative research methods and the approaches and strategies to carry out those methods.

Uncertainty About What to Do and How to Do It

The second major finding was that all participants expressed the need to gain knowledge about the content and to understand the process involved in conducting research and writing their dissertations. During the first 2 years, students are often more preoccupied with understanding theoretical concepts and meeting the demands of the course work than relating theoretical concepts to knowing what is involved in carrying out future research. A conclusion that can be drawn from this finding is that being grounded in theory alone is insufficient. Inexperienced student researchers also need the know-how (i.e., practical information about what to do and how to do it) to conduct research and write their dissertations, and they need to acquire this competency through more informal means. A related conclusion is that, in the absence of formal preparation, students need to be open to learning, be able to tolerate ambiguity, and have a compelling and fierce desire to succeed regardless of their circumstances.

Acquiring Information, Learning the Skills, and Developing the Attitudes Needed

The study's third major finding was that the majority of participants attempted to learn what they perceived they needed to learn by reaching out in dialogue with colleagues, rather than through more formal channels (i.e., advisement, other faculty, or post–course work seminars). A conclusion to be drawn from this finding is that (in the absence of formal preparation) dialogue with colleagues in a similar situation can serve as a catalyst for reflection and action and at the very least can provide a source of support to ameliorate feelings of isolation. Students may desire autonomy, but may not have the skills or even the motivation to learn the same material in isolation. Through dialogue, students have the opportunity to share information, exchange perspectives, challenge assumptions, test ideas, and play devil's advocate for one another, and all of these collaborative opportunities hold the potential for the development of new understanding, new learning, and the ability to take constructive action.

What Helps or Hinders Learning

The sample of students identified different factors that they perceived helped or hindered their learning. This study's fourth finding was that the majority of students indicated that, in the process of attempting to do their dissertation, they relied on themselves. More than half of these same participants also said that colleagues were instrumental in facilitating their progress. *There are two primary conclusions that can be drawn from this finding.* First, adults have a need to be self-sufficient and self-reliant, and most adult students have a preference for directing their own learning. Second, whether students progress well in the dissertation process is largely a function of their own personal characteristics and their motivation and drive to succeed.

The fifth finding was that the majority of students cited the lack of good, timely, and consistent advisement as a major barrier standing in the way of their progress. The primary conclusion that can be drawn from this finding is that, although students want to be self-reliant, good and consistent advisement must be an integral part of the doctoral experience. Dissertation work cannot and should not be a solitary endeavor. To move forward in the dissertation process, students need support, feedback, and guidance from advisors; without it, the ability to progress, in most cases, is limited.

Recommendations

The researchers offer recommendations based on the findings, analysis, and conclusions of this study. The recommendations that follow are for (a) doctoral program administrators and faculty, (b) current and prospective doctoral students, and (c) further research.

Recommendations for Doctoral Programs and Faculty

Given that there are multiple factors that affect attrition rates and acknowledging that these vary across universities, the recommendations put forth here for doctoral program administrators and faculty should be considered for their appropriateness on an individual basis. At the same time, it should be noted that there are many excellent university programs where the completion rate has steadily been improving. Therefore, some of the following recommendations may already be in place.

Recommendations for Doctoral Program Administration and Faculty

Administrators of doctoral programs should:

1. Revisit the reward and recognition system for faculty involved in advising and mentoring doctoral students by bringing forward to university leaders and decision makers any enhancements to the system that would create further incentives for faculty who provide advisement.
2. Consider the development and implementation of formal training programs in mentoring for faculty.
3. Review on an ongoing basis the criteria for acceptance of students into the university's doctoral programs. In addition, once students are enrolled in the program, guidelines and benchmarks should be put into place to monitor students' progress.
4. Conduct ongoing assessments of students' status to uncover on a timely basis any problems, issues, and/or challenges that may be blocking student progress, and identify resources to help students with such issues.

Recommendations for Current and Prospective Doctoral Students

Individuals contemplating enrolling in a doctoral program should

1. Take sufficient time to find out as much about not only criteria for acceptance and course requirements, but equally as important, the kind of support, direction, and guidance they can rightfully expect to receive during the entire time they are in the program.
2. Have realistic expectations about the investment in time and money involved in completing a dissertation.
3. Become knowledgeable about what recourse they have if they find they are not receiving the guidance and direction they require. For those students already involved at some stage of the dissertation process, they should be aware that, if they do not have a satisfactory relationship with their advisor, it is legitimate and appropriate to seek another advisor. Further, students should be aware that there should be neither a penalty nor any political implications for changing advisors.

Recommendations for Further Research

The researchers recommend further studies be conducted to develop a larger database of information to gain a more comprehensive understanding of why some students who complete the required course work do not go on to complete their dissertations.

In light of this, the following should be considered:

1. Based on the limitations of the current study and to correct for researchers' bias, a survey of a large sample of active and inactive doctoral students should be conducted to assess the extent to which the same or similar findings would be uncovered.

2. A further similar study using the same criteria should be undertaken among students who successfully completed their dissertations and obtained their doctoral degrees to compare and contrast the experiences of students who graduate with those in this study who remain at ABD status.

3. A comparison and analysis of research should be undertaken to assess the recent experiences of doctoral program administrators and faculty and students who have obtained doctoral degrees and those who remain ABDs. This research should be undertaken to uncover similarities and/or differences in perspectives as well as the implications for success or failure in doctoral programs.

Researcher Reflections

There are two ways of spreading light: to be the candle or the mirror that reflects it.

—Edith Wharton

As we come to the close of this study, we want to pause for a moment and reflect on the journey that we have undertaken with you. We hope we have been like the candle guiding those students struggling at various stages of the process, rekindling the flame of possibility for those who have abandoned this work, and shedding some light on what lies ahead for those who are contemplating taking up this work. This was our intention and sincere hope from the moment we began this project. But as with everything in life, the more we attempted to give, the more we received in return, and we came to understand how prophetic are the words of Joubert, who reminds us that "to teach is to learn twice." This study was a collaborative effort among ourselves, and it was greatly enhanced by the insight and feedback of the research participants who willingly gave of their time to share their experiences with us. Our fondest hope is that we lit the candle that may help demystify the process for you and that you have come to see this work, although difficult, as achievable. At the same time, by mirroring the process, we are grateful for all that we have learned and continue to learn as researchers, academics, and doctoral advisors.

Part II: Summary and Discussion

Content and Process: A Chapter-by-Chapter Road Map

Part II of this book mirrors each chapter of an actual dissertation. Chapters 5 through 7 set up the study and constitute the study's framework. As pointed out in Part I, these three chapters form your proposal. Chapters 8 through 10 discuss how you conduct research and write up your study. The problem identified in Part I, which addresses the issue of why people who have completed course work do not go on to complete the research and write their dissertations, is used throughout each of the chapters in Part II. In this way, you can follow the same idea as it threads through the different sections that constitute a dissertation. Each chapter in Part II is presented in two sections. Section I provides instructions regarding the specific content of each chapter and how that content is developed. Section II is the application that demonstrates what a written-up chapter would look like based on the content developed.

- The first chapter of your dissertation is the most critical, and everything that follows hinges on how well this first chapter is constructed. Chapter 1 of your dissertation begins with the *context,* which introduces the research by providing the background that sets the stage for the *research problem* to be investigated. The next step is to describe the *purpose* of the research—that is, *how* you will go about addressing the problem. To carry out the purpose, *research questions* are developed that, when answered, will shed light on the problem you have identified.

- The second chapter of the dissertation constitutes a review of topic-specific literature. A dissertation demonstrates your ability to write a coherent volume of intellectually demanding work. A key part of the dissertation that illustrates your scholarship is the way in which you have analyzed, organized, and reported the relevant literature. In conducting a literature review, you are forced to think critically and consider the role of argument in research. Thus, reviewing the literature is research in and of itself. We also address the conceptual framework as an integral element of the research process and provide detailed explanation regarding how to understand and develop this often misunderstood concept, where it would be introduced in the dissertation, and how it functions in analysis.

- Chapter 3 of the dissertation presents the research design and methodology used in conducting your study and includes various interrelated elements that reflect the sequential nature of qualitative research. This chapter is intended to show the reader that you have an understanding of the methodological implications of the choices you have made and in particular, that you have thought carefully about the linkages between your study's purpose and research questions and the research approach and research methods that you have selected.

- Once you have collected your data by way of the various data collection methods, your next step is to manage, organize, and make sense of all the separate pieces of accumulated information. Your task is to transform *raw data* into something meaningful by analyzing them and making inferences from discrete pieces of information. This process is based on induction: The researcher starts with a large set of data and seeks to progressively narrow them into smaller important groups of key data. The analytic procedure falls essentially into the following sequential phases: organizing the data, generating categories, identifying patterns and themes, and coding data.

- When you reach this point in the research process, it is essential to keep an open mind, remembering that qualitative research is all about discovery. You need to look carefully at all of your data, seeking to uncover important insights regarding the phenomenon that you are researching. These are your "findings," which are presented in Chapter 4 of your dissertation. The procedures you use to accomplish analysis of data and reporting findings need to be well thought out, explicitly documented, and directly connected to your research questions.

- Subsequently, in the following chapter, Chapter 5, "Analyzing and Interpreting Findings," you will synthesize all your data sources and insights, creating an interpretation that is holistic and integrated. Your goal in conducting analysis of findings is to discover what it means or, more precisely, what meaning you can make of it by integrating your findings with literature, research, and practice. Meaning comes from looking at differences and similarities and from inquiring into and interpreting causes, consequences, and relationships. This process requires a good deal of careful thinking and reflection.

- Because qualitative research depends on the skills, training, capabilities, and insights of the researcher, qualitative analysis and interpretation of findings ultimately depend on the analytical intellect and style of each individual analyst. Analyzing and interpreting is a highly intuitive process; it is certainly not mechanical or technical. As such, there is no clear and accepted single set of conventions for the analysis and interpretation of qualitative data.

- Analytical approaches are linked to particular forms of data collection and are underpinned by specific conceptual and philosophical traditions and their inherent grounding assumptions. Methodological congruence implies that there are analytic distinctions among traditions or genres. Each tradition is sensitive to particular analytic methods and strategies, as such demanding that the researcher think about data analysis and representation in a particular way, with the product of each tradition providing a perspective on reality that is specific to that tradition.

- In dealing with interpretation, we are unavoidably dealing with human subjectivity, and therefore there are differences in the ways we make meaning. Be sure to acknowledge that there are multiple ways of interpreting findings, that you have sought rival explanations, and that your interpretations are but one perspective. The human-as-instrument in qualitative inquiry is both its greatest strength and its greatest weakness. Nowhere does this ring more true than in analysis. This is indeed one of the greatest strengths of qualitative research, but also the source of one of the greatest critiques of the field.

- The final chapter of your dissertation, Chapter 6, is much more than just a cursory summary of findings. Presenting trustworthy conclusions and actionable recommendations is an opportunity to have the last word about your study and stimulate your readers to think more deeply about the findings of your study and the implications thereof in terms of both practice and future research.

NEARING COMPLETION

PART III

Finally, you have reached the "almost completion" stage of the dissertation process. We know how much time and effort you have invested up until now, and for this, you certainly deserve to give yourself much credit. Indeed, take a moment to reflect on the many varied activities you have engaged in to reach this point. This work has been no small accomplishment. Part III of this book addresses preparation with regard to the final stages of the dissertation process. Chapter 11 offers guidelines and suggestions regarding alignment of all key elements that constitute your study, selecting an appropriate title, writing the abstract, assembling your manuscript and making sure that all the necessary components of the dissertation's layout are addressed, and proofreading and editing the manuscript. The chapter also includes a comprehensive (and extensive!) quality assessment checklist for the entire dissertation. Chapter 12 addresses preparation for a successful defense and thinking about potential avenues for dissemination of your research.

Some Final Technical Considerations

Overview

As you near the end of a very long process, there are a few key elements that still need to be tackled and addressed. First, it is imperative that you make certain that all the elements that constitute your entire document are aligned (a) with your research questions and (b) with one another. Next, you need to craft an appropriate and relevant title that captures the essence of your study and that conveys this in clear and concise terms. You will also need to formulate a tight abstract. In addition, you will need to assemble your entire document. Finally!

Revisiting the Importance of Alignment

Part I of this book started out by indicating the elements that would need to be included in a completed dissertation. Table II.1, "Overview of Dissertation Content"

(p. 83), provides a visual outline of an entire dissertation—a prelude to the steps that are described and demonstrated in Chapters 5 through 10. In addition, Figure 5.1, "Road Map for Developing the Dissertation's First Chapter: Necessary Elements" (p. 91), illustrates the importance of alignment among the first three core critical elements: problem, purpose, and research questions.

At this juncture, as you reach the final stages of writing your dissertation, it is crucial that you once again make certain that all the necessary elements that constitute a dissertation are aligned with one another. In this regard, it is important to revisit the chapters of your dissertation, as if in detective mode, carefully and meticulously checking that the elements are all meaningfully tied together. Check specifically that each element (a) flows sequentially from the elements prior to it and (b) leads logically to the elements that succeed it. In particular, make sure of the following:

- Problem statement defines the subject of inquiry.
- Specific research problem is situated within a broader context.
- Purpose addresses the research problem.
- Research questions together shed light on purpose.
- Conceptual framework is based on research questions.
- Conceptual framework is the repository for the findings.
- Findings, which are objective, are the basis for interpretations, which are subjective.
- Findings and interpretations together are the basis for drawing trustworthy conclusions.
- Conclusions are the springboard for actionable/doable recommendations.

Ensuring that you have achieved all of these steps means that your study is tight and you have taken an important step in ensuring methodological integrity. This process is extremely important for the defense when, among other things, the methodological integrity of your research is finely scrutinized. Table 11.1 "The Alignment Flowchart" is, in effect, the final "dissertation picture," illustrating clearly the alignment that is required among all of the qualitative dissertation's key elements.

Crafting a Title

The title of your dissertation should catch the readers' attention while properly informing them of the main focus of your study. From the beginning of your research, and certainly from the initial proposal stage, you will have had some kind of guiding working title. You have most likely revised and re-revised the title as you proceeded. Now, at the end of the study, you hone that title so that it is crystal clear, meaningful, and appropriately worded. Most important, it should accurately reflect your work.

A title serves various functions. The first function is to identify the content of your study. The title is the first contact that your readers have with your research. It generates some anticipation of what is to follow and as such, must communicate a concise, thorough, and unambiguous picture of the content of your dissertation. The second function of a title is for retrieval purposes. By including the most applicable keywords, you enable another researcher doing a literature search to locate your study. Therefore, a title becomes an important factor in sharing research.

A well-crafted title conveys the essence of what is under study and the mode of inquiry. In composing a title, be sure to include the central phenomenon of your study, as well as the research approach you have used. The title should describe as accurately as possible the main elements of your study. Although such accuracy demands the use of specific language, the title should be clear (i.e., free of obscure technical terms, highly specialized language, and jargon). Mechanically, the title should be concise, to the point, and free of elaborate constructions, alliteration, and other literary devices that detract from the content of the title. Excessive length should be avoided, too, because that dilutes the impact of the key elements presented.

Generally, a two-part title structure offers you the scope to specify the key elements of your report: a few words capturing the essence of your study, followed by a colon that introduces a more specific and descriptive subtitle. One way to begin constructing an effective title is to list all the elements that seem appropriate for inclusion and then weave them in various ways until you are satisfied with the title both aesthetically and technically. As you do this, make a list of all possible two-part titles. Reverse the order. See which works best. Try to obtain feedback from advisors and critical colleagues, and revise accordingly.

In qualitative research, the title provides the researcher with a conceptual frame of reference for continuous reflection. As you immerse yourself in the context of your study, you become increasingly attuned to the key issues of your research—issues you may have been unaware of before starting your research. This process may lead you to shift the focus of your study and as a result, to change the title to more accurately reflect the new focus. It is a good idea to keep notes of how your title evolves, and we suggest that you keep all ideas of titles as memos. If systematically monitored, your changing title can become a means to track the evolution of your perspective as a researcher, as well as the ways in which the focus and direction of your study have shifted over time.

Writing the Abstract

You are required to write an abstract—a carefully worded comprehensive summary that precedes the main body of the report and that tells readers what to expect. An abstract condenses a longer piece of writing while highlighting its major points, concisely describing the content and scope of the writing, and reviewing the content in (very) abbreviated form. A research abstract concisely states the major elements of a research project. Writing a good abstract requires that you explain what you did and found in simple, direct language so readers can then decide whether to read the longer piece of writing for details. Although it is the first section of your paper, the abstract, by definition, should be written last since it will summarize the contents of your entire paper.

TABLE 11.1 ● Alignment Flowchart

Chapter 1: Introduction	Chapter 2: Literature Review	Chapter 3: Research Methodology	Chapter 4: Presentation of Findings (OBJECTIVE)	Chapter 5: Analysis and Interpretation of Findings (SUBJECTIVE)	Chapter 6: Conclusions and Recommendations
• Research problem must be situated within a broader context • Purpose statement must be formulated in such a way that it will shed light on the problem • Research questions must address the purpose	• Each body of literature that is reviewed must be tied to and address some aspect of the problem • Conceptual framework: Categories emanate from research questions; descriptors/subcategories emanate from "hunches" as well as from the literature • Conceptual framework becomes the repository for findings • Based on the findings and interpretations, make sure that all areas of literature reviewed are relevant and appropriate. Eliminate unnecessary sections, and add in what might still be needed	• Check that all data collection and data analysis methods have actually been done in the way that you have described • Be sure to eliminate any unnecessary material	• Findings are answers to the research questions • Each finding must be tied to a research question • Findings are basis for interpretation	• Interpretation is about what you think the findings really mean • Final synthesis includes findings from all data collection methods, integrated with the literature	• Each conclusion that is drawn should be tied to respective findings and interpretations • There should be at least one conclusion per finding • Conclusions are the springboard for actionable recommendations • Typically there are recommendations for (a) the organization or institution; (b) people in the particular discipline under study; and (c) for further research
			"If I find this…"	*"Then I think this means…"*	*"Therefore I conclude that…"*	*"Thus I recommend that…"*

The abstract allows readers to survey the contents of a study and like a title, is used by abstracting and information services to index and retrieve articles. The information included in your abstract influences whether readers proceed to look at your total study. In addition, your abstract is the means through which other researchers, searching for studies on your topic, will be able to evaluate whether your study is useful to them. Therefore, the abstract offers a valuable opportunity for your study to inform a wide audience. It is the means with which to capture potential readers' interests, thereby expanding your professional opportunities within the research community. As in the case of the title, focusing on the most significant elements and using precise wording are key. A sample abstract appears as Appendix FF.

Abstracts can differ in terms of style and word count. We suggest that you consult with your advisor, departmental regulations, and the relevant style manual regarding abstract requirements. In the social sciences, abstracts are usually published in the *Dissertation Abstracts International*, and for this there is a 350-word restriction. The content of an abstract typically includes the following elements:

- Title of your study,
- Research problem or issue that was addressed,
- Qualitative research tradition or genre,
- Theoretical basis that guided the study,
- Data sources that informed your study,
- Methods and procedures of data collection and data analysis, and
- Key findings, conclusions, and recommendations.

A well-prepared abstract can be the most important paragraph in your article. Most people will have their first contact with a dissertation by accessing the abstract, as they are doing a literature search through an electronic abstract-retrieval system. Readers frequently decide on the basis of the abstract whether to read the entire study. The abstract needs to be dense with information but also readable, well organized, concise, focused, and self-contained. Embedding keywords in your abstract will enhance the user's ability to find it. A good abstract is

- **Accurate:** Ensure that an abstract correctly reflects the purpose and content of the manuscript. Do not include information that does not appear in the body of the paper. If the study extends or replicates previous research, note this in the abstract, and cite the author (initials and surname) and year. Comparing an abstract with an outline of the paper's headings is a useful way to verify the accuracy of an abstract.
- **Self-contained:** Define all abbreviations (except units of measurement) and acronyms. Spell out names of tests and drugs (use generic names for drugs). Define unique terms. Paraphrase rather than quote. Include names of authors (initials and surnames) and dates of publication in citations of other publications (and give a full bibliographic citation in the article's reference list). Include keywords within the abstract for indexing purposes.

- **Concise and specific:** Each sentence should be maximally informative, especially the lead sentence. Begin the abstract with the most important information (but do not waste space by repeating the title). This may be the purpose or thesis, or perhaps the results and conclusions. Include in the abstract only the four or five most important concepts, findings, or implications. An abstract should not contain any lengthy background information or references to other literature.
- **Nonevaluative:** Report rather than evaluate; do not add to or comment on what is in the body of the manuscript.
- **Coherent and readable:** Write in clear and vigorous prose, use concise but complete sentences, and get to the point quickly. Use verbs rather than the noun equivalents and the active rather than the passive voice. Use the present tense to describe results with continuing applicability or conclusions drawn; use the past tense to describe specific variables manipulated or tests applied.

Writing Tips

1. Refer to academic journals for examples of abstracts.
2. Keep on hand a copy of your preferred style manual.
3. Write an initial draft that follows the guidelines.
4. To begin composing your abstract, take whole sentences or key phrases from each section and order them in a sequence that summarizes your paper. Then revise or add connecting phrases or words to make it cohesive and clear.
5. Obtain feedback on the draft from colleagues, preferably those who have not yet read the longer work. Note their comments and questions. This will be an indication of whether and to what extent your abstract is "doing its job."
6. Revise the abstract based on the feedback. Plan to revise repeatedly in order to craft it as well as possible, and to keep it within the word limit.
7. Be sure your abstract is grammatically correct with correct spelling, punctuation, and format. The abstract is typically a single paragraph that is double spaced.
8. If necessary, take your abstract to your school's writing lab for assistance.

Additional Tips

- An abstract always begins on a new page. On the first line of the abstract page, center the word "Abstract" (no bold, formatting, italics, underlining, or quotation marks).
- Beginning with the next line, write a concise summary of the key points of your research. (Do not indent.) Your abstract should contain your research topic, research questions, participants, methods, results, data analysis, and conclusions. You may also include possible implications of your research and future work you see connected with your findings.
- You may also want to list keywords from your paper in your abstract. To do this, center the text and type *Keywords* (italicized) and then list your keywords. Listing your keywords will help researchers find your work in databases.

- *Ways to conserve characters include* (a) using numerals for all numbers, except those that begin a sentence (consider recasting a sentence that begins with a number); (b) abbreviating liberally (e.g., use *vs.* for *versus*), although all abbreviations that need to be explained in the text must also be explained on first use in the abstract; and (c) using the active voice (but without the personal pronouns *I* or *we*).
- Remember that within the specified word limit, you will need to try to make your research summary as informative and comprehensive as possible. To achieve a final, solid version, go through various drafts. Usually you will start off by writing an extended abstract, and this is followed by various iterations in which you pare down the words so that the key elements are expressed concisely within the imposed limits.

Assembling the Manuscript

Although format and style is a function of individual taste and institutional and/or departmental regulations, several general rules can be adopted in design and layout:

1. Pages must be numbered consecutively throughout. Page numbers are usually centered at the bottom of the page or placed at the top right. Roman numerals (i, ii, iii, iv) are used for the preliminary pages or front matter (abstract, dedication, acknowledgments, list of tables and figures, table of contents). Note that the title page is always the first page (i), but it is not numbered. Arabic numbers (1, 2, 3, 4) are used throughout the rest of the manuscript.
2. The entire document, including page numbers and table captions, must be typed in the same typeface/font and size. The most common usage is 12-point type Times New Roman.
3. The body of the dissertation should be double spaced. Single spacing is permitted in the following text: (a) footnotes, (b) block quotations, (c) tables and figures and their captions, and (d) bibliography entries (if single spaced, you must still have double space between entries).
4. Don't "justify" (square off) on the right margin. This style is for published articles only.
5. It is customary to use 1-inch margins all round. In some cases, the margin on the left side may be required to be 1.5 inches for binding purposes.
6. Regarding headings and subheadings, refer to the standards set by your department's choice of style manual. Regardless of style, all heading and subheading format must be consistent throughout.
7. Paragraphs are distinguished by indentation. Make sure there are no skipped lines or extra spaces between paragraphs.
8. The reference list must include all sources that were directly used in writing your dissertation. Every source that you have cited should be included in the reference list, and every entry listed in the reference list must appear in the

manuscript. Because it is critical that the reference list is precise and accurate, we suggest that you carefully check all your citations.

9. Footnotes can be used for explanatory purposes where necessary.

10. Figures and tables must be consecutively numbered throughout. Alternatively, you may make use of combination chapter and figure and/or table number designations (e.g., Table 1.1, 1.2, 1.3, 2.1, 2.2). The number and caption of the table is placed above the table and must appear in the same typeface and size of the dissertation text. The number and caption of a figure is placed below the figure and must appear in the same typeface and size of the dissertation text. All tables that are working tools should be included as appendices, rather than in the main body of the text.

11. Appendices provide information that is pertinent to the study, but that is either too lengthy or not important enough to be included in the main body of the text. This information includes materials especially developed for the study, such as cover letters, data collection instruments, tables containing raw data, and tabulated data analysis. Appendices are lettered, not numbered (Appendix A, Appendix B, etc.).

12. The key point to remember when you include an appendix is that the information is nonessential; that is, if it were removed, the study would still be understandable to the reader. It is appropriate to include appendices (a) when the incorporation of material in the body of the work would make it poorly structured or (b) when the information is too long and detailed to be easily summarized in the body of the paper. Ensure inclusion of helpful, supporting, or essential material that would otherwise clutter or break up the narrative flow of the paper or would be distracting to the reader.

13. The final element to check is the table of contents, which must be clearly and logically organized. The function of the table of contents is to guide your readers, allowing them to follow a long and involved story. It should enable them to find their way easily around the different parts of your dissertation and quickly pinpoint those sections that they are most interested in reading. Therefore, it is essential that every heading and subheading that you use appear in the table of contents. Your style manual will indicate specified differences regarding the levels of subheadings and how these should be numbered. The list of tables and figures is presented on a separate page. This list must give the number and title of each table and figure and the page on which it can be found. A sample table of contents is presented as Appendix GG.

Proofreading and Editing

Getting the dissertation ready for submission refers to both the form and the content of the document. Although some revisions are required following the defense, what you present at the defense cannot be incomplete in any way, nor should it contain any grammatical and/or typographical errors. Although you anticipate some changes and alterations following the defense, you should consider your dissertation a polished final version, not a work in progress.

At this point, go back and, if necessary, adjust Chapters 1 through 3. Make sure all text elements are necessary and relevant. Check for items that need to be expanded. Also be aware that the literature review was an important early task. You now need to reread it and ensure that everything in your review is directly relevant to your study. If not, it needs to be eliminated. Equally important, if a section of literature review is missing, it needs to be added. Check throughout your document for correct tenses. In the proposal, you used the future tense because you were writing about what you were intending to do. In the dissertation, you are reporting on research that you have already completed, so you should change to past tense.

All manuscripts require editing and proofreading, and especially if English is not your native language, you might need editing assistance in this regard. If you feel that you need assistance with writing, be sure to contact your advisor or institution for additional resources and guidance. It should be obvious that the expectations for correctness and accuracy in academic writing are high. If you feel that you are unable to meet these demands at your current level of writing proficiency, you may need to seek outside assistance. It is quite acceptable to hire an editor or a proofreader to help meet academic writing expectations. In addition, most universities have writing centers with writing classes and/or workshops that offer an array of helpful writing resources.

A word of advice: After you complete your final draft, it is often helpful to set your manuscript aside for several days. Stepping back in this way creates the distance needed to change roles from "writer" to "reader," which is a way to approach and review your work with fresh eyes.

In rereading, you should be critically evaluating the completeness and quality of the contents of your work. In doing so, the following checklist (albeit extensive) might be useful:

Quality Assessment Checklist for Your Complete Dissertation: All Together Now!

Front Matter	**Title**
	✓ Does it convey the essence and purpose of the study?
	✓ Does it indicate the type of study and participants?
	✓ Does it include keywords that will promote proper categorization into databases?
	✓ Does it include author's full name, degree to be conferred, university, and year?
	✓ Are letters all in all capitals?
	Copyright Page (optional)
	✓ Are author's name and year centered between the margins on the lower half of page?
	✓ Do you include copyright symbol (©)?
	✓ Do you include the statement "All Rights Reserved"?

(Continued)

(Continued)

	Abstract ✓ Is it written in third person (active voice)? ✓ Does the first sentence describe the entire study? ✓ Do subsequent sentences expand on that description? ✓ Do you include all necessary material (i.e., problem, purpose, scope, research tradition, data sources, methodology, key findings and implications)? ✓ Does it include all keywords in order to promote proper categorization into databases? ✓ Is the format correct as per guidelines in your preferred style manual? ✓ Is the word count accurate? **Dedication and Acknowledgments** ✓ Is the heading ACKNOWLEDGMENTS capitalized? ✓ Does the heading appear centered between the left and right margins 2.0 inches from the top? ✓ Does text begin two spaces after the word ACKNOWLEDGMENTS? ✓ If included, is the dedication page separate from the acknowledgments page? ✓ Is the dedication text centered between the left and right, and between the top and bottom margins? ✓ Have you included the title for the dedication page? If so, it should be removed. **Table of Contents** ✓ Is the heading TABLE OF CONTENTS centered between the left and right margins, 2.0 inches from the top of the page? ✓ Are all chapters and major sections within chapters and is all back matter listed with page numbers? ✓ Are all headings and subheadings grammatically consistent (i.e., "Introduction," "Review of Literature" not "Introduction," "Reviewing the Literature")? ✓ Are the headings and subheadings worded exactly the same as those in the text? ✓ Is the entire table of contents correctly formatted as per guidelines in your preferred style manual? **List of Tables and Figures** ✓ Are all tables and figures that appear in the body of the dissertation included? ✓ Are all tables and figures worded exactly as they appear in the body of the dissertation?
CHAPTER 1	**Introduction** ✓ Do you provide an overview of purpose and focus of the study, why it is significant, how it was conducted, and how it will contribute to professional knowledge and practice? **Statement of Problem** ✓ Is the background to the problem clearly presented? ✓ Is adequate background information presented for a clear understanding of the problem? ✓ Is the problem clearly and logically articulated? ✓ Does the discussion move from the general to the specific? ✓ Is the problem situated within the literature? That is, does literature serve to place the problem in context? ✓ Do you make clear the relationship of the problem to previous research? ✓ Is there an appropriate amount of relevant literature cited? ✓ Is the researcher's perspective and relationship to the problem discussed? If so, are assumptions and biases made explicit? ✓ Do we know how this research might contribute to the knowledge base and practice?

✓ Is there a logical segue that leads directly to the purpose statement?
✓ Is your writing clear and readable?

Purpose Statement

✓ Is the purpose clearly, succinctly, and unambiguously stated?
✓ Is it clear as to how the research purpose will address the problem?
✓ Is your purpose relevant to your chosen research tradition?

Research Questions

✓ Are the research questions clearly focused?
✓ Are research questions open-ended so that they will foster exploration and discovery?
✓ Would answers to research questions shed light on the problem?
✓ Are all your research questions interconnected; that is, is there a natural and meaningful relationship among them?
✓ Is there alignment among problem, purpose, and research questions?

Research Design and Methodology

✓ Is the overall research design approach appropriate and feasible as a means of qualitative inquiry?

Role of Researcher

✓ Does this section inform the reader what the researcher brings to the study?
✓ Do you discuss how researcher experience and/or perspective are related to the problem?

Researcher Assumptions

✓ Are researcher assumptions and biases revealed and explained?

Rationale and Significance

✓ Is there a well-thought-out rationale that provides justification for this study?
✓ Is a convincing argument explicitly or implicitly made for the importance or significance of this research?
✓ Is it clear how this research will contribute to the knowledge base and/or practice and/or policy?

Definitions of Key Terms

✓ Does the chapter conclude with definitions and/or explanations of key terminology that might not have a commonly understood meaning?
✓ If you include definitions, have you properly cited all relevant authoritative sources?

CHAPTER 2	**Literature Review**

✓ Do you have a clear introduction to this chapter that includes your purpose statement (if required), as well as an explanation of how the chapter will be organized?
✓ Does your review show a clear understanding and critique of each topic?
✓ Is the review comprehensive? Does it cover the major issues and thinking around each topic?
✓ Have you included historical as well as current and most up-to-date coverage?
✓ Does the path of your argument flow logically?
✓ Make certain that you have written with authority: Is the review analytical and critical, and not merely summative and descriptive?
✓ Is the review well organized and systematically presented?
✓ Do you include an introductory paragraph that outlines the way you organize the different bodies of literature?

(Continued)

(Continued)

	✓ Are the methods for conducting the literature review sufficiently described? ✓ Does the order of headings and subheadings seem logical? ✓ Do you make use of transition phrases to link and integrate paragraphs? ✓ Do you include logical segues between sections? ✓ Do you include summary paragraphs at the end of each major section, as well as an overall summary at the end of the chapter? ✓ Do summary paragraphs highlight and clarify the main points of a section, especially if it is complex and long? ✓ Have you included too much paraphrasing and too many direct quotations that detract from the readability of the chapter? ✓ Are all authors who make the same point combined in a citation? ✓ Are all citations included in the reference list? ✓ Have all citations that you have not included been eliminated from the reference list? ✓ Have you checked your recommended style manual for format, punctuation, and grammar? **Conceptual Framework** ✓ Does your conceptual framework depict the overall "territory" of your research? ✓ Does your framework provide theoretical clarification of what you have investigated? ✓ Does your framework illuminate the relationships among theoretical variables, concepts, or constructs? ✓ Does your framework enable a reader to understand *what* your research seeks to achieve and *how* that will be achieved? ✓ Does your framework provide a strong methodological base for development of the study and for analysis of the findings? ✓ If you have developed a diagrammatic model, is this clearly, accurately, and meaningfully presented? ✓ If you have developed a diagrammatic model, is this accompanied by comprehensive descriptive narrative? ✓ If your conceptual framework underwent any developments, do you mention and describe its evolution? ✓ Does your conceptual framework add value to the way you and others understand your research? ✓ Does your conceptual framework enhance the conceptual quality of your dissertation?
CHAPTER 3	**Introduction** ✓ Do you restate your research purpose? ✓ Do you describe the general organization of the chapter? **Research Sample** ✓ Do you provide a comprehensive description of your research sample and the population from which it was drawn? ✓ Do you discuss and explain the research site (organization/program/institution)? ✓ Do you discuss in detail your sampling strategy/strategies, citing appropriate literature? ✓ Are the criteria for sampling selection stated and explained? ✓ Are the details and characteristics pertaining to the sample adequately discussed? ✓ Have you discussed issues of access and consent? **Information Needed** ✓ Is the information that was needed to conduct the study clearly and specifically outlined? (This should include demographic, perceptual, and contextual information.) ✓ Are you clear how and from whom the necessary information was obtained? ✓ Do you provide a logical connection between the type of information needed and the methods you have selected to obtain that information?

Research Design Overview

✓ Do you describe qualitative research as your chosen research paradigm, citing appropriate literature?
✓ Do you offer a convincing argument for choosing qualitative research?
✓ Do you provide a convincing argument for the particular qualitative tradition or genre (or combination of traditions) that you have chosen?
✓ Do you describe your chosen qualitative research methods including rationale for suitability regarding addressing the research questions?
✓ Is the study's methodology/research design documented in sufficient detail so that the study could be replicated?
✓ Have you described in chronological order each step taken in conducting the study?
✓ Is there a sequential progression inherent in the methodological design? That is, is the reader able to see how each stage of the study's design builds on and flows logically from the stage preceding it?
✓ Have you discussed all decisions made during the course of the study, and if applicable, have you mentioned any changes or modifications in focus, direction, and design?
✓ Do you include explanation of any field tests or pilot studies, including administration and description of findings (if appropriate)?
✓ If you include a timeline, have you described in chronological order each step taken in conducting the study?
✓ Are all charts and/or figures that you have included comprehensive and relevant?

Data Collection Methods

✓ Do you reference all tools, instruments, and procedures that you have used?
✓ Do you provide a rationale for the selection of instruments used?
✓ Do you discuss the strengths and weaknesses of each method of data collection, citing appropriate literature?
✓ If an instrument was developed specifically for this study, have you described procedures involved in its development, validation, and administration?
✓ Do you describe how, when, where, and by whom data were collected?
✓ Are the data collection methods congruent with the problem being investigated, and the specific qualitative tradition employed?
✓ Has triangulation of data collection methods been achieved?

Data Analysis and Synthesis

✓ Do you explain the procedures you use for recording, managing, and storing information?
✓ Are your methods of data analysis, synthesis, and interpretation sufficiently described and detailed?
✓ Are all charts and/or figures that you have included comprehensive and relevant?

Ethical Considerations

✓ Are the ethical considerations that you have identified clear and acceptable, and have you discussed the procedures followed to address them?
✓ Do you include how you have satisfied IRB requirements?

Issues of Trustworthiness

✓ Does your discussion of the key issues pertaining to trustworthiness in qualitative research show that you have a clear understanding of these issues?
✓ Does your discussion illustrate how you have considered and accounted for credibility, dependability, and transferability vis-à-vis your own study?

(Continued)

(Continued)

	Limitations and Delimitations
	✓ Do you acknowledge all limitations and delimitations pertaining to your study?
	✓ Do you indicate how you have attempted to address limitations?
	Chapter Summary
	✓ Does your culminating summary integrate all the elements presented in this chapter?
	✓ Do you include all key points?
	✓ Is your summary comprehensive and focused?
CHAPTER 4	**Presentation of Findings**
	✓ Is your introduction clear?
	✓ Does your introduction include your purpose statement (if required), as well as inform the reader as to how the chapter is organized?
	✓ Are your data analysis steps clearly identified?
	✓ Do you explain clearly how you have managed and organized your data for analysis?
	✓ Is your coding process adequately described?
	✓ Are your findings statements clearly and precisely stated?
	✓ Are the findings presented in relation to the research questions?
	✓ Are the findings presented in a logical sequence?
	✓ Are the findings clearly organized and easy to follow?
	✓ Are the findings directly responsive to the problem raised by the study? That is, do the findings provide an answer to the research questions?
	✓ Do the data presented in support of the findings (interview and/or focus group quotations, incidents from field notes, material from documents, etc.) provide adequate and convincing evidence for the findings?
	✓ Is this chapter free from interpretation? That is, are your findings reported accurately and objectively?
	✓ Are there appropriate lead-in sentences and clues?
	✓ Have you selected the strongest and most appropriate quotations to support your point(s)?
	✓ Have you trimmed your quotations, eliminating all unnecessary wording?
	✓ If you have made use of a road map, is this clear and precise?
	✓ Do the headings of your road map correspond with the headings in your narrative?
	✓ Do you include a summary paragraph that offers a logical link to the next chapter?
	✓ Are all tables and figures well organized, self-explanatory, and easy to understand?
	✓ Are the data that are presented in each table described in the text that either follows or precedes it?
	✓ Have you tightened up your writing, looking for how to make short, crisp sentences?
CHAPTER 5	**Analysis and Synthesis**
	✓ Does your introductory paragraph include purpose statement (if required) as well as explanation of how you went about analyzing and synthesizing the findings?
	✓ Does your argument flow logically and coherently?
	✓ Do you make one point at a time?
	✓ Are your interpretations clear, thoughtful, and reasonable?
	✓ Are your interpretations relevant to the research problem, purpose, and research questions?
	✓ Are the major themes interrelated to show a higher level of analysis and abstraction?
	✓ Is your analysis positioned and discussed in terms of the related bodies of literature and previous research?
	✓ Have you included relevant participant quotations to support your argument, making sure that these same quotations did not appear in Chapter 4?
	✓ Is all information presented in tables consistent with information that is presented in the narrative?

	✓ Have you acknowledged that there are multiple ways of interpreting findings, and that you remain open to other interpretive possibilities? ✓ If you have chosen to revisit and reflect upon your initial assumptions as stated in your opening chapter, do you flesh these out in terms of your study's findings? ✓ Do you offer a comprehensive overview that integrates all key points?
CHAPTER 6	**Closure** ✓ Do you include a brief but informative introduction? ✓ If you have included a final reflective piece, does this make a statement regarding your role as a qualitative researcher, and/or your experience in writing the dissertation? ✓ If you step back and review this, your chapter, do you think that it offers the reader a completed picture of your research? ✓ Will readers be likely to walk away with a good understanding of the study and with a general feeling of finality and closure? **Conclusions** ✓ Are your conclusions clearly derived from your study's findings? In other words, is it clear to the reader that your conclusions are warranted by the findings? ✓ Do you offer at least one conclusion per finding? In other words, even though conclusions can cut across findings, is each finding tied to at least one conclusion? ✓ Are your conclusions logical and clearly explained? ✓ Are you sure that your conclusions are not mere restatements of the findings? ✓ Are you sure that your conclusions are not "interpretations" but rather strong conclusive statements? ✓ Are your conclusions consistent? Do they flow logically from each other, and not contradict each other? ✓ Can your conclusions be challenged? If so, can you think of any flaws or limitations in the way in which you have stated and explained each conclusion? **Recommendations** ✓ Are all your recommendations justified by the findings? ✓ Are all your recommendations doable and actionable? ✓ Have you discussed applications for practice? ✓ Have you discussed applications for policy? ✓ Have you offered suggestions for further research? ✓ Have you selected strong recommendations for each of the above sections?
BACK MATTER	**Appendices** ✓ Are all research instruments used listed? ✓ Are all other relevant materials included (sample transcripts, sample coding schemes, summary charts, etc.)? ✓ Is each item that is included listed in the table of contents? **References** ✓ Have you included all works cited in the dissertation? ✓ Are all works cited listed in alphabetical order by author? ✓ Do all references adhere to proper style format (APA, MLA, Turabian, Chicago, etc.)? ✓ Have you checked spelling of all authors and titles?

(Continued)

(Continued)

AND FINALLY:	✓ Does the structure of your complete document comply with institutional and/or programmatic requirements? ✓ Is your writing throughout scholarly and academic? ✓ Have you checked throughout for unclear and/or ambiguous language? ✓ Have you checked for any incorrect grammar? ✓ Have you checked throughout for any incorrect spelling? ✓ Does the discussion throughout have a logical flow? ✓ Are headings and subheadings throughout used effectively in order to structure and present the discussion? ✓ Have you eliminated any needless repetition? ✓ Conversely, have you checked for insufficient detail, and areas that are "unfinished"? ✓ Refer and RE-REFER to Chapter 4 "Guidelines for Academic Writing"!!

Source: This chart first appeared in Bloomberg, L. D. (2009). *The qualitative dissertation: A content guideline.* Unpublished manuscript series.

Defense Preparation and Beyond

Overview

Your manuscript is finally ready! You now stand on the cusp of presenting your study to the academic community at your institution and beyond. As you head toward this final milestone in the dissertation journey, we provide you with some ideas and clues that will hopefully prepare you and stand you in good stead, in terms of both pre- and post-defense status. Much success to you!

Pre-Defense Preparation

Submitting Necessary Documentation

To stay within required time frames, you should plan ahead accordingly. When you approach your defense (sometimes referred to as the "dissertation hearing," "orals," or "vivas"), you should generally keep in regular contact with your institution's registrar and office of doctoral studies for their calendar of deadline dates and requirements for submissions of all the necessary documentation. Check dates carefully because your degree may be delayed if you have not complied with all the necessary submissions. Especially make sure whether you need to file the "intent to defend" form and do not exceed the required deadline. This form declares that you and your advisor believe that you can meet all the institutional demands for defense; this stage usually requires advisor approval.

As you near completion of your dissertation, you also should check that all your required courses have been completed in accordance with your approved program plan, that all necessary credits are entered on your transcript, that your proposal is on file, and that all your records are in proper order. If there are any discrepancies or concerns, you should bring these matters to the immediate attention of your program administrator and/or dissertation secretary in the office of doctoral studies. You certainly want no unwelcome surprises at this point.

Selecting and Forming Your Committee

As mentioned in Part I, each university has a different system regarding dissertation committee structure and the process of preparing for that structure. You need to find out what system is adopted in your particular institution; your advisor/sponsor and/or departmental chair are likely to be in the best position to inform you of these matters. A dissertation committee typically consists of three to six faculty members. In some instances, all committee members are from within the department of the student's major. Other times, the committee is multidisciplinary, with members representing various academic departments. In some cases, a dissertation committee consists of three faculty members who guide the development and completion of the dissertation. In these cases, a final oral panel is convened, consisting of the dissertation committee plus two outside readers selected by the graduate office.

In some universities, the doctoral committee structure is based on an apprenticeship model and is used as a vehicle to guide the student from course work through the defense. The dissertation committee is the group of faculty responsible for the student's progress right from the beginning, with all those involved contributing to the development of an acceptable dissertation. The committee is a hierarchical organization, with each member of the committee having a different responsibility vis-à-vis the student's research. Ideally, the doctoral committee is composed of faculty with different areas of expertise whose resources the student will be able to tap into during the dissertation process. Sometimes the same committee will stay with the student from the outset, guiding the apprenticeship. In other cases, this committee will evolve during the course of conducting research and writing the dissertation as the necessary expertise becomes evident based on the developing project.

At some universities, the student will be required to work with an advisor/sponsor and second reader from the proposal stage onward; it is only when the student has almost completed the dissertation that a dissertation committee needs to be formed. In this instance, you can usually select your committee from among those in your own and related departments, those whose courses you have taken, and/or those whose work bears some relation to the focus of your dissertation. Some of these faculty members may be involved in other programs or schools within your university. In some rare cases, experts beyond your university can be chosen. In most instances, faculty has the choice to accept or decline to serve on a doctoral committee. Given the voluntary nature of serving on a dissertation committee, faculty typically elect to work with those candidates whom they perceive to be academically strong and/ or easy to work with. Faculty frequently seek those students who demonstrate these characteristics in their course work. Bear in mind that because in most instances a faculty member has the choice to accept or decline to serve on a doctoral committee, be prepared to make alternative choices should the need arise. If you have difficulty in securing a committee, you might want to seek assistance from your sponsor/advisor and/or from your departmental chair.

Because you have known from the beginning of the program that faculty members will eventually have to be selected, rather than wait for the time close to the dissertation defense, you should start thinking early on about who might best serve on your committee. The more information you have about potential committee members, the easier it will be for you to make decisions regarding which individuals may be best suited in helping you achieve your goals. You certainly want your committee to enhance the quality of your academic work and to be supportive of your progress. Therefore, you need to identify the best match between your own learning style and the faculty who are available to work with you. We suggest that you seek faculty who can meet the following criteria:

- They are knowledgeable in your discipline and have an interest in your research topic.
- They are familiar with the procedures of your university.
- They are respectful of each other and value collegial relationships.
- They are cooperative and supportive of students' progress.
- They have the time available and are accessible based on their own busy schedules and time constraints.

In the process of selecting members for your committee, you want to remain cautious of offending others in the department—those who will become your professional colleagues once you graduate and/or those who may ultimately participate in the process of evaluating your dissertation. One never knows which committee members will need to be replaced, for a variety of reasons, and which colleagues might participate in your defense as the fourth reader. Academic institutions, by their nature, are highly political arenas. Therefore, selection of the committee requires careful planning, with an emphasis on maintaining respectful professional relationships at all stages of the dissertation process.

Once you have filed your intent to defend and your advisor/sponsor or dissertation chair has approved your defense, you should secure the necessary additional committee members. This process usually includes selecting and assigning additional readers. Each institution has its own way of going about setting up the defense meeting, and you should always consult with your institution's office of doctoral studies with regard to the correct procedures and protocol.

Preparing for the Defense

Generally, it is a safe rule of thumb to figure out that a complete draft of the dissertation should be in the advisor's hands within the first weeks of the semester in which you intend your defense to take place. This allows your primary advisor sufficient time to review your material and make recommendations, forward to the second reader for approval and recommendations, and secure third and fourth readers and comply with the institutions' scheduling procedures regarding the defense committee. You need to make sure that you have the necessary information regarding all required deadlines by consulting with your advisors as well as contacting your institution's office of doctoral studies for guidelines and rules.

The purpose of the dissertation defense is twofold: (a) to publicly discuss what you have researched and what you have discovered in the process and (b) to evaluate the acceptability of the study as a scholarly piece of research in your area of specialization and to make a collective decision that will determine the recommendations for revisions.

The defense, in effect, moves your dissertation from the private domain into the arena of public discourse, providing you with some sense of closure. Actual procedures for conducting the meeting and the formalities involved are likely to vary, not only among universities, but also among departments. Your advisor will most likely outline the proceedings of the defense, as well as explain to you the roles of the various committee members. As such, although each experience will certainly be unique, you should be well prepared as to what to expect in the session.

Each institution is concerned with maintaining an implicit academic standard for acceptable scholarship. You have just completed a rigorous piece of research, so your research apprenticeship is ending. The defense marks this transition as you are invited to sit at the table and talk about your research as a peer with your professors. With your knowledge from your just-completed research study, you are expected to provide authoritative insight into previously uncharted or contested issues. Your ideas are as highly valued as your committee members', and you have an equal place at that table.

In our view, no student should be allowed to schedule the defense if the dissertation is not regarded as complete and worthy of examination. Your advisor will no doubt have had the opportunity to review the final document prior to its official distribution to committee members and will already have determined that the document meets the necessary academic standards, thereby qualifying for formal review. Consequently, part of the function of the defense is a formal induction of the doctoral candidate into a scholarly community—the celebration of a major scholarly achievement and a symbolic rite of passage to the awarding of the doctorate.

Because it is the culminating aspect of a rigorous, traditional, and long-standing ritual, we understand that you will likely approach the defense with some sense of anxiety. The more you can frame the defense as an opportunity to present your research publicly and the more you take a proactive and nondefensive position, the better the experience is likely to be. View the defense as an opportunity to think about your study more deeply and creatively and to articulate the implications of your work. Your months of concentrated reading and research have contributed to unique knowledge on your topic that few possess. Think of the meeting essentially as an academic conversation among colleagues that involves the exchange of ideas and the sharing of knowledge—an opportunity to extend your thinking in new directions.

You can certainly prepare to make the defense a positive experience. Therefore, being fully conversant about all aspects of your study is crucial. The more familiar you are with the details of your study, including the relevant literature and research, the more you will appear as the expert. You have lived with your study for an extended length of time and have been totally immersed in it. The role that the committee can rightfully play is to provide some new lenses with which to review your work and to offer you some new perspectives.

Usually, at the defense, as the researcher you are given an opportunity to set the stage by presenting an overview of your study to the committee. Typically students are given anywhere from 10 to 45 minutes to do this. Although you can use your discretion in making the choice as to what points you want to get across in the time available, you should think carefully about this task beforehand. Rather than just summarizing the salient points of your study, you should think of that part of your research that is most critical, interesting, unique, and/or controversial. Committee members have read your study (or at least certain parts of it). Therefore, they are expecting not to hear from you what they already know, but rather to learn something new.

Think about whether there is anything that is deserving of further discussion. What is it about the content or process that might require additional emphasis, illustration, explanation, elaboration, and/or clarification? What might committee members not know that they might need or want to know more about? Also think about what predictable concerns or needs that committee members might have regarding your study. In what ways might the limitations of your study deserve special mention? What broader or more pressing social issues does your study connect with? Having completed the study and lived with your findings, are there any ways your work might be revised and/or extended so that it would make a useful contribution either theoretically and/or practically?

Try to remain as specific and focused as possible, rather than crowding too much detail into this opening discussion. An interesting, concise, topical, and meaningful researcher presentation usually lays the ground for the discussion to follow. Maintaining the close attention of committee members allows you to maintain some degree of control over what will be given attention in the conversation that ensues. Remember that you have only limited time available to make your presentation. Note your beginning and ending times. Inform the committee of what is to come and for how long you intend to speak. This, for them, is a sign of careful planning and will be appreciated.

In planning your presentation, prepare an outline of what you want to talk about, laid out in sequence. You also might want to prepare some graphic aids to organize, illustrate, and support your oral presentation, including flowcharts, diagrams, audiotape segments, or even photographs or video clips. Audiovisual materials can provide focus and heighten impact. However, in light of the limited time that you have available, if you do decide to use visuals, be selective; use only what is highly pertinent to your discussion. Be sure that these are *used* and not simply displayed. Present them, explain their significance, and allow readers the time to digest these materials and ask questions. Visuals should feel like an integral and relevant aspect of the conversation, rather than an interruption. Although visual materials can certainly be used effectively, an overreliance on handouts and visuals can be off-putting to faculty who come to the defense expecting to engage in substantive conversation with the candidate and each other.

Typically, the presentation of your study is followed by questions and comments from the various committee members, which usually generate a discussion of your study that can further establish your professional credibility. Part of the expertise of being an acknowledged specialist is the ability to explain your work logically and intelligently. In the days prior to your defense, read over your dissertation carefully so you can respond authoritatively to the questions asked. Be able to succinctly summarize your research problem as well as your key findings. Be prepared to defend your choice of research tradition (or combination of traditions), choice of data collection methods, and sample selection procedures, as well as your methods of data analysis. If there are any concerns over the quality of the inquiry or the document, these obviously will be a major focus of deliberation. Know that you can provide elaborate explanations on all aspects of your work and offer a rationale for your decision making. Also be ready to explain any figures and tables that you have included.

In the days leading up to your defense, reflect on the value of your dissertation. Recall the relevant literature in your field and bring yourself up to date with the most recent work. Think carefully about how your study contributes to the current knowledge base. Probe yourself about how your work relates to the literature, both theoretically and practically. Try to anticipate all possible questions that the committee members might ask. In this regard, play "devil's advocate" with yourself and try to identify as many of your study's strengths and weaknesses as possible. Following are some of the specific questions that examiners might predictably raise:

- What do you see as the main contributions of your research for your discipline, practitioners, and/or policy makers?
- In what ways, if at all, does your study contribute to the existing literature and/or prior research in the field? In what ways does it extend the literature? Contradict the literature? Fill gaps in the literature? Clarify contradictions in the literature?
- In planning and conducting this study, which major theorists influenced your thinking?
- What are the conflicting issues in your field (every field has conflicts—hence, the research problem), and what contributed most to your understanding of these issues?

- In what ways do you expect that your work will clarify the conflicting issues in your field?
- What motivated you to conduct this study? In other words, what brought you to explore this particular topic?
- What new learning about qualitative research have you come away with as a result of conducting this study?
- What, if any, are the unanticipated outcomes of your study? What surprises have you come away with?
- What new learning about yourself have you come away with having conducted this study? What additional insights has the dissertation experience afforded you?
- What were the high and/or low points for you in the dissertation experience?
- If you were to redo this study, how might you conduct this study differently? How might you change your research methodology? Why?
- How could you build on or extend this research in the future?
- What are the major strengths and/or limitations of your research design/ methodology?
- What might further strengthen this study?
- Why did you analyze the data in the way that you did? How might you have analyzed your data differently?
- What suggestions might you offer somebody about to conduct a study of this nature?

Remembering that your conceptual framework is the means through which you articulate the theoretical significance of your research, your chosen research design, the conceptual significance of your findings, and how your study makes a contribution to knowledge, consider some questions pertaining to your study's conceptual framework. Such questions might include:

- How did you arrive at your conceptual framework?
- What are the theoretical components of your framework?
- What informed your conceptual framework?
- How did you decide upon the components that you include in your conceptual framework?
- How did the components of your conceptual framework assist you in visualizing and explaining what you intended to investigate?
- How did you use your conceptual framework to design your research and analyze your findings?

The discussion during the defense can evolve in many directions and on many levels. It pays to be prepared for all the prior potential questions, as well as any that your advisor and other critics might have raised with you over the course of discussions about your research. You are certainly free to refer as needed to your dissertation as you respond to questions. Be sure that you understand what is being asked of you before attempting to answer questions. If you are uncertain as to any question that is posed to you, ask that the question be rephrased or restated. Try at all times to provide clear, logical answers. Present your reasoning carefully. Avoid overlong and verbose answers that might take you off course. Count on being asked a few questions that you may not have anticipated. If you do not have an answer to a particular question, acknowledge that you need more time to think about the issue.

As the defense meeting draws to a close, you will be asked to leave the room, affording the committee members privacy in their final deliberations regarding your dissertation. Having heard each other's perspectives, they collectively assess the extent to which their individual views are congruent. Depending on the quality of the dissertation, the meeting can conclude with one of several outcomes. What everybody hopes for, of course, is approval. What everybody dreads—and which is hardly likely to occur—are substantive revisions that might necessitate another meeting. Typically, some revisions are necessary, and the committee members arrive at agreement as to what changes they would recommend. Usually the primary advisor is charged with ensuring that these requests are addressed in the finally approved document.

Post-Defense Preparation

Making Revisions to Your Manuscript

On the basis of the committee members' discussion, there are likely to be a number of suggestions, additions, and/or corrections. In a few cases, substantive or major alterations may be required. The most likely outcome, however, is a pass with the request for minor revisions. These revisions can include some further analyses, expansions to the literature review, additional methodological details, and additional conclusions and/or recommendations. You might be required to reorder parts or sections of the text, clarify and/or elaborate some discussion points, and rewrite or omit sections that seem confusing, as well as attend to various technical, grammatical, and/or editorial details.

Generally a post-defense meeting is held with your advisor to discuss the necessary changes, reconcile any contradictory feedback, and make sure that you understand what needs to be done. We strongly suggest that, within a few days, with the defense discussion still fresh in your mind, you make a point of processing all the feedback you received. Be sure you understand what needs to be changed and how to proceed. Most minor revisions can usually be completed within a week or two. The sooner you tackle the required revisions, the sooner you will be able to submit a final copy of the document to your office of doctoral studies for a final round of proofreading. Allowing sufficient time for possible redrafting is especially important if you hope to graduate in the same semester in which the dissertation was completed and defended. Filing the final dissertation means that the approval of any revisions as indicated by your advisor is complete.

Although you have revised and refined your manuscript many times prior to the defense, following the required revisions, you need to carefully and meticulously edit your manuscript one final time. The purpose for this final review is to check accuracy regarding content as well as mechanics and style. There is no substitute for painstaking proofreading, preferably by somebody else. This is not simply because it is a tedious task, but because your familiarity with the text is likely to impede your effectiveness at the task.

In doing a final check of your entire manuscript, look for the following requirements:

- Have you addressed all issues that were raised by the committee members?
- Have you added the necessary sections in the most logical places so as not to interrupt the flow of the discussion?
- Regarding any added material, have you checked with your style manual regarding mechanics, style, and consistency?
- Are all headings and subheadings formatted in accordance with the guidelines specified in the style manual?
- If necessary, have you added and/or deleted any citations?
- Have you adjusted your reference list according to all additions and/or deletions of citations?
- Have you adjusted your abstract according to any changes that were made?
- Have you added your acknowledgments and/or dedication? This appears after the abstract and is an opportunity to express appreciation to those who have contributed significantly to the completion of your dissertation.
- Have you checked that your table of contents corresponds with all headings, subheadings, and pagination? This check is especially important if you have adjusted your margins for binding purposes.
- Have you checked that all tables and figures are correctly numbered and labeled throughout?
- Have you reread and edited your manuscript one final time?
- Have you performed a final spell-check on the entire manuscript?

The instructions for preparing final copies of your dissertation can be quite complex, and these differ from university to university. As such, we recommend that you consult with your institution's office of doctoral studies regarding format and style details, as well as the number of copies of the dissertation and abstract that you are required to submit and to whom. Generally, you can rely on your advisor to clarify procedures regarding your university's protocol for completion of the dissertation process, including final approval and sign-off.

Publishing and Presenting Your Research

The dissertation process comes to a definitive end when the final document is submitted and the doctoral degree is awarded. You have undoubtedly devoted an extensive amount of time and energy to your research. Finally, having reached the end of the trail, you should feel a well-deserved sense of accomplishment. This is a time to bring closure to your doctoral program. It is also a time to move forward and celebrate your enhanced knowledge and expertise. Completion of the dissertation is a significant milestone of an ongoing journey. As is usually the case, as one door closes, another door opens.

At this juncture, you might consider looking beyond the dissertation and contemplating new projects, particularly those you may have deferred while working on your dissertation. Think especially of how you can more fully share what you have researched with a broader audience than the academic community. Following your immersion in your research, you will certainly want to disseminate your findings to others, enabling others to have access to cutting-edge information as well as extending your own professional network. Presenting and/or publishing your findings is a way to contribute to the ongoing knowledge base and work toward advancing your professional career.

The dissemination of research is fundamental to its credibility and to its capacity to influence society. Research findings should always be subject to replication by others. Research findings should be brought into the public domain, not merely to facilitate their potential verification, but also to contribute to knowledge in the field, and enable other professionals or members of the public to act on them where appropriate.

Publishing Your Research Your dissertation does not and should not exist in an "intellectual vacuum." The academic journal is the principal medium for the dissemination and sharing of research findings to a wider audience. Moreover, in the broader academic job market, most positions require that candidates have an established or at least emerging publication track. Indeed, "publish or perish" is the injunction that rings true for most of us, especially if you aspire to a university career as a teacher and/or researcher.

All of the main subject areas of research in the social sciences, and many areas of minority interest, have academic journals devoted to them. Journals exist in many different languages, and are increasingly available electronically. It is clearly important that research published in academic journals is as trustworthy as possible. Toward this end, most academic journal submissions undergo a peer review process.

Each of the major journals provides information pertaining to application and submission details. It is important that you select a journal whose articles match your research topic and your particular study. Some journals focus on empirical research, while others publish theoretical or applied articles. Also be aware that journals are rated in quality based on refereeing systems and how often they are cited by other researchers. In this regard you might refer to the *Social Science Citation Index* and the *Arts and Humanities Citations Index.*

To initiate the process of publishing you may want to talk to your dissertation advisor or other established academics regarding advice on specific journals and realistic and appropriate publishing opportunities. You might also visit your university library and peruse all journals pertinent to your field of interest and potential audience. Remember that the style of your writing should be sensitive to and reflect the targeted audience, be it academics, practitioners, policy makers, or laypersons (general public). Communication should always be designed with an audience in mind. As the researcher you need to be aware of and remain accountable to the demands of the intended publication outlet and its audience(s), and as such adapt and frame your text accordingly. In this regard, writing remains an ongoing and socially embedded practice (Van Maanen, 2006). Marvasti (2011) makes an interesting point, however, when he states:

> As writing social science becomes more politicized . . . to the extent that alternative writing challenges mainstream tropes it should be encouraged as the fuel for change or scientific progress. Whether the landscape of writing practices and expectations should be expanded or curbed will likely remain a matter of contention in the field of qualitative research. (p. 394)

Indeed, the information revolution and its impact on genres and audiences of qualitative research remains an evolving process. Postmodernism (in its various forms) has alerted us to the diversity of writing styles and "textual shifts" in the social sciences, engendering different assumptions regarding textual representation (Silverman & Marvasti, 2008). Researchers' decisions about what to report, how, and to what audience involve reflexive political choices. Instant access to global audiences could indeed transform the review process as well as the ways in which audience expectations are addressed (Marvasti, 2011).

As Wolcott (2009) puts it, when writing a journal article you need to "de-dissertationize" your work. You will have to not only shorten your piece by avoiding too much detail (most journal articles cap the word count at around 6,000), but also be clearly focused on one aspect or topic that will make a compelling argument that will intrigue readers of the journal you have selected. The following resources address the process of turning a dissertation into a publishable manuscript, providing practical advice for writing a publishable qualitative article, and outlining the various features that will increase the chances of having your manuscript accepted for publication:

http://supp.apa.org/style/pubman-ch08.pdf

http://www.parint.org/isajewebsite/bookimages/isaje_2nd_edition_chapter6.pdf

Reworking a lengthy formal, and often technically intricate, dissertation requires a major rewrite and hence often lengthy time commitment. Moreover, in the review process, most articles (if not rejected) are returned—sometimes more than once—with a request for some degree of revision—sometimes substantial—adding more time to the already tedious process. You should treat "revise and resubmit" as a golden opportunity.

Presenting Your Research In addition to publications, completion of the dissertation provides you with an opportunity to present your study in other academic settings and research forums, such as graduate seminars and professional associations. A good first step is to present your research to professional associations or organizations in your field. Research conference formats include formal presentation of papers; participating in roundtables, panel discussions, or poster sessions; making formal addresses; and leading seminar or workshop sessions. Scan professional journals for "call for papers"—a formal invitation to submit an application to present research.

A key benefit to presenting your research after it is complete is that it helps you to summarize the dissertation for possible publication. Student researchers can also benefit from presenting their research at discipline-related conferences during the course of their research in that presenting preliminary research while the study is under construction is a valuable opportunity for feedback and critique from colleagues and other professionals and/or academics in the field.

The final chapter of your dissertation contains recommendations regarding implications for action, in which you make concrete and practical suggestions to practitioners in the field that are directly related to your study's findings. Often recommendations are made regarding creation of specific products such as handbooks, training materials, manuals, and programs. Taking time to follow up on creating some of these products makes a practical and worthy contribution to the field of practice.

As you go about considering different ways to disseminate your research, there are various resources that offer emerging and experienced scholars from all disciplines a comprehensive review of the essential elements needed to craft scholarly papers suitable for submission to academic journals. Included are discussions regarding the components of different types of manuscripts, submission and review processes, quality writing skills, suggestions for working collaboratively with editors and coauthors, dealing with rejection, and tackling the challenges inherent in rewriting and resubmission of one's work. In addition, some texts deal with fundamentals of a good review and offer guidance for becoming a manuscript reviewer—an emergent and often rewarding task when one reaches the postdoctoral phase.

Recommended resources that you might like to peruse include:

Loseke, D., & Cahill, S. (2004). Publishing qualitative manuscripts: Lessons learned. In C. Seale, G. Gobo, J. F. Gubrium, & D. Silverman (Eds.), *Qualitative research practice* (pp. 576–592). Thousand Oaks, CA: Sage.

Rocco, T., Hatcher, T., & Creswell, J. W. (2011). *The handbook of scholarly writing and publishing*. San Francisco: Jossey-Bass.

Wallace, M., & Wray, A. (2006). *Critical reading and writing for postgraduates*. London: Sage.

Wolcott, H. (2009). *Writing up qualitative research* (3rd ed.). Thousand Oaks, CA: Sage.

Part III: Summary and Discussion

Nearing Completion

Part III of this book addresses the final stages of the dissertation process, and we offer suggestions regarding the various activities involved.

- It is crucial that all the necessary elements that constitute a dissertation are aligned with one another. At the end of the process, it is necessary that you revisit the chapters of your dissertation and check that each element flows sequentially from the elements prior to it and that each element leads logically to the elements that succeed it.
- The first thing your readers will read, and something you will need to revise following the completion of your study, is the title of your dissertation. Therefore, the wording of your title deserves careful consideration. By conveying the key concepts of your study, the title attracts the attention of interested readers. The title also enables your work to be correctly catalogued, and effective wording is essential for retrieval purposes.
- You want your study's abstract to be an accurate representation of all the hard work you have devoted to this project. More important, you want people who are studying issues related to yours to find your study among all the others. Therefore, in your abstract, careful wording and attention to key elements are essential. An abstract should generally state the research problem, describe the research approach, and announce key findings, conclusions, and recommendations. There is usually a specified word limit. Within that word limit, try to make your abstract as comprehensive and informative as possible.
- Although format and style are a function of individual taste and institutional and/or departmental regulations, some general rules can be adopted in designing the layout of your manuscript. We offer various ideas on what to check in assembling your manuscript.
- In preparing for your defense, check that all necessary documentation is completed in a timely manner. You do not want any unnecessary delays at this point. Customs and routines surrounding the number of faculty who attend a dissertation defense vary among institutions and programs. Make sure that you are familiar with the system adopted by your university regarding the dissertation committee structure as well as the process for preparing for that structure. At most universities, students have the opportunity to request specific faculty members to serve on their dissertation committee. If you have the freedom to exercise some choice, committee membership should be designed to maximize the support and assistance available.
- The defense, in effect, moves your dissertation from the private domain into the arena of public discourse. As a result of your research, you are now considered

a specialist in your topic area. Part of the expertise of being an acknowledged specialist is the ability to explain your work logically and intelligently. Under all imaginable circumstances, everybody on your committee wants you to do well. With a solid, thoughtful, and well-prepared presentation, you are highly likely to be successful.

- Following the defense, there are almost always some revisions you will have to make. We strongly suggest that, within a few days, with the defense discussion still fresh in your mind, you make a point of processing all the feedback you received. The sooner you tackle the required revisions, the sooner you will be able to submit a final copy of your document to the office of doctoral studies for a final round of proofreading. As you incorporate the necessary revisions, make sure that any and all additions conform to the style manual that you are using.

• Afterword •

A dissertation is an extensive, challenging, and rigorous scholarly endeavor. As such, completing it represents the pinnacle of academic achievement. This book traces the path of the dissertation process from the time your research was the beginning of an idea to its final successful completion.

The intention is that this book provides the guidance and initiative for careful and systematic planning, preparation, and management of what might at first seem to be a nebulous and seemingly impossible task. Hopefully, with this road map in hand, you are now better equipped for the challenges ahead and are on your way to graduating with your doctorate. The dissertation journey is about achieving several milestones, one at a time. Once you have made the decision to complete your dissertation, which is a significant milestone in itself, do not allow one day to go by without doing *something*. Certainly you can expect your initial projections to be revised and re-revised. But keep a positive attitude, actively finding ways to move forward and *succeed*.

Based on globalizing forces, new theoretical perspectives, increasingly expanding critical research, enhanced technology, and other sociocultural changes that continue to impact the work of social scientists, innovative methods and approaches are emergent and evolving. The field of qualitative research continues to transform itself. Paradigm shifts and deep dialogues have become a constant presence within and across the theoretical frameworks that organize both qualitative inquiry and social and human sciences. The literature clearly reflects an ongoing need for a critical, interpretive, compassionate, multivoiced, civic social science that is directed to praxis and social change and that strives to combat repression and oppression in our daily lives. It has been gratifying to see that as graduate students continue to engage in their research, many are forging new pathways that challenge boundaries and build bridges across traditions and genres, thereby expanding and significantly enhancing the field. It is these bold efforts that continue to develop qualitative inquiry as a growing, thriving, dynamic, and ever-evolving multidisciplinary and interdisciplinary endeavor.

As an adult educator it is my philosophy that what matters ultimately in life is not only what one has learned, but also what one has taught. My hope is that if this book has given you some new knowledge, skills, and insight, you will pass what you have learned on to somebody else who is starting off on the qualitative dissertation process or who might be stuck along the way and attempting to move forward.

And may we all continue to apply what we learn to build a more compassionate and just world because I know and trust that learning powers change.

My best wishes for your continued success.

—Linda Dale Bloomberg

• Appendices •

Note: Those appendices that are completed samples of the various templates provided throughout this book, are included in the companion website **study.sagepub.com/ bloomberg3e.** This includes appendices E, G, H, K, L, M, N, O, P, S, T, U, V, W, X, Y, AA, BB, CC, DD, EE, FF, GG. Refer to page xix for a complete list.

Appendix A: Rubric for Evaluating a Completed Qualitative Dissertation

Topic	Outstanding	Acceptable	Minimally Acceptable	Unacceptable
Title Page	1. Title is complete within character limit. 2. Includes all keywords that will promote proper categorization into databases. 3. All relevant parts of the title page are included (author's full name, degree to be conferred, name of university, year). 4. APA style is completely correct.	1. Title is appropriate but may not be very concise. 2. Most key words are included. 3. All relevant parts of the title page are included (author's full name, degree to be conferred, name of university, year). 4. APA style is completely correct.	1. Title does not effectively convey all aspects of the study, or some needed elements are missing. 2. Key words may or may not be included. 3. All relevant parts of the title page may or may not be included (author's full name, degree to be conferred, name of university, year). 4. APA style is not completely correct.	1. Title is not appropriate for a dissertation. 2. Most key words are missing. 3. Most relevant parts of title page are not included. 4. Title page does not follow APA style.
Abstract	1. Abstract includes problem, purpose, scope of study, research tradition, number and type of participants, methodology, major findings. Implications/ limitations of these findings stated clearly and concisely. 2. Format and style are correct as per APA guidelines. 3. Word limit is accurate as per APA guidelines.	1. Abstract includes all essential information but is misleading due to a lack of concise sentence structure, or there may be some information missing. 2. Format and style are correct as per APA guidelines. 3. Word limit is accurate as per APA guidelines.	1. Abstract is missing essential information. 2. Format and style may or may not be correct as per guidelines in APA style manual. 3. Word limit may or may not be accurate as per APA guidelines.	1. Abstract has some incorrect information or does not accurately portray the study. 2. Format and style may or may not be correct as per APA guidelines. 3. Word limit has been significantly exceeded.
Literature Review Scoring Rubric	See Appendix B	See Appendix B	See Appendix B	See Appendix B

Introduction				
	1. The research topic is relevant to the program of study, and the content is current and timely in terms of the researcher's field of interest.	1. The research topic is somewhat relevant to the program of study, and somewhat current in terms of the researcher's field of interest.	1. The research topic is vague in its relationship to the program of study and to the researcher's field of interest.	1. The research topic has no or very little relationship with the program of study.
	2. Clear statement of research problem. Description of background to the problem is provided.	2. Statement of research problem, description of background to the problem, and relationship of the problem to previous research could be stated more clearly.	2. Statement of the research problem, description of background to the problem, and relationship of the problem to previous research is unclear or vague.	2. Statement of the research problem, description of background to the problem, and relationship of the problem to previous research is very unclear, messy, or missing.
	3. Relationship of the problem to previous research is clearly stated, and relevant literature is cited.	3. Explanation of how this research will contribute to the knowledge base and/or practice and/or policy is included, but it could be more specific.	3. There is little justification for how this research will contribute to the knowledge base and/or practice and/or policy.	3. There is no justification for how this research will contribute to the knowledge base and/or practice and/or policy.
	4. How this research might contribute to the knowledge base and/or practice and/or policy is clearly stated.	4. Researcher's perspectives and assumptions are provided but could be stated more clearly.	4. Researcher's perspectives and assumptions are unclear or vague.	4. Researcher's perspectives and assumptions are very unclear or missing.
	5. Researcher's perspective and relationship to the problem is discussed, and all researcher's assumptions and biases are made explicit.	5. Purpose of the study, how the purpose will address the problem could be explained more clearly.	5. Purpose of the study, how the purpose will address the problem is unclear or vague.	5. Purpose of the study, how the purpose will address the problem is very unclear or missing.
	6. Purpose of the study is clearly, succinctly, and unambiguously stated.	6. The relevance of the study's purpose vis-à-vis the chosen qualitative tradition could be explained more clearly.	6. The relevance of the study's purpose vis-à-vis the chosen qualitative tradition is unclear or vague.	6. The relevance of the study's purpose vis-à-vis the chosen qualitative tradition is very unclear, messy, or missing.
	7. It is clear how the purpose will address the problem.			
	8. Stated purpose is relevant to chosen qualitative research tradition.			

(Continued)

Research Questions	1. Research questions are open-ended, and answerable; answers will clearly shed light on research problem. 2. All research questions are interconnected; there a meaningful relationship among them. 3. There is clear and strong alignment among problem, purpose, and research questions.	1. Research questions are open-ended, but it could be made clearer how answers will shed light on research problem. 2. Relationship among the research questions could be clearer. 3. Alignment among problem, purpose, and research questions could be stronger.	1. Research questions are open-ended, but it is unclear how answers will shed light on research problem. 2. Relationship among the research questions is unclear or vague. 3. Alignment among problem, purpose, and research questions is unclear or vague.	1. Answers to research questions would not shed light on research problem. 2. There is no relationship among the research questions. 3. There is no alignment among problem, purpose, and research questions.
Research Design	1. Research design is appropriate and feasible as a means of qualitative inquiry. 2. The type of data being collected is clearly described. 3. A well-thought-out rationale is provided to justify the study. 4. A convincing argument is made for the importance or significance of the study.	1. Research design is appropriate and feasible as a means of qualitative inquiry. 2. The type of data being collected is briefly discussed but not clearly or sufficiently described or explained. 3. The rationale provided to justify the study is not clearly described or explained. 4. The argument made for the importance or significance of the study needs additional explanation or clarification.	1. Research design is not appropriate or feasible as a means of qualitative inquiry. 2. The type of data being collected is not clearly described or explained. 3. The rationale provided to justify the study is unclear or vague. 4. The argument made for the importance or significance of the study is unclear, vague, or weak.	1. Research design is both inappropriate and/or unfeasible as a means of qualitative inquiry. 2. Description or explanation of the type of data being collected is absent or unclear. 3. The rationale provided to justify the study is absent. 4. There is no argument made for the importance or significance of the study. If there is an argument made it is very weak.

Methodology: Participants and/ or Setting	1. Sample is ideal for the questions being asked. 2. Sampling strategy is appropriate, and criteria for sampling selection are stated and explained, including access and consent. 3. Participant information includes number and all necessary characteristics. [This should include demographic, perceptual, and contextual information.] 4. Transferability is adequately addressed regarding setting and time.	1. Sample is appropriate for the questions being asked. 2. Sampling strategy and criteria for sampling selection are not clearly or sufficiently described. 3. Participant information includes some but not all necessary characteristics. [This should include demographic, perceptual, and contextual information.] 4. Transferability is addressed regarding setting and time, but not in sufficient detail.	1. Sample is not appropriate for the questions being asked. 2. Sampling strategy and criteria for sampling selection are not clearly explained. 3. Participant information lacks clarity. 4. Transferability regarding setting and time lacks clarity.	1. Sample is undefined. 2. Sampling strategy and criteria for sampling are not discussed and/or are not appropriate. 3. Participant information is not provided. 4. Transferability regarding setting and time is either inaccurate or is not discussed.
Methodology: Data Collection	1. The process for collecting data is explained and methods are described with sufficient detail that a reader could replicate the study consistent with research questions. 2. It is clear what methods were selected to obtain data; when and from whom. 3. A clear rationale for selection of instruments used is provided. 4. If instruments are developed specifically for this study, procedures involved in development, validation, and administration are clearly documented. 5. All data collection methods are congruent with the problem being investigated, and the specific qualitative tradition employed.	1. The process for collecting data is briefly explained but needs additional detail so that a reader could replicate the study consistent with research questions. 2. Methods selected to obtain data; when and from whom could be described more clearly. 3. A rationale for selection of instruments used is provided but needs additional clarification or explanation. 4. If instruments are developed specifically for this study, procedures involved in development, validation, and administration need additional clarification or explanation.	1. The process for collecting data is identified but not described in detail and it is unclear if a reader could replicate the study consistent with research questions. 2. Methods selected to obtain data; when and from whom are vague or unclear. 3. A rationale for selection of instruments used is provided but is vague or unclear. 4. If instruments are developed specifically for this study, procedures involved in development, validation, and administration are vague or unclear. 5. Congruence between data collection methods, research problem,	1. The process for collecting data and methods selected are not explained. 2. There is no rationale for selection of instruments used. 3. If instruments are developed specifically for this study, procedures involved in development, validation, and administration are not explained. 4. There is no congruence between data collection methods, research problem, and the specific qualitative tradition. 5. There is no evidence of triangulation of data collection methods. 6. There is no evidence of dependability, or evidence that dependability was even addressed.

(Continued)

	6. Triangulation of data collection methods has been achieved. 7. Dependability has been satisfied, and clearly addressed and explained. One can track the processes and procedures used to collect and interpret data.	5. Congruence between data collection methods, research problem, and the specific qualitative tradition could be clearer. 6. Triangulation of data collection methods could be clearer or more specific. 7. Dependability has been somewhat satisfied. One can track some, but not all, of the processes and procedures used to collect and interpret data.	and the specific qualitative tradition are vague or unclear. 6. Triangulation of data collection methods is unclear. 7. Dependability has been only minimally or vaguely addressed.	
Methodology: Procedure	The procedure is appropriate for the research questions and is described in order or sequence, with enough detail that a reader could replicate the study. Instructions and protocol are included. In addition: 1. A convincing argument for choosing qualitative research and particular research tradition is provided. 2. All decisions made during the course of the study, including any changes or modifications in focus, direction, and design are discussed. 3. All limitations and delimitations pertaining to study are discussed, including how the researcher attempted to address limitations.	The procedure is appropriate and the description is mostly complete but some minor details may be missing, or some procedural aspects could be explained more clearly.	The procedure is appropriate, but description is not in order or sequence, and/or it may be difficult to follow, and/or a few major details are absent.	The procedure is not appropriate, and/or the description is unclear, and/or many major details are absent.

Analysis of Data and Presentation of Findings			
1. Data analysis steps are clearly identified, including clear explanation of how data was managed and organized for analysis.	1. Data analysis steps are identified, including explanation of how data was managed and organized for analysis, but explanation could be clearer.	1. Data analysis steps are identified, including explanation of how data was managed and organized for analysis, but explanation is vague or unclear.	1. Data analysis steps are not identified
2. The coding process is clearly described and coding scheme is included.	2. The coding process is described and coding scheme is included, but explanation and/or presentation could be clearer.	2. Coding process is described and coding scheme is included, but explanation and/or presentation are vague or unclear.	2. Coding process is not described and/or coding scheme is not included.
3. All findings statements are clearly and precisely stated.	3. All findings statements are stated, but could be clearer.	3. Some or all of the findings statements are unclear or vague.	3. Some or all of the findings statements are missing or inaccurately presented.
4. Findings are summarized and aggregated, and clearly presented in relation to the research questions.	4. Findings are summarized and aggregated in a way that mostly addresses the research questions. The process of summarizing data is spelled out, but may not be complete or comprehensive.	4. Findings are summarized and aggregated but are not organized according to research questions, nor does this summary address all the research questions. The process of summarizing data is not clearly spelled out.	4. Findings are summarized and aggregated but large portions of data are left out of the analysis. The process of summarizing data is very messy or absent.
5. Findings are free from interpretation, and are reported accurately and objectively.	5. Findings are generally free from interpretation, and are reported accurately and objectively.	5. Findings are not all free from interpretation, and/or are not always reported accurately and objectively.	5. Findings are not free from interpretation, and/or are not reported accurately and objectively.
6. The narrative and tables/figures are easy to understand and summarize the findings in a way that answers the study's questions.	6. The narrative and tables/figures summarize the findings, but in a way that sometimes does not address the study's questions.	6. The narrative and tables summarize the findings but might miss some key points of the study.	6. The narrative and tables summarize the findings but do not address the research questions.
7. Examples of specific evidence (quotations or other qualitative data including artifacts or visuals) are provided to support all the findings of the study.	7. Examples of specific evidence (quotations or other qualitative data including artifacts or visuals) are provided to support only some of the findings of the study.	7. Examples of specific evidence that support the findings of study are mostly inappropriate or absent.	7. Examples of specific evidence that support the findings of study are inappropriate or absent.
8. The study's conceptual framework clearly and logically illuminates the relationships among the study's theoretical and/or conceptual variables.	8. Some conceptual insights emerge from the analysis. The conceptual framework is clear and easy to understand.	8. Few conceptual insights emerge from the analysis. If a conceptual framework has been developed it is unclear or imprecise in parts.	8. No conceptual insights emerge from the analysis. Instead, the results simply reflect the idiosyncratic views of the author. There is no conceptual framework, or if there is one it is very unclear. messy and/or inaccurate and does not enhance the study in any way.

(Continued)

Discussion: Interpretation				
	1. The discussion includes a restatement of the findings. 2. Interpretations are clear, thoughtful, and reasonable. The argument flows logically and coherently. 3. Interpretations are relevant to research problem, purpose, and research questions. 4. Major themes are interrelated to show a higher level of analysis and abstraction. 5. Analysis is positioned and discussed in terms of relevant related bodies of literature and previous research. 6. All information presented in tables/figures is consistent with information presented in the narrative. 7. Researcher acknowledges multiple ways of interpreting findings, and is open to other interpretive possibilities. Often researcher revisits and reflects upon initial assumptions and/or biases.	1. The discussion includes a restatement of the findings, but this could be clearer and more focused. 2. Interpretations could be more clearly stated. The argument could flow more coherently. 3. Interpretations are mostly relevant to research problem, purpose, and research questions. 4. Major themes are interrelated to show a relatively high level of analysis and abstraction. 5. Analysis is discussed in terms of relevant related bodies of literature and previous research, but integration could be tighter. 6. Information presented in tables/figures is mostly consistent with information presented in the narrative. 7. Researcher acknowledges multiple ways of interpreting findings, and is open to other interpretive possibilities, but has not revisited and reflected upon initial assumptions and/or biases.	1. The discussion includes a restatement of the findings, but this discussion lacks clarity and focus. 2. Interpretations are unclear or vague. The argument does not flow logically and coherently. 3. Interpretations are sometimes relevant to research problem, purpose, and research questions. 4. Major themes are somewhat interrelated but show a low level of analysis and abstraction. 5. Analysis is discussed in terms of relevant related bodies of literature and previous research, but integration is lacking. 6. Information presented in tables/figures is sometimes consistent with information presented in the narrative. 7. Researcher infers that there are multiple ways of interpreting findings, but this point is not strongly made, and the researcher has not revisited and reflected upon initial assumptions and/or biases.	1. The discussion does not include a restatement of the findings. 2. Interpretations are unfounded, unrealistic, or naive. The argument does not flow logically and coherently at all. 3. Interpretations are not relevant to research problem, purpose, and research questions. 4. There is no interrelationship of major themes. 5. Analysis is not discussed in terms of relevant related bodies of literature and previous research. 6. Information presented in tables/figures is mostly not consistent with information presented in the narrative. 7. Researcher does not address that there are multiple ways of interpreting findings, and has not revisited and reflected upon initial assumptions and/or biases. 8. There is no evidence or discussion related to credibility.

8. There is clear and logical argument in support of credibility. By way of various appropriate strategies, the researcher has accurately represented what the participants think, feel, and do. 9. Comprehensive overview synthesizes and integrates all key points. 10. There is clear overall alignment among all dissertation elements.	8. Credibility has been somewhat satisfied. The argument for establishing credibility could be clearer and more substantial. 9. An overview synthesizes and integrates all key points, but this could be tighter and more comprehensive. 10. Overall alignment among all dissertation elements could be somewhat strengthened.	8. Credibility has been only minimally or vaguely addressed. 9. An overview summarizes key points, but there is no integration or synthesis. 10. Overall alignment among dissertation elements is unclear or vague.	9. There is no overview summary, integration, or synthesis. 10. Overall alignment among dissertation elements is unclear, incorrect, or missing.
Discussion: Conclusions and Recommendations 1. This chapter offers a completed picture of the research; that is, the reader has a good understanding of the study and its implications. 2. Any limitations of context, available evidence, and interpretation inconsistency are considered. 3. All conclusions are presented as strong conclusive statements, are clearly derived from study's findings and are warranted by the findings, are logical and clearly explained, and are not mere restatements of the findings. 4. All recommendations are justified by the findings, are actionable, and include applications for practice, policy, and further research.	1. This chapter offers an almost complete picture of the research; the reader has a relatively good understanding of the study and its implications. 2. Limitations of context, available evidence, and interpretation inconsistency are considered but not critically evaluated or taken seriously. 3. Most conclusions are presented as strong conclusive statements, are clearly derived from study's findings and are warranted by the findings, are logical and clearly explained, and are not mere restatements of the findings. 4. Most recommendations are justified by the findings, are actionable, and include applications for practice, policy, and further research.	1. This chapter offers an inconclusive picture of the research. 2. Limitations of context, available evidence, and interpretation inconsistency are mentioned briefly but not fully discussed. 3. Most conclusions are not presented as strong conclusive statements, and/or are not clearly derived from study's finding, and/or are mostly not warranted by the findings. 4. Most recommendations are not justified by the findings, and/or are not actionable, and/or do not have applications for practice, policy, and further research.	1. This chapter offers a very limited picture of the research. 2. Limitations of context, available evidence, and interpretation inconsistency are not discussed, and/or not considered, and/or not taken seriously. 3. The conclusions are mere restatements of the study's findings. 4. The recommendations are not justified by the findings, and/or are not actionable, and/or do not have applications for practice, policy, and further research.

[Continued]

[Continued]

References	1. References include all and only cited publications. 2. References are all appropriately scholarly and appropriate to the topic. 3. Sufficient recent sources make the review current, and relevant classic studies are included if applicable and available. 4. Original articles/chapters were clearly cited. 5. All references adhere to APA style format.	1. The reference list may leave out some cited article or include some that were not cited. 2. References are appropriately scholarly but may include some that are somewhat tangential. 3. Sources include a good mix of recent and classic, as necessary. 4. All references adhere to APA style format.	1. Some references may not be appropriate for the topic. 2. Key references are clearly cited from other sources and not integrated. 3. Sources do not include a good mix of recent and classic literature. 4. References may or may not adhere to APA style format.	1. The reference list is more like a bibliography of related sources. 2. References may not be scholarly sources or otherwise appropriate for the assignment (e.g., too many secondary sources], or they may not be current. 3. References mostly do not adhere to APA style format.
Academic Writing Style	1. There is clear organization to the document, and transitions are smooth and effective. Headings and subheadings are used effectively to structure and present the discussion. 2. Writing throughout is scholarly and academic. Tone is appropriately formal. 3. Topic sentences are appropriate for paragraphs, and key ideas are explained and described as needed. 4. Punctuation and grammar are correct, including correct tenses and voice. 5. All spelling is correct.	1. Organization of the document is effective, although improvements could be made. Transitions are generally but not always smooth, and paragraphs may stray from the central idea. 2. Writing throughout is mostly scholarly and academic. Tone is mostly appropriately formal. 3. Topic sentences are mostly appropriate for paragraphs, and key ideas are mostly explained or described as needed. 4. Punctuation and grammar are almost completely correct.	1. Organization of the document is inadequate, making the paper difficult to follow. Transitions are sometimes there but could be improved. 2. Writing is not always scholarly, and tone is occasionally colloquial. 3. Topic sentences are mostly inappropriate for paragraphs, and key ideas are mostly not explained or described as needed. 4. Punctuation and grammar are usually correct, but there are consistent mistakes. 5. There is some incorrect spelling throughout.	1. Organization of the document is messy or confusing. Transitions are missing or are very weak. 2. Tone is consistently too informal or colloquial. 3. There are mostly no topic sentences, and key ideas are mostly not explained or described as needed. 4. Punctuation, grammar, and spelling errors exist throughout. 5. Sentences are not concise and word choice is vague. 6. There is much needless repetition, and/or there are parts with insufficient or missing detail. 7. Author tends to string together quotations without sufficient original input.

	6. Sentences are concise and word choice is precise, with non-biased language. 7. Proper paraphrasing is used, and quotation marks are used appropriately when necessary.	5. Mostly, spelling is correct. 6. Sentences are generally concise and word choice is usually precise. 7. Paraphrases are usually used, and quotation marks are used appropriately if necessary.	6. Sentences are not always concise and word choice is sometimes vague. 7. Author includes many quotes or improper "paraphrases" that may constitute unintentional plagiarism.	1. Information is consistently included in the incorrect sections (e.g., materials described in procedure; discussion included in findings). 2. There are many inconsistent style errors throughout the document.
APA Style	1. Information is included in appropriately titled sections. 2. Title page, in-text citations, paper format, and Reference page are in APA style with no mistakes. 3. All headers, tables and figures, margins, captions, etc., are in APA style.	1. For the most part, information is included in the appropriately titled sections. 2. Style is generally correct and includes correct spacing, fonts, and margins. Page breaks are in appropriate places, and sections are in order. 3. There may be minor errors in punctuation, references, in-text citations, statistical copy, or headers.	1. For the most part, information is included in the appropriately titled sections. 2. There are consistent APA style errors in referencing, spacing, statistical copy, or headers.	

Source: This rubric is part of Bloomberg, L. D. (2015). *Qualitative dissertation evaluation.* Unpublished manuscript.

Appendix B: Rubric for Evaluating a Literature Review

Category	Criterion	Outstanding	Acceptable	Minimally Acceptable	Unacceptable
1. Coverage	**A. Justified criteria for inclusion and exclusion from review**	– Discussed exactly what should have been in the review and was neither over nor under inclusive.	– The review justified the inclusion and exclusion of literature.	– The review discussed the literature included and excluded.	– The review did not discuss the criteria for inclusion or exclusion.
2. Synthesis	**B. The review distinguishes what has been done in the field from what needs to be done**	– The review offered new perspective on the state of the field. – The topic was examined in a way that showed a new way of thinking about it in the scholarly literature.	– The review critically examined the state of the field. – The topic was clearly situated within the broader body of scholarly literature.	– The review discussed what has and has not been done in the field. – There was some discussion of the broader body of scholarly literature.	– The review did not distinguish what has been done and has not been done in the field. – The topic was not placed in the broader scholarly literature.
	C. Situates the topic or problem within the broader scholarly literature	– A new and insightful way of examining the history of the topic was revealed.	– The history of the topic was critically examined.	– There was some mention of the history of the topic.	– The history of the topic was not discussed.
	D. Situates the research within the historical context of the field	– New and insightful definitions of existing constructs and new constructs were attained.	– Ambiguities in definitions and/or vocabulary were resolved.	– The key vocabulary was defined.	– The vocabulary was not discussed.
	E. Articulates important variables and phenomena relevant to the topic	– New and undiscovered relationships in the literature were identified.	– The review noted ambiguities in the literature and proposed new relationships.	– There was some review of relationships among key variables and phenomena.	– The key variables and phenomena were not discussed.
	F. Synthesizes and gains a new perspective on the literature			– There was some critique of the literature.	– The literature was accepted at face value.

	Criteria			
3. Methodology	**G. Identifies the main methodologies and research techniques that have been used in the field, and their advantages and disadvantages** **H. Relates ideas, concepts and/or theories in the field to research methodologies**	– The review criticized the existing methods and offered new ways to think about the standard or predominant methodology. – The new methods suggested ways to resolve unjustified claims in the literature.	– The research methods common to the literature were critiqued. – The appropriateness of the research methods to warrant the claims was critiqued.	– There was some discussion of the research methods used to produce the claims in the literature. – There was some discussion of appropriateness of research methods that warrant claims in the literature.	– Research methods of the studies were not discussed.
4. Significance	**I. Rationalizes the practical significance of the research problem** **J. Rationalizes the scholarly significance of the research problem**	– A new perspective was added to the practical significance of the research that was not found before in the literature. – A new perspective was added to the scholarly significance of the research that was not found before in the literature.	– The practical significance of the research was critiqued. – The scholarly significance of the research was critiqued.	– The practical significance of the research was discussed. – The scholarly significance of the research was discussed.	– The practical significance of the research was not discussed. – The scholarly significance of the research was not discussed.
5. Rhetoric (writing effectively)	**K. The review is coherent, and the structure is clear and ordered**	– The writing was coherent and well developed so that it offered new ways to write about and think about this literature adding to the theoretical or applied knowledge base.	– The writing was well developed and coherent.	– There was some coherent structure.	– The paper was poorly conceptualized, haphazard, and/or messy.

(Continued)

[Continued]

6. Style	L. The writing is compelling M. The tone is consistently professional N. Grammar, spelling and writing mechanics are free of errors	– The writing is generally engaging. – The tone is generally professional and appropriate for an academic research paper. – There are only a few errors in grammar, spelling, and/or writing mechanics.	– The writing is engaging in some parts of the review but not in others. – The tone is not consistently professional. – There are various errors in grammar, spelling, and/or writing mechanics.	– The writing overall is dull and unengaging. – The tone is largely unprofessional. – There are many errors interspersed throughout the review.	– The writing is of a poor quality and difficult to follow. – It is difficult to discern the tone. – The writing is of a very poor quality, and sentence structure is very awkward.
7. Format	O. Length is appropriate as required P. Citations within the paper are accurate Q. References are professionally legitimate and correctly stated R. APA format is accurate and consistent	– The review is the correct number of specified pages. – Citations, references, and APA format are all accurate and consistent.	– The length exceeds the word or page limit, or does not meet the word or page limit. – Citations, references, and APA format are mostly accurate.	– The length exceeds the word or page limit, or does not meet the word or page limit. – There are frequent errors regarding citations, references, and/or APA format.	– The length exceeds the word or page limit, or does not meet the required limit. – The review is characterized by gross inaccuracies with citations, references, and APA format.

Source: This rubric is part of Bloomberg, L. D. (2015). *Qualitative dissertation evaluation.* Unpublished manuscript.

Appendix C. Commonly Used Electronic Library Databases

ABI/INFORM

Provides access to business information in more than 800 journals. Excellent source of information on management, the corporate environment, and business conditions. Consists of bibliographic entries and abstracts.

Academic Search Premier

This is a strong general purpose database that covers fields such as the social sciences, business and economics, general sciences, and humanities. Many of the articles are available in full text form.

Current Contents Search®

Provides access to tables of contents and bibliographic data from more than 7,000 of the world's leading scientific and scholarly journals and more than 2,000 books. Offers full, up-to-date journal information, as well as reprint and research addresses.

Education Full Text/Education Research Complete

Includes journal articles, monographs, and yearbooks related to education. There is substantial overlap with ERIC, but it does cover 40 journals not indexed in ERIC.

Emerald Management Xtra 150

This is the largest, most comprehensive collection of peer-reviewed management journals. It features access to 150 full-text journals, with reviews from the top 300 management journals, including, among others, *Cross Cultural Management, Education and Training, Development and Learning in Organizations, European Journal of Innovation Management, Handbook of Business Strategy, International Journal of Sociology and Social Policy, International Journal of Sustainability in Higher Education, Journal of Educational Administration, Journal of Health Organization and Management, Journal of Knowledge Management, Leadership and Organization Development Journal, The Learning Organization, Multicultural Education and Technology Journal, Quality Assurance in Education,* and *Strategy and Leadership.*

ERIC (Education Resources Information Center)

Provides access to approximately 1 million abstracts of documents and journal articles related to educational research and practice. These include conference papers, master's theses, doctoral dissertations, government reports, books, book chapters, reports, and unpublished documents. Most documents published by ERIC are available in full text and can be purchased from the ERIC Document Reproduction Service using the form and procedures found in the back of *Review of Research in Education*.

JSTOR

JSTOR stands for journal storage. This is a wide-ranging database and archive of important scholarly journals spanning both multidisciplinary and discipline-specific collections. The Arts & Sciences

Collections represent more than 600 journals in the arts, humanities, and social sciences. Because of *JSTOR's* archival mission, it is not a current issues database. *JSTOR* is a wide-ranging database containing back files from many scholarly journals.

MUSE

The foremost collection of more than 150 peer-reviewed interdisciplinary journals from leading university presses, not-for-profit publishers, and prestigious scholarly societies. It offers comprehensive coverage of journals in the humanities and social sciences, including education.

PAIS International (Public Affairs Information Service)

Index to political, economic, and social issues. This database covers the public and social policy literature of business, economics, finance, law, international relations, public administration, and political science, among others. Dating from 1972 to the present, PAIS contains abstracts of journal articles, books, statistical yearbooks, conference proceedings, research reports, and government documents from all over the world.

Political Science Abstracts

Important source for political science articles published since 1976. Contains abstracts of materials from professional journals, news magazines, and books. Useful resource for charting political issues and processes and public policy worldwide.

ProQuest Dissertations and Theses Database

This is one of the most comprehensive collections of dissertations and theses and is the official digital dissertations archive for the Library of Congress and the database of record for graduate research. The site includes 2.7 million searchable citations to dissertations and theses from around the world from 1861 to the present, together with 1.2 million full-text dissertations that are available for download in PDF format. Over 2.1 million titles are available for purchase as printed copies. The database offers full text for most of the dissertations added since 1997 and strong retrospective full-text coverage for older graduate works. More than 70,000 new full-text dissertations and theses are added to the database each year through dissertation publishing partnerships with 700 leading academic institutions worldwide and collaborative retrospective digitization of dissertations through UMI's Digital Archiving and Access Program.

PsycINFO®

Comprehensive international database covering the academic, research, and practice literature on topics in psychology and related disciplines, including education, social work, medicine, psychiatry, criminology, and organizational behavior. This database indexes more than 850 journals under 16 different categories of information. It allows you to limit your search to reviews of literature or specific types of research studies, such as case studies or experimental research, and provides a link to more recent studies that have cited the study that is presented. *PsycINFO®* also provides indices to journals, dissertations, book chapters, books, technical reports, and other documents from 1887 to the present, with optional access to *Historic PsycINFO®*, an archival file database.

Social Sciences Citation Index (SSCI)

Covers about 5,700 journals that represent virtually every discipline in the social sciences. Provides access to 300 major international periodicals in the social sciences and related disciplines: anthropology, environmental sciences, law and criminology, psychology, political science, public health, sociology, urban studies, and women's studies. Like *PsycINFO®*, it can be used to locate articles and authors who have conducted research on a topic. You can also trace all studies since the publication of the key study that have cited the work. Using this system, you can develop a chronological list of references that document the historical evolution of an idea or study.

Social Work Abstracts

Contains information on the fields of social work and human services from 1977 to the present. Provides coverage of more than 450 journals in all professional areas, including theory and practice, areas of service, and social issues. Useful for research in the areas of social sciences, public health, criminology, and education.

Sociological Abstracts

This database contains abstracts to articles in more than 2,500 journals as well as book reviews and abstracts for dissertations and books. Provides access to the most current worldwide findings in theoretical and applied sociology, social science, and policy science. Features journal citations and abstracts, book chapters, and software review citations. This database is useful for interdisciplinary research on social science issues and for practitioners seeking sociological perspectives on various disciplines.

Wilson Social Sciences Abstracts and Full Text

Contains abstracting and indexing coverage for all 513 periodicals included in Social Sciences Index, as well as the full text of more than 150 periodicals. Subjects include anthropology, criminology, psychology, public administration, and sociology.

Appendix D. Style Manuals for Social Sciences

Most universities require consistent use of a particular style manual to format your dissertation and to cite references. Most widely used primary text style manuals in the social sciences include the following:

American Anthropological Association. (2009). *AAA style guide.* Available from http://www.aaanet.org/publications/guidelines.cfm

American Psychological Association. (2007). *APA style guide to electronic resources.* Available from http://books.apa.org/cfm?id=4210509

American Psychological Association. (2010). *Publication manual of the American Psychological Association* (6th ed.). Washington DC: Author.

American Sociological Association. (1997). *American Sociological Association style guide* (2nd ed.). Washington, DC: Author.

Modern Language Association of America. (2008). *MLA style manual and guide to scholarly publishing* (3rd ed.). New York: Author.

Turabian, K. L. (2007). *A manual for writers of term papers, theses, and dissertations: Chicago style for students and researchers* (7th ed.). Chicago: University of Chicago Press.

University of Chicago. (2010). *The Chicago manual of style: The essential guide for writers, editors, and publishers* (16th ed.). Chicago: University of Chicago Press.

There are also some useful secondary sources available:

American Sociological Association. (2007). *Quick style guide.* Available from http://www.asanet.org/Quick%20Style%20Guide.pdf

Gibaldi, J. (2003). *MLA handbook for writers of research papers* (6th ed.). New York. Modern Language Association of America.

Hacker, D. (2010). *A writer's reference* (8th ed.). Boston: Bedford/St. Martin's. (This book can be consulted as needed to master the academic style of scholarly writing. The author provides details pertaining to word choice, grammar, sentence style, and punctuation. The author also discusses the most commonly used academic writing styles: APA, MLA, and CMS/Chicago.)

Lipson, C. (2006). *Cite right: A quick guide to citation styles—MLA, APA, Chicago, the sciences, professions, and more.* Chicago: University of Chicago Press.

Schwartz, B. M., Landrum, R. E., & Guring, R. A. (2012). *An easyguide to APA style.* Thousand Oaks, CA: Sage.

Appendix F. Overview of Purposeful Sampling Strategies

Purposeful Sampling Strategy	Explanation
Typical case sampling	Individuals are selected because they represent the norm and are in no way atypical, extreme, or very unusual.
Critical or crucial case sampling	The researcher samples those individuals who can "make a point quite dramatically, or are, for some reason, particularly important in the scheme of things" (Patton, 2015, p. 276).
Snowball, network, or chain sampling	A few participants who possess certain characteristics are selected, and they are asked to identify and refer others who are known to have the same or similar characteristics.
Criterion sampling	All participants must meet one or more criteria as predetermined by the researcher.
Extreme or deviant case sampling	Individuals are selected because they represent the extremes. The researcher seeks to learn from highly unusual manifestations of the phenomenon of interest.
Maximum variation of sampling	Individuals are selected because they represent the widest possible range of the characteristics being studied. Selection includes "a deliberate hunt for the negative" (Miles & Huberman, 1994). Diverse variations are included to identify patterns. This strategy was first identified by Glaser and Strauss (1967) in their presentation of grounded theory.
Homogenous sampling	In contrast to maximum variation, individuals with only similar experiences are selected.
Stratified purposeful sampling	Sampling in this way illustrates subgroups and facilitates comparisons among them.
Theoretical or theory-based sampling	Selection is ongoing: Sampling begins purposefully. The researcher analyzes data, and as the theoretical framework emerges, the researcher decides from whom to collect more data next. Sampling is thus an evolving process guided by emerging theory. This strategy was popularized by Glaser and Strauss (1967).
Intensity sampling	The researcher seeks information-rich cases that manifest the phenomenon intensely, but not extremely.
Convenience sampling	This is the least desirable sampling strategy. Tendency is to rely on availability. This can save time and effort, but is at the expense of information and credibility. It can produce "information-poor" rather than "information-rich" cases (Patton, 1990, p. 183).
Purposeful random sampling	One of the purposeful sampling procedures mentioned above is used, followed by a randomization procedure. This strategy supposedly adds credibility to the study, although the initial sample is based on purposeful selection.

Source: This summary chart first appeared in Bloomberg, L. D. (2007). *Understanding qualitative inquiry: Content and process* (Part I). Unpublished manuscript.

Note 1: The sample size in qualitative research is relatively small, but consists of "information-rich" cases. In-depth interviews and immersion in a culture make a large sample size unnecessary, particularly as qualitative researchers do not seek to generalize. It is generally recommended that researchers use their judgment regarding the numbers in the sample.

Note 2: Samples in qualitative research consist not merely of people, but also of texts, events, cultural phenomena, and artifacts.

Appendix I. Sample Flowchart of Research Design

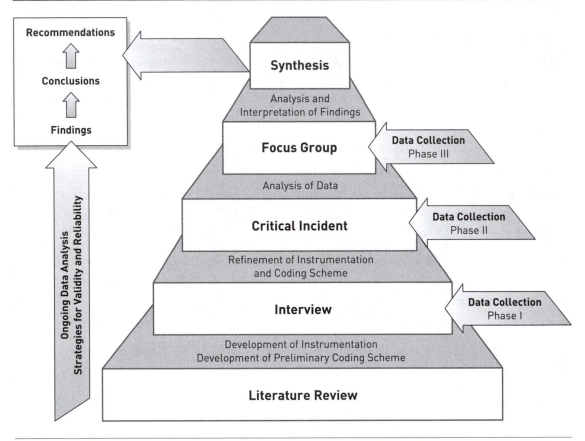

Source: This figure first appeared in Bloomberg, L. D. (2007). *Understanding qualitative inquiry: Content and process* (Part I). Unpublished manuscript.

Appendix J. Qualitative Data Collection Methods: A Summary Overview

Method	Function
Document review	• Data are collected in their natural setting • Records, documents, and artifacts provide contextual information and insights into material culture • Facilitates discovery of cultural nuances
Survey	• Provides demographic information • Provides contextual information • Provides perceptual information • Can include both quantitative (numerical) and qualitative (open-ended) elements
Interview	• Fosters interactivity with participants • Elicits in-depth, context-rich personal accounts, perceptions, and perspectives • Data are collected in their natural setting • Interviews can be unstructured, structured, or semistructured • Explains and describes complex interactions and processes • Facilitates discovery of nuances in culture
Focus group	• Notes or verbatim transcriptions are used to document the interview • Fosters interactivity and dialogue among participants • Describes complex interactions • Clarifies and extends findings yielded by other methods • Allows for increased richness of responses through synergy and interaction
Observation	• Notes or verbatim transcriptions are used to document the interview • The researcher observes and records behavior, but does not interact with participants • Provides data collected in their natural setting • Useful for describing complex processes and interactions • Runs the risk of observer effect and observer bias
Participant observation	• Field notes are used to document observations • Fosters face-to-face interaction with participants • Provides data collected in their natural setting • Facilitates insight into complex social and cultural nuances by allowing the researcher to develop relationships with participants • Runs the risk of observer effect and the potential for the researcher to become emotionally involved
Critical incidents	• Field notes are used to document observations • Engages participants in the reflective process • Draws on the personal meaning of experience
Life history	• Provides critical perceptual information • Discovers retrospective information • Enhances participants' critical thinking, reflection, and depth of response • Encourages participants to extract meaning from their own experience

Note: Rather than relying on any one method, qualitative researchers typically triangulate a variety of data collection methods.

Appendix Q. Template for Document Summary Form

Name or Type of Document: _____

Document No.: _____

Date Received: _____

Date of Document: _____

Event or Contact With Which Document Is Associated: _____

- ☐ Descriptive
- ☐ Evaluative
- ☐ Other _____

Page #	Keywords/Concepts	Comments: Relationship to Research Questions

Brief Summary of Contents:

_____

_____

Significance or Purpose of Document:

_____

_____

Is There Anything Contradictory About Document?

- ☐ Yes
- ☐ No

Salient Questions/Issues to Consider:

_____

_____

Additional Comments/Reflections/Issues:

_____

_____

_____

Source: Adapted from Miles & Huberman (1994, pp. 54–55).

Appendix R. Template for Participant Summary Form

Participant Name: _____

Type of Contact: (Check where appropriate)   **Contact Date:** _____

Today's Date: _____

    ☐ Face to Face

    ☐ Phone

    ☐ Videoconference

Summary of Information for Each Research Question:

Research Question 1

Research Question 2

Research Question 3

Research Question 4

Research Question 5

Additional Information Needed:

_____

_____

Overall Impressions, Questions, Concerns, Issues Still to Be Addressed:

_____

_____

_____

Source: Adapted from Miles & Huberman (1994, "Contact Summary Form," pp. 52–54); Miles, Huberman, & Saldana (2014, "Contact Summary Form," pp. 124–127).

Appendix Z. Qualitative Data Analysis Software Resources

Many software packages for qualitative data analysis are currently available. Searching for the most appropriate software package is important so that it directly supports and is usable in terms of your chosen research design and approach. "Code, search, and retrieve" are basic features of the major packages. AnSWR is especially suited for coordinating and conducting team-based analysis projects that integrate qualitative and quantitative techniques. Software can perform specialized searching and sorting tasks. However, be aware that the software does not do the thinking for you! These programs do not engage in interpretive work, nor were they designed to do this!

Program Name	Website
AnSWR (free of charge)	http://answr.software.informer.com/
ATLAS.ti	http://www.atlasti.com/
	Friese, S. (2014). *Qualitative data analysis with ATLAS.ti* (2nd ed.). Thousand Oaks, CA: Sage.
The Ethnograph	http://www.QualisResearch.com
HyperRESEARCH	http://researchware.com
NVivo	http://www.qsrinternational.com
	Bazeley, P., & Jackson, K. (2013). *Qualitative data analysis with NVivo* (2nd ed.). Thousand Oaks, CA: Sage.
	Bazeley, P. (2008). *Qualitative data analysis with NVivo.* Thousand Oaks, CA: Sage.
NUD*IST	http://www.qsrintenational.com
MAXQDA	http://www.maxqda.com/
Transana	http://www.transana.org/ (used for analysis of video, auditory, and still-image data)
Qualrus	http://www.qualrus.com/
Comparisons between ATLAS.ti and NUD*IST:	http://www.socresonline.org.uk/3/3/4.html
QDA Miner	www.provalisresearch.com
Weft QDA (free of charge)	www.pressure.to/qda/
Comparisons among all of the available software programs	http://projects.iq.harvard.edu/qualitative/files/QDA_panel_introduction_slides_0.pdf

Note: Some of the software sites offer links to interactive discussion groups.

• References •

American Psychological Association. (2010). *Concise rules of APA style* (6th ed.). Washington, DC: Author.

American Psychological Association. (2010). *Publication manual of the American Psychological Association* (6th ed.). Washington, DC: Author.

Andrews, M., Squire, C., & Tamboukou, M. (2013). *Doing narrative research.* (2nd ed.). Thousand Oaks, CA: Sage.

Anfara, V. A., & Mertz, N. T. (Eds.). (2015). *Theoretical frameworks in qualitative research* (2nd ed.). Thousand Oaks, CA: Sage.

Azad, A., & Kohun, F. (2006). Dealing with isolation feelings in doctoral programs. *International Journal of Doctoral Studies, 1.* Retrieved January 20, 2012, from http://ijds.org/Volume1/IJDSv1p021-033Ali13.pdf

Bair, C. R., & Haworth, J. G. (1999, November 18–21). *Doctoral student attrition and persistence: A metasynthesis of research.* Paper presented at the annual meeting of the Association for the Study of Higher Education, San Antonio, TX.

Bauer, T. N., & Green, S. G. (1994). Effect of newcomer in work-related activities: A longitudinal study of socialization. *Journal of Applied Psychology, 2,* 211–223.

Bazeley, P. (2008). *Qualitative data analysis with NVivo.* Thousand Oaks, CA: Sage.

Bazeley, P. (2014). *Qualitative data analysis: Practical strategies.* Thousand Oaks, CA: Sage.

Bazeley, P., & Jackson, K. (2013). *Qualitative data analysis with NVivo* (2nd ed.). Thousand Oaks, CA: Sage.

Beeler, K. D. (1991). *Graduate student adjustment to academic life: A four-stage framework.* Retrieved January 20, 2012, from http://eric.ed.gov/?id=EJ426739

Berg, J. (2007). Exploring ways to shorten the ascent to a Ph.D. *New York Times,* October 3, p. B9. Retrieved from www.nytimes.com

Bernard, H. R., & Ryan, G. W. (2010). *Analyzing qualitative data: Systematic approaches.* Thousand Oaks, CA: Sage.

Blaxter, L., Hughes, C., & Tight, M. (1996). *How to research.* Buckingham, United Kingdom: Open University Press.

Bloomberg, L. D. (2007a). *Revisiting research approaches.* Unpublished manuscript. –chap 3

Bloomberg, L. D. (2007b). *Understanding qualitative inquiry: Content and process* (Part I). Unpublished manuscript.

Bloomberg, L. D. (2009). *The qualitative dissertation: A content guideline.* Unpublished manuscript series.

Bloomberg, L. D. (2010). *Understanding qualitative inquiry: Content and process* (Part II). Unpublished manuscript.

Bloomberg, L. D. (2011). *Understanding qualitative inquiry: Content and process* (Part III). Unpublished manuscript.

Bloomberg, L. D. (2015). *Qualitative dissertation evaluation.* Unpublished manuscript.

Boeije, H. (2010). *Analysis in qualitative research.* Thousand Oaks, CA: Sage.

Bogdan, R. C., & Biklen, S. K. (2007). *Qualitative research for education: An introduction to theory and methods* (5th ed.). Boston: Pearson Education.

Boote, D. N., & Beile, P. (2005). Scholars before researchers: On the centrality of the dissertation literature review in research preparation. *Educational Researcher, 34*(6), 3–15.

Booth, W. C., Colomb, G. G., & Williams, J. M. (2008). *The craft of research* (3rd ed.). Chicago: University of Chicago Press.

Bourner, T., Bowden, R., & Laing, S. (2001). Professional doctorates in England. *Studies in Higher Education, 26*(1). Retrieved November 22, 2006, from *EBSCOHost* database.

Bowen, W. G., & Rudenstein, N. L. (1992). *In pursuit of the PhD.* Princeton, NJ: Princeton University Press.

Boyatzis, R. E. (1998). *Transforming qualitative information: Thematic analysis and code development.* Thousand Oaks, CA: Sage.

Brause, R. S. (2004). *Writing your doctoral dissertation: Invisible rules for success.* New York: Routledge Falmer.

Brinkmann, S. (2014). Doing without data. *Qualitative Inquiry, 20,* 720–725.

Brinkmann, S., & Kvale, S. (2015). *Interviews: Learning the craft of qualitative research interviewing* (4th ed.). Thousand Oaks, CA: Sage.

Brookfield, S. D. (1991). Using critical incidents to explore assumptions. In J. Mezirow & Associates (Eds.), *Fostering critical reflection in adulthood* (pp. 177–193). San Francisco: Jossey-Bass.

Brookfield, S. D. (2005). *The power of critical theory: Liberating adult learning and teaching.* San Francisco: Jossey-Bass.

Bryman, A. (2001). *Social research methods.* Oxford: Oxford University Press.

Cañas, A. J., & Novak, J. D. (2005). *A concept map-centered learning environment.* Paper presented at the Symposium at the 11th Biennial Conference of the European Association for Research in Learning and Instruction (EARLI), Cyprus.

Candy, P. C. (1991). *Self-direction for lifelong learning: A comprehensive guide to theory and practice.* San Francisco: Jossey-Bass.

Charmaz, K. (2014). Grounded theory in global perspective: Reviews by international researchers. *Qualitative Inquiry,* 20: 1074–1084.

Charmaz, K. (2015). *Constructing grounded theory* (2nd ed.). Thousand Oaks, CA: Sage.

Chase, S. (2005). Narrative inquiry: Multiple lenses, approaches, voices. In N. K. Denzin & Y. S. Lincoln (Eds.), *The Sage handbook of qualitative research* (3rd ed., pp. 651–680). Thousand Oaks, CA: Sage.

Clandinin, D. J. (Ed.). (2006). *Handbook of narrative inquiry: Mapping a methodology.* Thousand Oaks, CA: Sage.

Coffey, A., & Atkinson, P. (1996). *Making sense of qualitative data: Complementary research strategies.* Thousand Oaks, CA: Sage.

Connelly, F. M., & Clandinin, D. J. (2006). *Narrative inquiry: Experience and story in qualitative research.* San Francisco: Jossey-Bass.

Cohen, L., Lawrence, M., & Morrison, K. (2000). *Research methods in education* (5th ed.). London: Routledge Falmer.

Cooper, H. (2010). *Research synthesis and meta-analysis* (4th ed.). Thousand Oaks, CA: Sage.

Corbin, J.,& Strauss, A. (2015). *Basics of qualitative research: Techniques and procedures for developing grounded theory* (4th ed.). Thousand Oaks, CA: Sage.

Cozby, P.C., & Bates, S.C. (2012). *Methods in behavioral research.* Boston: McGraw Hill Higher Education.

Crabtree, B. F., & Miller, W. L. (Eds.). (1992). *Doing qualitative research: Multiple strategies.* Newbury Park, CA: Sage.

Creswell, J. W. (2013). *Qualitative inquiry and research design: Choosing among five traditions* (3rd ed.). Thousand Oaks, CA: Sage.

Creswell, J. W. (2014). *Research design: Qualitative, quantitative, and mixed methods approaches* (4th ed.). Thousand Oaks, CA: Sage.

Daiute, C. (2014). *Narrative inquiry.* Thousand Oaks, CA: Sage.

Denzin, N. K. (2001). *Interpretive interactionism.* Newbury Park, CA: Sage.

Denzin, N. K., & Lincoln, Y. S. (Eds.). (2011). *The Sage handbook of qualitative research* (4th ed.). Thousand Oaks, CA: Sage.

Denzin, N. K., & Lincoln, Y. S. (2013a). (Eds.). *Strategies of qualitative inquiry* (4th ed.). Thousand Oaks, CA: Sage.

Denzin, N. K., & Lincoln, Y. S. (2013b). *Collecting and interpreting qualitative materials* (4th ed.). Thousand Oaks, CA: Sage.

Denzin, N. K., & Lincoln, Y. S. (Eds.). (2013c). *The landscape of qualitative inquiry* (4th ed.). Thousand Oaks, CA: Sage.

Derrida, J. (1976). *Of grammatology* (G. C. Spivak, Trans.). Baltimore: John Hopkins University Press.

Derrida, J. (1981). *Positions* (A. Bass, Trans.). Chicago: University of Chicago Press.

Dewey, J. (1916). *Democracy and education.* New York: Macmillan.

Dominice, P. (2000). *Learning from our lives: Using educational biographies with adults.* San Francisco: Jossey-Bass.

Dunn, S. (2014). In hindsight: Former PhD students reflect on why they jumped ship. *The Chronicle of Higher Education.* Retrieved February 25, 2015, from https://chroniclevitae.com

Emel, N. (2013). *Sampling and choosing cases in qualitative research.* Thousand Oaks, CA: Sage.

Ercikan, K., & Roth, W. (2006). What good is polarizing research into qualitative and quantitative? *Educational Researcher, 35*(5), 14–23.

Fanger, D. (1985, May). The dissertation from conception to delivery. *On Teaching and Learning: The Journal of the Harvard-Danforth Center, 1,* 26–33.

Finfgeld-Connett, D. (2014). Use of content analysis to conduct knowledge-building and theory-generating qualitative systematic reviews. *Qualitative Research, 14*(3), 341–352.

Fink, A. (2014). *Conducting research literature reviews* (4th ed.). Thousand Oaks, CA: Sage.

Fink, A, (2013). *How to conduct surveys: A step-by-step guide.* Thousand Oaks, CA: Sage.

Flanagan, J. C. (1954). The critical incident technique. *Psychological Bulletin, 51*(4), 327–358.

Flick, U. (2013) (Ed.). *The Sage handbook of qualitative data analysis.* Thousand Oaks, CA: Sage.

Fontana, A., & Frey, J. H. (2003). The interview: From structured questions to negotiated text. In N. K. Denzin & Y. S. Lincoln (Eds.), *Collecting and interpreting qualitative materials* (pp. 61–106). Thousand Oaks, CA: Sage.

Fontana, A., & Frey, J. H. (2008). The interview: From neutral stance to political involvement. In N. K. Denzin & Y. S. Lincoln (Eds.), *Collecting and interpreting qualitative materials* (pp. 115–159). Thousand Oaks, CA: Sage.

Foucault, M. (1972). *The archaeology of knowledge and the discourse on language* (A. M. Sheridan Smith, Trans.). New York: Harper.

Fowler, F. J. (2014). *Survey research methods* (5th ed.). Thousand Oaks, CA: Sage.

Freire, P. (1970). *Pedagogy of the oppressed.* New York: Seabury.

Friese, S. (2014). *Qualitative data analysis with ATLAS.ti* (2nd ed.). Thousand Oaks, CA: Sage.

Gadamer, H. (1960). *Truth and method.* London: Sheed and Ward.

Galvan, J. L. (2014). *Writing literature reviews: A guide for students of the social and behavioral sciences* (6th ed.). Glendale, CA: Pyrczak.

Gay, L. R., Mills, G. E., & Airasian, P. (2006). *Educational research: Competencies for analysis and application* (8th ed.). Upper Saddle River, NJ: Pearson.

Geertz, C. (1973). *The interpretation of cultures.* New York: Basic Books.

Gibson, G., & Hartman, J. (2014). *Rediscovering grounded theory.* Thousand Oaks, CA: Sage.

Gibson, W. J., & Brown, J. (2009). *Working with qualitative data.* Thousand Oaks, CA: Sage.

Glaser, B. G., & Strauss, A. L. (1967). *The discovery of grounded theory: Strategies for qualitative research.* Chicago: Aldine.

Grbich, C. (2013). *Qualitative data analysis: An introduction* (2nd ed.). Thousand Oaks, CA: Sage.

Green, K. E., & Kluever, R. C. (1996). *The Responsibility Scale.* Paper presented at the annual meeting of the American Education Research Association, New York, April 8–12.

Green, K. E., & Kluever, R. C. (1997). *The dissertation barrier scale.* Paper presented at the annual meeting of the American Education Research Association, Chicago, March 24–28.

Guest, G., MacQueen, K., & Namey, E. E. (2012). *Applied thematic analysis.* Thousand Oaks, CA: Sage.

Hacker, D. (2010). *A writer's reference* (8th ed.). Boston: Bedford/St. Martin's.

Harding, J. (2013). *Qualitative data analysis from start to finish.* Thousand Oaks, CA: Sage.

Hart, C. (2005). *Doing a literature review: Releasing the social science research imagination.* Thousand Oaks, CA: Sage.

Hawley, P. (2003). *Being bright is not enough.* Springfield, IL: Charles C. Thomas.

Henderson, S., & Segal, E. H. (2013). Visualizing qualitative data in evaluation research. In T. Azzam & S. Evergreen (Eds.). *Data visualization, Part 1: New Directions for Evaluation* (pp. 53–72). San Francisco: Jossey-Bass.

Heinrich, K. T. (1991). Loving partnerships: Dealing with sexual attraction and power in doctoral advisement relationships. *Journal of Higher Education, 62*(5), 514–538.

Hesse-Biber, S. N., & Leavy, P. (2011). *The practice of qualitative research* (2nd ed.). Thousand Oaks, CA: Sage.

Hockey, J. (1994). New territory: Problems of adjusting to the first year of a social science PhD. *Studies in Higher Education, 19*(2), 177–190.

Houle, C. O. (1988). *The inquiring mind* (2nd ed.). Madison: University of Wisconsin Press.

Huck, S. W. (2000). *Reading statistics and research* (3rd ed.). New York: Longman.

Hycner, R. H. (1985). Some guidelines for the phenomenological analysis of interview data. *Human Studies, 8,* 279–303.

Jacobs, R. L. (2013). Writer's forum—developing a dissertation research problem: A guide for doctoral students in human resource development and adult education. *New Horizons in Adult Education & Human Resource Development 25*(3), 103–117.

Kane, M., & Trochim, W. (2006). *Concept mapping for planning and evaluation.* Thousand Oaks, CA: Sage.

Katz, E. (1995). *The dissertation: Academic interruptus.* Paper presented at the annual meeting of the American Education Research Association, San Francisco, April 18–22.

Kilbourn, B. (2006). The qualitative doctoral research proposal. *Teachers College Record, 108*(4), 529–576.

Kim, J. (2015). *Understanding narrative inquiry: The crafting and analysis of stories as research.* Thousand Oaks, CA: Sage.

Knowles, M. S. (1980). *The modern practice of adult education.* New York: Cambridge University Press.

Knowles, M. S. (1998). *The adult learner* (5th ed.). Houston, TX: Gulf Publishing.

Krathwohl, D. R. (1998). *Methods of educational and social science research: An integrated approach* (2nd ed.). Reading, MA: Addison-Wesley.

Kreuger, R. A., & Casey, M. A. (2015). *Focus groups: A practical guide for applied research* (5th ed.). Thousand Oaks, CA: Sage.

Kuckartz, U. (2014). *Qualitative text analysis.* Thousand Oaks, CA: Sage.

Lazerson, M. (2003). *Navigating the journey: A case study of participants in a dissertation support program.* Unpublished doctoral dissertation, University of Pennsylvania.

Leedy, P.D., & Ormrod, J. E. (2013). *Practical research: Planning and design* (10th ed.). Boston, MA: Pearson.

Lenz, K. (1995). *Factors affecting the completion of the doctoral dissertation for non-traditional aged women.* Paper presented at the annual meeting of the American Education Research Association, San Francisco, April 18–22.

Leshem, S., & Trafford, V. (2007). Overlooking the conceptual framework. *Innovations in Education and Teaching International, 44*(1), 93–105.

Lewin, K. (1935). *A dynamic theory of personality.* New York: McGraw-Hill.

Lewis, C. W., Ginsberg, R., Davies, T., & Smith, K. (2004). The experiences of African American Ph.D. students at a predominantly white Carnegie I research institution. *College Student Journal, 38*(2), 231–235.

Liamputtong, P. (2011). *Focus group methodology: Principles and practice.* Thousand Oaks, CA: Sage.

Lichtman, M. (2014). *Qualitative research for the social sciences.* Thousand Oaks, CA: Sage.

Lincoln, Y. S., & Guba, E. G. (1985). *Naturalistic inquiry.* Beverly Hills, CA: Sage.

Lincoln, Y. S., & Guba, E. G. (2000). Paradigmatic controversies, contradictions, and emerging confluences. In N. K. Denzin & Y. S. Lincoln (Eds.), *Handbook of qualitative research* (2nd ed., pp. 163–188). Thousand Oaks, CA: Sage.

Locke, L. F., Spirduso, S. J., & Silverman, S. J. (2000). *Proposals that work.* Thousand Oaks, CA: Sage.

Loseke, D., & Cahill, S. (2004). Publishing qualitative manuscripts: Lessons learned. In C. Seale, G. Gobo, J. F. Gubrium, & D. Silverman (Eds.), *Qualitative research practice* (pp. 576–592). Thousand Oaks, CA: Sage.

Lovitts, B. E. (1996). *Leaving the ivory tower: A sociological analysis of the causes of departure from doctoral study.* Unpublished doctoral dissertation, University of Michigan, Ann Arbor, MI.

Lovitts, B. E. (2001). *Leaving the ivory tower: The causes and consequences of departure from doctoral study.* Lanham, MD: Rowman & Littlefield.

Lovitts, B. E., & Nelson, C. (2000). *The hidden crisis in graduate education: Attrition from Ph.D. programs.* Retrieved January 20, 2012, from http://www.aaup.org

Madden, R. (2011). *Being ethnographic: A guide to the theory and practice of ethnography.* Thousand Oaks, CA: Sage.

Marshall, C., & Rossman, G. B. (2015). *Designing qualitative research* (6th ed.). Thousand Oaks, CA: Sage.

Marvasti, A. (2011). Three aspects of writing qualitative research: Practice, genre, and audience. In D. Silverman (Ed.), *Qualitative research* (3rd ed., pp. 383–396). Thousand Oaks, CA: Sage.

Mason, J. (1996). *Qualitative researching.* Thousand Oaks, CA: Sage.

Maxwell, J. A. (2012). *A realist approach to qualitative research.* London: Sage.

Maxwell, J. A. (2013). *Qualitative research design: An interactive approach* (3rd ed.). Thousand Oaks, CA: Sage.

May, T., & Perry, B. (2014). Reflexivity and the practice of qualitative research. In U. Flick (Ed.), *The Sage handbook of qualitative data analysis* (pp. 109–122). Thousand Oaks, CA: Sage.

McNiff, J. (2014). *Writing and doing action research.* Thousand Oaks, CA: Sage.

Meloy, J. (1992). *Writing the qualitative dissertation: Voices of experience.* Paper presented at the annual meeting of the American Education Research Association, San Francisco.

Meloy, J. (1994). *Writing the qualitative dissertation: Understanding by doing.* Hillsdale, NJ: Lawrence Erlbaum Associates.

Merriam, S. B. (1998). *Qualitative research and case study application in education.* San Francisco: Jossey-Bass.

Merriam, S. B. (2009). *Qualitative research: A guide to design and implementation.* San Francisco: Jossey-Bass.

Merriam, S. B., & Caffarella, R. S. (1999). *Learning in adulthood: A comprehensive guide.* San Francisco: Jossey-Bass.

Mertler, C. A. (2012). *Action research: Improving schools and empowering educators* (3rd ed.). Thousand Oaks, CA: Sage.

Mezirow, J. (1981, Fall). A critical theory of adult education. *Adult Education, 31,* 3–24.

Mezirow, J. (1991). *Transformative dimensions of adult learning.* San Francisco: Jossey-Bass.

Mezirow, J., & Associates. (2000). *Learning as transformation: Critical perspectives on a theory in progress.* San Francisco: Jossey-Bass.

Miles, M. B., & Huberman, A. M. (1994). *Qualitative data analysis: An expanded sourcebook* (2nd ed.). Thousand Oaks, CA: Sage.

Miles, M. B., Huberman, A. M., & Saldana, J. (2014). *Qualitative data analysis: A methods sourcebook* (3rd ed.). Thousand Oaks, CA: Sage.

Miller, M. M. (1995). *ABD status and degree completion: A student's perspective.* Paper presented at the annual meeting of the American Education Research Association, San Francisco, April 18–22.

Mills, J., & Birks, M. (Eds.). (2014). *Qualitative methodology: A practical guide.* Thousand Oaks, CA: Sage.

Morse, J. M., Barrett, M., Mayan, M., Olson, K., & Spiers, J. (2002). Verification strategies for establishing reliability and validity in qualitative research. *International Journal of Qualitative Methods, 1*(2), 1–19. Retrieved January 20, 2012, from http://ejournals.library.ualberta.ca/index.php/IJQM/article/view/4603

Moustakas, C. (1994). *Phenomenological research methods.* Thousand Oaks, CA: Sage.

Neuman, W. L. (2000). *Social research methods: Qualitative and quantitative approaches* (4th ed.). Boston: Allyn & Bacon.

Novak, J. D. (1998). *Learning, creating, and using knowledge: Concept maps as facilitative tools in schools and corporations.* Mahwah, NJ: Lawrence Erlbaum Associates.

O'Dochartaigh, N. (2012). *Internet research skills* (3rd ed.). Thousand Oaks, CA: Sage.

O'Dwyer, L. M., & Bernauer, J. A. (2014). *Quantitative research for the qualitative researcher.* Thousand Oaks, CA: Sage.

Patton, M. Q. (1990). *Qualitative evaluation and research methods* (2nd ed.). Newbury Park, CA: Sage.

Patton, M. Q. (2015). *Qualitative research and evaluation methods* (4th ed.). Thousand Oaks, CA: Sage.

Pellegrino, V. C. (2003). *A writer's guide to powerful paragraphs.* Wailuku, HI: Maui'ar Thoughts Company.

Penslar, R. I. (1993). *IRB guidebook.* Retrieved January 3, 2012, from the U.S. Department of Health and Human Services Office for Human Research Protections: http://www.hhs.gov/ohrp/archive/irb/irb_guidebook.htm

Phillips, D. C., & Burbules, N. C. (2000). *Postpositivism and educational research.* Lanham, MD: Rowman & Littlefield.

Piantanida, M., & Garman, N. B. (1999). *The qualitative dissertation: A guide for students and faculty.* Thousand Oaks, CA: Corwin.

Pinnagar, S., & Daynes, J. G. (2006). Locating narrative inquiry historically: Thematics in the turn to narrative. In D. J. Clandinin (Ed.), *Handbook of narrative inquiry* (pp. 1–34). Thousand Oaks, CA: Sage.

Pring, R. (2000). *Philosophy of educational research.* London: Continuum.

Punch, K. F. (2000). *Developing effective research proposal.* London: Sage.

Ravitch, S. M., & Riggan, M. (2012). *Reason and rigor.* Thousand Oaks, CA: Sage.

Reason, P., & Bradbury, H. (2008). (Eds.). *Handbook of action research: Participatory inquiry and practice.* Thousand Oaks, CA: Sage.

Reichardt, C. S., & Rallis, S. F. (1994). The qualitative quantitative debate: New perspectives. *New Directions for Program Evaluation, 61,* 5–11.

Reybold, L. E., Lammert, J. D., & Stribling, S. M. (2013). Participant selection as a conscious research method: Thinking forward and the deliberation of 'Emergent' findings. *Qualitative Research,* 13: 699–716.

Richards, L. (2015). *Handling qualitative data: A practical guide* (3rd ed.). Thousand Oaks, CA: Sage.

Richards, L., & Morse, J. M. (2013). *Readme first for a user's guide to qualitative methods* (3rd ed.). Thousand Oaks, CA: Sage.

Ritchie, J., Lewis, J., Nichols, C., & Ormston, R. (2014). (Eds.). *Qualitative research practice: A guide for social science students and researchers.* Thousand Oaks, CA: Sage.

Rocco, T., Hatcher, T., & Creswell, J. W. (2011). *The handbook of scholarly writing and publishing.* San Francisco: Jossey-Bass.

Rossman, G. B., & Rallis, S. F. (2012). *Learning in the field: An introduction to qualitative research* (3rd ed.). Thousand Oaks, CA: Sage.

Roulston, K., & Shelton, S. A. (2015). Reconceptualizing bias in teaching qualitative research methods. *Qualitative Inquiry, 21,* : 332–342.

Rubin, H. J., & Rubin, I. S. (2012). *Qualitative interviewing: The art of hearing data* (3rd ed.). Thousand Oaks, CA: Sage.

Rudestam, K. E., & Newton, R. R. (2001). *Surviving your dissertation: A comprehensive guide to content and process* (2nd ed.). Thousand Oaks, CA: Sage.

Ryan, G., & Bernard, H. (2003). Techniques to identify themes. *Field Methods, 15*(1), 85–109.

Saldana, J. (2013). *The coding manual for qualitative researchers* (2nd ed.). Thousand Oaks, CA: Sage.

Saldana, J. (2015). *Thinking qualitatively: Methods of mind.* Thousand Oaks, CA: Sage.

Schein, E. H. (2010). *Organizational culture and leadership* (4th ed.). San Francisco: Jossey-Bass.

Schram, T. H. (2003). *Conceptualizing qualitative inquiry.* Columbus, OH: Merrill Prentice Hall.

Schwandt, T. A. (2000). Three epistemological stances for qualitative inquiry. In N. K. Denzin & Y. S. Lincoln (Eds.), *Handbook of qualitative research* (2nd ed., pp. 189–213). Thousand Oaks, CA: Sage.

Schwandt, T. A. (2015). *The Sage dictionary of qualitative inquiry* (4th ed.). Thousand Oaks, CA: Sage.

Schwartz, B. M., Landrum, R. E., & Guring, R. A. (2012). *An easyguide to APA style.* Thousand Oaks, CA: Sage.

Seidman, I (2012). *Interviewing as qualitative research: A guide for researchers in education and the social sciences* (4th ed.). New York: Teachers College Press.

Silver, C., & Lewins, A. (2014). *Using software in qualitative research: A step-by-step guide.* Thousand Oaks, CA: Sage.

Silverman, D. (2011). (Ed.). *Qualitative research: Issues of theory, method, and practice* (3rd ed.). Thousand Oaks, CA: Sage.

Silverman, D. (2013). *Doing qualitative research* (4th ed.). Thousand Oaks, CA: Sage.

Silverman, D., & Marvasti, A. (2008). *Doing qualitative research: A comprehensive guide.* Thousand Oaks, CA: Sage.

Smallwood, S. (2004). Survey points to mismatch in doctoral programs. *The Chronicle of Higher Education, 47*(20), A14–A15.

Smith, J. A., Flowers, P., & Larkin, M. (2009). *Interpretive phenomenological analysis: Theory, method, and research.* London: Sage.

Spencer, L., Richie, J., & Ormston, R. (2014). Analysis: principles and processes. In J. Ritchie, J. Lewis, C. Nichols, & R. Ormston (Eds.), *Qualitative research practice: A guide for social science students and researchers* (pp. 269–293). Thousand Oaks, CA: Sage.

Stake, R. E. (1995). *The art of case study research.* Thousand Oaks, CA: Sage.

Stake, R. E. (2000). Case studies. In N. K. Denzin & Y. S. Lincoln (Eds.), *Handbook of qualitative research* (2nd ed., pp. 235–254). Thousand Oaks, CA: Sage.

Stake, R. E. (2001). The case study method in social inquiry. In N. K. Denzin & Y. S. Lincoln (Eds.), *The American tradition in qualitative research* (Vol. II, pp. 131–138). Thousand Oaks, CA: Sage.

Sternberg, D. (1981). *How to complete and survive a doctoral dissertation.* New York: St. Martin's Griffin.

Stewart, D. W., & Shamdasani, P. N. (2015). *Focus groups: Theory and practice* (3rd ed.). Thousand Oaks, CA: Sage.

Strauss, A. (1987). *Qualitative analysis for social scientists.* New York: Cambridge University Press.

Stringer, E. T. (2014). *Action research* (4th ed.). Thousand Oaks, CA: Sage.

Strunk, W., & White, E. B. (2000). *The elements of style* (4th ed.). New York: Longman.

Taylor, K., Marienau, C., & Fiddler, M. (2000). *Developing adult learners.* San Francisco: Jossey-Bass.

Tinto, V. (1993). *Leaving college: Rethinking the causes and cures of student attrition.* Chicago: University of Chicago Press.

Torraco, R. J. (2005). Writing integrative literature reviews: Guidelines and examples. *Human Resource Development Review, 4*(3), 356–367.

Tracy, S. J. (2010). Qualitative quality: Eight "big-tent'" criteria for excellent qualitative research. *Qualitative Inquiry, 16*(10), 837–851.

Urquhart, C. (2013). *Grounded theory for qualitative research: A practical guide.* Thousand Oaks, CA: Sage.

U.S. Department of Health and Human Services (HHS). 2005. Retrieved February 3, 2015, from 42 CFR Parts 50 and 93: Public Health Service Policies on Research Misconduct; Final Rule.

Van Maanen, J. (1988). *Tales of the field: On writing ethnography.* Chicago: University of Chicago Press.

Van Maanen, J. (Ed.). (1995). *Representation in ethnography.* Thousand Oaks, CA: Sage.

Van Maanen, J. (2006). Ethnography then and now. *Qualitative Research in Organizations and Management, 1*(1), 13–21.

van Manen, M. (1990). *Researching lived experience: Human science for an action sensitive pedagogy.* New York: State University of New York Press.

Wallace, M., & Wray, A. (2011). *Critical reading and writing for postgraduates* (2nd ed.). London: Sage.

Watkins, K. E., & Marsick, V. J. (2009). Trends in lifelong learning in the US workplace. In P. Jarvis (Ed.), *The Routledge international handbook of lifelong learning* (pp. 129–138). New York: Routledge.

Weaver-Hart, A. (1988). Framing an innocent concept and getting away with it. *UCEA Review, 24*(2), 11–12.

Weitzman, E. A., & Miles, M. B. (1995). *Computer programs for qualitative data analysis: A software sourcebook.* Thousand Oaks, CA: Sage.

Wertz, F. J., Charmaz, K., McMullen, L. M, Josselson, R., Anderson, R., & McSpadden, E. (2011). *Five ways of doing qualitative analysis: Phenomenological psychology, grounded theory, discourse analysis, narrative research, and intuitive inquiry.* New York: Guilford Press.

Wheeldon, J., & Ahlberg, M. K. (2012). *Visualizing social science research: Maps, methods, and meaning.* Thousand Oaks, CA: Sage.

Willig, C. (2014). Interpretation and analysis. In U. Flick (Ed.), *The Sage handbook of qualitative data analysis* (pp. 136–149). Thousand Oaks, CA: Sage.

Wlodkowski, R. J. (1985). *Enhancing adult motivation to learn.* San Francisco: Jossey Bass.

Wlodkowski, R. J., & Ginsberg, M. G. (1995). *Diversity and motivation: Culturally responsive teaching.* San Francisco: Jossey-Bass.

Wolcott, H. (1994). *Transforming qualitative data: Description, analysis, and interpretation.* Thousand Oaks, CA: Sage.

Wolcott, H. (2009). *Writing up qualitative research* (3rd ed.). Thousand Oaks, CA: Sage.

Yin, R. K. (2014). *Case study research: Design and methods* (5th ed., Vol. 5). Applied Social Research Methods Series. Thousand Oaks, CA: Sage.

• Author Index •

• Subject Index •